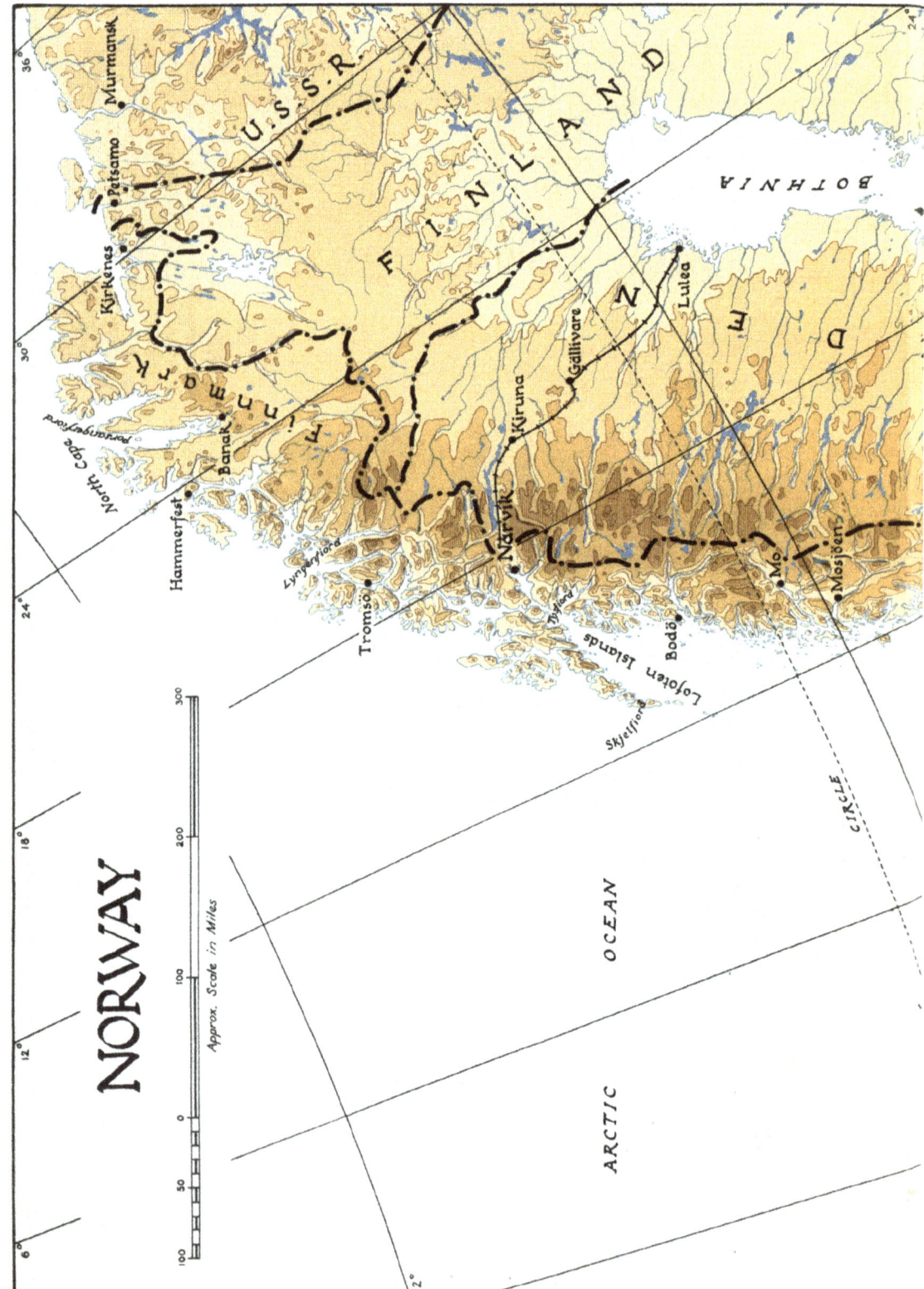

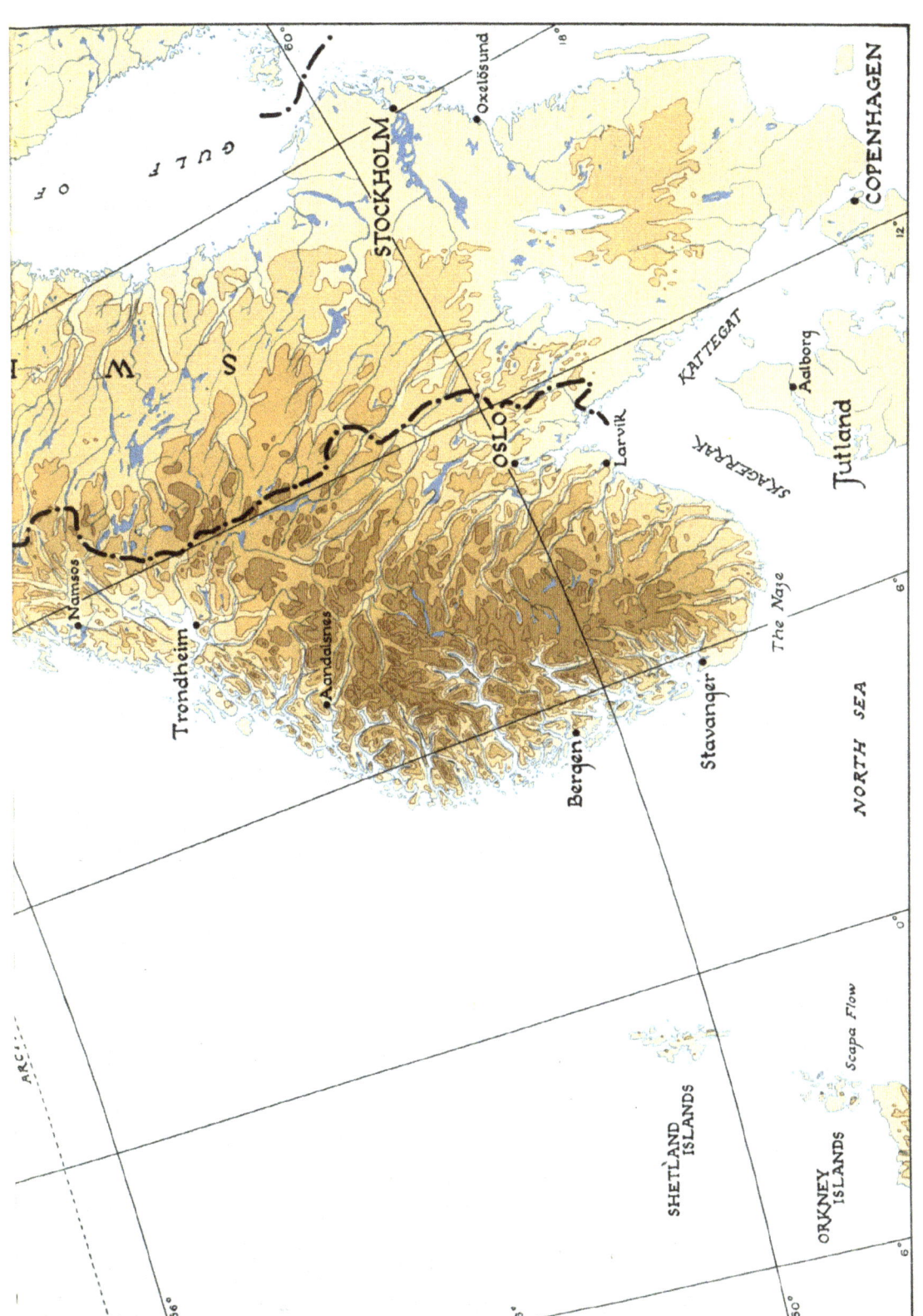

HISTORY OF THE SECOND WORLD WAR
UNITED KINGDOM MILITARY SERIES

Edited by J. R. M. BUTLER

The authors of the Military Histories have been given full access to official documents. They and the editor are alone responsible for the statements made and the views expressed.

Air view of Narvik from the north-west

Norsk Telegrambyraa

Frontispiece

THE CAMPAIGN IN NORWAY

BY

T. K. DERRY

D.Phil. (Oxon)

The Naval & Military Press Ltd

Published by

The Naval & Military Press Ltd
Unit 5 Riverside, Brambleside
Bellbrook Industrial Estate
Uckfield, East Sussex
TN22 1QQ England

Tel: +44 (0)1825 749494

www.naval-military-press.com
www.nmarchive.com

Front cover image:
French, British and Norwegian soldiers
aboard a Royal Navy warship, 8 May 1940.

In reprinting in facsimile from the original, any imperfections are inevitably reproduced and the quality may fall short of modern type and cartographic standards.

CONTENTS

	Page
EDITOR'S PREFACE	vii
AUTHOR'S PREFACE	xiii
TABLE OF OPERATIONS	xv
CHAPTER I: A Note on Norway	1
CHAPTER II: Norway and the War: British and German Military Plans	9
CHAPTER III: 9th April—The German Plan in Action	25
CHAPTER IV: British Counter-Measures by Sea and Air	43
CHAPTER V: Land Operations: General Strategy (Part 1)	57
CHAPTER VI: The Advance towards Trondheim	83
CHAPTER VII: Initial Operations in Gudbrandsdal	97
CHAPTER VIII: Gudbrandsdal—The Second Phase	113
CHAPTER IX: The Evacuation of Central Norway	129
CHAPTER X: Narvik—The First Landings	145
CHAPTER XI: Land Operations: General Strategy (Part 2)	161
CHAPTER XII: Narvik—Delaying Operations to the Southward	177
CHAPTER XIII: The Capture of Narvik	193
CHAPTER XIV: The Evacuation of North Norway	213
CHAPTER XV: The Campaign in Retrospect	229
APPENDIX A Instructions to Commanders	247
APPENDIX B Lists of Forces Engaged	261
APPENDIX C List of Published Sources	269
INDEX	271

MAPS

Orientated north and south unless otherwise indicated.
Place names are indexed with map reference.

Norway	*End Papers*
	Facing Page
1 (a). Naval Movements, 7th–9th April	42
2. Narvik: Battles, 10th and 13th April	50
1 (b). Naval Movements, 9th–13th April	56
3. The Environs of Steinkjer	96
4. South Norway	112
5. The Approaches to Trondheim	128
6. Romsdal and Gudbrandsdal	138
7 (a). British Air Operations in Norway: Bomber Limits and Fighter Bases	144
7 (b). German Air Operations in Norway: Bomber Limits and Fighter Bases	144
8 (a). The Road to the North: Mosjöen to Mo	186
8 (b). The Road to the North: Mo to Bodö	192
9. The Capture of Narvik	212
10. The Approaches to Narvik	220
11. Naval Movements, 8th–13th June	228

SKETCH MAPS

	Page
Action at the Balbergkamp, 22nd April	109
Action at Tretten, 23rd April	111
Action at Kvam, 25th–26th April	119
Action at Kjörem, 27th April	125
Action at Otta, 28th April	127
Action at Stien, 17th May	185
Action at Pothus, 25th–26th May	190

PHOTOGRAPHS

Air View of Narvik from the north-west	*Frontispiece*
	Facing Page
Namsos town and harbour, looking inland towards Grong	83
Aandalsnes and the mouth of the Romsdal	98
Kvam, seen from a point north of the church	120
View of Otta from the north, showing the two spurs	126

EDITOR'S PREFACE

THE military series of the United Kingdom History of the Second World War, of which Dr Derry's volume on the campaign in Norway is the first to appear, has been planned in accordance with a Government decision announced to the House of Commons on 25th November 1946. The purpose of the history, said the then Prime Minister, was 'to provide a broad survey of events from an inter-Service point of view rather than separate accounts of the parts played by each of the three Services'. The historians have thus felt themselves under no obligation to tell the story of operations in the same detail as was thought appropriate in the case of the war of 1914–18. For such detailed narratives the student must turn to the unit or formation histories of which many have already appeared. We have set ourselves to present a single series of volumes in which the whole military story, and every part of it, is treated from an inter-Service aspect. Here and elsewhere throughout our work the word 'military' is used to cover the activities of all three fighting Services, as distinct from the other sides of the national war effort which are treated in the Civil Histories edited by Professor W. K. Hancock.

Even on the military side, however, it seemed that a 'broad survey' which confined itself to a description of campaigns and operations would fail to give a satisfactory account of how the war of 1939–45 was waged. The vast area over which operations were progressively extended, the number and the variety of the campaigns being fought simultaneously, the constant need of co-ordinating policy and strategy with governments overseas, together with the centralisation of command rendered possible by modern systems of communication —all these increased the range and importance of the part played by the supreme authority at home and seemed to demand that a fuller treatment of the higher direction of the war should be attempted than has been usual in military histories. It was accordingly decided to allot several volumes to Grand Strategy as devised in Whitehall and at Washington, including one volume on developments prior to the actual outbreak of war in September 1939.

For the rest, the history has been planned to cover the following themes or theatres: the defence of the United Kingdom, the maritime war viewed as a whole, the two campaigns of the early period in Norway and in north-west Europe, the strategic air offensive, and the three epic series of military operations on the grand scale in the Mediterranean and Middle East, in the Far East, and again in the north-west of Europe in 1944 and 1945. Additional volumes have been allotted to the history of Civil Affairs or Military Government in view of the novelty and importance of the problems involved in this field of military responsibility.

In order to avoid undue detail, the standpoint from which campaigns have been viewed is that of the theatre commander. The intention has been to treat all the campaigns on the same scale; but it must be confessed that in some cases when the total forces involved were small, as in Norway in 1940 and in the Western Desert in the early phases, the narrative has descended to describe the operations of detached units in greater detail than their size would normally justify.

No doubt the proposed dual treatment of strategic problems, at the Whitehall level and at the level of theatre headquarters, involves a risk, indeed a certainty, of some overlapping. This would be the case even if it were not our aim, as it is, to make each group of volumes intelligible by itself and to that extent self-contained. We cannot, unfortunately, assume that the general reader, for whom as much as for military students our history is intended, will be prepared to buy or read the whole of our twenty or thirty volumes. We think that a moderate amount of overlapping is excusable and may even be welcomed if it avoids the necessity of constant reference to other volumes.

The description of a war waged by allies, in which 'integration' was successfully carried to lengths unattempted in previous campaigns, raised further problems. Granted that our commission is to write the history not of the Second World War as a whole but of the military effort of the United Kingdom, on what principle ought we to handle campaigns or actions in which men from the United Kingdom and from other nations fought side by side? Where United Kingdom forces served under foreign or Dominion command, or vice versa, it seems clear that decisions or actions of our fellow combatants must be described with sufficient fullness to preserve a proper balance in the story. On the other hand it is not desirable to duplicate the accounts given in the histories sponsored by our Allies and the other nations of the British Commonwealth, especially when the primary sources are under their control. Arrangements have indeed been made with them for mutual information on points of special interest and for an exchange of drafts; it is hoped that these arrangements will at least reduce the likelihood of controversy due to ignorance of another nation's point of view, though they will not, of course, eliminate differences of interpretation. It has not been possible to make such arrangements in the case of the U.S.S.R.

With regard to German military records, however, the Allied historians are fortunate, to an unprecedented degree, in having access to a mass of original documents, some of them of the highest importance, which were captured during the occupation of Germany and are now held under joint Anglo-American control. In the case of the other enemy Powers both the volume and the value of the documents captured are considerably less and details of their military plans and operations have of necessity been obtained from more conventional sources of information.

To the official United Kingdom records we have been allowed full access, and we have done our best to supplement them by reference to unofficial accounts, published and unpublished, written and oral. We have felt bound, however, to respect the requirements of military 'security', and in some cases cipher telegrams have been paraphrased, though not in such a way as to affect the sense. In accordance with the recognised British constitutional principle we have not held ourselves free to reveal individual differences of opinion within the War Cabinet nor, as a rule, to lift the veil of Civil Service anonymity.

We have taken it as our prime duty to present an accurate narrative of events. But events, properly speaking, include plans and intentions as well as actions, and it is the duty of a historian, as opposed to a mere annalist, to say why, as well as how, things happened as they did. He must interpret, not merely narrate, and interpretation implies a personal judgement. In any case the need to select from the vast mass of material implies a personal judgement of what is most relevant and important.

We all share the contemporary outlook, and some of us are laymen in military matters; it would be unbecoming in us to attempt to pronounce what a commander should have done or should not have done in a particular situation. Our ideal would be to let the facts speak for themselves, to point out how such a decision led to such a result, and to leave speculation and moralising to the strategists; but the facts can only speak to our readers as we have selected and presented them, and we have not shrunk from stating what seemed to us the lessons that emerged from a particular course of events.

Lord Tedder has remarked that as a nation 'we have a tendency to concentrate too much on our successes and our enemies' failures and consequently to draw our lessons too much from the final stages of war', when 'after some years of lavish expenditure' the Commander knows that he can more or less 'count on a blank cheque'. 'Surely', he says, 'it is the problems of the early stages of the war which we should study. Those are the difficult problems; those are the practical problems which we and every democratic nation have to solve. There are no big battalions or blank cheques then. Here is the real and vital test of our defence policies'.[1]

Lord Tedder's words may serve as a reply to any critic who objects that in a 'broad survey' of the Second World War the space allotted,

---

[1] *Air Power in War*, p. 25.

in Dr Derry's volume, to what was after all a minor campaign is excessive. The Norway episode was, it is true, in a sense a sideshow; the forces engaged, except on the naval side, were comparatively small and the losses light. But it was the first campaign of the war in which all three Services were involved and it revealed before the eyes of the world how lamentably deficient were our military preparations and organisation compared with our political commitments and our urgent needs. It is right that not only the results of our unpreparedness should be indicated in broad outline, but enough detail should be given to show where and why the shoe pinched. The lessons of the Norway campaign were learnt and applied, with triumphant effect, before the end of the war. But, if Lord Tedder is correct, that does not make them less worthy of study now, when once again democracies are living in dangerous times and have critical decisions to take.

It is normally the duty and desire of a historian to support his assertions and arguments by detailed references to his authorities. Such references serve partly as an indication of his sources, partly as a challenge to his readers to verify his statements. Where, however, the main authorities are official documents which are not at present, and for some time are not likely to be, open to public inspection, published references have comparatively little point, since the challenge cannot be taken up. The nature of the material used can, we think, in most cases be sufficiently indicated in the prefaces or bibliographical notes to the several volumes. Accordingly our usual practice has been that explained by Professor Hancock in his introduction to the Civil Histories.[1] 'It has been decided not to clutter the published pages with references to official files which are not yet generally available to students. In the published series, footnotes have been confined to material that is already accessible. The completed documentation has been given in confidential print. There it will be immediately available to critical readers within the Government service. No doubt it will become available in due time to the historians of a future generation. The official historians of this generation have consciously submitted their work to the professional verdict of the future'.

In the use of the enemy documents the historians' labours have been immensely lightened by the help of their colleagues charged with the collection, collation and interpretation of this vast mass of material. Work on the German and Italian documents has been directed by Mr Brian Melland; Colonel G. T. Wards has advised with regard to the Japanese. Valuable assistance in this matter has also been rendered by Commander M. G. Saunders, R.N., of the

---

[1] *British War Economy*, p. xii.

Admiralty Historical Section, and by Squadron Leader L. A. Jackets, of the Air Historical Branch.

The maps have been prepared under the experienced direction of Colonel T. M. M. Penney, of the Cabinet Office Historical Section. The spelling of the place-names follows in the main the system approved at an informal conference of the British and American experts in October 1947, but current usage has been adhered to where not to do so would be pedantic. In the representation of Allied and enemy troops the conventional symbols and colours, where used, are those officially recognised during the war. Apart from the fact that work on some of our maps had begun before November 1950, when the British Army changed its system, it seemed natural to follow the convention used in contemporary maps.

The appointment of a civilian editor to be responsible for the production of the military histories made it desirable that on general questions as well as special points he should be able frequently to consult authorities whose opinions on Service matters would command respect; I am fortunate to have had so helpful a panel of advisers as Vice-Admiral Sir Geoffrey Blake, Lieutenant-General Sir Henry Pownall, Air Chief Marshals Sir Douglas Evill and Sir Guy Garrod, and Lieutenant-General Sir Ian Jacob. These distinguished officers not only have given me the benefit of their experience and judgement in the planning of the history and the selection of writers but have read and commented on the volumes in draft; in all these matters, however, responsibility rests with the Editor alone.

The history could not have been written without the constant assistance of the Service Historical Sections, and the historians would express their gratitude to Rear-Admiral R. M. Bellairs, Brigadier H. B. Latham and Mr J. C. Nerney, and also to Lieutenant-General Sir Desmond Anderson, of the War Office, and their staffs. The monographs, narratives and summaries produced by the Service Departments have greatly reduced the labours, though not the responsibilities, of the historians, and the staffs concerned have been lavish of their help in supplying information and comment. Similar acknowledgements are due to the authors of the Civil Histories, and we are grateful to Mr. Yates Smith, of the Imperial War Museum, and to other librarians for the loan of books.

Finally, the historians in general and the Editor in particular are deeply indebted to Mr A. B. Acheson, of the Cabinet Office. His advice and help have been of the greatest service to us in many ways; indeed, without the relief provided by Mr Acheson in administrative matters, a part-time editor could hardly have performed his task.

J. R. M. B.

AUTHOR'S PREFACE

THE two-months campaign in Norway is justly famous for its record of arduous duties faithfully performed, in many cases by newcomers to the trade of war, for some notable acts of individual gallantry, for more than one fighting withdrawal finely conducted, and for the two naval victories which lend lustre to the name of Narvik. But these by themselves would constitute an incomplete and largely uninstructive story. For, as the Editor has indicated, it is also the function of the historian to attempt the ungrateful task of showing how deficiencies in our preparation for war, psychological as well as material and technical, handicapped and even thwarted the efforts of the three Services to check the German advance in this small and relatively unimportant field, where the first main clash of arms occurred. We were heavily outnumbered. On the ground the enemy mustered seven divisions against the Norwegians and their helpers, that is, about three men for every man we landed to give that help; his predominance in the air was still greater; only at sea were we in superior strength. But numbers alone do not explain the sense of frustration which seems to brood over the scene, so that more than one leading participant has found the closest parallel to his experience in that tragic misadventure, the Walcheren expedition of 1809.

In his use of the official papers, which are the main source of his narrative, the author has had the benefit of two special guides. One was the recollections and opinions of distinguished officers who commanded in, or otherwise controlled, the operations in Norway: they have given very readily and fully of their time and patience to unravel the tangle of events. The other was what could be learnt by enquiry on the spot—from the Historical Section of the Norwegian Ministry of Defence, who threw open their carefully maintained records with a generosity all too rare, and from a journey covering every district and place in which our forces served. Sometimes the rugged ground spoke for itself; often there were eye-witnesses to be found of what our men did and endured nine years before.

It is hoped that the addition of photographs and the rather numerous maps and plans, on which great care has been lavished by expert colleagues, will help the reader to reconstruct for himself the adverse physical conditions which played so large a part. Of the Appendices, the first two set out exactly what our generals were instructed to attempt in Norway and with what forces; the third gives a full reference to every published work on the campaign which is cited in the text, and will enable the student in some measure to judge for himself where it might seem that the author, like the subject of Kipling's verses, merely 'wrote that another man wrote Of a carl in Norroway'.

T. K. D.

TABLE OF OPERATIONS

1940	Narvik-Harstad	Mosjöen-Bodö	North of Trondheim	South of Trondheim
Apr. 8		British mines laid north of Bodö	Loss of *Glowworm*	
9	*Renown* v. *Gneisenau* and *Scharnhorst*			*Köln* sunk (off Kristiansand)
10	Destroyer attack, Narvik			*Königsberg* sunk (Bergen)
13	*Warspite* attack, Narvik			
14	Scots Guards at Sjövegan		Naval party at Namsos	
15	24 Brigade at Harstad			
16			146 Brigade at Namsos	
17				Naval party at Aandalsnes
18				148 Brigade at Aandalsnes
19			Chasseurs Alpins land	
20			Namsos heavily bombed	
21			Action at Vist begun	148 Brigade in line near Lillehammer
22			Vist area lost	Action at Balbergkamp
23				Action at Tretten
24	Narvik bombarded			15 Bde. at Aandalsnes Aandalsnes heavily bombed
25				Gladiators at Lesjaskog. Action at Kvam begun
26			Counter-offensive planned (Namsos)	
27				Action at Kjörem
28	Chasseurs Alpins land			Action at Otta
29	South Wales Borderers at Haakvik			
30		Scots Guards Company at Bodö		
May 2				Evacuation of Aandalsnes completed a.m.
3			Evacuation of Namsos completed a.m.	
4		No. 1 Independent Company at Mo		
6	Foreign Legionaries land			
8		4 and 5 Independent Companies at Mosjöen		
9	Poles land	3 Independent Company at Bodö		
10		Action at R. Björnaa; loss of Hemnesberget		
12		Scots Guards (3 Companies) at Mo		

xv

1940	Narvik-Harstad	Mosjöen-Bodö	North of Trondheim	South of Trondheim
May 13	Bjerkvik captured	2 Independent Company at Bodö		
15		Loss of *Chrobry*		
16	South Wales Borderers leave Ankenes area			
17		Action at Stien Loss of *Effingham*		
20		2 Companies South Wales Borderers at Bodö		
21	Gladiators at Bardufoss	Irish Guards at Bodö		
22		Action at Krokstrand		
25	Evacuation orders received	Action at Pothus begun		
26	Hurricanes at Bardufoss	Gladiators at Bodö		
28	Narvik captured			
31		Evacuation of Bodö completed		
June 4	Evacuation of troops begun			
8	Evacuation completed a.m. Loss of *Glorious*			

CHAPTER I
A NOTE ON NORWAY

To understand the British operations in Norway it is important to bear in mind the main physical features of the country—the barren mountains, thin and unevenly distributed population, great distances, and (sea transport excepted) very poor internal communications. One half of the land lies at a height of more than 2,000 feet and the whole cultivated area amounts to the insignificant fragment of three per cent.; thus to English eyes the landscape (except in the south-east) seems almost invariably to be dominated by wild hills, their lower slopes clothed with featureless forests of conifers and birch, an occasional clearing the only obvious sign of human habitation except in the valley bottoms. Even there our soldiers found that digging-in usually meant a hopeless struggle of spade against rock and had to make do with loose stone parapets and sangars, still to be seen.

Three million Norwegians are spread over an area larger than the whole of the British Isles. Not only so, but such centres of population as may be found are widely separated—the valley mouths in the south-east round Oslo; the ports of the south and west coasts as far as Trondheim and its hinterland, which are divided from the Oslo area by a vast mountain plateau rising at the Dovrefjell (north of Dombaas) to a maximum height of nearly 8,000 feet; and the isolated North Norway ports of Bodö, Narvik, and Kirkenes. These last are approached from the south by a narrow strip of territory, 300 miles long and at one point only $3\frac{1}{2}$ miles wide, which broadens at the North Cape to form the Finnmark plateau stretching east towards the Russian steppes. From the Naze to the North Cape is a distance of more than a thousand miles, from Bergen to Oslo about 200 miles, measuring in a straight line—which the steep configuration of the land makes utterly unrealistic. For so small a population the cost of grappling with its transport problems is almost overwhelming. Railways are few (in the north nearly non-existent) and single-tracked; the roads are narrow, hazardous, and rough-surfaced; the steamer routes slow; even air communications (except by seaplane) were under-developed because of the prohibitive expense of landing-grounds.

Furthermore, the difficulties of travel and transport are accentuated by the climate. East Norway experiences severe cold in winter with a thick, long-continued snow cover, and the nearness of the principal watershed to the west coast causes the traveller from any western port to climb into the eastern winter with surprising speed.

The west coast, in contrast, has a mild, wet, Atlantic climate, which in the latitude of Bergen approximates to the humidity of our own west coast. But farther north, although the influence of the Gulf Stream keeps the harbours open and encourages the growth of something more than Arctic vegetation, the long hours of winter darkness, the blizzards, and the spring thaw, all make movement more difficult. Hence the rigours which confronted and perplexed our troops in April 1940. There was the snow, deepest of course in the Narvik area, which is well north of the Polar Circle, but deep by English standards in every area concerned except for the immediate environs of the west-coast port of Aandalsnes; the cold, intense at night not only in the far north but in the eastern valley of the Gudbrandsdal, where every lake was a sheet of black ice; the formidable contrasts of temperature between the woods and the bare mountain plateau, between the sunny and the shady sides of the same valley, between calm and sudden wind; and finally the thaw, which would make rivers into torrents and the roads into quagmires axle-deep. Central Norway, however, was evacuated by our forces just as the thaw began. From Mosjöen northwards to Harstad operations continued through the period in which road transport is normally suspended, area by area, because the break-up of the frost in deeply frozen earth involves the break-up of road surfaces—which are loosely constructed for this very reason. The operations finished in what was for North Norway the early spring, a time of unending daylight, swollen rivers and cloudless skies. When the last troops left the shore in the early morning of 8th June, the background was still a majestic vista of snow mountains climbing to the Swedish frontier, but in the foreground, where the brightly-painted houses of the villages by the fiords had seemed almost incongruous in the harsh landscape of April, green fields now varied the pattern of grey rocks beside the warming sea.

Norway is, indeed, in a special sense a country created by the sea. Whatever the difficulties of life in North Norway, the fact remains that the Gulf Stream has enabled civilisation to press farther into the Polar wastes there than at any other point in the northern or southern hemisphere. The sea has given Norway its characteristic trades—the fisheries, the relatively huge mercantile marine, the whaling—and the proximity of the sea to the waterfalls and the mines has been a main reason for the prosperity of the newer metallurgical industries as far north as Kirkenes. More strictly to our purpose, the sea provides an unfailing means of communication in the fiords and the Leads. The deep and narrow fiords, some stretching for a hundred miles into the interior of the country, are ideal for inland navigation —except indeed under air attack—and form throughout western Norway the normal means of access to the settlements, which more often than not lie at the foot of mountain precipices. In the south and east the hinterland is as a rule less unapproachable, but even so there is no inland town of more than 15,000 inhabitants. The Leads are the continuous passages, without counterpart in Europe, which lie between the island archipelagos or skerries and the mainland; they constitute a fully sheltered, deep-water route for shipping along almost the whole coast from Stavanger to the North Cape. They have played a dominant part in making the Norwegians and their history: Norway is said to mean 'The way to the North'. It is indeed the sea which chiefly explains the apparent paradox that a country which cannot hope to feed from its own soil even so small a population as three millions, which has so few inherent resources and so many deficiencies, has managed in recent years to maintain an average standard of life among the highest in western Europe.

An outstanding example of this is provided by the mushroom growth of the town of Narvik on a barren peninsula of rock in the Ofotfiord, at the inner end of the Arctic Vestfiord. This locality had hitherto provided a meagre living for a handful of fishermen, to whom the warm water was more important than the inhospitable land. But in 1902 a railway was brought through from the Swedish frontier, involving a descent of 1,700 feet through nineteen tunnels in twenty-three miles, and next year the iron ore mined in the mountains at Kiruna (seventy-seven miles beyond the frontier) began to find its outlet to the world market along the ice-free waters. In a single generation a completely new town arose, the second largest in North Norway, with the Swedish iron company as virtually sole sponsors. Hemmed in by gloomy piles of rock and scree, its modern villas and blocks of offices stretched down to the ore-crushing plants, the busy railway sidings, a 1,200-foot ore quay of wood and granite, and a natural anchorage for thirty ships, ships which wore the flags of many nations but plied mainly to Germany.[1]

Norway seemed more remote from British interests than it was. The British Army had never served on Norwegian soil, and few English people had even heard of the episode which Norwegian history calls 'the hunger years' (1807–14), when Denmark-Norway was one of Napoleon's satellites and the Royal Navy maintained a close blockade of the coastline, with occasional forays by landing parties at Hammerfest and other remote harbours. As for British opinion in general, it was coloured by Norway's reputation as a tourist country. The scenic splendours were well known, but even basic facts about the economic and social life of the people remained unfamiliar. Since the dissolution of the union between Norway and

---

[1] Rickman, A. F.: *Swedish Iron Ore* (August 1939), pp. 139–43.

Denmark in 1814, Anglo-Norwegian relations had been harmonious but unimportant: they figured in general history only twice. In 1855 Sweden and Norway under their common Swedish monarchy were nearly but not quite induced to take our side against Russia in the Crimean War. In 1905 King Edward VII played an active part in the establishment of an independent monarchy for Norway by throwing British influence on to the side of the candidature of his son-in-law, Prince Charles of Denmark, who in that year was elected King Haakon VII of Norway.

But the attitude of the Norwegians to Britain was far more definite and positive. They were traditionally attracted to Britain by economic, social, and political considerations. Their mercantile marine, for instance, dates its meteoric rise from the repeal of the British navigation laws in 1849, while the tourist trade with England—and the lure of the salmon fishing—had for nearly a century added a substantial item to the Norwegian national income. Socially, they were inclined to find the English—and still more the Scots—the most congenial of foreigners outside their Scandinavian brethren, and to attach more importance than we did to the common historical heritage from the days of the Scandinavian settlements in Britain. Politically, the Norwegian saw in the growth of democracy in nineteenth-century Britain a movement with which his own national development was closely and sympathetically related. The earliest standard English guide-book assured its mid-Victorian readers that 'The Norwegians like the English, as every Englishman who has travelled in Norway can bear witness'.[1] It is safe to say that in 1940 England still had a considerable stock of goodwill to draw upon in Norway, quite independent of the international situation of the moment.

We may briefly compare the traditional Norwegian attitude to Germany. Politically, relations had been far less sympathetic: Norwegian volunteers took an active part in the Danish defence of Schleswig-Holstein, both in the successful campaign of 1848 and in the disastrous year 1864. Imperial Germany, particularly as personified in Kaiser Wilhelm II, who was a frequent visitor to the Norwegian fiords, was always viewed to some extent distrustfully; while the close relations between Sweden and Germany meant that anti-Swedish sentiments also tended to turn independent Norway in the other direction. Nevertheless, there were important links both cultural and economic. Germany was usually Norway's second-best customer (Britain coming first); and the thoroughness of German organisation was often more congenial than British amateurishness. In education, the arts, and such industrial branches as building and

---

[1] Murray's *Handbook for Travellers in Norway* (7th edition, 1880), p. [81].

engineering, Norway owed most to German models. This practice may have been stimulated to some extent by the ancient link of the German Hanseatic merchants, who dominated Norwegian trade almost to the seventeenth century. It was certainly fostered by Norwegian neutrality in the First World War, which made it relatively easy for Norway to enter into immediate friendly relations with the Weimar republic. In the 'twenties and 'thirties among visitors from outside Scandinavia German tourists were second only to the British in numbers and assiduity, though later events were to prove them to have been less disinterested sightseers.

Among the many aspects of Norwegian life in which British visitors, at least, took little interest was the state of the country's defences. This was conditioned in the first place by the recollection of a century of unbroken peace. In 1905, during the separation from the common Swedish monarchy, war against Sweden had for a few months seemed possible or even probable; but the upshot of the crisis was the demilitarisation of the Norwegian-Swedish frontier. Only ten years later the likelihood that Norway and Sweden if involved in the general war would take opposite sides proved to be an important factor in keeping Scandinavia neutral. That neutrality was not maintained without cost. On the one hand Allied blockade measures pressed very heavily upon Norway, especially in the last eighteen months of the war, when the entry of America into the struggle rendered the Allies less careful about the susceptibilities of the remaining neutrals. In particular, severe pressure was brought to bear in September 1918 to make the Norwegians lay an anti-submarine minefield in territorial waters so as to complete our existing Northern Barrage, though the work was still left undone when the war ended.[1] German action, on the other hand, bore much more hardly upon them as the owners of the principal neutral mercantile marine. Almost fifty per cent. of its tonnage was sunk and about two thousand Norwegian seamen lost their lives, primarily as a result of the unrestricted submarine warfare waged by the Germans. Many Norwegians believed, perhaps with reason, that the destruction of a rival trading fleet, larger in pre-war days than their own, was to the Germans an end in itself, apart from the loss to the Allies by whom it was chartered.

But in the post-war period the record of neutrality, whatever the cost at which it had been maintained, was one of several factors that brought about a steady neglect of defence which was to cost Norway dear. Idealist in outlook, the Norwegians were active champions of the League of Nations viewed as a substitute for national defence. The neglect of defences was also a concomitant of the rise of the Labour

---

[1] Newbolt, Sir Henry: *History of the Great War: Naval Operations*, Vol. V (1931), p. 349.

Party, which regarded the professional cadre of the armed forces as an inevitable stronghold for reactionaries and which, in Norway as elsewhere, thought that money spent on defence was money lost to social services. Moreover, even after Hitler's accession to power in Germany, when left-wing politicians were forced to suspect that arms might be necessary to protect social services, the geographical position of Norway and the character of its terrain still encouraged the dangerous belief that 'The country is easy to defend' (*Norway Year Book, 1938*)[1]—a statement which probably refers not only to the supposed invulnerability of the mountainous hinterland but to the comfortable belief (not confined to Norwegians) that recent developments had made no difference to the traditional and almost automatic protection of their coasts by the British Navy.

At the outbreak of war in September 1939, however, the neglect of defence was by no means absolute. The military condition of Norway was the product of three main influences. Firstly, a system of compulsory service dating back to the seventeenth century had been kept up as a badge of independent nationhood, though the period of training was thirteen weeks (which had even been reduced in practice to eight), the shortest for any army in Europe, with a rather longer period for the Navy. Secondly, the Labour Government which came into office in 1935 had been forced to reckon with the possible consequences of the ill-will of Nazi Germany, as for instance in 1936, when the Nobel Committee of the Norwegian Parliament awarded the Nobel Peace Prize to one of Hitler's victims, and in the spring of 1939, when Norway parted company from the equally pacific Danes by refusing to make a non-aggression pact with Germany. Consequently the defence budget, which had sunk to its lowest level in the significant year 1933, began to rise again, and by 1938 the sum allocated to defence reached the modest total of £1 per head of population. Finally, there survived from 1914-18 a realisation of the importance of proper measures to protect neutrality, though the stringent economies of the earlier inter-war years were to reduce the scale of Norwegian action this time to the establishment of a neutrality watch in lieu of their former neutrality defence.

The Royal Norwegian Navy was kept mobilised from the outset of hostilities in Europe, as the importance to both sides of the long sea route off Norway's deeply indented coastline made the task of enforcing the laws of neutrality both hazardous and complicated. The naval forces in question were, however, largely obsolete, and one vessel still in commission dated from 1858. The most important items were four antiquated coast defence ships, of which we shall hear more, seven destroyers, including four of modern design, and two mine-

---

[1] P. 100 (Article on National Defence by Captain R. Graff).

layers. As for the army, the Russian invasion of Finland (30th November 1939) caused the mixed Field Brigade of the 6th Division, stationed in the far north, to be fully mobilised in case the Russians should move against East Finnmark, and a state of reasonable preparedness obtained thereafter as far south as Narvik. Elsewhere, the neutrality watch was used mainly as a convenient chance to call in single battalions for training at the other five so-called Divisional Headquarters, each of which in the event of war was due to produce one mixed brigade. The total number of men under arms on 8th April 1940 was about 13,000, of whom nearly one-half were in the north (Denmark had mobilised 14,550). Norwegian aircraft were not a separate force or a factor of major importance. About thirty seaplanes were disposed at seven coastal stations to assist the naval control; and eighteen scouting aircraft and six fighters were in service on five airfields under army command. Lastly, we may notice that there were five coastal fortresses, which had their guns partly manned, but no infantry garrisons to protect guns or gunners from a landing-party.

CHAPTER II

NORWAY AND THE WAR: BRITISH AND GERMAN MILITARY PLANS

See Map of Norway, on end papers

FROM the outbreak of war between Britain and Germany on 3rd September 1939 Norway had in several ways a special importance for both belligerents, over and above the pressure which each side naturally sought to exercise upon all accessible neutral powers. The Norwegian coast provided the eastern limit of the main sea route from German ports to the Atlantic, and the control of that route was again, as in 1914–18, a cardinal factor in the British naval blockade. Within a fortnight after the outbreak of war the Government issued a declaration, made after consultation with the Chiefs of Staff, that a German attack upon Norway would meet with the same resistance as an attack on Great Britain. This was designed to encourage Norwegian co-operation with our blockade, which might have an important influence in two respects. Firstly, our naval measures, particularly those aimed against egress of enemy ships between Norway and the Shetlands, would be helped if the Norwegians gave a sympathetic interpretation to their rights as neutrals under international law. Secondly, there was the pressure to be exercised through negotiation of trade agreements, so as to maximise the usefulness of Norway's economic resources to ourselves and minimise it to our enemies. By agreement dated 11th November 1939 the Norwegian Shippers' Association chartered to Britain the largest and most modern vessels of the Norwegian merchant fleet, which more than offset the subsequent German-Norwegian trade agreement (23rd February 1940) providing for exports to Germany not in excess of those for the year 1938. This involved a hole in the British blockade, but Britain forbore to exercise any greater counter-pressure upon Norwegian economic life than the restriction of British supplies to Norway to approximately the same level, i.e. that of 1937–38 (agreement of 11th March 1940).[1]

The general situation outlined above was complicated from the outset by two special considerations. One was the existence of the Leads, which enabled German ships to enter territorial waters at remote points well inside the Arctic Circle and travel under their protection almost as far as the entrance to the Skagerrak, where the

---
[1] See Medlicott, W. N.: *The Economic Blockade*, Vol. I (1952), Chapter IV, Sec. 3.

proximity of German air and submarine bases made the rest of the voyage comparatively safe from British interception. Logically, the matter might have been complicated further by the traditional Norwegian claim to a wider limit for territorial waters than was accorded by international custom elsewhere, but the Norwegian Government resolved at the outbreak of war not to claim privileges of neutrality beyond the three sea-miles recognised by the other Powers. As it was, the course through the Leads gave virtually continuous protection to German shipping—a leakage through the blockade which was of constant concern to the Admiralty, although it only attracted public attention on special occasions, as when the German Atlantic liner *Bremen* slipped through from Murmansk or when the boarding of the *Altmark* revealed a graver anomaly.[1]

The other consideration assumed an importance in the Allied counsels which it did not perhaps altogether deserve. It was believed from the outset of the war that Germany had two main economic weaknesses—her dependence upon oil imports, with which it would be hard for the Allies to interfere effectively, and her dependence upon imports of high-grade iron ore, which came partly from Central Sweden via the port of Oxelösund but chiefly from deposits at Kiruna and Gällivare in North Sweden. This ore reached Germany by two main routes, from Swedish Lulea at the northern end of the Baltic and, especially during the months from December to April when Lulea was ice-bound, from the alternative railhead at the ice-free port of Narvik. The Chiefs of Staff when consulted about Norway had placed the iron-ore supplies received via Narvik in the forefront of their argument that access to Norwegian resources was more important to Germany than to Britain. This opinion was supported by a statement emanating from the formerly prominent German industrialist Fritz Thyssen, who informed the French Government from his place of refuge in Switzerland of a momentous report which he had once made to the German authorities showing the Swedish iron-ore to be all-important.[2] Thyssen's credentials as an expert in this matter do not appear to have been officially examined, but in answer to an inquiry from the War Cabinet on 30th November the Ministry of Economic Warfare gave its authority to the view that, once deprived of the ore, Germany could not wage active war for a period exceeding twelve months. In 1938 Germany was believed to have imported 22 million tons of iron ore, $9\frac{1}{2}$ million tons of it coming from sources which the Allied blockade had since cut off and nine million tons from Sweden, the loss of which would therefore bring Germany down to a sixth of her pre-war importation.[3]

---

[1] See p. 13.
[2] Reynaud, Paul: *La France a sauvé l'Europe*, t. II, p. 23.
[3] See Medlicott, Vol. I, Chapter IV, Sec. 6.

There were some unknown—or partly unknown—factors to be taken into account, including the importance of scrap iron to the German steel-makers, the domestic output of low-grade ore, and the amount of stockpiling. But the high value of any stroke which would cut off the entire Swedish supply was evident to any inquirer, so long at least as he indulged in no speculation about the many and violent ways in which the Germans might react to it. The value of a stroke to cut off the supply through Narvik only, which was the most that we could make sure of at the moment, was obviously less. The Ministry of Economic Warfare estimated that this would produce a deficiency in German supplies of one million tons spread over the four winter months, which 'would certainly mean acute industrial embarrassment'. A paper prepared by the German High Command in February, showing that the Germans counted on an extra million tons of Swedish ore in 1940 (and 10 million tons in all), gives reasons why the fulfilment of this programme was incompatible with a reduction from $2\frac{1}{2}$ million to one million tons of the share to be transported via Narvik, though there is evidence from Swedish sources that it might have been 'technically possible'.[1] While these figures support the general basis on which the Ministry of Economic Warfare was arguing, the German Naval Commander-in-Chief, Grand-Admiral Raeder (for whose use they were compiled), did not apparently infer that the closure of the Narvik route would be catastrophic for Germany, even if '2,500,000–3,500,000 tons per year would be lost'.

To return to the position as seen by the Allies during the winter of 1939–40, it is clear that the existence of the route through the Leads and its use for an essential German war import gave the Allies strong reasons for putting Norway in the forefront of their strategical calculations. Within a month from the outbreak of war Mr Churchill, as First Lord of the Admiralty, had pressed the Cabinet for leave to mine the Leads at some point north of Bergen, but at that time it was still possible to hope that our war trade agreements with the Scandinavian Powers might bring about a sweeping reduction in the export of Swedish iron to Germany. In November the Cabinet decided as a long-term programme to reconstruct the Northern Barrage of anti-submarine mines across the North Sea, which would eventually make mine-laying in the Leads necessary (as in 1918), and the Chiefs of Staff were instructed to report on the military factors which would be involved in stopping the iron-ore traffic from Narvik. In December, both before and after a meeting of the Supreme War Council on the 19th, at which the Thyssen memorandum was produced by the French, Mr Churchill pressed again for the immediate mining of the Leads or the patrolling of the waters by the Royal Navy—whichever

---

[1] Statement by the Foreign Minister, Herr C. Günther, cited in *Norwegian Parliamentary Report* (1947), Appendices, Vol. I, p. 237.

alternative might involve less risk of an armed clash with the Norwegians in defence of their neutrality. By this time the same active mind had other more delicate schemes in view for bottling up Oxelösund and, when the spring came, Luleå as well. On 6th January this sequence of events culminated in an attempt to secure Norwegian and Swedish acceptance of our proposed entry into Norwegian territorial waters by diplomatic representations, which pointed to their notorious violation by German submarines torpedoing British ships there. But the Cabinet was still far from being persuaded to mine the Leads without more ado if permission were refused, as it quickly was.

Meanwhile, the whole question of action in Scandinavia had been complicated by the unprovoked attack launched by Russia against Finland on 30th November. Its first effect was to align France and Britain with Sweden and Norway as eager supporters of the Finns, so far as voluntary effort and supplies of material were concerned. The Royal Air Force, for example, released nearly 150 from its scanty supply of aircraft for Finnish use. It was also believed that the threat of Russian aggression, viewed with benevolence by Germany as the friend of Russia, would bring the Scandinavian countries to interpret their neutrality in a manner more favourable to our interests and almost to welcome our intervention. When the initial successes of the Finns caused the danger from Russia momentarily to recede, it was still hoped that the Scandinavian Powers would so interpret their obligations as members of the League of Nations as to allow Allied forces to cross their territories to help the Finns against acknowledged aggression. The result was a prolonged diplomatic wrangle. Both Norway and Sweden were genuinely desirous of helping the Finnish cause by all means short of their own implication in the war. But they consistently refused to court the fate of Poland, for whose defence the Western Powers seemed to have done absolutely nothing, by allowing Allied forces even in the guise of 'volunteers' to cross their territory into Finland, either to preserve Finnish independence or for their own protection against a hypothetical Russian (or German) advance directed to the Swedish orefields or the warm-water ports of northern Norway.

The Allies for their part, while sincere in protesting their desire to save Finland, certainly had other objects in view to which they gave less publicity—objects so important that the original scheme for a naval operation against the Narvik traffic was for the time being virtually abandoned lest it might prejudice the larger hope. The French wanted the establishment of a Scandinavian field of operations almost as an end in itself, and were prepared to run the risks of establishing a naval blockade against Russian supplies shipped to north Finland from Murmansk or of trying to wrest Petsamo, the Finnish Arctic port, from Russian hands rather than forgo the chance to keep the main action of the war away from the Franco-German front. The plans, however, which the British sponsored were less widely open to criticism than the Petsamo project, which seemed to combine the maximum provocation to the Russians with the minimum of strategic advantage to ourselves. Accordingly, what was approved by the Supreme War Council at its first meeting of the year 1940 on 5th February was a British scheme, which contemplated the provision of two or more Allied brigades on the Finnish front, but laid its chief emphasis elsewhere. This was timed for action by mid-March.

On its way to rescue the Finns the main striking force was to land at Narvik and advance along the railway to Kiruna and Gällivare, the two centres of the North Swedish orefield, and on to the Baltic port of Luleå; it was hoped to establish the equivalent of two Allied brigades along this line before the latter part of April, when weather conditions would normally open the Baltic to German seaborne expeditions and also facilitate a German advance overland through Sweden. A second force of five British Territorial battalions was to occupy three ports in southern Norway, so as to provide us with bases for the general defence of Scandinavia (and an alternative route to Finland) and to deny those bases to the Germans. Trondheim (with Namsos) would be the principal Allied base, Bergen an important subsidiary base and the terminal point of our northern mine barrage; Stavanger, on the other hand, would probably not be occupied longer than was necessary to demolish the airfield, which is the nearest on the Continent to Scapa Flow. Two British divisions were held back from France for these immediate tasks. But the plan also provided for much larger forces, drawn from both French and British sources, to be passed through Trondheim for an eventual campaign in southern Sweden. The British would in the end put about 100,000 men in the field, the French perhaps 50,000. Forty destroyers would be needed for close escort duty, besides making the protection of the convoys the main preoccupation of the Home Fleet. The air component totalled six and a half squadrons of aircraft, including three of fighters, and four squadrons of home-based heavy bombers would also be employed. These are for that period of the war big figures, but not extravagantly so, if the Chiefs of Staff were right to call the scheme our 'first and best chance of wresting the initiative and . . . shortening the war'.

On 16th February a new turn was given to the situation when the destroyer *Cossack* was sent into Jössingfiord, south of Stavanger, in order that a boarding party might rescue 299 British merchant seamen incarcerated in the German auxiliary warship *Altmark*, to which they had been transferred from the pocket battleship *Graf Spee* before the latter was caught by the Royal Navy off the River Plate early in

December. The Norwegian Government complained bitterly of the infringement of territorial waters by our ships; the British Government found in this startling revelation of the misuse of these waters for German military purposes, which the Norwegians had shown themselves powerless to prevent, an additional justification for the long-considered action against the Narvik iron-ore traffic. It was very nearly touched off, but at the last moment postponed again in favour of the larger plan.

For this the French Prime Minister, M. Daladier, desired *une opération brusquée*,[1] but the British did not. The Chiefs of Staff canvassed the pro's and con's of rushing our 'volunteers for Finland' ashore at Narvik and perhaps the southern ports in the hope that Norwegian opinion might accept or even welcome a *fait accompli*. But it was not until the eleventh hour or later, namely at 6.30 p.m. on 12th March, three days after the Finns were known in London to be negotiating for terms with the Russians, that instructions to commanders for action along these lines received Cabinet approval—and even then the execution of our plans still presupposed some degree of acquiescence, at least, on the part of the Norwegian and Swedish Governments. This had not been secured when the Finnish surrender, announced on the night of the 12th/13th, put an end to the only argument which had any chance of persuading the Scandinavian Governments or peoples to hazard their neutrality.

On 14th March the British War Cabinet decided, with the reluctant assent of the French, that in the altered circumstances our plans would meet with positive resistance from Norway and Sweden and might drive them into the arms of Germany. The War Office stood down the three forces which had been got ready, and the 5th Scots Guards, a volunteer battalion of skiers trained at Chamonix, was actually disbanded. But a change of government in France, which brought M. Reynaud into power on 21st March as the champion of a more aggressive policy, renewed the demand for action. It was now decided to start by solving the original problem of the passage of the iron ore south from Narvik by the original method, namely, the mining of the Leads so as to drive enemy shipping out of Norwegian territorial waters. This operation, christened 'Wilfred' by Mr Churchill as being 'minor and innocent',[2] nevertheless required some justification in the eyes of the world for the breach of neutral rights which it would undoubtedly involve. The *Altmark* episode having been allowed to fade into the past, a more formal procedure was now to be adopted. Norway and Sweden were to be warned that their conduct as neutrals worked out in practice to the advantage of Germany; that this was the more intolerable because Germany in

---

[1] Reynaud: t. II, p. 26.
[2] Churchill, Winston S.: *The Second World War*, Vol. I, 1st ed. 1948, p. 599.

principle was the enemy of the independence and rights of small Powers, of which the Allies were the champions; and that in consequence the Allies reserved the right to take appropriate action. This was to be followed by the laying of minefields in Norwegian waters, of which no previous warning would be given to the Norwegian Government. This in turn, it was supposed, might be followed by German counter-action against Norwegian territory; and this, by the acceptance by Norway of an Allied occupation of Narvik and the three southern ports, for which troops (but no aircraft) would be held in readiness. Expectations about Sweden were less clear, but it was hoped that circumstances would enable the force landed at Narvik to reach the orefields as the champions of Sweden against aggression, actual or hypothetical. Once established in the far north, we had a further scheme for blocking Lulea harbour with mines laid from the air.

In detail, Operation Wilfred and the associated military Plan R.4 involved, firstly, the laying of two minefields, in the approaches to the Vestfiord north of Bodö, so as to close the passage south from Narvik, and off Stadland (between Aalesund and Bergen), with the pretended laying of a third near Molde. This operation, though not previously announced to the Norwegian Government, entailed the double risk of Norwegian counter-action in defence of neutrality and of action by German warships which fortune or foresight might bring into the vicinity. The plan therefore involved as its second feature the disposition of units of the Home Fleet so as to protect the mine-laying. There would be a small covering force to consist of one cruiser and two destroyers. Two other cruisers and three destroyers at Rosyth and —at longer notice—three more cruisers from Scapa were to be available as a striking force against any German sortie that might result. Thirdly, the plan provided for a military expedition to take immediate advantage of the somewhat vaguely defined moment when 'the Germans set foot on Norwegian soil, or there is clear evidence that they intend to do so'. Narvik and its railway as far as the Swedish frontier formed the primary objective. To this port there was assigned a force of one infantry brigade with one light anti-aircraft battery, of which the first battalion was to set sail in a transport escorted by two cruisers a few hours after the mines were laid. The forces to occupy Bergen and Trondheim and to raid Stavanger were on a smaller scale, totalling five battalions plus technical troops; but the timing of the operation would have sent them from their embarkation port on the same day as the Narvik expedition and, as the four battalions for Stavanger and Bergen were to be sent in cruisers, there was a reasonable supposition that they could forestall a German landing. The Trondheim battalion would reach the Norwegian coast two days later.

It was intended to make Narvik into a regular base, with local defence forces and fuel supplies. The Allied strength there was to be built up from French sources to a total of 18,000 men, and there was even a prospect of air support (one fighter squadron and one army co-operation flight) in the event of a move on Gällivare. The battalions at Bergen and Trondheim would be less fortunate. Not only were they left without any prospect of air support (though so much nearer the German bases), but on the ground they depended for their build-up upon the hope that the two battalions at Stavanger might succeed in rejoining them, if the latter were attacked by superior German forces, and the intended provision at a date unspecified of 'such reinforcements as may prove necessary . . . in the face of German action'. Lastly, it should be noticed that each of these expeditions was to be 'organised and equipped on as light a scale as possible' and was envisaged as landing in a friendly port or at worst in the face of sporadic, temporary resistance from misguided Norwegians, not Germans—a limited scope which in the sequel was all too quickly forgotten or ignored.

The ideas which found expression in the German plan *Weserübung* can be traced back to controversies regarding German naval strategy in the First World War, in which the views of Admiral Wegener played a leading part. His book *Die Seestrategie des Weltkrieges*, published in 1929, was well known in naval circles in Britain and America and even Norway, with its study of the implications of Germany's geographical situation and its insistence that the main function of a navy is to open and maintain access to ocean trade routes. This had not been achieved by defending 'the dead angle of a dead sea' (the German North Sea ports languishing under the effects of a British blockade) and would not in the Admiral's opinion have been achieved even if the German navy had successfully occupied the coast of Denmark.

> The Norwegian position was certainly preferable. England could then no longer maintain the blockade-line from the Shetlands to Norway but must withdraw approximately to the line of the Shetlands—the Faeroes—Iceland. But this line was a net with very wide meshes. The fresh wind from the ocean then already blew from afar into the stifling atmosphere of the hunger-blockade. Moreover, this line was hard for England to defend: for in the first place it lay comparatively near to our bases; but above all, as the map shows, we should considerably outflank the English strategic position to the north.[1]

Although the pressure of the British naval blockade in the first winter

---

[1] Wegener, Vice-Admiral Wolfgang: *Die Seestrategie des Weltkrieges* (Mittler, Berlin 1929), p. 49.

of the Second World War was far from reconstituting the hunger-blockade of Admiral Wegener's argument, his general theory at least prepared the way; it is even alleged that Hitler treated Wegener's writings as his 'naval bible'.[1] Grand-Admiral Raeder, the earliest advocate among German war leaders of aggression against Norway, first laid the matter before the Führer on 10th October 1939, when the latter promised consideration of his suggestion of 'how important it would be for submarine warfare to obtain bases on the Norwegian coast, e.g. Trondheim, with the help of Russian pressure'. Almost two months later Raeder returned to the attack on a different score, pointing out that a German occupation of Norway was the only effective way of blocking the trade routes from Norway to England, because they started from so many scattered points on the Norwegian coast, and conversely, that a British occupation would endanger the control of the Baltic, on which German naval warfare essentially depended.

At this juncture the strategic was fortified by the political argument, when Vidkun Quisling, the leader of the tiny 'National Union' party in Norway, was brought before Hitler by Raeder and Rosenberg, the expert on Nazism for export, as the leader of a promising national-socialist movement which would facilitate a bloodless invasion of his country. This caused the operation, as conceived and authorised by Hitler, to be based at the outset on the two alternative hypotheses: that it might be carried out by peaceful methods, with the German forces entering Norway at the invitation of a Norwegian Government, real or sham, or by an invasion without such pretext. In the end, German confidence in Quisling's proposals was so small that he was not informed of the German military plans in time for him to take any advance measures of co-operation before the landings: the German military authorities let him into the secret at Copenhagen on 4th April, only five days before the invasion, when he furnished some mistaken intelligence about the gun defences of Narvik in return.[2] Nevertheless, he has double importance in relation to *Weserübung*, because he held out the prospect of co-operation by treacherous Norwegians, which made the plan seem less foolhardy, and also because he directly influenced Hitler to favour such a plan by his allegations that British intervention in Norway was imminent. On the whole, it appears that Hitler himself regarded the occupation of Norway primarily as a preventive measure and that, although instructions to make a plan date from Hitler's first meeting with Quisling on 14th December, the effective decision to implement it resulted from the *Altmark* episode of 16th February, which showed

---

[1] Article by Dr H. Rosinski in *Brassey's Naval Annual 1945*, p. 144.
[2] Sundell, Colonel Olof: *9 April*, p. 106.

that in certain circumstances Britain was ready to infringe Norwegian neutrality.[1] Meanwhile Quisling's accomplice, Hagelin, a Norwegian long resident in Berlin who was conveniently engaged in selling German anti-aircraft guns and coal in Norway, was assiduous in providing reports of British military preparations arising out of the Finnish campaign.

A study for a possible operation against Norway and Denmark was accordingly authorised on 14th December: it was to be made by officers of the three services under the auspices of the Supreme Command of the Armed Forces (O.K.W.). An order of 27th January 1940, signed by General Keitel, marks the transition from theoretical consideration of the project as 'Study North' to detailed preparation of *Weserübung* (Weser Exercise) by a planning staff which was to be the nucleus of a future operational staff. The Chief Planning Officer was Captain Krancke, who worked to a large extent under Hitler's personal supervision, and from 21st February the project took final shape with the appointment of a commander. This was General von Falkenhorst, who had been suggested by Keitel; he had served as Chief of Staff to von der Goltz when the Germans intervened in Finland in 1918. Hitler's order to complete arrangements for the execution of the plan was signed on 1st March and included a definition of its strategic aims. 'This operation will prevent British encroachment in Scandinavia and the Baltic; further, it will guarantee our ore base in Sweden and give our navy and air force a wider start-line against Britain'.[2] From this date the only matter still left for decision was the actual timing of the operation and its official pretext.

By this stage the plan used separate names for the two aggressions against Norway and against Denmark, the latter being designed chiefly to make the attack on Norway easier, but it will be convenient to use the term *Weserübung* throughout for the Norwegian operation, properly known as *Weserübung Nord*. The success of the plan must not blind us to the difficulties under which it laboured—difficulties arising from personal jealousies of both the Army and the Air Force (including Göring) against a plan sponsored by the Navy; difficulties arising from its superimposition upon the main plan for the attack in the west, which had been postponed from November to the spring; and difficulties arising from the naval odds. These weighed so heavily against Germany that Raeder himself at a conference with Hitler on 12th December entered the *caveat* that the German Navy could not yet 'cope for any length of time' with severe surface warfare off the Norwegian coast. *Weserübung* had therefore to be based essentially on secrecy, speed, and deception—secrecy of preparation,

---

[1] See p. 13.
[2] Martienssen, A.: *Hitler and His Admirals*, p. 50.

speed of execution, and deception as to the objective. In view of these considerations the number of troops to be employed was kept to a minimum and General von Falkenhorst was debarred from occupying certain minor ports, including Namsos and Aandalsnes. But the occupation of Oslo, the capital; Kristiansand on the south coast; Stavanger, Bergen, and Trondheim, the principal west-coast ports; and Narvik in the north—which was considered to be the minimum for holding the country and excluding the British—was judged to require a force of six divisions. Therefore the essence of the plan was to find a means of conveying and landing the six divisions which would meet the requisite conditions, particularly those of secrecy and speed.

The plan was accordingly based in the first instance on finding an alternative for the orthodox method of transporting a military expedition overseas. Six divisions would normally have required more than half a million tons of transports protected by warships, constituting an armada which Germany could not in fact have mustered in full strength, and which would in any case have clearly advertised its intentions to the British and the Norwegians long before it could have reached Norwegian waters at transport speed. Instead, the Germans decided to embark their first échelon of 8,850 men in warships; these would move fast and would not proclaim their destination, but would, of course, be seriously handicapped by their load in the event of a naval engagement. Moreover this decision involved the use, for conveyance or protection, of the entire German fleet. But the warships could not carry the equipment, so by an elaborate and carefully timed series of operations slower-moving merchant vessels were to go on ahead—one group of seven steamers figuring as normal traffic for Murmansk, others travelling singly and trusting to luck to escape investigation. Some would lie in Norwegian harbours as coal ships, awaiting *der Tag*; all were to be at their port of destination in the course of the first day. The equipment force, as we may call it, carried also a small additional provision of troops, but the first serious reinforcements were not due until the third and fifth days of the invasion. These would be directed to Oslo only and redistributed thence by land or air (or possibly by sea) as occasion served. Thus very small initial forces were expected to take their separate objectives by surprise; some equipment would quickly be made available and they were then to hold on pending reinforcement. There was to be an immediate turn-round of the shipping used, and all warships —with the exception of two destroyers, which Hitler decided to retain for harbour defence at Trondheim—were to try to get home to German waters as quickly as possible, those from Bergen and farther south slipping back along the coast, those from the two northern ports attempting a combined break-through. It was however assumed that in the Skagerrak area British counter-measures would not prevent the passage of reinforcements northwards continuing over a period of several weeks.

Finally, we may notice that the naval plan included elaborate arrangements for using, or rather abusing, the British flag, names of British warships, and communication in English so as momentarily to confuse the issue if the invaders were challenged at Norwegian harbours. For that moment of penetrating the harbour defences was foreseen as being in all probability the crisis of the whole expedition, the more so as the latest Intelligence reports from Norway suggested an increase of alertness on the part of the naval authorities. But with or without deception the plan assumed, on much the same arguments as had brought Hitler triumphantly through Munich and other crises, that the Government of a peace-loving people would sooner let the moment for action pass than risk the charge of precipitating total war.

The 10th Air Corps at Hamburg was to support the attack on Norway and Denmark with a force of 1,212 aircraft (1,008 immediately serviceable). Rather more than one-half of these were transports used by Germany's civil air lines before the war, which would drop paratroops to seize the big airfield at Stavanger (Sola) and the main Oslo airfield of Fornebu and would subsequently be used to fly-in airborne troops and the more urgent supplies. There would be a hundred fighters to deal with Norwegian air units, which it was hoped to catch on the ground, and later with the expected intervention of the Royal Air Force, and about four hundred long-range bombers would be available to support the German landings from the sea and to engage British naval forces on their approach to Norwegian waters. They had also a more general task, to induce the submission of Government and people by the threat of devastation which their mere appearance in Norwegian skies would convey.

Army Group XXI, the force placed at the disposal of von Falkenhorst, had been formed by the army authorities under orders which specified the employment of first-class troops. Of the six divisions, however, only one had been in action before, namely the 3rd Mountain Division, and its experience in Poland amounted to very little because it was not motorised and in that quick-moving campaign usually arrived too late. General Dietl, who commanded it, was a personal friend of Hitler and a mountain expert—he had even attended winter manœuvres in Norway before the war. It seems probable that these mountain troops with their special training and equipment, first embodied as a division under the same leader at Graz in 1938, were set aside for Narvik in the expectation of a spectacular success. The other five divisions received no special training or equipment, and for security reasons only their commanding officers were given any advance information about the intended campaign.

The history of British and German planning for the eventuality of war in Norway makes two things clear. One is that the Germans enjoyed an enormous advantage because the carrying out of their plan did not depend upon Norwegian goodwill, whereas the Allied military advisers had considered and rejected in advance the idea of forcing an entry into Norway in the face of positive resistance by Government or people. But the advantage which the Germans enjoyed through their consistent disregard for neutral rights was liable to be cancelled out if Britain took the first step; and her control of the seas made it possible at any time by mining or similar action to deny to the Germans the use of territorial waters. The timing of operations in fact largely determined their immediate outcome.

The main considerations for both sides were the established facts of climate and weather, the general political situation, and what was known or guessed as to enemy intentions. Neither side would have chosen to fight in Norway under winter conditions; but the British had hoped originally to enter Norway with a sufficient margin of time for their forces to be in a position to defend Lulea by the second half of April, when the break-up of the ice in the northern part of the Baltic might make a German seaborne attack on that port possible.[1] For the Germans, on the other hand, a limit was set by the period of generally low visibility, frequent storms, and long nights, needed to give the German ships a reasonable chance of reaching Trondheim and still more Narvik without interception. Politically, as we have seen, Allied hopes were for a long time tied up with the Finnish campaign, which might enable forces sent to defend Finland under the general auspices of the League Covenant to get a footing in Scandinavia. After the Finnish surrender the Allies had to consider instead how to present their general argument, to the effect that the Norwegian interpretation of neutral rights conferred an unreasonable advantage upon Germany, in such a way as to conciliate American and other neutral opinion. As for Germany, Jodl's diary describes Hitler on 13th March 1940 as 'still looking for some justification' for *Weserübung*,[2] but as no new excuse was found during the succeeding month it is probably more realistic to suppose that in its political aspect the important decision was that taken on 3rd March, when after a good many changes of plan the attack on Scandinavia was given precedence over the attack upon the Low Countries.

---

[1] The opening of Lulea to traffic was to be expected between 26th April and 28th May (*Baltic Pilot*, 3rd ed., 1937, Vol. III, p. 13).

[2] *Nazi Conspiracy and Aggression* (*Proceedings of the International Military Tribunal at Nürnberg*), Vol. IV, p. 392.

The part played on either side by knowledge of enemy intentions is more difficult to determine, because the period of the so-called 'phoney war' was one in which Europe seethed with rumours of plans and counter-plans, making it almost impossible for Governments to separate truth from fiction, still more to base action upon appreciation. Thus the British Foreign Office noted as early as 19th October 1939 an unsupported rumour of an impending partition of Scandinavia between Germany and Russia. Then on 8th January 1940 the Foreign Secretary informed the War Cabinet of a secret report, dated 29th December, that the Germans were ready to act in southern Scandinavia. On 3rd February, we find the War Cabinet examining a circumstantial report despatched by our military attaché from Stockholm on 20th January: a neutral colleague had explained to him in some detail plans to secure the Narvik-Lulea railway route and subsequently to occupy both southern Sweden and southern Norway, on which the Germans were said to be now actively engaged. On 26th March, the British Minister in Stockholm reported the concentration of German aircraft and shipping, possibly for the seizure of Norwegian airfields and ports, as information obtained from a Swedish officer which was corroborated by other news of shipping massed at Kiel. On the 30th the French Admiral Darlan, desiring authority to requisition merchant ships so as to put the French expeditionary force for Norway at one week's notice for embarkation, argued that 'Recent information shows that Germany has collected the means for an expedition against the bases in south Norway, Stavanger, or Sweden: it is not unreasonable to imagine that she will react on the morrow of our diplomatic *démarche* or of the minelaying'.[1] His letter, addressed to Daladier and General Gamelin, does not indicate the sources on which he relied in his appreciation, but reports of various kinds were by now fairly widespread; the possibility that they 'might portend an invasion of Scandinavia' was put, for instance, to the British Chiefs of Staff at their meeting on the morning of 3rd April. The final preparations for a large-scale expedition could not be wholly concealed from neutral eyes, and it has been suggested that Admiral Canaris, head of the German Intelligence Service, and other highly placed officers who opposed Hitler were deliberately indiscreet.[2] The most circumstantial, and in retrospect the most interesting, report was one received through a neutral Minister in Copenhagen on 6th April, to the effect that a division conveyed in ten ships was due to land at Narvik on the night of the 8th. It was not for a moment believed that the Germans could anticipate us so far north; but by this time special arrangements had been worked out between the Cabinet and the

---

[1] Reynaud: t. III, p. 31.
[2] Sundell: pp. 91-92, 107, 132.

Chiefs of Staff to avoid any last-minute hitch in authorising our expeditions to sail at once, when the moment came, because the Germans might forestall us at Stavanger or possibly involve us in a race for Bergen or even Trondheim.

The Germans knew less of Allied plans; there was less to know. But, as we have seen, the fear that the other side might get their blow in first was strong in Hitler's mind at least from the time of his interview with Quisling in December. It would not require much in the way of secret military intelligence to inflame his fears: even before the *Altmark* episode the speeches of the First Lord of the Admiralty implied that German misuse of Norwegian territorial waters would not be tolerated for ever, and the manœuvres in which the Allies engaged in order to secure an official Finnish appeal for their help were precisely the kind of stratagem of which Hitler would be quick to detect the earliest traces. Thus on 30th December his naval conference was considering the 'danger that volunteers from Britain, in disguise, will carry out an unobtrusive occupation of Norway'. As for specific operations, according to information which reached the British War Cabinet on 20th February, French officials in Stockholm were then talking openly of an expedition to Narvik, and a fortnight later the details of proposed arrangements for securing Norwegian ports seemed to be more or less public property in the same capital, which was notoriously honeycombed with German espionage. The German naval staff at this juncture had even listed the countermeasures, including invasion of South Norway, to be taken 'on receipt of the first intelligence of any British landing in northern or western Norway'—an event which up to the time of the Russo-Finnish peace treaty was considered imminent. But Admiral Raeder's final forecast, given to the Führer on 26th March, was that Britain was more likely to strike first at Germany's trade in neutral waters, in hopes of a German reaction which would occasion a British landing.

The German operation *Weserübung* was framed originally so as to be ready on 20th March. The British plan, accepted by the Supreme War Council on 28th March, was to come into effect with the minelaying on 5th April, as a sequel to the despatch of justificatory Notes to the Scandinavian Powers on 1st or 2nd April. This meant that the Germans would have got their blow in first and the world might never have heard of the mining operation; but the persistence of ice in the Baltic and the Great Belt caused a German postponement and it was not until 2nd April that Hitler, after reference to the period of moonless nights—the new moon was on 7th April—finally decided upon 9th April. This would have given the Allies a small margin of time after their minelaying, in which the west coast of Norway could have been occupied with Norwegian agreement according to plan, if—and it is a big 'if'—the immediate German reaction had been sufficient to warrant, but insufficient to impede, our intervention. But at the meeting of the Supreme War Council the decision to initiate the action in Norway had been linked, with the consent of the French Prime Minister, to the initiation of another action—the sowing of fluvial mines in order to disrupt traffic along the Rhine. The British authorities had long been pressing for this operation (which the French opposed as being likely to provoke German air attacks) and we believed that its novelty and boldness might distract American attention from the possible illegality of our intended action off the Norwegian coast. The French War Committee, under the influence of M. Daladier, now in effect went back on the agreement, and this caused a three-day postponement of the Norway plan for fruitless expostulation. The Notes therefore were not delivered in Stockholm and Oslo until 7 p.m. on the 5th, by which time a newspaper agitation about our supposed intentions had developed in the two capitals; the actual minelaying was due to follow on the 8th.

Thus it came about that the naval forces of both sides were in motion simultaneously for the execution of their respective plans, some of the Germans having started from their more distant bases a little earlier. But the German plan provided for landing operations unconditionally at all points at 4.15 a.m. on 9th April, whereas the British plan provided for a succession of conditional landings, which would only take place if evidence of a suitably hostile German reaction to the minelaying were available immediately, and in that event would follow it at an interval ranging from one to four and a half days. Even then, the British landings were to be further conditioned by our ability, through diplomatic pressure at the centre and local liaison, to avoid serious and active resistance by the Norwegians. In point of fact, there would have been token resistance and consequent delays.

CHAPTER III

9th APRIL—THE GERMAN PLAN IN ACTION

See Map 1(a), facing p. 42

IN the first week of April British preparations for the intended stroke were duly completed. Admiral Sir Edward Evans was to command the naval side of the expedition for Narvik and had hoisted his flag at the Clyde on the 4th in the cruiser *Aurora*. This ship, together with a second cruiser still at Scapa, was to escort a big transport which took the first troops on board on the morning of the 7th. By the same date the single battalion for Trondheim was aboard a second transport in the Clyde and the four battalions for Stavanger and Bergen had embarked with ninety tons of stores to each in four more cruisers lying in the Forth. The cruiser *Birmingham*, which was already in the Lofoten area in search of a German fishing fleet, was originally intended to support the minelaying in the north; but it was finally decided to send the battle cruiser *Renown*, flagship of Vice-Admiral W. J. Whitworth. Her presence would discourage any counter-action by the Norwegians, who had moved two of their coast defence ships to Narvik on 1st April, and were believed by us to have moved all four, though the other two were actually at Horten and out of commission: the British orders were to 'refrain from replying to Norwegian fire until the situation becomes intolerable'. To meet the graver and more probable contingency of German retaliation in the form of a seaborne expedition against Norway, two cruiser forces were available, one at Rosyth and the other on convoy duty in the latitude of Scapa. Support was also provided by an increase in the number of submarines on patrol: under orders given on the 4th nineteen vessels (including two French and the Polish submarine *Orzel*) were directed to the Kattegat-Skagerrak-southern North Sea area. Lastly, some provision had been made for air assistance by moving No. 204 Squadron (Sunderland flying-boats) to the Shetlands station of Sullom Voe.

The *Renown*, screened by four destroyers, sailed from Scapa on the evening of 5th April for her rendezvous with the cruiser *Birmingham* (which the latter was unable to keep owing to bad weather) and was joined *en route* by the northern minelaying force of eight destroyers, including four for escort. These carried out the laying of the minefield in the approaches to the Vestfiord north of Bodö at 4.30 a.m. on the

8th. The second minefield, off Bud near Molde, was duly created by two destroyers warning traffic of the non-existent danger. The third, off Stadland still farther south, was entrusted to the minelayer *Teviot Bank* and four destroyers, which left Scapa on the 5th but were recalled before zero hour. The British action was simultaneously announced in Oslo in a Note covering all three areas, and the Norwegian authorities protested energetically both in Oslo and at the scene of action. The Norwegian Navy quickly detected the fact that there was no minefield off Stadland and took over the patrol of the supposed minefield off Bud from the British destroyers, which then withdrew. The Norwegians also began preparations to sweep the mines in the Vestfiord, though the British force at first remained there.

The rest of our plans were then cancelled piecemeal on account of the news that the German fleet was out. It was for this reason that the third minelaying expedition had been abandoned. Then at 10.45 a.m. on the 8th the northern minelaying force was ordered by the Admiralty to leave the neighbourhood of its minefield—where (as we now know) it would have been likely to intercept the Germans making for Narvik—and rejoin the *Renown*, which was patrolling farther off-shore. Meanwhile the dispositions of the Home Fleet under the command of Admiral Sir Charles Forbes were being revised in the hope of bringing heavy German units to battle. The Admiralty decided that every ship was needed for strictly naval purposes and that in any case no expedition should be risked until the naval situation was cleared up. Shortly after midday they informed the Commander-in-Chief accordingly: the cruiser *Aurora* which had been intended for Narvik would leave the Clyde for Scapa instead, and the four cruisers lying with troops in the Forth would complete disembarkation by 2 p.m. and sail northwards, also to rejoin the fleet. This critical step, which involved the abandonment of a carefully considered military expedition, seems to have been taken by the Admiralty independently and to the surprise of the Prime Minister. The First Sea Lord issued the order; the Commander-in-Chief, Home Fleet, who already had superior forces at his disposal, was not consulted. Thus the measures adopted to secure the traditional object of a decisive encounter at sea, which was not secured, deprived us of our best chance to restore the position on land.

The execution of the British Plan R.4 had now given place to counter-measures against *Weserübung*. The execution of the German plan had in fact begun a little earlier with the despatch of the pretended coal ships, etc., on 2nd April, but the vital operations were those of the main naval forces and troops which began to leave North

German harbours on the evening of the 6th. Three days later there was not a single warship left in port (unless under repair), while some twenty-eight submarines—about two-thirds of the force available for all purposes—were also engaged in the protection of this operation. These German forces were organised in eleven groups, five of which had decisive parts to play. The battle cruisers *Gneisenau* and *Scharnhorst*, under command of Vice-Admiral Lütjens, accompanied ten destroyers carrying the two thousand soldiers who were to seize Narvik. A second group, composed of the heavy cruiser *Admiral Hipper* and four destroyers, set out upon the shorter but still venturous voyage to Trondheim, where 1,700 men would be landed; and the *Hipper* was then to rejoin the two battle cruisers for an excursion into the southern half of the Arctic Sea, in the hope of diverting British naval forces from pursuit of the smaller German units operating farther south. There were two groups of light forces for the landing of 900 men at Bergen and about 1,100 at Kristiansand and Arendal; and a larger group including the heavy cruiser *Blücher* and the pocket battleship *Lützow* had orders to penetrate the long Oslofiord and land about 2,000 men for the occupation of the capital. The only serious hitch in the initial stages of the plan was the occurrence of engine damage in the *Lützow*. This had necessitated the transfer of this powerful ship from its position in the Trondheim group, in which it also had a special task assigned to it of breaking through into the Atlantic, to the less exacting Oslo assignment, the possibility of serious resistance by the coastal artillery being apparently discounted.

Oslo was to be secured by the 163rd Division under General Engelbrecht, which was also to supply the men to occupy Kristiansand, the Norwegian naval and military headquarters for the south coast, and the smaller port and cable station of Arendal. The 196th Division, commanded by General Pellengahr, would follow up, spreading eastwards from Oslo to the Swedish frontier. The 69th Division was to occupy Egersund (with the cable to Peterhead) and the main south-western ports of Stavanger and Bergen; Kristiansand and Stavanger would later be handed over to the 214th Division. General Dietl's 3rd Mountain Division was to make the initial seizure of Trondheim as well as Narvik, but it was intended to bring the 181st Division to Trondheim six days later, so that the whole of the 3rd Mountain Division could be concentrated under its commander at Narvik, the post which was most likely to remain for a long time in isolation and under attack.

The route of the German expedition was as follows. The Oslofiord was approached through the Great Belt and the Kattegat from the German bases in the Baltic. The other groups proceeded north from Wilhelmshaven, leaving the shelter of the Jade and the Weser estuary at dawn for the advance into the North Sea. The smaller forces for the more southerly ports made directly for their destinations, subject to the fact that great care was taken to synchronise the actual entry into Norwegian coastal waters. The more heavily escorted forces for Trondheim and Narvik advanced together, moving farther out into the North Sea to the west of the route taken by the smaller expeditions, until the afternoon of the 8th, when they separated into two forces in a latitude considerably north of Trondheim. The first part of the plan was in general carried out to time, heavy weather and poor visibility acting less as a hindrance to precise navigation than as a defence against the search of wide areas of sea by numerically superior British forces.

The Admiralty had had substantial news of a foray by German ships on the 7th. One cruiser and six destroyers, accompanied by eight fighter aircraft, were sighted by R.A.F. Hudsons at 8.5 a.m., about 150 miles south of the Naze. The enemy ships were steering northwards. The information first reached the Commander-in-Chief, Home Fleet, at 11.20 and more fully half an hour later, to be considered in the light of the discovery of the *Gneisenau* and *Scharnhorst* in Wilhelmshaven Roads by the R.A.F. three days before and the unusual lights and activity seen near various North German ports by bombers returning from a leaflet-dropping raid the previous night. Later in the morning the Admiralty sent him the following telegram:

> Recent reports suggest a German expedition is being prepared; Hitler is reported from Copenhagen to have ordered unostentatious movement of one division in ten ships by night to land at Narvik, with simultaneous occupation of Jutland. Sweden to be left alone. Moderates said to be opposing the plan. Date given for arrival at Narvik was April 8th.
>
> All these reports are of doubtful value and may well be only a further move in the war of nerves. Great Belt opened for traffic April 5th.

The intelligence was good but belated (it had been received in London at 1.20 a.m. the previous day), the appreciation most unfortunate. The information came from a neutral Minister in Copenhagen, as we have previously noticed, but seems to have been interpreted in the light of a further message (received in London on the afternoon of the 6th) giving his evaluation of the report as 'in principle fantastic'. Unfortunately also the Commander-in-Chief had just received another aircraft report, this time of three destroyers in approximately the same area but now steering south. However, in any case he had already decided to await the result of an R.A.F. attack on the German ships, pending which he brought the fleet to one hour's notice for steam. Twelve Blenheim bombers of No. 107 Squadron found the enemy shortly before 1.30 p.m., seventy-eight miles farther north than before. The attack, though followed up with a search by a second force (of Wellingtons), had no success, but they had reported the Germans much more accurately as one battle cruiser or pocket battleship, two cruisers, and ten destroyers. Having received this report at 5.30—delayed because the bombers had been told not to break wireless silence—Sir Charles Forbes sailed from Scapa at 8.15 that evening in the *Rodney*, with the capital ships *Valiant* and *Repulse*, two cruisers, and ten destroyers, and steered at high speed N.N.E. in search of the enemy. A further sweep in the North Sea would be carried out by two cruisers and eleven destroyers from Rosyth (2nd Cruiser Squadron) under Vice-Admiral G. F. B. Edward-Collins, who sailed an hour later to join the Commander-in-Chief. Two more cruisers under Vice-Admiral G. Layton (18th Cruiser Squadron) lay to the west of the Home Fleet, protecting a convoy for Norway which was now ordered back into Scottish waters. On the last occasion when the Germans were known to be advancing through the North Sea in strength and the Fleet had sailed to find them, in the same month twenty-two years earlier, we had been able to deploy thirty-five capital ships, twenty-six cruisers, and eighty-five destroyers.

For twenty-four hours the Commander-in-Chief kept on towards the north, searching beyond the latitude of Trondheim, but in vain. The only contact made by surface ships with the enemy that day was by accident. The *Glowworm*, forming part of the destroyer screen for the *Renown*, which had left Scapa on the 5th to cover the minelayers,[1] fell behind in the heavy weather after stopping to pick up a man fallen overboard. As she followed the *Renown* northwards towards the Vestfiord at a little after seven o'clock in the morning of the 8th, in a position W.N.W. of Trondheim, she sighted two enemy destroyers belonging to the Narvik expedition which had likewise lost contact through the weather. The first German destroyer made off at high speed followed by two salvoes from the *Glowworm*, and a running fight ensued against the second. This action, begun just after 8 a.m., went in our favour, but the German ship was able to call for help from the heavy cruiser *Hipper*, which opened fire on the *Glowworm* within an hour. Utterly outmatched, she replied with a salvo of torpedoes, and then disappeared momentarily in a smoke-screen. The *Hipper* avoided the torpedoes but ran into the smoke-screen and, after failing to answer her helm in the high seas, came into the path of the British ship, which rammed her to such effect that 130 feet of armour belt and the starboard torpedo-tubes were torn away from her side. The *Glowworm* blew up a few minutes later; her captain, Lieutenant-Commander G. Broadmead Roope, when the full story became known was posthumously awarded the Victoria Cross.

[1] See p. 25.

The first duty of the destroyer, however, had been to report her sighting of the enemy—a part of the German force of which the whole fleet was in search. This she had done in a series of signals from 7.59 until she sank: the reported position was about 140 miles from the *Renown*, 300 from the main fleet. The Commander-in-Chief detached the *Repulse*, with the cruiser *Penelope* and four large destroyers, in a vain attempt to make contact. Admiral Whitworth in the *Renown* was nearer—though the Germans may have been as much as sixty miles farther south than the *Glowworm's* reckoning—and turned more hopefully southward to intercept the enemy. His search was, however, impeded by the heavy seas, which caused the flagship to show signs of damage, and poor visibility, and only one of his four destroyers remained at his disposal. But during the morning the Admiralty (as we have already noticed) directed the eight destroyers which had been minelaying in the Vestfiord to join him, and also gave the Admiral a message that the previous day's report of a German expedition to Narvik might after all be true. He therefore turned back north again to rendezvous with the destroyers.

While the Home Fleet likewise continued northwards, something of the German intentions was being disclosed farther south, where the Polish submarine *Orzel* was on watch near the mouth of the Skagerrak. About mid-day she challenged and sank off Lillesand the German transport *Rio de Janeiro*, from which about a hundred German soldiers were brought ashore by Norwegian fishing boats. On interrogation they disclosed to the Norwegian authorities that they were on their way, with guns and transport, to 'protect' Bergen.[1] But this event, though known at the Admiralty in the early afternoon and published by Reuter from Oslo at 8.30, was not reported to the Commander-in-Chief, Home Fleet, until 10.55 p.m. This was the more unfortunate as all that day the North Sea weather had been most unfavourable to air reconnaissance. The only new local information which Sir Charles Forbes received came from a Sunderland flying boat of No. 204 Squadron scouting ahead of the fleet. This spotted a German battle cruiser, with two cruisers and two destroyers, seen momentarily through a gap in the clouds of rain at 2 p.m. in a position W.N.W. of Trondheim, well out to sea and steering west. Damaged by anti-aircraft fire the Sunderland could not remain to observe the enemy, whom a second flying boat and the *Rodney's* aircraft were unable to rediscover. This was in reality not surprising, as these ships were not on a set course but cruising to and fro while they awaited zero-hour for their entry into the Trondheimsfiord next day. The Home Fleet, however, was misled by this unlucky chance into

---

[1] Scheen, Captain R.: *Norges Sjökrig*, Vol. I, p. 140.

altering its course to N.N.W., away from the Norwegian coast. Further information from the Admiralty, originating with the Naval Attaché at Copenhagen (and later confirmed by two of our submarines posted off the Skaw), complicated the picture by indicating that there were other large vessels in the Kattegat or Skagerrak. A German force had evidently passed northwards ahead of our main fleet—in actual fact it had got beyond the latitude of Scapa before the Commander-in-Chief weighed anchor: but we could still hope to intercept its return journey. The second German force presented a more promising objective at the moment, especially as an additional squadron, composed of four more cruisers from Rosyth (now minus troops), one French cruiser, and two French destroyers, was now also on its way north under the command of Vice-Admiral J. H. D. Cunningham (1st Cruiser Squadron).

Accordingly, at 8 p.m. on 8th April, the Commander-in-Chief turned south and made arrangements for a patrol line of cruisers to sweep northwards during the night. The Admiralty, however, fearing that the cruisers might be caught between two enemy forces, altered the dispositions in the small hours, ordering Admirals Cunningham and Edward-Collins to meet and steer towards the fleet as Admiral Layton was already doing from farther north. The change of plan did not lead to success; the Germans, preparing to enter the fiords of West and South Norway, were favoured by poor visibility and all made their destinations, though the expedition bound for Bergen escaped our cruisers by a narrow margin.

There remained the possibility that, if the Germans were making for Narvik, they might still be caught by Admiral Whitworth's force farther north. The eight destroyers, struggling through heavy seas, had duly joined him off the Skomvaer light (about 70 miles to the west of Bodö) at 5.15 p.m. Then, after weighing the advisability of entering the storm-bound Vestfiord, he moved out to sea for a time instead, with the hope that he might intercept the squadron which had been sighted by the flying boat W.N.W. of Trondheim. While thus employed he received definite Admiralty orders 'to concentrate on preventing any German force proceeding to Narvik'; but the weather remained extremely severe and Admiral Whitworth felt obliged to keep his nine destroyers close together and to hold his course more to the northward than he would otherwise have done. The *Repulse* and her little squadron were ordered to join him, but did not arrive until 2 p.m. next day. In all the circumstances it is not surprising that he failed in his mission to intercept the ten German destroyers, which parted company with their escort off the Vestfiord about eight o'clock that night and set their course for Narvik unmolested through the waters from which the minefield patrol had so recently withdrawn. But Admiral Whitworth made contact instead, as it happened, with the big ships proceeding from their escort duties to create a diversion in the Arctic.

At midnight (8th/9th April) there was a temporary improvement in the weather, and the squadron had turned south-eastwards at early dawn when, about 50 miles west of Skomvaer Light, they sighted two darkened ships in the direction of the Norwegian coast just emerging from a snow squall. Admiral Whitworth reported them as a battle cruiser and a heavy cruiser, though they were in fact the *Gneisenau* and the *Scharnhorst* together—a very natural mistake, since similarity of design in different classes of German ships had given them similar silhouettes, but one which left the Admiralty still guessing as to the whereabouts of the second battle cruiser. The *Renown* opened fire just after 4 a.m. at a range of rather more than ten miles, engaging the *Gneisenau* with her main armament and the *Scharnhorst* with her 4·5-inch guns. A heavy sea from ahead was now rising again, so that the destroyers rapidly fell astern of the conflict and even the British battle cruiser was handicapped by having to slow down to fight her fore-turret, whereas waves breaking over the forecastle would not affect the use of their after-turrets by the enemy. But the *Renown*, though less strongly armoured than either of her opponents, sustained no serious damage from the heavy shell which struck her three times. The *Gneisenau*, on the other hand, when the range had closed to about eight miles received a hit on the foretop, which destroyed the main fire-control equipment and temporarily disabled her main armament. She therefore altered course to break off the action, and the *Scharnhorst* crossed her stern to make a smoke-screen. The *Renown* turned northward in pursuit of the *Scharnhorst* but did not succeed in hitting her, though two more hits were registered on the *Gneisenau*. Then just before five o'clock the German ships disappeared in one of the snow squalls which from time to time obscured all but the flashes from the guns, and when the weather cleared some twenty minutes later they were farther off than before. For a few minutes the *Renown* raised her speed to twenty-nine knots, but after some more ineffective firing by both sides the enemy ran out of sight into the north. About eight o'clock Admiral Whitworth for a short time turned west, hoping to cut off the enemy if they had broken back to southward—in actual fact the German ships did not turn south for more than twenty-four hours, by which time they were far out to the west in the neighbourhood of Jan Mayen Island. But the British Admiral was already coming back towards the Vestfiord when, soon after 9 a.m. on the 9th, he received the Admiralty instructions to the Commander-in-Chief for a watch to prevent the Germans from landing at Narvik, with which port the later operations of his force are connected.

That morning the situation was simplified, inasmuch as the Commander-in-Chief had learnt in the small hours from the Admiralty, and to a less extent from the reports of submarines, that German ships were being engaged by shore defences in the Oslofiord and had also approached Trondheim, Bergen, and Stavanger. His immediate reaction to the fact of invasion was to prepare an attack on Bergen by Admiral Layton's cruisers, which were then joining the fleet (6.20 a.m.); two hours later, as Sir Charles Forbes steamed on southwards to the rendezvous with his two other cruiser forces, he received the Admiralty's orders to prepare attacks against German warships and transports in Bergen and if possible Trondheim. It should be noted that the coastal defences were believed to be still in Norwegian hands. The attack on ships in Trondheim was however cancelled by the Admiralty before noon, to avoid an undue dispersion of forces pending the location of the German battle cruisers known to be at large. As for Bergen, the Commander-in-Chief reported that his ships could go in by the fiords north and south of the port in three hours from the receipt of a definitive order to do so. A force of four cruisers and seven destroyers under Admiral Layton was detached for the purpose at 11.30 a.m., by which time the fleet had moved a considerable distance southward, so that in the face of a strong northwest wind some time was lost in making the approach to Bergen. The plan was for the destroyers to penetrate the fiords and destroy the enemy forces, believed to include one light cruiser, while the British cruisers remained in support at the entrances. Just after two o'clock the Royal Air Force, which made nineteen reconnaissance flights over the Norwegian coast that day, reported that there were two enemy cruisers at Bergen: this belief, together with a growing uncertainty as to whether the enemy did not control the shore defences, caused Admiral Layton to regard an attack by destroyers as unduly hazardous. The cruisers might nevertheless have gone in, and we now know that the Germans in Bergen were not at this stage able to operate the shore batteries—though they quickly laid mines which they had brought with them—and had made ready to take refuge in the hills, if our ships had appeared. But at this juncture an Admiralty telegram, timed just before the aircraft reconnaissance report, arrived to cancel the attack. Sir Charles Forbes had, however, an alternative in view, namely a torpedo attack by aircraft from the carrier *Furious*.

But during the afternoon a new factor caused serious modifications in the plan for the Home Fleet. Since about eight o'clock in the morning it had been shadowed by German aircraft in clear weather, and although the fleet turned north again at mid-day this did not take them out of the range of shore-based bombers, which made a series of attacks from about half past two until 5.30. Their first objective was Admiral Layton's force returning from its sally towards Bergen. Two cruisers were slightly damaged by near misses and the destroyer *Gurkha* was sunk. The Germans then turned their attention to the main body of the fleet and a diving aircraft dropped a 1,100-lb. bomb on the deck of the flagship (H.M.S. *Rodney*): structural damage was slight and casualties were remarkably low, but the implications of the event seemed very serious. In later attacks several more bombs fell near ships, including the *Rodney*, and three cruisers sustained minor damage, though there were no more direct hits. The Home Fleet's anti-aircraft barrage brought down one enemy aircraft; some units had thrown up forty per cent. of their 4-inch ammunition. The Commander-in-Chief held on northward for some hours after the attack, cruised westward during the night, and turned towards the Norwegian coast again on the morning of the 10th, when a third battleship, *Warspite*, joined the flag, as did the aircraft carrier *Furious*. But the prime result of the German air attacks had been that the Commander-in-Chief proposed to the Admiralty an important change of plan. His 'general ideas' now, he stated, were to attack the enemy in the north with surface forces and military assistance, but to leave the southern area mostly to submarines, on account of the German air superiority in the south. In particular he reported that the *Furious*, which had been hurried to sea by Admiralty orders without its fighter squadron (Skuas), could not work so far south and should be diverted to Trondheim, leaving Bergen to the R.A.F.

Twelve Hampden and twelve Wellington bombers were sent to the Bergen area in the early evening, while the full German force, including two light cruisers, two torpedo boats and an M.T.B. depot ship, still lay in the harbour. There were several near misses but little damage was caused, and one light cruiser (*Köln*) accompanied by the two torpedo boats put to sea on the return journey an hour later, though they went into hiding for the first night at the head of the narrow Maurangerfiord. Apart from the air attack, cruiser forces and destroyers, including two French destroyers, had been disposed under Admiralty instructions to pin down the ships at Bergen and Stavanger and to prevent their reinforcement; but this patrol terminated at 4 a.m. on the 10th without contact. By the next evening the Admiralty had formally ruled that 'Interference with communications in southern areas must be left mainly to submarines, air, and mining, aided by intermittent sweeps when forces allow'.

Farther south, however, an important success was scored by a submarine off Kristiansand. The light cruiser *Karlsruhe* was torpedoed by *Truant* at 7 p.m. on the 9th, one hour after leaving port, and sank about three hours later. Submarines had indeed begun to take toll of enemy transports and supply ships in the Skagerrak and Kattegat the previous day, when they also sank a tanker in much the same area as the *Rio de Janeiro*. Within a week, helped by Cabinet permission to attack shipping off the coasts of South Norway at sight, they sank nearly a dozen vessels (including the escort ship *Brummer* and one enemy submarine) and damaged the pocket battleship *Lützow* and others. But these operations, which ultimately cost us four submarines, became increasingly hazardous because of the shortening of the nights and the progress of the German counter-measures, which were unchallenged by surface ships. The strength and effectiveness of the patrol were therefore gradually reduced.

The ports which the Germans seized on 9th April included each of the four biggest towns in Norway and a clear majority of the principal mobilisation centres. In a single swoop they had established themselves at a series of points stretching round the coast from Oslo to Bergen; at Trondheim, 250 miles north of Bergen; and at Narvik, 360 miles north of Trondheim. It is hoped that a separate account of the crucial events in and near the capital, followed by a still more cursory note of what happened in the other areas from south to north, will not obscure the fact that the simultaneity of the attacks was itself a most important element in achieving the bewilderment of the Norwegian people and the success of the German aims.

The approach to Oslo involved a long passage up the Oslofiord and the Norwegians received considerable warning, since the German ships were challenged at the mouth of the fiord at 11.6 p.m. on 8th April by the Norwegian patrol boat *Pol III*, a 214-ton whaler, which raised the alarm (and rammed a German torpedo boat) in the very few minutes before the machine guns of an undeclared enemy had gravely wounded her captain and set the vessel on fire. He died in the water, the first victim of Grand-Admiral Raeder's instruction that resistance was to be ruthlessly broken. A little farther in, the island fort of Rauöy engaged the leading German ship without effect in the fog; but the real function of Rauöy and its sister fort of Bolaerne on the other side of the fiord was to guard a minefield, the key defence of the area—but no mines had been laid, for reasons which included the hope of British naval assistance. Having passed, the Germans stopped in the fiord to organise landing parties, which eventually captured these outer forts from the rear, and to detach a small force against Horten, the Norwegian naval base, which lay farther up on the west shore. A courageous defence was made by the minelayer *Olav Tryggvason*, but the Admiral surrendered the base at 7.35 a.m. under the usual German threat of remorseless bombing from the air. Meanwhile the main convoy, due to reach Oslo at 4.15, had resumed the advance at low speed, with some lights showing and its most valuable units leading the way. But there was another Norwegian fortification—built originally at the time of the Crimean War, when it was reputed the strongest in northern Europe—at Oscarsborg, where the navigable channel narrows to five or six hundred yards at a point about ten miles short of the capital. Here the Norwegian batteries, armed with three 28-cm. guns (Krupp model of 1892), some 15-cm. guns, and torpedo tubes, and manned with particular enthusiasm, scored a success of some significance to the naval war at large as well as to the time-schedule for the occupation of Norway. Germany's latest cruiser, the *Blücher*, was set on fire, torpedoed, and sunk with the loss of about 1,000 men, including most of General Engelbrecht's staff for the occupation of Oslo. The *Lützow*, which had also been damaged, and the other ships had therefore to turn and land their forces on the east bank of the fiord, whence they advanced towards the capital more slowly. The forts were eventually reduced by naval and air bombardment and the sea route reopened after more than twenty-four hours' delay. But at 8 a.m. a separate attack had been launched against the Oslo airfield at Fornebu. A part of the airborne forces landed by mistake in advance of the paratroops, who were delayed by fog, and the anti-aircraft defences destroyed three German aircraft and damaged five. But the situation was hopeless, as the only modern fighters the Norwegians had, nineteen Curtis Pursuits just received from America, were still lying on the ground in their crates. The small military field (Kjeller) offered no resistance. By midday six companies of airborne troops had been landed, to whom Oslo was surrendered as an open city. But the important fact is that Oslo, unlike the other ports, was not firmly in German hands during the vital period of the morning of the 9th. Had it been, the Government could not have organised resistance and the success of the German *coup* would have been complete.

Only twenty-four hours earlier the attention of the Norwegian Government had been engrossed by the sudden *fait accompli* of the British mining and the call for an immediate and urgent protest against the breach of neutrality which it involved. But from 10 a.m. on the 8th messages began to flow in from Sweden and Denmark, reporting the ominous procession of German ships northwards through the Great Belt and the Kattegat. These might have been taken to show that this was not a case of false alarm, as on former occasions in December and February, and that there was substance in the telegram received from their Berlin Legation on the evening of the 5th—'Rumours of an occupation of points on the south coast of Norway'.[1] Then came the news of the sinking of the *Rio de Janeiro* and at 5.15 p.m. a report from the Divisional General at Kristiansand about the indubitably military character of the ship and its alleged

---

[1] *Norwegian Parliamentary Report*, Appendices, Vol. II, p. 148.

destination.[1] This was followed almost at once by a detailed confirmation from the Legation in London of a warning that a German attack on Narvik might be expected from 10 p.m. onwards; the Deputy Chief of Naval Staff had given this in an interview at the Admiralty soon after one o'clock, and the gist of it had been telephoned immediately to Oslo. No effective action was taken, however, either during the parliamentary sitting that evening or in the meeting of Ministers which followed. The coastal fortresses had been alerted, but were not authorised to lay the essential mines; north of Bergen the beacons were not even extinguished; the decision to mobilise the army was after three days' discussion at Ministerial level still postponed.

The fact of invasion became clear a little before midnight of the 8th/9th with the initial attack on the outermost fortifications of the Oslofiord, and the nationality of the invading force was definitely established in a report from Bergen at 1.35 a.m. The Government had entered into a midnight session, which was still in progress when the German Minister (Dr Brauer) arrived with his demands at the appointed hour of 4.15. The War Commands for the Services had already come into operation, and at 2.35 a.m., when the British Minister was informed by telephone of the naval attack, the Foreign Minister, Dr Koht, had used the words, 'So we are now at war'. Even then the Government decision was for a partial and unproclaimed mobilisation (the call-up to be by post), affecting the four southern divisions of the army and watch detachments on both sides of the Oslofiord, with Thursday the 11th as the first day on which troops were to present themselves at their prescribed centres. Such was the purport of the official Mobilisation Order, despatched to the Divisional Commands about 6 a.m. by telegram; but there was put out over the Norwegian broadcasting system an hour and a half later a chance interview with the Foreign Minister at the railway station. He then spoke of general mobilisation, as a result of which many of those concerned believed the call-up to be immediate and comprehensive and reported accordingly, only to find that they were not expected. Since German infantry was already being landed within ten miles and German aircraft were actually over the city, the one project was now scarcely more hopeful than the other as regards Oslo or indeed any of the main centres of population. Norwegian public opinion has not been disposed to censure the Government of April 1940 in retrospect for its desperate reluctance to take any action which might precipitate war, but its members have been censured for their ignorance of the mobilisation machinery when at last they had to set it in operation.[2]

In the long run, however, what mattered most to Norway was the

---

[1] See p. 30.
[2] *Norwegian Parliamentary Report*, Appendices, Vol. II, p. 212.

decision which at this crisis kept the Government in being. Dr Koht, in his early morning conversation with the British Minister, had expressed the opinion that the defences of Oslo were strong enough for the Government to stay there. But wiser counsels prevailed, and about 7.30 a.m. a special train conveyed the Royal family, the Cabinet, most members of the Parliament, and a small proportion of civil servants about seventy miles inland to Hamar. The immediate result was to make the capital an easy prey to rumour; to allow a confused situation to develop there, in which a handful of German troops with some air support were able to take a town of 250,000 inhabitants by bluff; and to give Quisling his chance to assume governmental authority, including control of the broadcasting station. His first official act, at 7.30 p.m. the same day, was to cancel the mobilisation. This heightened the confusion, but did not succeed in obstructing the political developments which centred on Hamar.

A short breathing-space had been secured. This was spent in the first place in taking plenary powers for the Government, which would give legal validity to its actions if the Parliament were no longer free to meet and even if the Government were forced to operate from outside the country. At Elverum, to which the Parliament adjourned its sittings the same evening in the belief that Hamar was already insecure, they were within fifty miles of the Swedish frontier (which the Crown Princess and her children crossed that evening). More important than the powers was the decision slowly arrived at to use them for war. The Parliament had apparently begun by approving of the Government's rejection of the German demands, but later in the day depression set in. The loss of Narvik became known for the first time, as well as the completeness of the disaster at Bergen and Trondheim; the British and French promises of help were found to be less immediate and comprehensive than had been hoped; and the example of the Danish surrender was not without effect. Accordingly, before the Parliament had completed its sittings and dispersed from Elverum, it gave its approval without a division to the renewal of negotiations, which the German Minister had proposed, and appointed a small delegation for the purpose. The long day ended with a last-minute decision, for which a certain Colonel Ruge was partly responsible, that in spite of the pending negotiations the troops were to defend a barricade on the road to Elverum against the approach of a small German detachment in lorries. The Germans lost some men there, including the Air Attaché from the Oslo Legation, who had planned to settle the matter by capturing the King, and they withdrew. The negotiations next day were conducted by King Haakon himself (at the insistence of the German Minister) and Dr Koht, but the formal decision was taken subsequently at a Cabinet meeting. The German demands in general had gone up, not down, and in particular they now included the acceptance of an unconstitutional government under Quisling; for Hitler had already erected that name into a shibboleth. The King informed his Ministers that he would abdicate rather than be a party to this breach of constitutional principle; they at once followed his lead; and the Germans were informed by telephone that 'resistance would continue as far as possible'.[1] The decision was now final. A Government which knew less than most about the art of war, as the events of these three days clearly demonstrated, nevertheless had the faith and courage to accept a challenge which much larger countries than theirs shirked facing. This was the more remarkable because they were already virtually fugitive. From the moment when the Parliament dispersed on the morning of 10th April the contact between the Government and the rest of the country was inevitably disrupted. While they maintained themselves as best they could in inland valleys, where King and Ministers were the target of German bombers, the enemy strengthened his hold on each of the main centres of population on the western seaboard as well as in the south and east.

Kristiansand, the port which dominates the north side of the entrance to the Skagerrak, with its small but useful airfield (Kjevik), had obvious attractions for the German armada known to be proceeding northwards; the *Rio de Janeiro* had been sunk not far away. Thick early-morning fog embarrassed the Germans on arrival and their approach was met by resolute fire from the fortifications. Two attempts were repulsed, and in a third the *Karlsruhe* nearly ran on to the rocks. Then there arrived an order to the effect that British or French forces were not to be fired on, with the result that the flag of the German squadron, when it came into sight again shortly afterwards from the west, was read or more probably misread as French. During the ensuing confusion the cruiser *Karlsruhe* and her consorts passed into the harbour, where resistance ended about 11. The occupation then proceeded so smoothly that the German cruiser, in company with the smaller forces detached to Egersund and Arendal, was able to put to sea again the same evening, only to be torpedoed about ten miles out, as previously related.[2]

Farther west, at Stavanger, a Norwegian destroyer sank one of the so-called German 'coal-boats' (actually loaded with anti-aircraft and other artillery) on suspicion soon after midnight on the 8th/9th, but there the Germans employed the then novel method of airborne invasion. Although the Sola airfield, eight miles south-west of Stavanger, was by far the most considerable in Norway, it had no regular anti-aircraft protection, and the few Norwegian aircraft on

---

[1] *Norwegian Parliamentary Report*, Appendices, Vol. II, p. 276.
[2] See p. 34.

the ground were ordered to fly eastwards at 8 a.m., just as the first Germans arrived. These were six Messerschmitt 110s, which destroyed two Norwegian aircraft but had as their main object an initial bombing of the airfield and its two concrete machine-gun posts. They were followed by ten transport aircraft carrying some hundred and twenty paratroops, who dropped and captured the field after a short struggle. Then came the main force, half destined for Sola and half for the seaplane harbour nearby; a total of 180 aircraft flew in during the day.

Stavanger was in any case unfortified; more remarkable was the taking by surprise of the defended west-coast ports, Bergen and Trondheim. Norway's second- and third-largest towns were in the event securely gripped by German hands while the population was still waking to its day's work. At Bergen, the outlying fortification was passed by the German squadron in the darkness without difficulty, though some mines were laid at the last moment which caused losses to German convoys later on. There were, however, two more powerful forts on high ground nearer in, whose commanders refused to be hoodwinked by a signal in English, 'Stop firing! We are friends!' and did serious damage to the cruiser *Königsberg*. But they could not prevent the landing of troops from the smaller ships, who overran the town in an hour, and the forts then surrendered to the first bombs of the German air force over Norway. The safety of Trondheim depended on the two forts, Brettingen and Hysnes, which command the entrance to the fiord on the north bank near Agdenes, some thirty miles north-west of the town: a third fort existed on the south bank, the manning of which was still under active discussion when the Germans arrived. The batteries received a warning of hostilities a little before 1 a.m. and of the approach of German warships just two hours later. Nevertheless, the German squadron, consisting of the *Hipper* and four destroyers, was able to force the entrance at a speed of twenty-five knots, materially helped by the fact that the first salvo with which they answered Brettingen's fire destroyed the electric cable on which both forts depended for their searchlights. This enabled the Germans to put their troops ashore about 7 a.m. in Trondheim, which offered no resistance. One destroyer was left behind with the landing parties for the forts, but Hysnes opened fire with some effect, causing the destroyer to be beached, and the defenders did not surrender until the afternoon; by then the *Hipper* had been brought back from Trondheim to support the assault. Vaernes airfield, sixteen miles east of the town, held out until midday on the 10th, but the Germans had immediately improvised an airstrip on the ice for their transport 'planes, without which the position could scarcely have been consolidated.

Lastly, there were the ten German destroyers which had eluded the

British search and made for Narvik.[1] Coastal batteries at the mouth of the Ofotfiord existed only in Quisling's imagination, though the Germans (and to a less extent the British later on) made careful search for them; the defence lay much nearer in, in the shape of the two 4,000-ton ironclads, *Norge* and *Eidsvold*, both dating from 1900, but as coastal defence vessels not to be despised. They received the alarm, given at 3.12 a.m. on the 9th by watch boats stationed at the mouth of the Ofotfiord, and made ready for action; but because of the thick weather and the possibility that the approaching ships were British (whom instructions received in the last hectic quarter of an hour had told them no longer to oppose) *Eidsvold* sought to identify them first. There was a parley, which would have been followed by resistance at heavy but not hopeless odds, as only three of the German destroyers had yet arrived off Narvik; but a salvo of torpedoes fired by the German flotilla leader at a range of a hundred yards, on a signal illicitly given by the ship's boat while returning from the parley, blew the Norwegian vessel to pieces.[2] Her consort, lying nearer in by the harbour, heard the crash and was able to fire seventeen rounds before she too succumbed to torpedoes launched by a destroyer which had already reached the quay. Resistance to unprovoked aggression had cost nearly three hundred Norwegian lives. The garrison of about 450 men, which was being hurriedly reinforced at the moment of the German arrival, could still have made some defence with the help of its two newly constructed pillboxes; but its commander, Colonel Sundlo, who was one of the very few followers of Quisling in occupation of a key post, at the critical moment refused to fight. By the time he had been superseded at the order of Divisional Headquarters the Germans were in the town, and it was too late for his successor to do more than extricate one half of the garrison by a bold act of bluff. Meanwhile three other destroyers captured without resistance the important stocks of military equipment at Elvegaard, the regimental depot for the area, about eight miles north-east of Narvik. Thus the stage was set for a naval struggle such as had never before wakened the echoes in those lonely fiords.

---

[1] See p. 31.

[2] The justification offered for General Dietl's action in approving the naval decision to open fire is that the German destroyer was in danger of being rammed by her 40-year-old opponent (Dietl, G.-L. and Herrmann, K.: *General Dietl*, 1951, p. 56).

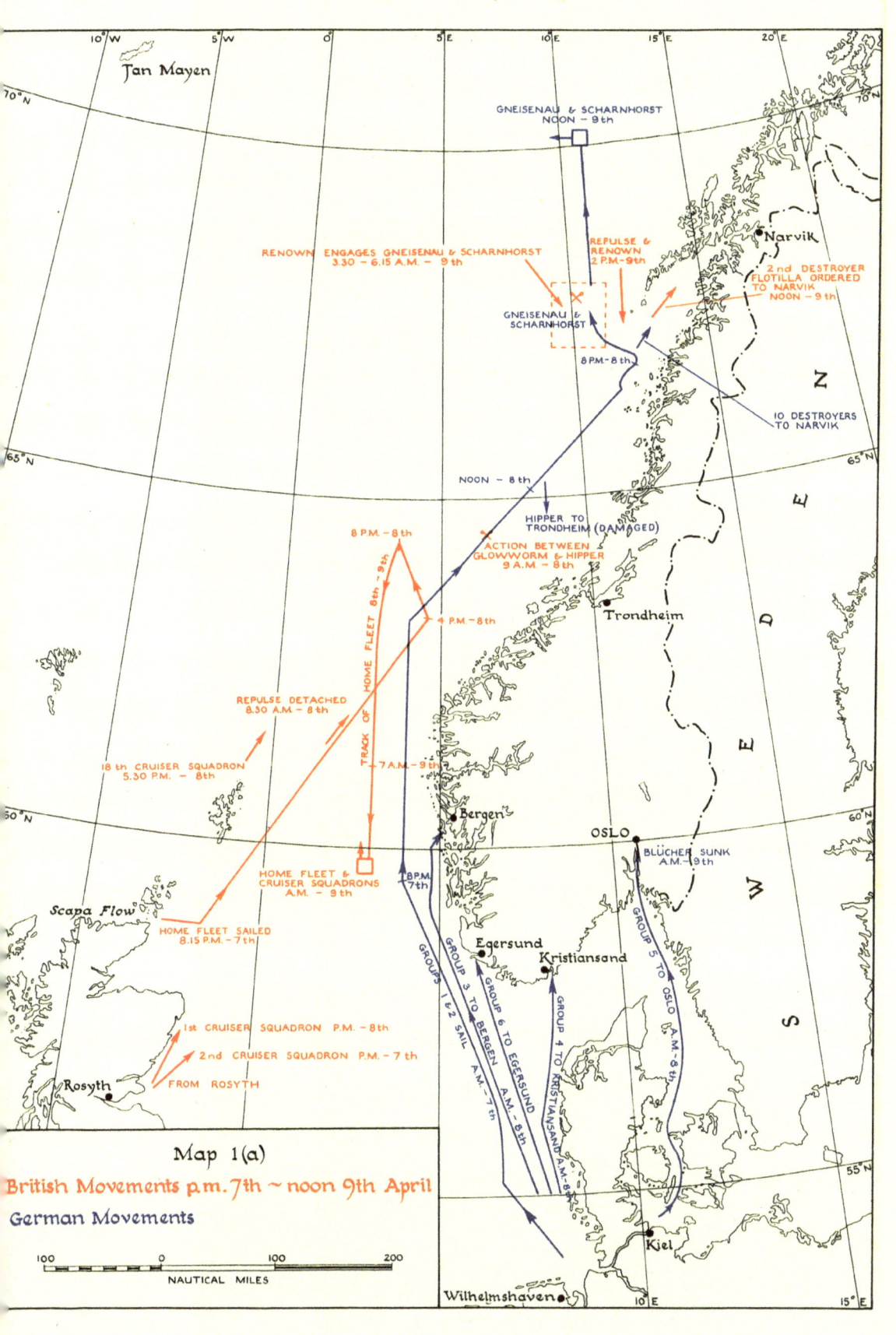

CHAPTER IV

BRITISH COUNTER-MEASURES BY SEA AND AIR

See Map 2, facing p. 50, and Map 1(b), facing p. 56

ON 10th April the story of the initial German successes blends with that of the British counter-thrusts by sea and air. These thrusts were delivered by sea more than by air because of the air supremacy which the Germans had already demonstrated in southern Norway over land and sea, and in the north more than in the south for the same reason. At Narvik the Germans, as they well knew, were running in any case a heavy risk by venturing ten of their relatively few modern destroyers on a voyage so far to the northward that the slightest hitch in the turn-round would enable them to be bottled up by superior British forces. Ruthlessness, as we have seen, had achieved the rapid surrender of the port to the formidable German expedition in the early morning of the 9th. But for reasons which are not wholly clear the British Admiralty remained dependent upon press reports stating that one German ship had arrived at Narvik, no better information being obtained until 4 p.m., when an officer was sent ashore at the Vestfiord pilot station of Tranöy, some fifty miles to the west. His ship belonged to a force of four (later increased off Tranöy to five) destroyers of the 'H' class, about one-third lighter than the German destroyers, which had been despatched by Admiral Whitworth in the early morning to patrol the entrance to the Vestfiord, pending a rendezvous with the *Renown* (still chasing the *Gneisenau* and *Scharnhorst*) and the *Repulse*. But the Commander-in-Chief and the Admiralty had later given direct orders to the flotilla commander to proceed to Narvik, and they were actually on their way in when they learnt approximately what had happened there.

Captain B. A. W. Warburton-Lee, in the flotilla-leader *Hardy*, was told by the Norwegian pilots that six ships larger than his and a submarine had been sighted making for Narvik, which the Germans held very strongly, and that the harbour entrance was mined. He reported this to the Admiralty, the Commander-in-Chief, and Vice-Admiral Whitworth, and at the same time announced his intention of attacking at dawn high water (dawn for surprise, high water for protection against mines) in accordance with the instructions which the Admiralty had sent him at midday on the strength of the misleading press reports referred to above. Admiral Whitworth had already been considering the possibility of reinforcement, with the knowledge that the ships at his disposal would shortly include the *Repulse*, the *Penelope*, and four additional destroyers.[1] But he maintained his decision that he could only reinforce at the cost of the postponement of the attack, for which the order had been issued direct to his subordinate officer. The final Admiralty telegram at 1.36 a.m. on the 10th, which suggested that the two Norwegian men-of-war, in addition to the coastal batteries, might now be in the hands of the enemy, still left it to Captain Warburton-Lee to decide. 'You alone can judge whether, in these circumstances, attack should be made. We shall support whatever decision you take.'[2] If the Admiralty had chosen to address either the Commander-in-Chief, Home Fleet, or Vice-Admiral Whitworth rather than their subordinate officer, then the decision would probably have been to send in a more powerful force even at the cost of some delay; this might have lost the advantage of surprise but would almost certainly have finished off the German naval forces in one engagement instead of two and might even have provided the opportunity for an immediate landing. But Captain Warburton-Lee for his part took the more heroic course.

By this time the five destroyers had passed Tranöy again on their way in, under weather conditions so appalling that they only sighted land once and that when they were about to run aground. The speed of approach along the Ofotfiord was therefore very slow, stern lights being in use to keep formation, but the poor visibility also contributed to the completeness of the surprise. Our ships were not spotted by the German submarines stationed in the outer fiord, which had been misled by sighting them the previous evening sailing in the opposite direction to fill in time; and the one destroyer on patrol had returned to harbour without replacement ten minutes before the British flotilla made its attack. Five destroyers then lay in the harbour itself, including two which were alongside the tanker *Jan Wellem* refuelling: the slowing-up of this process (between seven and eight hours for each pair of ships) through the non-arrival of a second tanker was in fact the reason why the German flotilla had not already left for home. Two destroyers were at anchor in the Ballangen fiord on the south side of the main fiord, about twelve miles short of Narvik; and the other three lay at a lesser distance along the small Herjangsfiord beyond the town.

At 4.30 a.m. the *Hardy* entered the harbour followed by the *Hunter* and *Havock*, while the *Hotspur* and *Hostile* stayed outside with orders to watch the supposed coastal fortification, the sea approaches by which they had come, and the two fiords which open past Narvik to

---

[1] See p. 31.
[2] Despatch by Rear-Admiral R. H. C. Hallifax: Commander H. F. Layman's Narrative, Sec. 8.

the north-east (where three German ships lay) and to the east. The surprise was complete. As the three destroyers in turn made the circuit of the harbour up to the narrow channel (since bridged) which forms the entrance to the Beisfiord, firing fifteen torpedoes and also using their guns, the Germans were still under the impression that it was an air attack. The first torpedo caused a formidable explosion on board the German flotilla-leader, which killed Commodore Bonte, the naval officer in charge of the expedition, and caused the ship to capsize twenty-four hours later; a second destroyer broke in two and sank on the spot; the fire-control equipment was smashed in a third; and the other two destroyers in the harbour were temporarily disabled. The *Hotspur* was then sent in separately to fire her torpedoes, which sank two merchant ships. No counter-action having been observed from outside the harbour, a second attack was made: all five British ships engaged with their guns at the harbour mouth, particularly against the merchantmen lying inside, which were reported to contain military stores. By this time an hour had passed, and although the German warships in the harbour had returned our fire and received some help from the rifles and machine-guns of the soldiers on land, the British flotilla was still virtually unscathed.

A short consultation was then held off Skjomnes. Captain Warburton-Lee concluded that not more than two enemy destroyers were located outside the harbour (four out of six were computed to be inside the harbour, which actually contained five out of ten), and ordered one more attack. The *Hardy* led the line, which was snaked so as to keep guns bearing continuously on the misty harbour entrance, where each ship fired as she turned; the *Hostile*, in the rear, discharged her torpedoes. The number of German merchantmen destroyed rose to six; as the seventh had been beached the previous day, there remained only the important tanker *Jan Wellem* from Murmansk, which was by the pier and somehow still escaped damage. In substance, Captain Warburton-Lee had now completed the task he had set himself, since the German force was clearly too large for there to be any hope of silencing opposition completely, so as to land at the ore-quay. It was at this point that his luck changed.

Towards 6 a.m., as the British flotilla, having completed its third attack, was about to retire down the Ofotfiord, it sighted the three German destroyers which had been lying away to the north-east at the head of the Herjangsfiord. They had received the alarm at 5.15 and were making their way to the scene of action as fast as their depleted oil supply would allow. The British flotilla increased its speed while engaging the enemy at a range of about four miles. But only a few minutes after the *Hardy* had made the signal for withdrawal two more ships appeared out of the mist, coming up the Ofotfiord and cutting the line of retreat. These, which for a brief moment were taken for a supporting force of British cruisers, were in fact the last two of the German destroyers—those which the British had passed unseen in the Ballangen fiord on their way in. Our ships were thus caught between two fires, but poor visibility helped them to force their way past to the south of the enemy, making it once more a stern chase. The flotilla continued to act upon Captain Warburton-Lee's final signal, 'Keep on engaging enemy,'[1] but the heavier German guns now began to take their toll. A shell burst on the *Hardy's* bridge with such effect that for a few critical minutes the Captain's Secretary was the only officer left there to take command. The ship had now lost steam and was on fire forward, so he ordered her to be beached, and she made the south shore about three miles east of Ballangen, where her crew, including many wounded, struggled ashore through the icy water and found safe shelter in the village. Captain Warburton-Lee, when at last persuaded to leave his ship, died of his wounds on the beach; his Victoria Cross was the first to be awarded in the war. The *Hunter* and *Hotspur* were both hit, collided, and drew heavy fire while locked together. The *Hunter* as a result sank in midfiord, but the *Hotspur* though struck by seven 5-inch shells was saved by the two remaining ships, which turned back from their position two miles ahead to cover her retirement. But the German ships which had done the damage—the two from Ballangen—had now received hits affecting their gunfire and the others were short of fuel (as already noted), so after half an hour they broke off the running fight and allowed the three British destroyers to withdraw unhindered.

These then scored a further important success by the destruction of the German ammunition ship *Rauenfels*, which they met and blew up on their way out. The German ships in Narvik had used up half their ammunition. When the two which had completed their refuelling and were in a condition to sail reached Tranöy that evening, they could discern a patrolling cruiser on the horizon and knew their fate was sealed.

During the next few days, Admiral Whitworth was instructed to prevent both the escape of enemy forces from Narvik and the arrival of reinforcements there, while the Admiralty prepared for a further attack. This was complicated by uncertainty as to the strength of the German force remaining and by simultaneous preparations for escorting a military expedition into the area. At one stage the cruiser *Penelope* was designated by the Admiralty to carry out a new operation, but while this was still under consideration she went in search of a rumoured enemy supply ship for Narvik—which, as it turned out, had already been secured by the destroyer *Icarus*—and grounded on

---

[1] Despatch by Rear-Admiral Hallifax: Commander H. F. Layman's Narrative, Sec. 21.

a rock near Bodö. She had therefore to join the *Hotspur* at Skjelfiord,[1] near the southern extremity of the Lofotens, where ships were stationed to cover the approach to the Vestfiord and a repair depot was organised.

One remarkable feat had meanwhile been achieved farther south, when the unrewarded R.A.F. bomber attack on the German ships at Bergen was renewed by the Fleet Air Arm[2] at extreme range from their land base at Hatston, Orkneys, in the early morning of the 10th. Fifteen Skuas scored three direct hits by dive bombing on the damaged cruiser *Königsberg*, which sank in the harbour within three hours. This was the first major warship of either side to be destroyed by attack from the air. But it was not until the early hours of 11th April that the generally northward movement of the Home Fleet enabled the carrier *Furious*, which the Admiral had diverted from her intended employment in the Bergen area,[3] to launch her aircraft against Trondheim. In the meantime the Germans were busy there, as at Bergen, in landing their forces and turning their ships round as quickly as possible. Accordingly, late in the evening of the 10th, after the Royal Air Force had completed its reconnaissance on which the plans for the Fleet Air Arm attack were based, the main prize, namely the *Hipper*, went to sea down the long Trondheimsfiord. Shortage of fuel had reduced her escort to a single destroyer, and this was forced to put back on account of the heavy seas; but the *Hipper* broke through to the north-westward, eluding the watch kept by destroyers close inshore and then all but running into the Fleet itself, which patrolled farther west of the approaches to the port. Her luck held, however, and at the time when our aircraft were over Trondheim she was already preparing to swing southwards towards Germany. The objects of attack were thus reduced to four destroyers, of which the one mentioned above was still making its return journey to Trondheim. Eighteen torpedo-carrying Swordfish aircraft left the *Furious* at 4 a.m. in a position ninety miles from the town and attacked two of the destroyers, which were all they could see except one submarine and merchant ships. Several torpedoes grounded in shallow water and exploded before reaching their targets; no hits were registered. On the return of the airmen, for whom this was their first taste of action, to the *Furious*, the fleet continued northwards towards Narvik, though two destroyers, detached on reconnaissance, made an approach independently to the batteries at the mouth of the Trondheimsfiord, were fired on, and fired back.

---

[1] Pronounced 'Shalefure'.

[2] This title, strictly speaking obsolete since 1937, when the Admiralty resumed full control of naval aviation as an integral part of the Navy, is retained for convenience throughout this volume.

[3] See p. 34.

It was becoming clear that the larger elements in the German fleet had on this occasion slipped through our hands, though at midnight the submarine *Spearfish*, lying in wait off the Skaw, had succeeded in torpedoing the pocket battleship *Lützow* (as previously mentioned)[1] and put her out of commission for a year. The Home Fleet therefore continued north on the 11th, when a second of its destroyers was disabled (but not sunk) by German aircraft, and next day it became possible to launch an air attack on Narvik harbour from the carrier *Furious*. The leading squadron left the ship soon after 4 p.m. on the 12th on a round flight of about 300 miles. There had been no prior reconnaissance, and only Admiralty charts were available which lacked contours. No German destroyer was hit, but some damage was done to enemy positions on land and three small units of the Norwegian Navy, taken over for German use, were sunk. Two of the eight aircraft were lost through enemy fire, but the crews were saved. The second squadron, starting forty minutes later, ran into very heavy snow and turned back without reaching its objective to land on the carrier in the gathering darkness.

On the same day the Admiralty finally gave orders to the Commander-in-Chief to employ a battleship with strong destroyer escort for the destruction of enemy forces and batteries in Narvik. This attack, timed for the afternoon of the next day (13th April), was entrusted to Admiral Whitworth, who therefore transferred his flag to the *Warspite* overnight in a heavy sea. It is safe to say that no 30,000-ton battleship, even one whose history stretched back to Jutland, had ever seen action in inland waters like these before. She would be exposed to the threefold risk of a suspected minefield, possible submarines (we now know that four had been sent to the Vestfiord area), and the torpedoes of enemy destroyers concealed in the side fiords. Nine destroyers were made available for a screen and striking force. Aircraft of the *Furious*, cruising with the heavy units of the Home Fleet to seaward of the Lofoten Islands, were also to conduct supporting operations against Narvik and supposed enemy positions farther out.

The squadron passed the Tranöy light about 11 a.m. next morning. A bomber from the *Furious* met them an hour later but found nothing to attack in the outer reaches of the fiord. More important was the help received from the scouting aircraft of the *Warspite*, serving as the eyes of the fleet. Not only did it sink a submarine at the head of the Herjangsfiord (the first such success in the war), but it was able to observe and report the manœuvres of the first two German destroyers, found in and around the narrows off Hamnesholm. One German destroyer retired, exchanging fire with the British ships at a range of

---

[1] See p. 35.

about seven miles, which was the limit of visibility. The other could not retire as she had been damaged by running aground two days previously—she had in fact been brought out with a view to future employment as a floating battery. This vessel made for Djupvik Bay on the south side of the fiord, where her torpedoes might have been used with effect against the *Warspite*, had not the battleship's aircraft enabled the British squadron to make ready to put the German ship out of action as they passed the mouth of the bay. Our destroyers engaged her with torpedoes and gunfire, so that her own torpedoes passed clear, and her destruction was then completed by the *Warspite*.

By this time the rest of the German squadron had received the alarm and were emerging from the harbour, whereupon a general action began about a dozen miles from Narvik. The leading destroyers went up the fiord as much as three miles in advance of the battleship, which was engaging the enemy with her main armament in so far as the smoke and manœuvres of the destroyer battle permitted. Only three out of six German destroyers could raise steam in time to unite with the *Künne*, the vessel which had fallen back before the British after giving the alarm. These four, to which a fifth was added later, joined action with the British destroyers. Their torpedoes, however, were without effect; and although their gunfire was at first a serious threat to the leading British destroyer, which was acting as guide of the fleet and also had minesweeping duties to perform, they were gradually forced back towards the harbour. At 1.50 p.m. the Germans, still undamaged but running short of ammunition, received the order to retire up the Rombaksfiord lying north and east of Narvik, though the *Künne* made for the Herjangsfiord instead. There she beached herself and was almost immediately torpedoed by the pursuing British destroyer *Eskimo*.

At this stage in the action the British secured a further success, as another of the ships still left in the harbour had now raised enough steam to leave, but was almost immediately overwhelmed. The only casualty among our ships had been the *Punjabi*, which was forced to withdraw with her main steampipe damaged but returned within an hour. Unfortunately, however, the ten aircraft from the *Furious*, arriving over Narvik in good weather conditions after flying there through snow squalls, apparently failed to score any direct hits: two aircraft were lost. Stubborn opposition was also offered by the last destroyer, which was lying in an unseaworthy condition alongside the quay and was engaged for a time by the *Warspite* under the impression that it was a shore battery. But after the retirement of the other Germans three British destroyers entered the harbour and sank the enemy with torpedoes, which are said to have broken the quay as well. In the course of this attack the *Cossack* was hit and went aground at the south side of the entrance, just east of Ankenes.

But the main problem was the pursuit into the Rombaksfiord. Five miles up, the fiord narrows at Straumen to a neck only a quarter of a mile across, with the fairway further reduced by rocks and by the tidal current from which the name derives. It subsequently opens out again between its sombre mountain walls, but there is no view through. The *Warspite* therefore did not proceed farther in, but sent up her aircraft (which spotted two of the German vessels already at the far end of the fiord) and prepared for indirect bombardment if necessary. Four British destroyers led by the *Eskimo* passed through the narrows and engaged two German ships, which were lying in wait with torpedoes in a very strong position just beyond. The *Eskimo's* bows were blown off, so that the progress of her three consorts was held up until she could make her way back stern-first through the narrows, where the wreckage struck bottom. Meanwhile two of the three had almost exhausted their ammunition and one of them also had two of her forward guns put out of action. However, when these and two other British destroyers finally made their way through, they found that their most determined opponent had now run herself on to the rocks three miles up the fiord and that the other three all lay at the very end deserted by their crews, who had made off up a track to the railway. There was nothing more to be done but to search and finally to torpedo one ship which, although aground, remained upright. But the situation might well have been critical, because the configuration of the fiord made it impossible for more than two ships under way to operate simultaneously against an enemy ensconced in its farther end, and we had no means of knowing that the German retreat was conditioned, in part at least, by the exhaustion of their ammunition supply. The three hulls, one of them marked with a huge swastika, are still to be seen in that remote wilderness of barren rock, bearing silent witness to the long arm of British naval power.

By 5.30 p.m. the *Warspite* had returned to a position off Narvik, where the grounded *Cossack* was exchanging a desultory fire with small guns across the harbour; but nothing was left afloat in it except thirteen merchantmen, which it was hoped in due course to investigate. Vice-Admiral Whitworth, having (at 5.42) signalled the sinking of all the German destroyers plus one submarine, then 'considered the landing of a party to occupy the town as the opposition had apparently been silenced'.[1] He decided, however, that the men available were too tired and too few to risk against 2,000 German soldiers whose morale would speedily recover, at any rate unless *Warspite* remained off the town risking submarine and air attack. About a dozen German aircraft were in fact sighted within half an

---

[1] Despatch by Vice-Admiral W. J. Whitworth, Sec. 44.

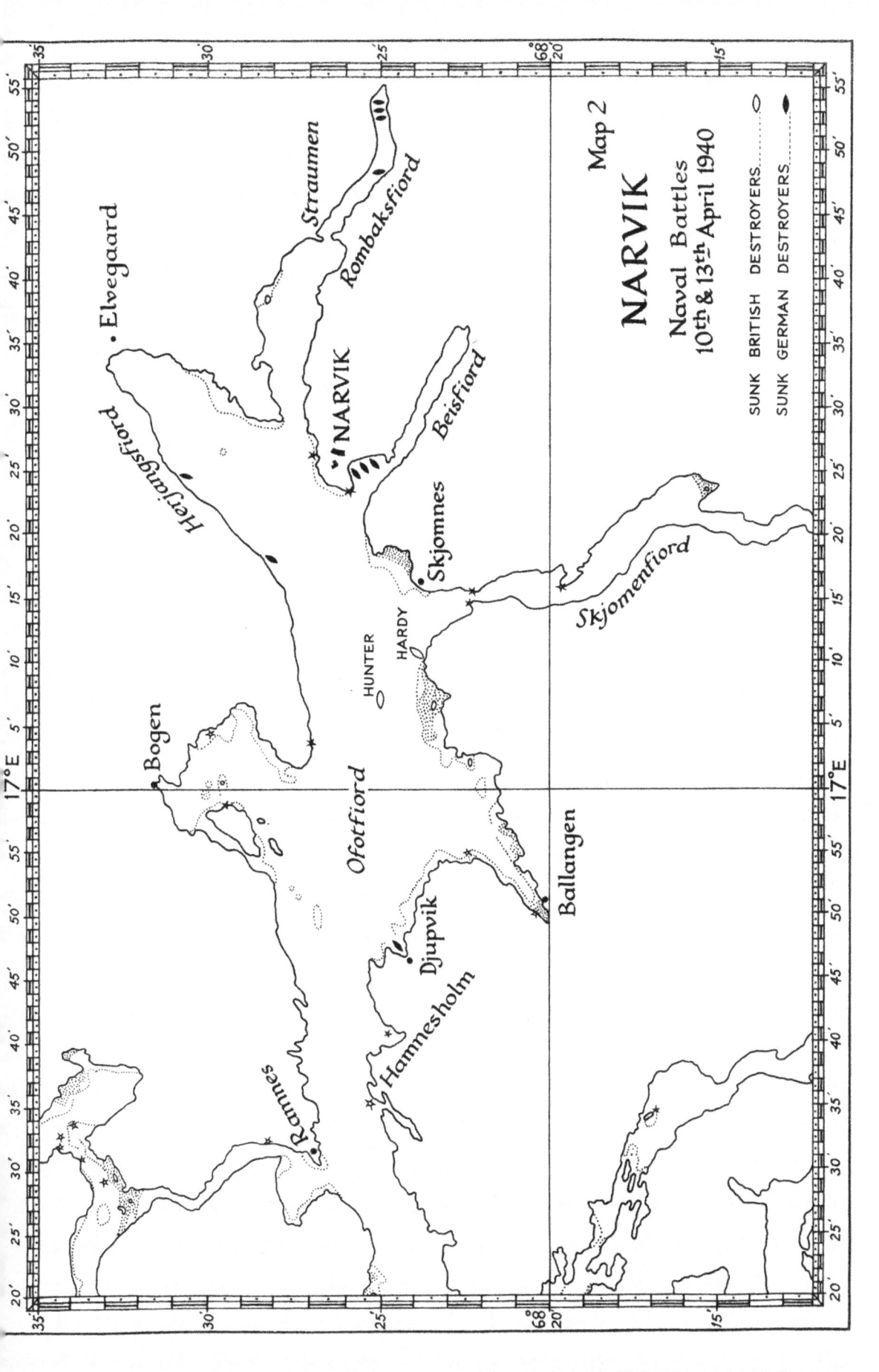

hour. The main force accordingly started down the fiord about 6.30, though the *Warspite* later turned back and remained through the night taking wounded on board. Our casualties were twenty-eight killed and fifty-five wounded, but one of two additional destroyers which had been sent up the Ofotfiord to Narvik at the close of the action picked up off Ballangen the survivors from the *Hardy* as well as some other British seamen from sunk merchant ships. The squadron did not actually withdraw into the Vestfiord until the following morning. Two destroyers were then left at Narvik to make a further investigation of the merchant ships, but this was abandoned the same day, apparently on account of a call for a submarine hunt.

An Admiralty telegram, timed at 9.15 p.m. on the 13th, had urged the Commander-in-Chief to occupy the town of Narvik so that there could be no opposition to a landing later. It is not clear whether Vice-Admiral Whitworth knew of this signal, wireless conditions inside the fiord being very poor, but he did later that evening report his 'impression that enemy forces in Narvik were thoroughly frightened' and recommend that the main landing-force should occupy the town without delay; he also stated his intention of taking the *Warspite* in again.[1] He followed this up next morning with an informational message which pointed out that *Cossack* was not seriously molested by the Germans although aground in Narvik Bay for twelve hours, and suggested that a small landing force could complete the task, given naval support of the strength of his own squadron.[2] But by the 15th Vice-Admiral Whitworth in the *Warspite* was cruising farther west, under orders from the Commander-in-Chief to keep outside the Vestfiord unless required for an operation; the landing of the long-projected Narvik expedition was then in progress fifty miles away at Harstad instead.[3]

Though the 1st Cruiser Squadron under Vice-Admiral Cunningham also stayed behind to examine the fiords northwards to Kirkenes, the naval operations arising directly out of the German naval thrust terminated on the departure of the Commander-in-Chief with the *Rodney* and *Renown* from his station off the Lofotens for Scapa on the evening of 15th April. The *Gneisenau* (with foretop and one turret damaged) and the *Scharnhorst* had passed far to the west of the Home Fleet and made their way back safely to Wilhelmshaven on the 12th. Our resounding successes at Narvik must be balanced against the fact that for six vital days the Germans had had a battle cruiser force at sea and largely unlocated, which necessitated the concentration of the Home Fleet and its exposure to air attack and distracted attention at

---

[1] Signal made at 10.10 p.m. to Commander-in-Chief, Home Fleet, and repeated to Admiralty; see Admiral Whitworth's Despatch, Sec. 57.

[2] Despatch by Vice-Admiral Whitworth, Sec. 66.

[3] See Chapter X.

the critical moment from the *coup* directed against the Norwegian ports. The Germans had lost one heavy cruiser, two light cruisers, and ten modern destroyers. In relation to their total naval resources this was a big price to pay.[1] But they had secured a big military advantage in return—a chance of overrunning the whole southern half of Norway, which the soldiers were quick to exploit. They had also obtained a compensatory advantage in terms of sea power, since a brief trial of strength had enabled the German air force to deny the British Home Fleet its control of the Skagerrak and eastern North Sea within range of Stavanger and the Danish airfield at Aalborg.[2]

Having failed to crush the German invasion of Norway by naval action, Britain turned to a counter-invasion instead. But logically a third alternative was possible—a sustained attack by air against the communications which were the enemy's life-line. It will be convenient to trace the history of our efforts to achieve this now, although they in fact continued *pari passu* with the landings in Norway over a period of almost exactly one month. Against the German Navy the Royal Air Force at this time had no success. In the early morning of 12th April the strenuous reconnaissance work on which it had been engaged throughout the invasion period was indeed rewarded by the detection of the elusive German battle cruisers, when they had just been rejoined by the *Hipper*, south of Norway, on the last lap of their return journey. But a force of no less than ninety-two bombers scoured the misty North Sea for them in vain; and when part of it went on to attack another warship reported at Kristiansand, six Hampdens fell victims to the German fighters. The attack on enemy supply ships and transports had then already begun with a night raid in the Oslo area, remote and difficult of access, in which twenty-three Whitley bombers secured one direct hit. Such raids were continued from time to time by bomber forces, by aircraft of Coastal Command making their regular reconnaissance patrols, and (to a small extent) by Skuas sent out from the Fleet Air Arm station at Hatston in the Orkneys. At this stage of the war, however, the bombing of ships at sea was not technically at all easy, and in the all-important Skagerrak-Kattegat area the R.A.F. could not do more than supplement our submarine activities. But the Air Force also gave direct support to surface craft which revisited the area to help the submarines, when three French destroyers made a dash into the Skaggerak on the night of 23rd/24th April; these sank two enemy motor torpedo boats and a trawler, but

---

[1] See p. 231.

[2] For the subsequent operations of the Home Fleet elsewhere than off the coast of Norway, on which the safety of the North Sea routes for our landings depended, the reader is referred to Roskill, Captain S. W.: *The War at Sea*, Vol. I, Chapter 10.

their air escort on the return journey was heavily attacked by German fighters from Kristiansand.

A more sustained effort was directed against the German-held airfields. There was even a hope that the enemy might not be 'able to develop ground aerodromes', as a War Office appreciation puts it, during the period before the thaw would deprive them of the use of frozen lakes. The Stavanger airfield, Sola, besides being the largest in Norway, was the nearest to our bases (325 miles from Lossiemouth) and approachable directly from the sea: this was the obvious target. Unfortunately, the niceties of Franco-British bombing policy, as it had been announced on 2nd September 1939, in response to an appeal by President Roosevelt, imposed a delay of two vital days, in which machine-gun attacks were authorised but bombing was barred, until the Germans were known to have bombed some other landing ground that was still in Norwegian hands. Thereafter small raids, by an average of seven aircraft, were made at the rate of nearly one a day. The second objective in order of importance was the large Danish airfield at Aalborg in North Jutland, the third the partly developed civil airport of Oslo, Fornebu. We also tried to extend the attack to Kristiansand, Rye in Jutland, and even Trondheim. This last was at extreme distance for the bombers of those days, but a long-range Wellington—a type of which our total stock was two—counted twenty-two enemy aircraft on the frozen surface of Lake Jonsvand, south-east of the city, as a result of which two raids were made, on the nights of 22nd/23rd and 23rd/24th April, but neither found the target. The intensity of our efforts against the airfields was varied in accordance with their supposed usefulness to particular phases of the campaign, as we shall see in due course. But their general scale can be judged from the fact that they cost Bomber Command twenty-seven aircraft in a month. This was at a time when the total number of aircraft available with crews, including those posted to the Striking Force in France, was only 216. Coastal Command, which had few aircraft to spare from other duties, lost five out of the twenty-three made available for the purpose.

Distance was a severe handicap—only one of our raiding forces had even a small fighter escort (Blenheims) and the bombers, though their range was of course greater, were severely restricted in the time they could afford for locating targets. The Germans were quick to organise the defence of the fields they had seized: heavy anti-aircraft fire was put up from Sola as early as the evening of the 10th and their fighters were in action when we attempted a daylight raid on the 11th. But, as modern navigational aids were then in their infancy, our most powerful enemy in the changeable North Sea area was the weather. Some operations failed (or were cancelled) because of fog over Britain, others because of storms over the water, others again because of the lack of cloud over the target. The want of large-scale maps increased the uncertainty of the landfall among the intricate network of fiords and islands and hampered the search for the objective. It appears that our main resource was the town plans in Baedeker's *Scandinavia* (revised 1912): to the pilot battling with snow and ice in the upper air it was small consolation to reflect that the absence of target maps and photographs at least argued our innocence.

But in any case the attack on the Norwegian and Danish airfields would have been at best a *pis aller*. The airfields of Germany lay nearest to us and were the real basis of the campaign, as we knew from both common sense and captured pilots; the official policy, however, was to take no action which might provoke, or at least help to touch off, retaliation against British or French soil. This means that the maximum result that we could have hoped to achieve was to limit the impact of the German air force in Norway to such activities as were practicable from bases situated at about the same distance from the theatre of operations as our own. It is therefore fortunate that we had an alternative way of employing our bombers in the struggle for Norway, which at least did not suffer from the same fundamental defect. This was the sowing of shallow waters with magnetic mines, for which urgent preparations had been in progress ever since the Germans began the practice in October 1939. By a coincidence the decision to make the first dropping in the next moon period had been taken for reasons unconnected with Operation Wilfred on 8th April: it was easy to extend the area of action from the North German estuaries northwards along their vital supply route to Norway.

Not all types of bombers were suitable for a task which involved dropping a weight of 1,500 lb., including 750 lb. of explosive, from a height of about 500 feet into some 30 feet of water, at a speed not exceeding 200 miles per hour, and with such unobtrusiveness and accuracy that the enemy would not notice the fall of the mine, much less recover it. Good weather as well as moonlight was essential. But operations began on the night of 13th/14th April and were continued until the 25th/26th, from which date fog in the North Sea rendered them impracticable up to 1st May, and they were then resumed for a second fortnight. The main area covered from north to south was the mouth of the Oslofiord, the Sound, the Great and Little Belts, Kiel Bay, the approaches to Lübeck, and the estuaries of the Elbe and Weser. Two hundred mines were ready for use in each of the two lunar months with which we are concerned, and about two-thirds of these were duly dropped at a cost of eleven aircraft. The results were difficult to assess at the time, though the foreign press was combed for significant items, but we now know that the Germans lost twelve ships totalling 18,355 tons. Neutral losses were also considerable, including at least two Danish train-ferries. Minelaying aircraft therefore share with the submarines—which themselves accounted for at least 7,000 tons of shipping by mines in addition to their other activities[1]—the credit for the fact that from 13th April until the end of the campaign German troop transportation was diverted to the railway through Jutland and the shorter sea passage across the Skagerrak to South Norway.

The German invasion of the Low Countries put an end to all serious operations against German air bases and sea supply routes for the Norway campaign: our bombers were needed too urgently elsewhere. But even in the preceding month, the situation had been such that the Instructions to the Commander-in-Chief, Bomber Command, told him on the one hand not to hold back his heavy force for 'operations on the Western Front which may not materialise', and on the other hand to remain prepared to 'switch . . . to Germany with the least possible delay should the situation develop'. Coastal Command, planning on 14th April for a big raid on Stavanger, found the force reduced to six aircraft by a special Cabinet decision. The overriding consideration throughout was the smallness of our bomber force, computed to have been at that time not more than one-quarter the size of the German. In fine, the bombers of the R.A.F. were not freely expendable, and could therefore play only an ancillary part in necessarily expensive projects for the recovery of Norway.

---

[1] See p. 34.

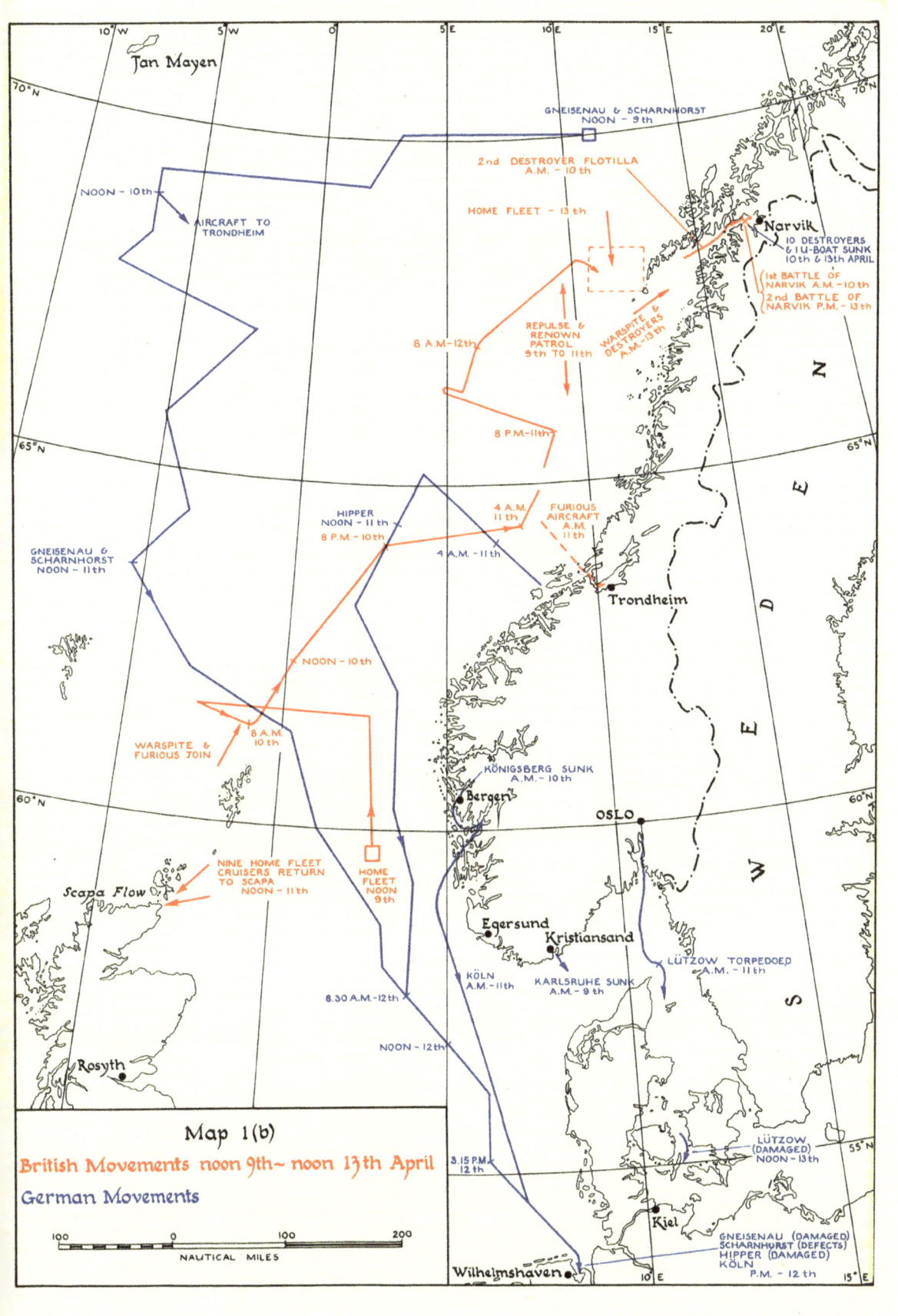

CHAPTER V

LAND OPERATIONS: GENERAL STRATEGY (PART 1)

See Map 5, facing p. 128

THE Supreme War Council had by a decision of 5th February 1940 delegated the command of Scandinavian operations to the United Kingdom Government, the Allied Military Committee in London having purely subordinate functions. This decision was never rescinded, the Council at its meetings on 9th, 22nd and 27th April being content in the main to accept the British line in relation to the new situation created by the German invasion. The French readily agreed to release their troops for the new front, which they hoped would be a valuable distraction of the enemy, and were on the whole disposed to make light of difficulties. Morally the French were for the moment in a strong position. It was not their navy which appeared to have been taken by surprise; Admiral Darlan at least had shown considerable prescience as to the German intentions;[1] and the responsibility for making the first Allied landings in Norway had throughout the long period of discussion been accepted, if not appropriated, by the British. Moreover, the French were to find (and point out) that the various échelons of their troops were ready to leave French ports more quickly than British transport arrangements and the improvised base areas in Norway could be made ready for their reception. France also lent a cruiser and six destroyers to operate at this juncture with the Home Fleet.

The British War Cabinet was, then, the authority by which all major decisions affecting the Norway campaign were taken or at least ratified. But there was no Theatre Commander with powers corresponding in any way to those which were being exercised by General Gamelin as Generalissimo over the Allied military forces in France. The small scale of the operations in Norway would scarcely have warranted such an appointment, even if circumstances had not caused them to be started piecemeal so that the question did not arise. Moreover, the topography of western Norway, so far from indicating some inevitable centre from which control ought manifestly to be exercised, lent itself rather to the use of London as the not-too-distant point through which communications to and from

---

[1] See p. 22.

each sector along the Norwegian coast should pass. The War Office did, indeed, on 17th April state the view that, 'Once the Allies are in full control of the Trondheim area, a corps commander should be appointed to command all British, French, and Norwegian forces in Scandinavia'.[1] But the occasion named never arose, and if it had arisen there is little to suggest that the Norwegians would ever have consented: in North Norway, where their forces were most effective, they fought mainly in isolation from us. The most important point, however, is not the lack of cohesion between sector and sector or between British (or French) and Norwegian military efforts; it is the lack of a single control over the three Services engaging for the first time in a campaign which required their full and continuous co-operation. Our generals in Central Norway did not command either naval or air force units which were associated with their operations. The Navy took command until the moment of landing, after which the land forces were dependent upon friendly agreement for whatever further services they needed. The one squadron of Air Force fighters which came into action had been sent to co-operate with the Army as an attachment but remained under Air Ministry orders. In North Norway the naval Flag Officer appointed had command by land as well as sea from 20th April and he also commanded the air component which arrived the following month. But the area within which he had naval control was circumscribed by the Admiralty to within a hundred miles of Vaagsfiord; he was dependent upon the *ad hoc* decisions of the Admiralty for the support of aircraft carriers and any other reinforcement from the Home Fleet; and if home-based bomber operations had been feasible, as they were in the south, it would have been in accordance with current practice for the Air Ministry to keep the bombing programme entirely in its own hands.

In these circumstances particular importance attaches to the machinery available in London to supply some of the elements of control which, in the later campaigns of the war, were supplied by Theatre Commanders of two or more Services or by an Allied Supreme Commander. One main link between the making of major policy and its execution by the separate Services was provided at this time by the Ministerial Committee on Military Co-ordination, which met twenty-three times in the hectic month between 9th April and its demise on the fall of the Chamberlain Government. This committee of four Ministers had been formed in November 1939 to discuss strategical plans, with the Chiefs of Staff in attendance as its expert advisers and Major-General H. L. Ismay as the usual head of its secretariat. Under the less exacting conditions of the winter lull the Committee had performed useful functions of review and examination

---

[1] See Appendix A (4), p. 253.

on behalf of the War Cabinet, particularly in the field of supply. On 4th April, after the lapse of the office of Minister for the Co-ordination of Defence, the chairmanship of the Military Co-ordination Committee passed to the First Lord of the Admiralty, Mr Winston Churchill. The other members at this time were Mr Oliver Stanley as Secretary of State for War, Sir Samuel Hoare as Secretary of State for Air, and Mr Leslie Burgin as Minister of Supply, no one of whom rivalled the representative of the Senior Service in knowledge and experience of warfare. The consequence was that under the pressure of events discussions easily became somewhat unbalanced, even after the First Lord induced the Prime Minister to promise to take the chair himself when 'matters of exceptional importance' were for discussion,[1] a condition which applied to nine out of ten meetings held in the second half of April. Supply now disappeared from the agenda, but although much time was given to the discussion of our strategy in Scandinavia, including even technical details of operations, the Committee did not develop a common personality, expressed in a common doctrine, nor did it succeed in matching the needs and reconciling the claims of the three Services. Its weakness is sufficiently shown by a note which Mr Churchill wrote for the Prime Minister a fortnight later (when further changes of structure pended),[2] urging the need for effective control to be exercised over the Committee either by his correspondent, 'if you feel able to bear this burden', or by a deputy acting on the Prime Minister's behalf. At the moment, the writer points out, 'There are six Chiefs of Staff, three Ministers, and General Ismay, who all have a voice in Norwegian operations (apart from Narvik). But no one is responsible for the creation and direction of military policy except yourself'.[3]

The Chiefs of Staff Committee, consisting of Admiral Sir Dudley Pound, General Sir Edmund Ironside, and Air Chief Marshal Sir Cyril Newall, found itself in an equally difficult position. Its members had a dual function—as individual and collective advisers to the War Cabinet and its Military Co-ordination Committee, and as high departmental officials serving their three respective Ministers. They held forty-three meetings in April, and it was not until the 23rd of the month that the appointment of Vice-Chiefs of Staff, who could attend the War Cabinet in their place—hence Mr Churchill's enumeration of six Chiefs of Staff—gave some relief from meetings other than their own. Their joint subordinate Staff was minute in relation to the demands made upon it. The Joint Planning Sub-Committee consisted of nine Staff Officers (of whom three had been added only at the beginning of April for the particular benefit of

---

[1] H. of C. Deb., Vol. 359, Col. 699 (11th April).
[2] See p. 165.
[3] Churchill, Vol. I, p. 505.

long-term plans) working under the Directors of Plans of the three Service Departments. The Joint Intelligence Sub-Committee had an even smaller whole-time staff, working under the three Service Directors of Intelligence plus a Foreign Office chairman. Further links were provided only by such organisations as the Inter-Services Planning Staff, which brought together the Planning Staffs of the three Service Departments for occasional tasks of administrative planning at the direction of the Chiefs of Staff. But sudden demands for big strategical papers, of which there are several instances at this time, meant all-night work by the Joint Planners on tasks which at a later period of the war would have been completed inside a Theatre Headquarters; and this left them less free to focus their attention and that of their masters upon the joint aspects of the conduct of the campaign at large.

In general, the Chiefs of Staff, who were to become so closely integrated a body later on, had not yet become fully accustomed to team work and still represented primarily the interests and viewpoints of their several Departments. The pressure of operations involving all three Services—for which our experience in 1914-18 left us administratively unprepared—had not yet made it necessary that they should be empowered to issue collective orders to commanders in the field; in fact they had not even a common series of telegrams. The Prime Minister nominated one of their number to act as chairman—at this time the Chief of the Air Staff; but their views were as often as not conveyed to the War Cabinet by each Chief of Staff treating separately whatever appeared to belong mainly to the business of his own Department. Thus the directions issued from London for the conduct of the combined operations in Norway came from an Admiralty which had a greater immediate interest in blockade measures, a War Office all too conscious of its heavy commitments in France, and an Air Ministry whose first concern was the air defence of Great Britain.

The military forces available for the counter-attack in Norway were, in the first instance, the forces which had been ready for operations arising out of Plan R.4.[1] The 24th (Guards) Brigade had one of its three battalions (1st Scots Guards) ready embarked in the Clyde for Narvik and the two others on their way to embarkation. One battalion of the 146th Infantry Brigade (Hallamshire) was likewise in readiness in the Clyde for Trondheim; its other battalions were ashore in the Rosyth area, having been hurriedly disembarked from the cruisers which were to have conveyed them to Bergen.[2] The

---

[1] See pp. 15, 25.
[2] See p. 26.

two battalions of the 148th Infantry Brigade had been similarly disembarked from the projected expedition to Stavanger. Thus one half of the British force was temporarily immobilised, as some of the equipment, left on board ship in the confusion, would take five days to replace. In addition to these eight British battalions Plan R.4 envisaged the employment, at Narvik, of French troops, beginning with the mixed brigade of Chasseurs Alpins (six battalions), which had been raised in January for the proposed move into Finland; but their first échelon was not (even according to the latest schedule)[1] intended to sail until eight days after the first British forces. The list is not numerically unimpressive—about fourteen thousand men for a contingent operation compared with the German provision of twenty-four thousand in the first week of a fixed invasion—though the fact that they could not all be used for an immediate riposte put us at a serious disadvantage.

But a much worse disadvantage lay in the circumstance that these troops were organised and equipped to land in friendly ports, where they hoped to have some help from Norwegian garrisons and fixed defences in preparing to repel possible attacks by an out-manœuvred opponent. The reality was very different. The original hypothesis, however, explains the light scale of equipment[2]—no artillery (except one light anti-aircraft battery for the far north), no armour, and no transport, whereas Base details had been allotted for Narvik in a profusion which was later to prove embarrassing. It also explains why an expedition with no air component had seemed justifiable: to provide aircraft to accompany any Scandinavian expedition had all along been difficult, to find airfields on the other side for them to use was problematic at this time of year, and the German air force was somehow envisaged as carrying troops rather than bombs against our three widely separated garrisons stretching far into the north. These grave deficiencies on land and in the air were, in a situation now changed so drastically to our disadvantage, desperately hard to remedy.

With these reservations, however, the surprising fact is not that we mustered so little strength for the Norwegian campaign but that we scraped together so much. Barely a fortnight had passed since the presentation of a Memorandum by the Chiefs of Staff, giving the third year of war as the period by which concentrated efforts would provide 'a very powerful air force' and stating that a land offensive on the Western Front would not be justifiable in 1940, 'even if all new British divisions were to be allocated to France'. As other volumes in this series clearly show, we were at this time committed up to the hilt in the defence of France, and whatever we, or the French, could spare

---

[1] Gamelin, Général (Maurice): *Servir*, t. III, p. 328.
[2] See p. 16.

from that commitment was needed to build up the Allied position in the Middle East, where also 'a defeat would be a disaster'. Nevertheless, additional troops were readily made available for Norway. At a meeting of the Supreme War Council on 9th April the British offered a fourth infantry brigade (the 147th, Territorials) with artillery. Allocated as a second flight to each of three projected expeditions, this brigade in the end did not set foot on Norwegian soil, nor did an extra battalion allocated to bring the 148th Brigade (which had been left one battalion short for several months) back to full strength. The French at the same time offered the rest of their original expeditionary force for Finland, which unlike the British had never been formally dispersed—two battalions of the Foreign Legion and four battalions of Poles. The French brigade of Chasseurs Alpins, now renamed a light division, included in any case one group of artillery (75s), one battery of small anti-aircraft guns and one company of small tanks. The British strengthened their forces with one battery of twelve 25-pounders for the Narvik area, and provided at the expense of home defence all the serious anti-aircraft protection by light or heavy guns which reached any of the Allied expeditions.

Further expansion was only possible at the cost of the forces in France. The French mitigated the drain on their main front by deciding on 12th April that two more light divisions, which were to follow the first, should be constituted principally from the Army of the Alps and units in course of formation. Alpine divisions stationed on the main front were to sacrifice only one-fourth of their strength and remain where they were. This made a total French force available of about 40,000 men, subject to the provision of British transport to move its later elements to Norway. The British likewise formed ten Independent Companies by recruitment from the Territorial Divisions, a total of some 3,000 men; but our general intention was to reinforce the Norway expeditions by the diversion of existing units which were stationed, or due to be stationed, in France. General Gamelin believed that we were contemplating the transfer of two divisions when the decision to evacuate Central Norway removed the need;[1] this was about what the Chiefs of Staff had expected to transfer 'in certain eventualities' under the old Plan R.4. In actual fact one infantry brigade (the 126th), which was due to sail for France on 17th April, was considered for diversion but was eventually let go; one other (the 15th) was only a day or two later brought back from France and transferred to Norway via Scotland. Two battalions of Canadians, whom the French regarded along with the Scots as peculiarly fitted for warfare under Norwegian conditions, were, as we shall see, also earmarked for Norway but never went.

---

[1] Gamelin: t. III, p. 364.

Thus Britain sent four infantry brigades to make and maintain the landings in Norway. Two of these, the 24th and 15th, composed of Regular soldiers, were handicapped chiefly by deficiencies of material for which pre-war policy and the will of the electorate were mainly responsible; but even they had received no special training or preparation for the conditions with which they were to be confronted. The other two, the 146th and 148th, were Territorial brigades. Their five battalions represented the high traditions of the pre-war Territorial Army, but they had suffered all the confusions and strains which resulted from its doubling in March 1939 and from the sudden introduction of compulsory service two months later; at best they had received only seven months' continuous training of any kind. The five (out of ten) Independent Companies which reached Norway were also Territorials, as we have already seen: they were specially selected volunteers, but had had even less chance to train together and 'shake down' than other units. The position of the French was not very different. The Foreign Legionaries, who included many Spanish Republicans and even a few Germans, were men to uphold a great tradition; but the Chasseurs Alpins were new units which had recruited their rank and file in a hurry from the general run of *poilus* as much as from the villages of Upper Savoy; and the Polish Brigade was made up of miners and other workers long resident in France serving under officers who had escaped in 1939.

Yet another factor which strongly influenced the landing operations from the outset was the extreme uncertainty of the international position. We could not assess the strength of the Norwegian intention to resist the invasion in the form it had taken, much less what would happen if the Germans also entered Sweden, about which there was a new alarm a fortnight after their entry into Norway. The attitude of Russia to the German advance in the north was likewise a complete enigma. Most important of all, the possibility had always to be borne in mind that the German intention was to distract our eyes from a sudden development on the western front, where the main thrust through Belgium was now expected almost daily. As for Italy, relations were so uncertain that on the very day of the German stroke in the north our Commanders-in-Chief in the Middle East, aware of acute deficiencies, addressed a whole series of questions to the Chiefs of Staff in London about our intentions if and when Italy should enter the war against us.[1]

On 9th April the main task, given the German achievement of surprise, was the selection of an objective commensurate with the size

---

[1] Playfair, Major-General I. S. O.: *The War in the Mediterranean and Middle East*, Vol. I, Chapter 5.

and nature of the military forces immediately available to land in Norway. The Chiefs of Staff, roused from their beds by the disconcerting news, met first at 6 a.m.; they believed then that the Germans were not established at Narvik, for which destination a British battalion would be 'leaving at once', and decided accordingly that our first object was to prevent consolidation by the Germans of their positions at Bergen and Trondheim—in that order. At 8.30 a.m., when the War Cabinet was convened at the request of the Chiefs of Staff to consider their proposals, there was the same assumption that Narvik could still be peacefully occupied; attention was mainly concentrated upon the provision of troops, to include the Chasseurs Alpins diverted from the original Narvik expedition, for the recapture of Bergen and Trondheim. But the War Cabinet also directed that no troops were to be moved towards any of the three Norwegian ports until the naval situation had been cleared up. Accordingly, the Chiefs of Staff, at their second meeting on that fateful morning, when it had just become known that the Germans might be in Narvik, having expressed again the view that Bergen was the most important objective on political grounds and Trondheim on military, moved the first battalion to Scapa. They also ordered the seven other available battalions to be got ready to sail (from the Clyde) by the evening of the 12th, if possible; but they did not commit themselves as to which of the three ports would be their destination.

The Supreme War Council, which met in London in the late afternoon, likewise called for attacks to be mounted against all three ports. The French made it clear that they attached paramount importance to Narvik because of the orefields, but the Council dispersed under the impression that its recapture would be easy. By evening, however, the situation at Narvik was regarded more seriously by the First Lord, the telegrams received at the Admiralty being the main source of information. At the meeting of the Military Co-ordination Committee (which started at 9.30 p.m. and had other business on its agenda preceding Norway) he advised against any military operation at Trondheim or, by implication, at Bergen. The Chief of the Imperial General Staff took the same line, emphasising that the recapture of Narvik would fully tax Allied resources which comprised 'some three fully-trained battalions, about 13,000 lesser-trained troops and a brigade of Chasseurs Alpins'. It was accordingly resolved to mask the other points of German occupation, to explore the possibility of getting a foothold at Namsos and Aandalsnes, and to make Narvik the immediate objective. This decision fortunately coincided with the preference expressed by the French, and it was readily endorsed by the War Cabinet next morning. But the fog of war and the multiplicity of committees between them had caused the Allies to lose one whole day.

On 10th April the Chiefs of Staff proceeded to execute the decision by authorising the Joint Planning Sub-Committee to prepare a directive for the combined operation, on the basis of which the Inter-Services Planning Staff could arrange for the assembly and embarkation of forces; the first stage was subsequently omitted. Simultaneously the commander was to prepare his plan of operations, for which the staff of the Inter-Service Training Centre would be placed at his disposal. That evening the Military Co-ordination Committee distinguished our first two objects as the establishment of a naval base at Narvik and the use of the port as a means of entry to the orefields. The newly appointed naval commander of the expedition, Admiral of the Fleet the Earl of Cork and Orrery, was in attendance at this meeting, while the instructions for the military commander, Major-General P. J. Mackesy, were flown from the War Office to Scapa, where he arrived with his first battalion in the early morning of 11th April. Sir Edmund Ironside had told the War Cabinet that General Mackesy with half of this battalion would sail from Scapa at 11 a.m. that day, which would have brought him to the latitude of Narvik on the 13th, his earliest reinforcements (four battalions) following two days behind. But although the Chiefs of Staff, meeting at 9 a.m. on the 11th, accepted this arrangement (for one company at least) without demur, the movement of troops at Scapa Flow from transport to cruiser did not begin until the afternoon, under naval orders which fixed their sailing for 1 p.m. next day. In this way we lost some of the advantage which might have accrued from the second naval battle, at the end of which the *Warspite's* guns, as we have seen, dominated the town. Nevertheless the quick dash for Narvik, to which the historic name of 'Rupert' had been given, presumably by Mr Churchill, had already been organised and set in train before the news of the Navy's triumph encouraged the authorities in London to suppose that Narvik was as good as captured, and therefore to look more closely than hitherto at other objectives in less distant areas of the Norwegian coast. It was moreover at about this time that it became possible to build up some picture in London of how the Norwegians—for nine-tenths of whom Narvik was in every sense remote —were reacting to the German attack.

Ever since the early morning of 9th April our official link with the Norwegian Government through the British Minister had lost most of its value, not merely or chiefly because the Germans had severed the cables, but because the Government was forced to move from place to place and lost touch with its own representatives in most parts of the country. Moreover, the military High Command became separated from the Government and in any case we had at that moment no military attaché in Norway. A stop-gap supply of information came through the British Legation in Stockholm, which was well served with news from Norwegian sources because the Germans did not at first control either the telephone service to the east or the actual frontier: on 11th April the Military Attaché in Sweden reported with approximate accuracy that the enemy intention was to employ five divisions for Norway. There was also the neutral press. The Swedish public had the maximum interest in what was happening in Norway, and Swedish reports were supplemented by the work of American journalists, two of whom had been in Oslo when the Germans entered the city. But on the whole the newspaper reporting tended to exaggerate the bewilderment or apathy of the general public as well as the numbers and enterprise of the fifth column, or quislings.

In general, the British Government's information from Norway was little better than that of the newspaper reader: thus at 4 p.m. on the 9th, twelve hours after the German *coup* at Narvik, the Prime Minister was still informing the House of Commons that it was 'very possible' to believe that the landing in question was at Larvik, not Narvik,[1] though the distance between the two ports is nearly a thousand miles. Two days later the uncertainty was still so great that at a meeting of the Military Co-ordination Committee one of the matters for discussion was whether the Germans were in Tromsö. At that time the War Office gave as the most reliable estimate an enemy strength of two divisions in Norway, and the Air Ministry put the number of aircraft, other than coastal aircraft, used to invade Norway and Denmark at about two hundred. The Military Co-ordination Committee then placed the collection and collation of intelligence for the campaign under the general control of the War Office, to which other departments submitted material, and a Scandinavian intelligence summary began to appear daily from 13th April under the authority of the Director of Military Intelligence.

The delicate position of Sweden had already led to the despatch of a special Anglo-French Mission to Stockholm, with the object of stiffening Swedish resistance to likely German demands, especially as regards the use of the railway to Narvik or a possible *coup* at Lulea. One of its members, Admiral Sir Edward Evans, who until 8th April had been designated to sail for Narvik[2] and was well known in Norway as a polar explorer, was entrusted also with a personal mission to the King of Norway and his Ministers. His journey from Sweden was delayed by diplomatic difficulties, but he eventually found the King in the Gudbrandsdal area on the evening of 21st April. The information which the Admiral took with him from London was encouraging rather than accurate in detail: King Haakon and the Norwegian Commander-in-Chief might be led to expect a naval

---
[1] H. of C. Deb., Vol. 359, Col. 511.
[2] See p. 25.

assault on Trondheim starting that day, and a Norwegian Cabinet Minister, met on the return journey, was told of 40,000 Allied troops available for the land attack 'to begin with'. Admiral Evans brought back direct impressions of the havoc wrought by German air power and first-hand news, obtained as he travelled by car into Sweden, of the German advance up the Österdal.[1]

Meanwhile the newly appointed British Military Attaché, Lieut.-Col. E. J. C. King-Salter, with the French Military and Naval Attachés, reached Norwegian Headquarters from Finland (where he had held the same post) late on 14th April. The following morning he sent his first messages to London, one of which described the situation in Trondheim. The Norwegians believed that there were about 3,000 Germans holding the town itself with automatic weapons and light guns, pushing out small detachments to the south and occupying more strongly the outlying districts to the east and north-east. Reinforcements were reaching Trondheim by air from Oslo and Stavanger; on 12th and 15th April about fifty transport aircraft were seen going in that direction. The number of seaplanes at Trondheim was given at twenty to thirty, with eight bombers on the racecourse, but the German strength at the main Vaernes airfield was unknown. The positions of three anti-aircraft batteries were roughly stated, and one enemy cruiser and three destroyers reported to be in the harbour. Next day the Military Attaché added some details of the Norwegian military position in relation to Trondheim: there were 2,800 men north of Steinkjer, 300 men and some guns at Hegra, 400 men south of Trondheim preparing demolitions at Stören and elsewhere, and a regiment (two battalions) based on Aandalsnes. On the 17th a further telegram reported that the German transport planes flying between Oslo and Trondheim were largely Junkers 52s, which the Norwegians thought our day bombers could attack, and the extreme urgency of the situation was further emphasised by passing on certain information dated 13th April which had now reached the Norwegian Government from Oslo. This was to the effect that ten store-ships and six other ships had come into the harbour, from which about 10,000 men had been landed as well as field artillery, and that fifty troop-carrying aircraft were arriving daily with thirty men apiece.

On 18th April towards midnight British units began to land at Aandalsnes, with which Colonel King-Salter made contact next day, and he ceased to be the sole regular source of military information from South Norway. On that evening he and his French colleagues had sent the War Office a final picture of the position on the southern front as follows:

The Norwegian troops are opposing the German advance in the four

---

[1] See Admiral Lord Mountevans: *Adventurous Life*, Chapter XXVIII.

principal valleys running generally northwards from the region of Oslo . . . culminating eventually about 100 miles north of Oslo in easily defended defiles. These troops are the equivalent of only a few battalions and batteries . . . and consist of varied elements, many of which are completely untrained or very incompletely mobilised.

Hitherto the Germans have not concentrated in any sector and their operations appear to have been conducted by single battalions reinforced by some artillery and sometimes by light tanks.

The Norwegian detachments, too weak to resist in the open valleys, are now falling back by large bounds. . . . These withdrawals have given place to a number of rearguard actions in which a few prisoners have been taken. These actions have given the troops some confidence. But there are no reserves behind them and the men are without relief in the front line.

Such was the knowledge of the situation on which the Allies based their plans to extend the military counter-attack in Norway beyond Narvik.

It will be remembered[1] that on the evening of 9th April the Military Co-ordination Committee had the seizure of footholds at Namsos and Aandalsnes already in view, and the Chiefs of Staff next morning recorded the intention of attempting this if the Narvik operation did not require the whole of the Allied forces available. On the 11th, however, the Chief of the Air Staff referred at the meeting of the Military Co-ordination Committee to the desirability of an operation against Trondheim or Bergen which would follow up a success against Narvik, and authority was given to the staffs to study, but not to prepare for, what was now called 'Maurice' as the intended successor to 'Rupert'. On 12th April the War Cabinet itself became aware of pressure from the Norwegian Government for the recapture of Trondheim, to which the alternative might be the collapse of Norway, followed by that of Sweden. It was thereupon agreed that landings on the Norwegian coast even on a small scale would have an important political effect and from that point of view were desirable. The Military Co-ordination Committee ordered a plan to be prepared for landing such forces as could immediately be made available, but on the morning of the 13th the Chiefs of Staff were clear that the integrity of Rupertforce must not be compromised for operations elsewhere and that in any case the French contingent was the only part of it capable of diversion as a self-contained unit. Information about the Namsos-Trondheim area was badly needed, and the Chiefs of Staff welcomed the prospect that two parties of 150 men were to be landed at Namsos from cruisers. The War Cabinet, meeting an hour or two later than the Chiefs of Staff, were influenced by the Foreign

---
[1] See p. 64.

Office, which was concerned about opinion in Sweden as well as Norway, and by pressure from the French War Committee[1] to say that we must envisage operations at the outlying ports and at Trondheim itself. At this stage the force earmarked for 'Maurice' stood at five battalions, with four anti-aircraft guns taken from the Air Defence of Great Britain.

The experimental landing by seamen and Marines at Namsos was, however, postponed for 24 hours on account of a submarine scare, and meanwhile the situation as viewed in London was transformed by the news from Admiral Whitworth of his sweeping naval success at Narvik. In the late evening of 13th April the Military Co-ordination Committee believed that 'the landing of the "Rupert" force might possibly be made in the town itself' and, subject to confirmation of the view that serious opposition at Narvik was unlikely, authorised the diversion of the 146th Brigade from Narvik to Namsos. The naval authorities had pressed for this, informally, as early as the night of the 11th and had to some extent arranged the convoy accordingly. Its arrival would follow that of the cruiser parties and would coincide with the landing of another small naval force at Aalesund, south of Trondheim. On the afternoon of the 14th, after further consideration by the Chiefs of Staff, this diversion was ordered, and it was followed almost at once by the transfer with French permission of the first demi-brigade of Chasseurs Alpins (three battalions) to reinforce 'Maurice' instead of 'Rupert'. Optimism regarding the situation at Narvik now reached its zenith: the Military Co-ordination Committee passed a resolution which apparently anticipated a speedy resumption of ore exports to the United Kingdom, and some authorities in London even began to contemplate the transfer to the south of the 24th (Guards) Brigade—the only brigade now left to General Mackesy—as its task in the north would soon be completed.

Meanwhile, the naval landing south of Trondheim expanded to form an integral part of the general plan. Its main weight was transferred from the islands at Aalesund to the mainland at Aandalsnes, and the seamen and Marines were used to secure a base for the 148th Brigade (two battalions) which had previously been earmarked for Namsos: by a relatively small advance inland they would in effect invest Trondheim from the south, a manœuvre in which the French Generalissimo Gamelin saw great possibilities. Further reinforcement was contemplated for the new Sickleforce, as it was called, from both French and British sources, including British troops allotted to the B.E.F. in France.

The optimism regarding the success of 'Rupert' quickly gave place to disillusionment. On 14th April telegrams were sent to the naval

---

[1] Gamelin, t. III, p. 338.

and military commanders which implied that they had only to get together to decide the details of their entry into Narvik. In actual fact their first meeting disclosed a disagreement in principle both as to their instructions and as to the possibility of carrying them out. When General Mackesy refused to be hurried it was pointed out to him from home that it was no use his waiting for reinforcements assigned elsewhere, and strong pressure was brought to bear by the Government, which was willing to accept responsibility for whatever losses might be incurred in an immediate attack. But the General continued to regard a landing in deep snow from ships' boats against machine guns as utterly impracticable. On the 18th, the Director of Military Operations appreciated, on the basis of the information received in London, that Narvik was on the whole unlikely to be taken until troops could be released from the Trondheim area; thus the objective which had originally been allowed to overshadow the attack on Narvik because the latter operation was so easy now continued to predominate because that operation was so hard. Although the command at Narvik was changed, supreme authority being given to Lord Cork in the hope that he might force the issue, and although a naval bombardment after long deliberation was attempted on 24th April, the deterioration in the weather, the delay in reinforcement, and the determination of General Mackesy kept the situation in the Narvik area static throughout the period in which the operation against Trondheim was being developed.

The naval battle of the 13th, from which the situation described above had mainly resulted, had had an additional indirect effect upon what was to be attempted farther south. At the meeting of the Military Co-ordination Committee that evening, after the *Warspite* had successfully penetrated the entire length of the Ofotfiord, the suggestion was for the first time made that part of Mauriceforce might be landed straight at Trondheim. This was the start of the conception known as Operation 'Boots'—better known by its later and more expressive name of 'Hammer'—a direct attack on Trondheim which would meet the increasingly urgent demands of the Norwegian Government and Commander-in-Chief for immediate help; it was in turn facilitated by the information which the Norwegian authorities put at our disposal.

From a Norwegian point of view it was clear that the prompt recapture of Trondheim would be an almost ideal counter to the German thrusts. Politically, the city is of great importance as the medieval capital of the country, the crowning-place of Norwegian kings, and the traditional centre of the second-richest agricultural area. Economically, it is the third-largest town in Norway (population 56,000), having considerable industries, especially in timber, and an extensive harbour with outlying accommodation for vessels of deep draught. Strategically, it can almost be described as the key to Scandinavia. Looking south, Trondheim is at the head of two alternative routes through the mountains to Oslo; looking north, it is the starting point of the only road or rail link with North Norway; and looking east, it guards the approach to two valleys which throughout history have afforded a main route from Norway to Sweden. It follows automatically that, once the modern capital of Oslo was effectively in German hands, Trondheim assumed supreme importance as the natural alternative centre on which to base the reestablishment of the Government's authority and the movement for the expulsion of the Germans.

Accordingly, on 12th April at 2.25 p.m. the British Government had received a telegram from the Minister in Norway, Sir Cecil Dormer, informing them that the Norwegian Government urgently desired the recapture of Trondheim to maintain their authority in the country. This was also the policy of the Norwegian Commander-in-Chief, General Ruge, who asked for a British division to be sent and held two or more of his own battalions in readiness for an attack on the city from the south. This harmonised well with the first stage in the plan as given to Mauriceforce, which was to make a rapid push forward from the north, so as to secure at once as much of the area between Namsos and Trondheim as was not effectively denied to them by the enemy. On the 16th the Norwegian Commander-in-Chief sent another telegram through the British Military Attaché requesting a decision about the recapture of Trondheim. Colonel King-Salter then pressed the matter further by reporting certain topographical details furnished by the Director of Military Intelligence at General Ruge's Headquarters. This officer recommended a direct attack past the Agdenes forts or, if the Agdenes defences proved too strong, an attack based on positions at Vinje and Surna, sixty miles to the south-west of the town. His opinions were founded on extensive local knowledge, as he had previously acted as Chief of Staff to the division based on Trondheim, which had in peacetime considered the practicability of the forcing of Agdenes and of a landing for the capture of the town based on Kyrksaeterōra, Vinje, and Surna.

Otherwise no information was available except the general facts about the position and armaments of the three forts at Agdenes. Brettingen is built into the side of a rocky promontory, commanding the entrance on which the four sea approaches to Trondheimsfiord converge at the Agdenes lighthouse. Hysnes lies in a rather more accessible position about two and a half miles farther in on the same east bank of the fiord, with the third fort, Hambaara, opposite. The first two were known to have two 8-inch guns apiece and of 6-inch guns three and two respectively. Some smaller guns were not in commission, and there was no anti-aircraft defence (before the Germans took over), but the two forts had three heavy machine guns each and Brettingen a serviceable air-raid shelter. Hambaara had two 6-inch guns not in commission. The mouth of the fiord is very deep, nearly 300 fathoms between Hysnes and Hambaara, and nearly two miles wide. Beyond Agdenes it broadens still further to form a perfect seaway for vessels of any size, which runs s.s.e. for about thirteen sea miles and then due east for another eleven to Trondheim, lying on the south bank with ten miles of water before it. Some inference could however be drawn from the experience of the two British destroyers which had approached the mouth of the fiord in the early afternoon of 11th April.[1] The two forts opened fire on them, but the shooting was very wild.

Meanwhile, with the approval of the French Government and the implied support of the British public (which was eagerly canvassing the pro's and con's of a direct attack on Trondheim, especially the former), the Military Co-ordination Committee became engaged in the hurried adaptation of its Mauriceforce arrangements to prepare the way for Operation Hammer. As regards the military force for the Trondheim landing, it was proposed at first to employ ten battalions, half of them British (Regulars) and half French; but the troops finally allotted to the task were the 15th and 147th Infantry Brigades and two Canadian battalions. Of these the 147th Brigade (Territorials) was to be embarked separately as a reserve; the remainder, including Divisional and Brigade Headquarters, constituted the assault force, to which the Navy contributed a Royal Marine battery of 3·7-inch howitzers. The expedition was to be commanded by Major-General F. E. Hotblack; he received his instructions[2] on 17th April but suffered a stroke the same evening. His successor was Acting-Major-General H. P. M. Berney-Ficklin, from the 15th Brigade, but his command was terminated by an air accident on the morning of the 19th. Major-General B. C. T. Paget then received orders to leave immediately for the north, presumably to take over the same command.

Air operations against Trondheim were also envisaged. Bomber Command was instructed to develop its existing attacks on enemy-held airfields so as to include a half-squadron raid nightly on Vaernes, the use of which by the Germans had been reported (erroneously) on the 12th, in preparation for 'the combined operations against Trondheim, which might last several days'. During the actual operations it was to neutralise enemy air activity by attacks at maximum strength, which it was hoped would amount to a full-squadron raid each night on Vaernes, Sola, and Fornebu. But the main burden

---

[1] See p. 47.
[2] See Appendix A (4), p. 25.

of the struggle for mastery in the air would have to be borne by naval aircraft, operating as an integral part of the Fleet. We may therefore turn to the naval aspect of the undertaking.

Late in the evening of 13th April, the day of the second naval success at Narvik, when the Military Co-ordination Committee first considered the idea of a direct landing at Trondheim by part of Mauriceforce, it was reported that the Naval Staff anticipated no difficulty in silencing the shore batteries outside Trondheim, and the Service Staffs were instructed to prepare their plans accordingly. On the afternoon of the 15th, the Committee was told that the Navy would be ready for the direct attack in about a week. On the 16th, the First Lord of the Admiralty said that another seven or eight days would be required to mount the operation, of which it was assumed that the enemy would receive not more than two hours warning, so that they could not make much call upon their air strength in Denmark or Germany. Two carriers would put up 80 aircraft to deal with enemy air forces based in Norway; the Navy would then smother gunfire from the land. On the 17th the Committee determined the date of the operation as the 22nd, but on the 18th—after the news of the collapse of General Hotblack—a postponement to the 24th was contemplated as having the additional advantage of providing the troops with time for disembarkation practice. On the morning of the 19th agreement as to the naval preparations was completed, when the Committee decided that the *Warspite* must be withdrawn from the Narvik operations in order to take part. It had been resolved, however, to avoid the bombardment of the city itself, if at all possible; the initial landing points would be beyond, in the bay near Vaernes and at Levanger.

The feasibility of the Navy's share in this operation was much canvassed at the time. It may therefore be of interest to record the discussions between the Admiralty and the Commander-in-Chief, Home Fleet, on whose shoulders the immediate responsibility would rest. Sir Charles Forbes was informed of Operation Hammer in the early hours of 14th April, while he was still at sea off the Lofotens in the *Rodney*, with a request for his opinion as to the possibility of destroying or dominating the shore batteries so that transports could enter, and for particulars of the ships required. In his answer, at midday on the 14th, he said that the operation was not feasible unless the Government was prepared to face very heavy losses in troops and transports, because German bombers would have sufficient warning to provide continuous air attack. The Admiral also pointed out that no ships of the Home Fleet had on board the high-explosive bombardment shells which would be needed for their main armament. But the Admiralty answered, 'Pray consider this important project further': large troopships would have to be brought into the danger zone somewhere, and for this operation we should be in a position to put both Stavanger and Trondheim airfields out of action—the former by R.A.F. bombing followed up by bombardment from the cruiser *Suffolk*, the latter by the attacks of naval aircraft and Fleet bombardment. The Admiralty also said that high-explosive shell for 15-inch guns had been ordered to Rosyth and that the aircraft carrier *Furious* and the 1st Cruiser Squadron would be employed.

Sir Charles Forbes, having received particulars of the defences and confirmation of the fact that the Germans had seized the batteries at the entrance of the fiord, replied to the Admiralty on the 15th, deprecating the withdrawal of the 1st Cruiser Squadron from Kirkenes and that of the *Furious* from Narvik, and proposing a force to consist of the aircraft carrier *Glorious*; the three capital ships *Valiant*, *Renown* and *Warspite*, of which the last-named was to carry out shore bombardments; at least four anti-aircraft cruisers; about twenty destroyers; and 'numerous landing craft.' The Admiral added that his previous reply had been misunderstood: he did not 'anticipate any great difficulty from the naval side', provided the troops were conveyed in men-of-war instead of transports. The Admiralty went ahead with its preparations, and on the 19th the *Valiant* sailed for Rosyth to ship the special shell for the bombardment. Meanwhile the plan had been received by the Commander-in-Chief on his arrival with the Home Fleet at Scapa, and arrangements were made for the whole of the military assault force to be embarked according to his wishes in cruisers, destroyers, and sloops, which would also carry the stores, howitzer battery, and six landing craft. Embarkation was fixed for the 21st at Rosyth, whence the expedition would proceed to Scapa to pick up the reserve brigade and rendezvous with the aircraft carriers *Ark Royal* and *Glorious*. These last were not available until the 23rd, so the attack was in effect put back to 26th April at earliest.

But before the Admiral, busy examining the general requirements of the Home Fleet at Scapa, had become wholly committed to the proposed operation, which he regarded as a gamble, a more cautious policy, of limiting the risks to which we exposed our very slender resources, came suddenly to prevail in London. The forts might not prove a serious obstacle, but the German air force, knowing that we were bound to proceed up the fiord to Trondheim, might take a heavy toll of our ships. We may notice that the *Suffolk* reached Scapa Flow on the morning of 18th April with the sea 'lapping over the quarter-deck': she had bombarded Sola airfield, Stavanger, and so far from putting it out of action had suffered nearly seven hours of counter-attack from the air. Sent on northwards from Stavanger with additional orders to pursue some alleged enemy destroyers, the cruiser could not be found by her intended R.A.F. fighter escort (which expected her to be closer inshore), and although the Commander-in-Chief despatched naval aircraft from Hatston as well as both his battle cruisers to the rescue, it was too late to prevent a direct hit from a 1,000-lb. bomb. There were even four more air attacks after nine fighters had arrived to protect the cruiser. Similar, if less dramatic, reminders of the incalculable (or at least uncalculated) menace of air power had come in from our ships now operating in the Namsos area. There were also fears that, even if ships could be successfully defended by their own anti-aircraft armament and the Fleet Air Arm, the troops would be badly bombed as they went ashore to capture Trondheim and the Vaernes airfield. By the morning of the 19th, the Chiefs of Staff had drawn up a paper in this sense, which seemed to confront the Prime Minister with the alternatives of accepting their advice, backed as it was by the newly appointed Vice-Chiefs of Staff, or making (as Mr. Churchill tells us)[1] at least one change among his principal Service Advisers. The First Lord supported the more prudent course, and the decision became known at a late night meeting of the Military Co-ordination Committee on the 19th. The order for General Paget to go north had already been withdrawn by the War Office, about one hour after it was issued. An Admiralty telegram to the Commander-in-Chief formally announced the cancellation of 'Hammer' at 11.40 a.m. next day.

The papers of the Military Co-ordination Committee show that at the time of the decision to abandon the direct assault on Trondheim and concentrate on Namsos and Aandalsnes erroneous impressions of the strength of our positions at these two ports played a big part. As the First Lord of the Admiralty put it, 'we move from a more hazardous to a less hazardous Operation',[2] and by using these bases to the full we should be getting more men on to Norwegian soil sooner. It was also believed that the operations against Narvik would be brought to a quick completion through the release of the *Warspite* and important military reinforcements. Two birds in the bush were perhaps being over-valued to make up for the one which was not after all in the hand; but the Chiefs of Staff (or their principal assistants) were able to enumerate no less than six reasons for abandoning 'Hammer'. The establishment of our forces at two other bases is naturally given prominence, together with the enhancement of our prospective difficulties at Trondheim by German work on the defences and the indiscretions of our press in calling attention to the likelihood of a major Allied attack there. It is also pleaded that there had been 'insufficient time for that detailed and meticulous preparation which is so necessary in operations of this character and magnitude', and that, in the absence of previous reconnaissance or

---

[1] Churchill, Vol. I, p. 496.
[2] Churchill, Vol. I, p. 497.

air photography, it would be risky to proceed on a map and chart basis. But the chief drawback of the Trondheim operation, important in relation to later events of greater moment, is plainly stated as 'the concentration of almost the whole of the Home Fleet in an area where it could be subjected to heavy air attack'.

In retrospect it does not seem likely that the Agdenes forts would have been a serious obstacle. We now know that the third fort (Hambaara) had been disabled by the prompt action of a single Norwegian N.C.O. and a watchman and that, although artillerymen for the coastal batteries accompanied each of the German naval expeditions, they had serious technical difficulties to contend with, such as the restoration of the electric cables for Brettingen and Hysnes. A provisional torpedo-battery was laid out on floats; but there were no mines. The German naval strength in the fiord was reduced by the departure of two destroyers on the night of the 14th/15th to two ships, both suffering from engine-room defects. The German military force, which had at first totalled only 1,700 men, was indeed increased by successive airlifts of an infantry battalion less half a company on the 14th, a reinforced company on the 18th, and a further battalion, a troop of mountain artillery, and the Divisional General on the 20th. But about half of the 4,000 troops were dispersed to the north and south and even towards the Swedish frontier on the east, leaving a garrison of only two battalions equally divided between Trondheim (including Vaernes airfield) and the mouth of the fiord. Moreover, the Germans were still very short of material. The two largest of three supply ships and the only tanker which had been sent off in advance for Trondheim had been intercepted; two camouflaged trawlers carrying guns to supplement captured Norwegian artillery also failed to get through; the first two submarines with urgently needed supplies did not arrive until 18th April; and as late as the 22nd they were preparing to send three more with aviation spirit and anti-aircraft guns.

The crux of the matter, however, was the exposure of our ships to air attack during the voyage up the fiord in confined waters without the possibility of surprise and the similar risk to ships and men during the subsequent landing. Would the anti-aircraft armament of the fleet and the work of 100 naval aircraft (the final figure), of which only forty-five were fighters, have given sufficient protection? The Germans cleared Vaernes airfield of snow as fast as they could, but as late as the 19th the only operational forces at Trondheim were two flights of seaplanes; the resources of the Sola airfield, Stavanger, on the same date amounted to one squadron of heavy fighters and one flight each of dive bombers, Junkers 88s, and coastal reconnaissance aircraft. Clearly the cost of the venture increased with every day that was allowed to pass before we attacked, and although it is not now believed that the loss of one capital ship would have induced the Italians to declare war on us, the history of the next twelve months shows how narrow our margin of safety was. A paper by the German Naval Staff, whose retrospective generalisations on such matters are not necessarily objective judgements, suggests that the failure to attack on this occasion 'cannot be held against the British.' But the same authority also says, perhaps more revealingly, that 'a direct assault on Trondheim would only have been possible in the first days of the German operations, while coastal batteries were still unprepared and before the German air force was able to operate effectively against the attacker.'

Looking back, it seems quite clear that if we had captured Trondheim we could not have held on to it indefinitely, since we should have been short of both fighter aircraft and anti-aircraft artillery to meet the inevitable weight of German attack—a consideration on which the Joint Planning Sub-Committee had laid great stress as early as 15th April. On the other hand, we cannot tell how great the temporary advantages for the further conduct of Scandinavian operations might have been. If then we confine our judgement to the feasibility of the initial attack, which was the main contested issue at the time, it is difficult to resist, though impossible finally to establish, the conclusion that sufficient promptness of action, even with relatively small forces, could have won back the port.

The new strategy, however, still envisaged the capture of Trondheim, though more slowly, by a pincer movement. The landing of our forces at Namsos and Aandalsnes had been intended originally to work in with the combined operation for a landing about Trondheim, as the Commanders' instructions clearly show.[1] But the fact that, while the combined operation was being planned, prepared, and abandoned, first the seamen and Marines and then an infantry brigade had been landed at each of these ports without loss of life or shipping, and that the troops had been able to advance inland unimpeded except by the snow, made it now attractive to argue that to put larger forces ashore at the same bases would be equally feasible and produce correspondingly good results. The proposal therefore was to allocate both demi-brigades of Chasseurs Alpins to Mauriceforce (under Major-General Sir Adrian Carton de Wiart) at Namsos and two British brigades of infantry released from 'Hammer' to Sickleforce (now under Major-General Paget) at Aandalsnes. The Canadians were the only troops withdrawn from the Norway operations as a result

---

[1] See Appendix A (2) and (3), pp. 249 and 250.

of the change of plan, and the French notified the Allied Military Committee on the 20th that their second light division could commence embarkation in three days' time, thus doubling the number of their troops in Norway. The siege operations were expected to take a month to complete, but it was assumed that on the north side the German ground forces would remain on the defensive, leaving us free to choose the time for an attack, subject only to the evident danger from the air. Meanwhile on the south side there would be sufficient troops available both to press on towards the city and to establish a front along the two railway and road routes for holding back the German advance from Oslo to the relief of the garrison. General Gamelin in particular welcomed the prospect of a long-continued struggle in the mountains south of Trondheim, whither Germany's manpower might be increasingly diverted to fight at a disadvantage, and was pressing for this to be a French assignment under a French commander. But the British view was that the more mobile troops, namely the French, ought to be employed in the northern jaw of the pincers.

Lieut.-General H. R. S. Massy, who as Deputy Chief of the Imperial General Staff had been closely concerned with all the earlier phases of the operations, was appointed at this juncture to command all Allied forces in Norway except in the Narvik area.[1] The fact that the General and his headquarters never left London illustrates not only the speed with which the tide of events overtook his plans but the geographical complexity of the operations against Trondheim, the northern and southern halves of which had no communications except through home bases.

The pincer movement as a strategic concept lasted one week, as a practical venture even less. The Chairman of the Military Co-ordination Committee had noted already (on 19th April) of Mauriceforce that the position was 'somewhat hazardous, but its commander . . . used to taking risks.'[2] On the night of the 20th/21st General Carton de Wiart reported the devastating impact of the first serious German air attack upon his base at Namsos, which was followed in the next two days by a defeat in the forward area at Steinkjer, where his right flank rested upon the Trondheimsfiord. A bold face was put upon the situation for the meeting of the Supreme War Council on the 22nd, at which the French still spoke of sending in enough men to free all Scandinavia; their second light division was now at Brest, ready to embark in their own transports, and the third only awaited the promised British transportation in order to follow. Trondheim was still regarded officially as our first objective: but Carton de

---

[1] See Appendix A (5), p. 255.
[2] Churchill, Vol. I, p. 497.

Wiart's statement that the base had been rendered unusable caused the possible need to evacuate his force to be canvassed at once in London. However, the fact that the Germans on the north side of Trondheim were palpably outnumbered and that the French half of the Allied force had as yet seen no action made it difficult to picture the situation there as being irretrievable. The troops based on Namsos might still serve to contain the Germans until Sickleforce was ready to cut a way through to Trondheim from the south. But on the 22nd Mr Churchill was urging the need to reinforce in the Narvik area, so that our troops might be on the Swedish frontier before Lulea became open to a German seaborne expedition, and the second demi-brigade of Chasseurs Alpins was accordingly sent there. Two battalions of the French Foreign Legion and four Polish battalions, which were then on their way from France to Scotland, were held in Scottish waters from 16th April to 1st May, when they followed the Chasseurs.

What strength the second jaw of the pincers might possess was very quickly tested. Sickleforce had the advantage of a modest quantity of air support from a squadron of Gladiators which was flown to a frozen lake near Aandalsnes and from two carriers operating off the coast, but it had the greater disadvantage of a position between two enemy forces, which must both be driven back if we were ever to win, or at least kept apart if we were not immediately to lose. Material for demolitions had been sent over and its use repeatedly urged, but neither of the two valley routes leading north towards Trondheim was properly blocked. Even before the failure of our air projects the speed of the German advance both up the Gudbrandsdal, where tanks had completed the discomfiture of our 148th Brigade on 23rd April, and the Österdal, where Norwegian resistance was equally ineffective, made the prospect of stabilising the front as a necessary preliminary to any aggressive action on our part look remote. On the 24th there were plans in London for putting a third infantry brigade, a mechanised brigade, a regiment of tanks and the French demi-brigade from Namsos successively through Aandalsnes, with possible relief from subsidiary landing points not yet reconnoitred. But even apart from the likelihood of heavy air attack as at Namsos—which Aandalsnes was in fact experiencing that very day—it was obviously unlikely that the Germans having gained so much ground already would now give us time for any such build-up; and the virtual elimination of the Gladiator squadron within twenty-four hours then made the prospect of holding them in the valleys still more remote.

While bad news accumulated, a last attempt was made to find a solution. General Massy had already indicated to General Paget a minimum area south of Trondheim, into which he could withdraw without enabling the Germans either to raise the siege or to block the arrival of his reinforcements. At Namsos, on the other hand, the situation appeared to have been stabilised with the arrival of some anti-aircraft artillery, though General Massy proposed also to bring down to Namsos the guns and tanks which had accompanied the French to the Narvik area. To give the necessary impetus to the operations, the First Sea Lord revived the idea of 'Hammer'. Indeed, the notion of a naval bombardment directed against Trondheim, to divert attention at a critical stage in the pincer movement, had never been formally abandoned, and the French Admiralty in private (and Sir Roger Keyes of Zeebrugge fame in public) had continued to press for some such action. On 23rd April it was proposed that the Royal Navy should capture or neutralise the forts at the mouth of the Trondheimsfiord, so as to achieve command of the waters between Trondheim and Steinkjer, thereby securing the flank for a renewed advance from Namsos; a small force might also be landed to help. This grew into a more definite plan, 'Hammer 2,' which the Chiefs of Staff outlined as follows: naval bombardment was to neutralise the forts, which would be captured by a force of two battalions with four howitzers, to be disembarked from landing craft and paddle steamers. The assault on the forts from the land side was advocated by Norwegian officers escaped from the area, who had been interviewed at Namsos; but they were unaware that the Germans had strengthened the defences by bringing in mortars. Once Agdenes was in our hands, German ships in the fiord would be destroyed and we should disembark troops 'at points to be decided upon' to dislodge the German garrison of Trondheim. But the plan required the use of two brigades of Regulars: their withdrawal from France meant a delay of ten days, of which two would be used to train at Scapa for the landing—and what might not happen during that time to our troops hard pressed elsewhere? The operation was certain to be 'somewhat hazardous', and if it succeeded there was still the problem of holding Trondheim. This would require a greater provision of aircraft, anti-aircraft guns, naval escorts, and shipping than we could afford to make, as a Report from the Joint Planning Sub-Committee to the Chiefs of Staff at this juncture again pointed out. After anxious consideration of 'Hammer 2' by the Chiefs of Staff on the 25th, when the Prime Minister gave preliminary orders through Mr Churchill for the operation to be put in hand, the Military Co-ordination Committee at 10 a.m. next morning decided to abandon it, in view of the dearth of air defence available both for the assault and for the protection of the port when taken; and they resolved to evacuate Central Norway instead. The War Cabinet accepted the arguments of the Committee, noting the additional danger that a serious setback might precipitate the intervention of Italy in the war, and came to the belated conclusion that our resources were too small to undertake the capture of Trondheim as well as Narvik.

The French had still to be convinced, as it was only three days since the Supreme War Council had taken the opposite decision, and their second light division sailed for its rendezvous in the Clyde that morning. General Gamelin flew at once to London to protest, chiefly on the grounds of the blow to Allied morale. The resulting imbroglio was made worse by the disclosure to the Cabinet next morning (27th April), while the French Generalissimo was still suggesting alternatives to any evacuation, that on the contrary it must take place much more quickly than had been imagined even twenty-four hours earlier. General Massy while preparing his plan for evacuation had received further news from General Paget, in the light of which he now appreciated the alternatives as being to leave Aandalsnes on 1st/2nd May, in which case we ought also to leave Namsos the same night, or else to allow the build-up of Sickleforce to continue and prepare for a much larger operation of withdrawal, commencing about 10th May and taking 35 days to complete. At the meeting of the Supreme War Council, which followed, the French Prime Minister accepted that there had been a 'technical mistake' in ignoring the absence both of an adequate port and of air bases,[1] and agreed to evacuate whenever it should become a military necessity. But M. Reynaud was still allowed to hope that there would be time to take Narvik first, and that his French troops might not have to be evacuated from Namsos at all but could be withdrawn to the north overland. The first of these illusions was destroyed just after midnight of the 27th/28th, when the Chief of the Imperial General Staff notified General Gamelin by letter that the evacuation had to be made at the earliest possible moment, the second in the middle of the following night, when the French learnt that the first of their troops were actually being re-embarked.

The rather devious way in which the British decision to cut the losses was conveyed to the French may be attributed in part to our awareness of the strength of their feelings. The French Government had all along favoured the maximum diversion of the German war effort towards Scandinavia, thought that to admit a failure now might bring Italy in against us, and feared the effects of a second crisis of confidence at home following so quickly upon that which had overthrown the ministry of M. Daladier. In addition, they had a report of their own observer at Namsos, received just after the meeting of the Supreme War Council, on the basis of which they claimed that the port could and should be used for landing further troops and material. But there was also a natural reluctance on our

---

[1] Reynaud, t. II, p. 42.

part to state unequivocally so bitter a decision. For by it we gave up all hope of seizing the initiative in Norway at large, though the campaign at Narvik might serve other purposes. A single argument runs through the story of three disappointing weeks: because we had no airfield, we could not mount the air strength to secure one; because we had no proper base, we could not assemble the men and material to capture one; because we had no consistently held objective, no one of our objectives had been achieved.

Namsos town and harbour, looking inland towards Grong

Norsk Telegrambyraa

CHAPTER VI

THE ADVANCE TOWARDS TRONDHEIM

See Map 3, facing p. 96

As has been explained in the last chapter, plans for the capture of Trondheim by direct assault were linked up with plans for an advance from other, smaller ports north and south of the city, in which we persisted although the abandonment of Operation Hammer left German naval forces in undisputed control of Trondheimsfiord. The history of earlier wars, in which Swedes and Norwegians fought for possession of the city, showed clearly enough that strategically the long fiord was the thing that mattered. Nevertheless, these small and inconvenient ports outside the fiord might also have been in German hands already if von Falkenhorst had been allowed to spread German naval resources a little more widely,[1] and the British remained uncertain up to the last moment whether the Germans might not indeed have reached them. Namsos is 127 miles N.N.E. of Trondheim by road; the distance by rail is 170 miles, involving a detour eastwards as far as Grong. With a population of under 4,000 dependent mainly on the timber industry, the town had a stone railway quay, two wooden wharves, and good anchorage close by; the open sea is about 15 miles away along the winding fiord.

Major-General Sir Adrian Carton de Wiart, V.C., a soldier with a remarkable fighting record in the First World War and Belgian connections which were also to prove useful, was appointed to the command of Mauriceforce on 13th April, on which date the original plan of operations was given in outline at the War Office. Naval landing parties were to go ashore at Namsos first, to be followed by the two battalions of the 148th brigade and other units, French and British, in succession. On the 14th the plan was elaborated in Instructions[2] which set out three objects—the encouragement of the Norwegian Government, the provision of a rallying-point for that Government and its armed forces, and the acquisition of a base for 'any subsequent operations in Scandinavia'. From this it followed that the immediate objective was to secure the Trondheim area and then the use of its road and rail communications, particularly to the east, the operations being based initially on Namsos. These instruc-

---
[1] See p. 19.
[2] See Appendix A (2), p. 249.

tions also made the timing of the operation more definite, since the General was now informed that the 146th Brigade would be available next day (15th April), the 148th Brigade about dawn on the 17th, two battalions of Chasseurs Alpins on the 18th, and the 147th Brigade with artillery and ancillary troops on the 20th or 21st.

In the absence of adequate Intelligence, General Carton de Wiart's instructions were to seek Norwegian co-operation and not to land in the face of opposition. Both these matters were cleared up on 14th April, when a small cruiser force under Captain F. H. Pegram (H.M.S. *Glasgow*), one of two which were now searching the Leads from Aalesund to the north, executed orders for a preliminary landing, known as Operation Henry. About three hundred and fifty seamen and Royal Marines under Captain W. F. Edds, R.M., were landed by destroyers at dusk, men from the cruiser *Sheffield* taking post east of Namsos, those from the *Glasgow* south of the village of Bangsund. They met with no opposition, though Captain Pegram was certain that their presence had been spotted from the air; in point of fact the enemy had intercepted a naval signal on the 12th which mentioned Namsos (with Mosjöen)[1] as suitable for a landing. A small military advance party which accompanied the expedition sent a report home in the small hours of the following morning, after consultation with Norwegian officers. This was to the effect that the enemy made a daily air reconnaissance; that there was very small chance of concealment for any considerable force at Namsos or Bangsund; that local deployment was impossible owing to the snow; and that a move southward at anything above battalion strength would be slow, and conspicuous from the air. General Carton de Wiart himself crossed the North Sea by flying boat on 15th April, but was delayed by an air raid in the Namsenfiord, in which the only staff officer accompanying him was wounded.

Meanwhile, the first flight of Mauriceforce was on its way. According to the original plan, this should have consisted of the two battalions of the 148th Brigade, which were embarked in two cruisers and a large transport ready to sail on the evening of the 14th. But at the last moment, as we have seen,[2] the Government decided to divert the 146th Brigade to Namsos, so the battalions belonging to the 148th Brigade were relegated to the second flight and after further delays found themselves at Aandalsnes instead. The 146th Brigade, 2,166 strong, comprised the 1/4th Royal Lincolnshire Regiment, the Hallamshire Battalion (1/4th York and Lancaster Regiment), and the 1/4th King's Own Yorkshire Light Infantry, and was accompanied by one section, 55th Field Company R.E. It was due to reach Namsos at dusk on 15th April in two large transports, *Chrobry* and

---

[1] Ninety miles farther north (pronounced 'Mooshern').
[2] P. 69.

Empress of Australia, escorted by the cruisers *Manchester*, *Birmingham*, and *Cairo* and three destroyers under command of Admiral Layton. But at this point reports from Namsos caused a further change. Captain R. S. G. Nicholson, whose destroyer flotilla was to assist in the landing, urged that facilities for this were very inadequate and that there would be very grave risk to town and transports unless command of the air was certain. Even before the General's arrival, the Admiralty told Admiral Layton that it would probably be decided to transfer the troops to destroyers at Lillesjona, a remote channel about 100 miles farther north, where the German air force would be less likely to locate big ships. This was the more urgent because bad weather had prevented a second anti-aircraft ship from reinforcing the *Cairo*.

General Carton de Wiart on his arrival at Namsos late on the 15th agreed to the change; the convoy had already been diverted, and he followed it to its destination in a destroyer to concert arrangements with Admiral Layton. Brigadier C. G. Phillips, who commanded the 146th Brigade, was embarked in a different ship from his troops and had unfortunately been carried on with the Narvik expedition. By midday the Lincolnshire and the Hallamshire had been transshipped into five destroyers. They started out for Namsos and Bangsund during an air raid, but duly reached their destination that evening, and the seamen and Marines were then withdrawn. The remaining battalion was intended to travel as a second flight in the same destroyers, while the *Chrobry* brought in the stores. This meant awaiting the return of the destroyers at Lillesjona, where air attacks, though small as yet, were, as the Admiral says, 'practically continuous' and imposed a serious strain on the troops cooped up in the liner. It was therefore decided to make do with the *Chrobry* alone. The K.O.Y.L.I. were accordingly transferred, minus 170 tons of stores which there was no chance to shift, and these stores were taken home next day in the *Empress of Australia*. The troops left Lillesjona at dawn, so that *Chrobry* and her escort might cruise unmolested until evening, when it was deemed safe to go in to Namsos. *Chrobry* put the battalion ashore without loss, but 130 tons of supplies and equipment were still on board when unloading operations were suspended at 2 a.m.; the ship came back the next night (18th/19th April) to complete the task.

By the late evening of 17th April, then, Mauriceforce was ashore but operating under difficulties. The snow—two feet deep on an average but very much deeper in the hidden drifts and at the sides of the roads, which were kept open by frequent ploughing—was potentially the greatest; but to begin with, other wants loomed larger than the absence of skis and snowshoes and of the ability to use them. The troops were heavily equipped, with three kitbags of clothing apiece— the lambskin-lined Arctic coat alone weighed 15 lb.—but no motor transport had accompanied the expedition, which must therefore depend upon a single-track railway and whatever vehicles could be hired or commandeered locally with local drivers. No artillery of any kind had been provided for land or air defence. One battalion had lost its 3-inch mortars in the confusion of the voyage; the troops, who were Territorials, had in any case had no practice with these mortars and very few of them, in the General's opinion, 'really knew the Bren'. There was no Headquarters Staff, so the General was dependent upon Brigade Headquarters, which had been rejoined (on the 17th) by Brigadier Phillips. The fact that these were battalions which had originally been destined under Plan R.4 for the garrison of Trondheim and Bergen and had been disembarked from cruisers on 8th April in just over one hour[1] helps to explain the deficient initial provision; the losses *en route* had now reduced their supplies from two weeks' to two days'. At this juncture further instructions arrived, still envisaging a threefold attack against Trondheim (to include Operation Hammer) and placing the Chasseurs Alpins, who would be landed in two échelons of three battalions each, under General Carton de Wiart's command. The prospect of their early arrival encouraged the deployment of the British troops, which had already started.

The advance was rapid and unhindered. While Force Headquarters was established at Namsos, a detachment was at once moved up the railway eastwards to Grong, while from the smaller landing place at Bangsund there was a move south by road transport to secure both sides of the Beitstadfiord. This fiord is the innermost reach of the long Trondheimsfiord; a position gained on its western bank at Follafoss would serve as a safeguard against a German overland advance along that bank from the shore opposite Trondheim. But the advance along the east bank of the fiord was the crux of the expedition, since it gave direct road access via the town of Steinkjer to Trondheim itself. By the afternoon of the 17th, Steinkjer and Follafoss had both been reached. The general policy was to build up forward as quickly as possible: by the evening of the 19th, Brigade Advanced Headquarters was in the northern outskirts of Steinkjer and detachments were posted at Röra and Stiklestad, up to seventeen miles farther south. Having passed right across the base of the Inderöy peninsula, with the narrows of the same name beyond, our troops had now touched the main Trondheimsfiord at a point which was only about sixty miles from Trondheim. The snow did not seriously interfere with the advance, which was along the line of road and railway, the use of the rail route east to Grong and thence in a big loop south to Steinkjer being supplemented by the employment of twenty 30-cwt. Norwegian lorries, with others for local service.

---

[1] See p. 26.

The smooth working of the transport arrangements was the first-fruits of co-operation with the Norwegian military command. The 5th Division, based on Trondheim, was out of touch with the Commander-in-Chief, but was in communication with the more fully mobilised 6th Division north of Narvik. Its commanding officer, General Laurantzon, received an officer of our small advance party on 15th April at his headquarters, and decided to make liaison with the British base at Namsos his personal responsibility. He did not, however, favour any advance beyond Steinkjer until Agdenes had been taken and had, before the British arrived, adopted a rather passive attitude towards the German invasion. On 27th April General Laurantzon finally went on sick leave. For practical purposes our concern was with a younger and more vigorous officer, Colonel Getz, who on the 17th was put in direct command of all Norwegian troops in the area as Officer Commanding 5th Brigade. This had a potential strength of four battalions, but on the 18th, when Brigadier Phillips first conferred with Colonel Getz, the latter disposed in effect of only two battalions, one from each of the two locally recruited regiments. These, after completing their mobilisation, had been withdrawn to the district north of Steinkjer: there they could still guard the strategic position of the isthmus only seven miles wide between the head of the fiord and the big lake Snaasavatn, but they would no longer be directly exposed to a German landing on their flank as the fiord ceased to be ice-bound. A machine-gun squadron of dismounted dragoons held a small outpost at Verdalsöra, west of Stiklestad.

Colonel Getz described his troops as inexperienced militia, and emphasised the fact that their stock of ammunition amounted to only one day's battle issue (100 rounds per rifle, 2,500 per machine gun, etc.). When this was exhausted they would be dependent on securing British weapons, since ammunition of the right calibre for their own was unobtainable outside Norway. It seemed that their immediate usefulness would be chiefly through ski detachments, which they readily undertook to provide. Colonel Getz urged the seizure of the Fetten defile beyond Aasen, where the road from Levanger again touched the fiord, about thirty miles short of Trondheim. The defile was a strong position in itself and from Aasen our troops could have continued south by an inland route into Stjördal, the valley by which the railway from Trondheim climbs eastwards into Sweden. Just where they would debouch into the valley a Norwegian garrison of less than 300 men held the hilltop fort of Hegra. Under the determined leadership of Major Holtermann they stood siege successfully as long as our troops were in the area and longer; but Colonel Getz, though he had been recently in touch with the garrison, does not appear to have made clear to the British the help that Hegra, with its four 10·5-cm., two 7·5-cm., and two old field guns, might provide along that line of advance. At all events, the British view was that there was no hurry: within three days the Germans were past Aasen. In addition, there seems to have been little attempt to profit by local knowledge as to the date at which the thaw would make the water route up the fiord from Trondheim to Steinkjer fully available. The importance of this omission will appear in the sequel.

In its later stages the British advance from Namsos was hastened to clear the port for the arrival of the French reinforcement. This was the 5th Demi-brigade of Chasseurs Alpins, composed of the 13th, 53rd and 67th Battalions under Brigadier-General Béthouart and under the superior authority of the divisional General Audet, accompanied by his full staff. Leaving the all-important anti-aircraft guns, transport, skis, and snowshoes with much other material for a second flight, the main body sailed in four troopships from the Clyde, where they had been waiting for two days, escorted by the French Admiral Derrien with the cruiser *Emile Bertin* and some French destroyers; the British anti-aircraft cruiser *Cairo* was sent from Namsos to lead the way in. The landing was carried out at top speed during the night of the 19th/20th, as the convoy had been attacked from the air during the passage of the fiords and the flagship damaged so that she returned home. General Audet's plan, approved by General Carton de Wiart and Brigadier Phillips, who met him at the quay, was to disperse his troops to strategic positions outside the town, and all but two hundred bivouacked out on the wooded hills. It was not, however, possible to dispose of stores before daylight, as only two of the French ships could berth by the quay simultaneously and there was a shortage of French officers to control the hectic activities on the quayside. The best that could be done was to improvise a camouflage suggesting that the port was overloaded with timber. This was the less likely to deceive the Germans as the British landings 'at several points in Norway' had been officially announced on the 15th.

This was indeed the moment of time at which the prospects seemed brightest. General Carton de Wiart now had at his disposal more than 4,000 French troops partly accustomed to conditions of mountain and winter warfare; General Audet anticipated that his ski patrols—when they had their skis—might cut the railway east to Sweden and operate as far south as Elverum. The British brigade was in a posture for a rapid advance astride the rail and road route to Trondheim: the section of Royal Engineers was moved to Verdalsöra to consider the reconstructing of the railway bridge there, over-hastily blown by the Norwegians. Our eastern flank was secured by a Norwegian force numbering nearly as many men as our own brigade, knowing the country through which the advance was to be made, and eager to help in the recapture of the city which was their provincial capital. Meanwhile, liaison with the Norwegians was likely to provide valuable information for the sea-borne assault on Trondheim, in preparation for which the Commander-in-Chief, Home Fleet, had now ordered home almost every British ship operating in this area. As for the enemy, the latest War Office intelligence report, received just before the French landed, estimated the forces based on Trondheim at 5,000 men, in general well equipped but having no artillery; the report added that a further 6,000 reinforcements might reach the Germans by air, but this was primarily an argument for speed of action. The sea-borne assault, with which General Carton de Wiart was expecting to co-operate, was officially cancelled (as we have seen)[1] the next morning, but he was not at once informed. It would have been in any case too late to affect the rapid tempo of his advance, for which a heavy price was now to be exacted.

The reversal of fortune which quickly followed was due to two main causes, both foreseeable and one foreseen. Since the outset of the campaign, General Carton de Wiart had emphasised repeatedly his exposure to air attack. It was for this reason that the disembarkation of the British and French forces had taken place at night. By the 19th, awareness of the activity of German reconnaissance aircraft and of its implications was such that Brigade Orders discouraged any troop movement by day, forbade firing on enemy aircraft except as an urgent defence measure, and required wireless silence to be maintained 'until such time as it was really necessary to break it'. But the attempt to avoid attracting enemy attention could not be more than a temporary makeshift. More positive measures included the protection of the Namsos base by two anti-aircraft ships, but the *Curlew* had to go home for oil, and the *Cairo*, which led the French convoy in to Namsos, escorted the empty troopships back across the North Sea. No landing ground existed in the area held by Allied troops; no aircraft carrier was immediately available. There remained only the possibility that R.A.F. bombers could put out of action the Trondheim airfield of Vaernes or the seaplane alighting area on Lake Jonsvand nearby, of which the Germans were believed to make use pending the thaw. Small forces of Whitleys twice made the attempt, on the nights of 22nd and 23rd April; but at a range of over 750 miles they failed to locate their target. In any case, interrogation of captured German pilots subsequently confirmed the view that German bombers made the outward flight direct from more distant bases.

The bombing of Namsos began about 10 a.m. on the morning of the 20th after early reconnaissance, and continued at intervals up to 4.30 p.m. Some sixty-three aircraft were reported over the town that

---

[1] P. 75.

day. The civil population had for the most part left and the number of fatal casualties was only twenty-two, but the wooden houses were easily destroyed, together with the railhead, rolling stock, and much of the wooden wharves and the superstructure of the quay. The water mains and electricity supply were also cut. The French Headquarters had been hit, but the Rear Headquarters of the British Brigade escaped destruction and was easily moved forward. The French also lost a small part of their supplies and ammunition. When the destroyer *Nubian* came back that night to find 'the whole place a mass of flames from end to end', General Carton de Wiart was already speaking of the possibility that the expedition was doomed. Early next day he reported to the War Office as follows:

> Enemy aircraft have almost completely destroyed Namsos, beginning on railhead target, diving indiscriminately. . . . I see little chance of carrying out decisive or, indeed, any operations, unless enemy air activity is considerably restricted.

The British General, who was very much senior to any naval officer present, demanded that no more ships should enter Namsos, since every storehouse on the quay had been destroyed and Norwegians evacuating had taken all local vehicles with them. The French transport *Ville d'Alger* had therefore to be sent out again until the night of the 22nd, when a further disembarkation was allowed to complete the French demi-brigade. But the ship was too large to berth at the quay. Some 800 out of 1,100 men together with a stock of skis (mostly without bindings) and some rations were duly landed—partly from an accompanying storeship—but the heavy stores, including an anti-aircraft battery and the brigade transport, were not put ashore until nearly a week later. In any case the usefulness of Namsos as a base had been disastrously reduced. The difficulties of unloading ships might not be insuperable, as the big stone quay was intact, but there was no longer any proper storage. The railway had several breaks in it, the road approaches to the quay had been reduced to chaos, and transport facilities further impaired by the destruction of petrol and of lorries. Moreover, it was reasonable to assume that what the Germans had done at Namsos they could do at any other point along our intended line of advance. The large-scale bombing of Namsos was continued on the 21st and resumed again on the 28th; it involved a tremendous strain upon the anti-aircraft defence, which was provided in default of anti-aircraft artillery for eighteen hours of the twenty-four by the ships of the Royal Navy. In the end, Swedish correspondents were moved to describe Namsos as 'the most thoroughly bombed town in the world';[1] the description even at that date was inaccurate, but the event had all the effects of novelty.

---

[1] *Norges Krig*, p. 354.

The following day, 21st April, the use of air supremacy gave place to the use of localised naval supremacy. As early as the evening of 9th April, one German destroyer had penetrated as far as the neighbourhood of Inderöy, where a narrow channel leads from the main Trondheimsfiord into the smaller Beitstadfiord. It was joined by a second German destroyer on the morning of the 10th, but the ice prevented them from breaking through to Steinkjer. It was because of this threat, solely dependent for its execution on the date of the annual thaw, that the Norwegian troops (as we have seen) had withdrawn north of Steinkjer, and this was explained to Brigadier Phillips when he met the Norwegian Colonel Getz at Grong on the afternoon of the 18th.[1] On the 19th at 2 p.m., it was known that a number of small vessels had sailed northwards through the narrows into the Beitstadfiord, and the War Diary of the 4th Lincolnshire on the same day, after referring to a conference at which their commanding officer had been present, on the subject of the situation round Steinkjer, remarked: 'The fjord is beginning to thaw and danger of enemy destroyers approaching is imminent'. Orders were drawn up that night for a retirement from the exposed positions at Verdalsöra and Stiklestad as far as the line Strömmen-Röra, to begin at 7.30 p.m. next day; but in the meantime the enemy had arrived.

About 4 a.m. on the 21st, a vessel of 300 tons passed through the narrows followed by an enemy destroyer. This was the first of a series of German naval movements observed by the 4th Lincolnshire and by the Norwegian Dragoons and reported back to their respective Brigade Headquarters, which exchanged information. By 6 a.m., however, the Norwegian troops were in action against a German advance along the road from Trondheim, which threatened the position they held at Verdalsöra, where they had the support of the Royal Engineers. The German attack at this advanced point was strengthened by a landing to take Verdalsöra in the rear, whereupon the Norwegian machine-gun squadron and Royal Engineers withdrew inland to Stiklestad, where one British company was already posted. A second company, sent south from Strömmen after the Germans had got ashore to the north of Verdalsöra, was also forced to retire more gradually in the same direction. By half past seven it was believed that the British brigade, strung out along the road between the Verdal area in the south through Steinkjer to Namdalseid in the north, was threatened by at least two German attacks on its right flank. Besides the move against Verdalsöra, which had already succeeded, about 400 Germans were reported coming north-eastward along the coast towards Vist, just south of Steinkjer; another German force of unknown strength was supposed to be proceeding from the

---

[1] Getz, Colonel O. B.: *Fra Krigen i Nord-Tröndelag, 1940*, p. 55.

same landing place—the quay belonging to a sawmill at Kirknesvaag—south-eastward to cut the main road about 10 miles south of Vist. In addition to the actions of these parties, the British had also to reckon with the possibility of further landings and the probability of gunfire from the German warship or warships. It is not clear that the Germans in fact had any superiority in numbers (a battalion operated against Vist, two reinforced companies and a troop of mountain artillery in the advance against Verdalsöra from north and south), but they were for the most part mountaineers, their equipment was better suited to the situation, and they had both air and sea support.

The south-eastward advance from Kirknesvaag came to nothing: we had a very good defensive position at Strömmen bridge, closing the only way out from the south of the Inderöy peninsula. In any case the Germans, who had landed with guns and mortars but no transport except half a dozen motor cycles, had their work cut out to advance in one direction, their main objective being the neck of the peninsula round Vist. While the Germans busily ransacked the farms for carts, sledges, and an occasional motor vehicle, the 4th Lincolnshire were being moved up to form a front through Vist facing west and the K.O.Y.L.I. prepared to hold the main-road attack as far south of Vist as possible. The Germans might also push north by a secondary road which begins at Verdalsöra, runs roughly parallel with the main road from Stiklestad along the east shore of the Leksdalsvatn to Fisknes, and eventually through Ogndal about six miles east of Steinkjer. But the British and Norwegian detachments, already referred to, were able to retire unmolested from Stiklestad in the late afternoon and evening. The condition of the road over which they went back, which caused the Norwegian Dragoons to exchange their motor transport for horse sledges, probably explains why our extreme left was not seriously attacked that day. This was the flank on which the Norwegians were to be found, with their Headquarters at Ogndal, but a British suggestion that their ski troops should counterattack along both sides of the Leksdalsvatn in the hope of taking the Germans in the rear was rejected because we could not guarantee their line of retreat. About 8 p.m. the small ski patrols which the Norwegians established only at the head of the lake spotted the first Germans as they approached, 110 strong.

Against Vist, however, the pressure soon became severe. The distance from Kirknesvaag is about a dozen miles by a very hilly, narrow, winding lane, but the first motor cyclist made contact by 9.30 a.m. Intensive fire from trench mortars, carried in the side-cars of the motor cycles, as well as from machine guns, and the skilful use by the Germans of the numerous farm tracks to outflank our detachments made it very hard for our men to establish a firm line across the peninsula. The enemy may well have collected a few pairs of skis from the farms as they went along, and some no doubt used snowshoes, but for the most part they were confined to the roads just as our men were and their superior mobility was chiefly a result of superior fitness. Moreover, they had a tremendous asset in the light field guns, which they dragged up to commanding positions, first at Gangstad and later at Hustad Church. From midday onwards a series of heavy air attacks was launched against Steinkjer, five miles behind our line, the town in which both Brigade and Battalion Headquarters were now situated, and through which communications with Vist must pass. By late afternoon it was all ablaze, with its water supply cut, road bridge destroyed, and railway immobilised. At nightfall the situation in the whole area was already precarious. Two companies plus a headquarters detachment of the Lincolnshire were in the line, but a third company, having borne the brunt of the fighting at the critical point where the road from Kirknesvaag skirts the shore one mile west of Vist, had had to be withdrawn with a twenty-per-cent. casualty list to high ground farther east. On the main road one half of the area between Verdalsöra and Vist was relinquished to the enemy at dusk, when the two companies of K.O.Y.L.I. which had been stationed at Strömmen and Röra fell back respectively to a point on the main road just south of Sparbu and to Maere, between Sparbu and Vist.

Accordingly, Brigadier Phillips reported to the General that no position was now tenable in the neighbourhood of the fiord and proposed a withdrawal along the north bank of the Snaasavatn towards Grong. General Carton de Wiart, who came into the forward area next morning with the knowledge that the French were not yet ready to move, approved the proposed withdrawal but changed its direction towards the north, so as not to interfere with Norwegian troop movements along Snaasavatn.

The second day's fighting began at 7.45 a.m. with the dropping of flares by enemy aircraft to mark the position of the K.O.Y.L.I. south of Sparbu. The road itself was easily held, but with the help of sledge-borne mortars and machine guns the Germans came on quickly on the flanks, and the K.O.Y.L.I. had to withdraw both companies with some loss eastwards through the woods to Fisknes. In that area they were rejoined by the two companies from Stiklestad. The Lincolnshire held their front during the morning, though constantly engaged by the enemy infantry, by some gunfire from the destroyer and by machine-gunning from the air. But in the early afternoon they received after much delay an order issued by their second-in-command three hours before for a withdrawal to Steinkjer, which he regarded as necessary to conform with the action of the K.O.Y.L.I., and then fell back rapidly. The commanding officer tried to organise a further stand half way to Steinkjer, but 'the withdrawal once commenced was impossible to check'. He himself remained to reorganise the men of his battalion up to 8.45 p.m., by which time the enemy after shelling the town from the fiord had begun to land there. He then took the road north-east to Sunnan.

The defeat was undoubted. But it was less complete than the immediate situation suggested, because of the skill and determination with which units were extricated from a very difficult position. Thus, a company and a half of the 4th Lincolnshire who had been cut off on our right flank emerged from the woods west of Vist after the Germans had occupied the village, and succeeded in getting away past the enemy by a night march across country through three or four feet of snow; the first one and a half miles cost them four and a half painful hours. In the case of the K.O.Y.L.I., the entire battalion was already exhausted by its march when it left Henning at 9 p.m. to try to work round the flank of the Germans, before whose anticipated advance east from Steinkjer the Norwegian Dragoons were falling back to the south of Snaasavatn. But they found an unbroken and unguarded bridge half a dozen miles up the river from Steinkjer and got through without losing a man, though it meant a total march of fifty-eight miles in forty-two hours, winding their way along snow-bound forest tracks mainly at night.[1] The Lincolnshire, who had done most of the fighting, were now located only a few miles south of Bangsund. The K.O.Y.L.I. stretched beyond them as far as Namdalseid, and the Hallamshire (who had been in reserve throughout the two-day action) held the southward slope of the road from Namdalseid to where it reaches fiord level at Hjelle, about 15 miles north-west of Steinkjer.

Thus the attack on Trondheim had in the course of three days been changed from a hopeful offensive to a precarious defensive. General Carton de Wiart sent a telegram to the War Office on the afternoon of the 23rd, before the process of extrication was complete, which described Phillips's brigade as having been 'very roughly handled', stressed the danger of increasing enemy air activity, and discussed ways and means of evacuation. But as viewed from home the situation was by no means desperate. Before the news of the defeat in front of Steinkjer had reached England and been assessed, the news of the earlier disaster in the shape of the destruction of the base at Namsos had already been acted upon. Before midday on 22nd April, an Admiralty message was sent to advise the General that anti-aircraft guns were on the way; that an aircraft carrier with fighters would arrive on the 24th; and that shore fighters would 'probably' be established on the 25th. Accordingly, the new policy as expressed in the orders to General Carton de Wiart in the field, and in more detail in a memorandum drawn up by Lieut.-General

---

[1] Hingston, Lieut.-Col. W.: *Never Give Up*, pp. 74–77.

Massy in London, was to keep Mauriceforce in being and in position as 'a standing threat to the Germans at Trondheim'.

Actually the British force, in the short interim period before evacuation was finally determined on, remained so strictly on the defensive that there is nothing bigger to record than a patrol advance by night to Maere, although snowstorms and then the arrival of our aircraft carriers, which launched a successful attack on Vaernes airfield, were followed by a complete cessation of enemy air activity on the 23rd, 24th, and 25th. On the 26th General Carton de Wiart learned that the second demi-brigade of Chasseurs Alpins was to be sent to Narvik—General Béthouart left next day by destroyer to take command there. This information at least counterbalanced the encouragement given by the arrival at long last of some transport (fifteen lorries) and the receipt of a Bofors anti-aircraft battery without predictors and a Royal Marine 3·7-inch howitzer battery which had no ammunition. The British commander had already telegraphed on the 23rd that, even with air superiority, he would require more troops, 'say a brigade', before he could advance again south of Bangsund. But Generals Audet and Béthouart, who were perhaps encouraged by the lull in the air attack to minimise the significance of the reverse which the British troops had sustained, had been concerting a counter-attack with the Norwegians on the left flank under Colonel Getz.[1] The Norwegians were in good heart because their position on either shore of Snaasavatn had not been seriously attacked by the Germans: the latter, as we now know, had taken longer than they expected to enter Steinkjer and did not propose to advance past Sunnan, the occupation of which on the evening of the 24th gave them full control of what they called the Steinkjer Pass. In such skirmishing of patrols as had occurred the Norwegians, helped by conditions of terrain and climate, had given a fair account of themselves. The French had not been in action at all.

The 13th Chasseurs Alpins accordingly went forward to Namdalseid to the positions held by the Hallamshire, whom they would relieve, and also began to send ski patrols up the valley of the Bongaa east of the main road on to the heights. French and Norwegian patrols were there to join forces, the immediate object being to assert control of the isthmus east of Hjelle and reconnoitre further towards Steinkjer. The K.O.Y.L.I. as well as the 67th Chasseurs Alpins would be in the rear area and at the disposal of the French General for the operation. This arrangement, which had the Force Commander's approval, left two British battalions and one French battalion under Brigadier Phillips to hold our base and the line of communications east from Namsos towards the Norwegian base area round Grong.

---

[1] Sereau, R.: *L'Expédition de Norvège, 1940*, p. 34.

Though a Norwegian intelligence report of 27th April, which put the number of Germans in and around Steinkjer at 300, was highly optimistic—three battalions is nearer the mark—the enemy remained strictly on the defensive and (in point of fact) did not consider themselves capable of a forward movement without a further reinforcement of two battalions of mountain infantry. But early on the 28th, when the French anti-aircraft batteries had at last been landed with their stores and set up, an activity which monopolised the quay so completely that 7,000 rifles and 250 Bren guns with ammunition for the Norwegians had not left the *Chrobry*, General Carton de Wiart received his expected orders to evacuate the Allied forces. For security reasons the Norwegians were not to be told, so the delay in obtaining the weapons which they needed and had been promised for the counter-attack was used to explain away its indefinite postponement.

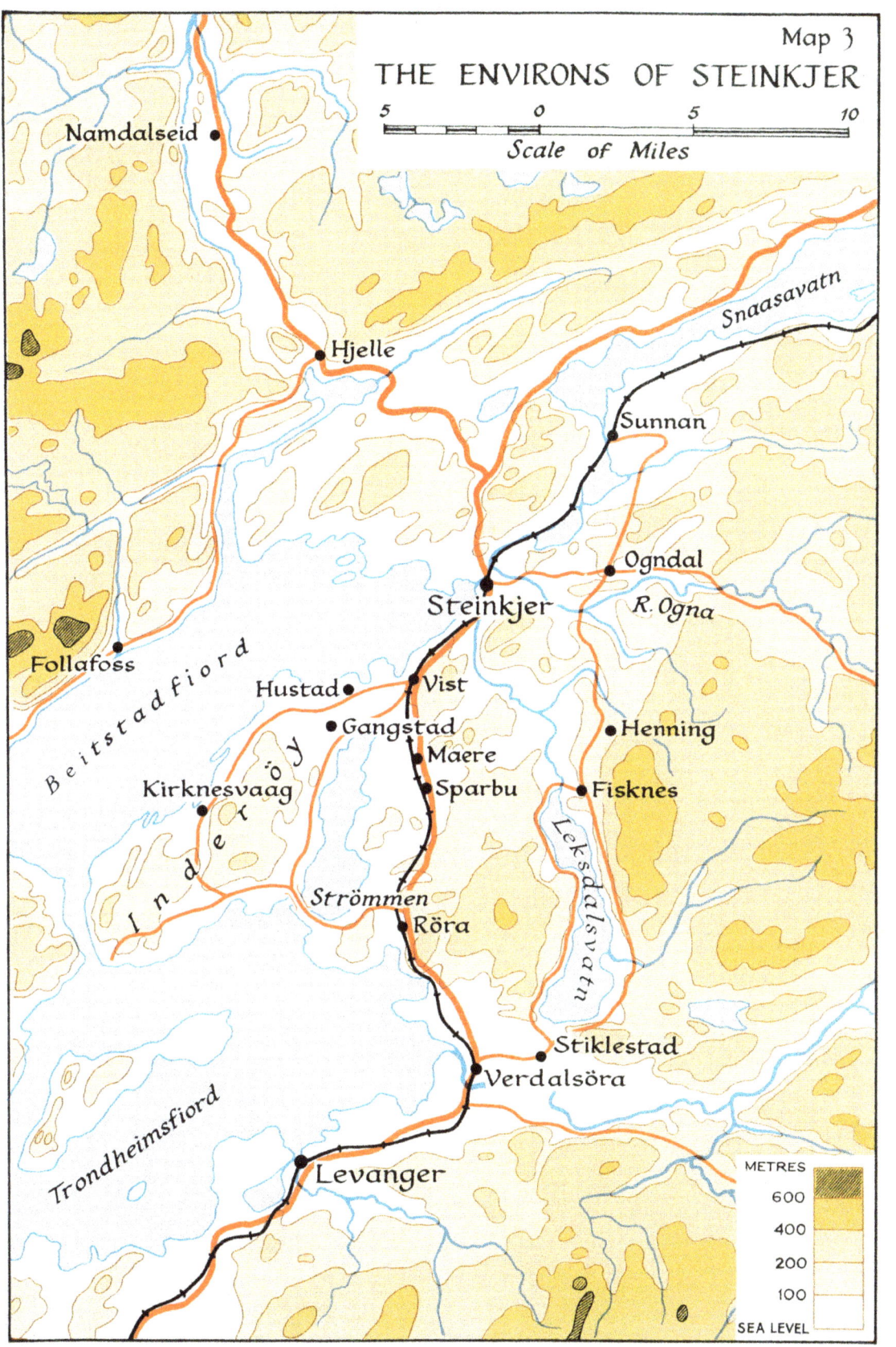

CHAPTER VII

INITIAL OPERATIONS IN GUDBRANDSDAL

See Map 4, facing page 112, and Map 6, facing page 138

THE attempt to retain Mauriceforce as a useful factor in defence implied a belief that Sickleforce, the expedition to the south of Trondheim, might still save the attack on Trondheim from developing into a complete fiasco. This line of thought was perhaps tenable because the operations based on Aandalsnes, after an opening phase far more disastrous than the struggle for Steinkjer, had just at this time entered upon a second phase with new troops under a new commander. But before we can trace the adventures of Major-General Paget and the 15th Brigade, we must in the present chapter go back to consider the first advance from Aandalsnes, which had begun a little later than the landing at Namsos and failed at almost the same time.

Aandalsnes is a much smaller port than Namsos: though frequented by tourists in the summer season, it was hardly more than a fishing village, until the completion of the Raumadal Railway in 1924 brought some additional trade. This railway, a masterpiece of engineering, follows in general the old road route from Dombaas down the Romsdal, linking the Oslo-Trondheim main line with the long fiord which has Aandalsnes at its head; the larger port of Molde (roughly comparable to Namsos) lies about 23 miles farther out towards the sea. Molde, though its harbour facilities were of course considerably better, never ranked as more than a subsidiary base because it had no direct road communications with Aandalsnes and its hinterland the Romsdal. From Aandalsnes, on the other hand, there was ready access to the southern approaches of Trondheim and the means of contacting the Norwegian forces in the east of the country. Hence its selection as a base, although there was but a single concrete jetty about 150 feet long, of which only one side could be used, one 60-foot wooden quay, and one 5-ton travelling crane. A less immediately obvious drawback was the fact that the four huge mountains which tower above the little town would hide approaching aircraft until they were over their target.

One of the first steps proposed to facilitate the intended assault on Trondheim was the occupation of Aalesund, the largest port between Bergen and Trondheim, whose island position commands the route north through the Leads. A party of 45 officers and 680 Royal Marines and seamen under Lieut.-Colonel H. W. Simpson, R.M., was drawn from three battleships then in dockyard hands, embarked in such haste that the searchlight detachments went without their searchlights, and sent off in four sloops for Aalesund. But while the overloaded ships were held up by a gale at Invergordon their destination was changed at Norwegian request to Aandalsnes. Hence the rather absurd situation, not uncharacteristic of the atmosphere of improvisation in which the campaign began, that the main military force, half-expecting to find the Germans in occupation or at least the Norwegian population in need of some persuasion, was greeted at the quay by a British consul in company with a lieutenant-colonel of Marines.[1] The Marines had landed twenty-four hours before, in the evening of 17th April, and had dispatched a subsidiary detachment to Aalesund. At Aandalsnes throughout the period of operations the seamen provided working parties and the Marines guards for the base; the anti-aircraft defence of the harbour was undertaken by the 21st (Royal Marine) Light Anti-Aircraft Battery, armed with eight naval 2-pounders on improvised mountings. Two 3·7-inch howitzers were also available, manned by seaman crews, but two 4-inch naval guns had been taken on to Aalesund to command part of the sea approach to Trondheim. These last, however, were never mounted and lacked several essential articles of equipment, as did two 3-inch high-angle guns with which they were later supplemented. Aalesund was repeatedly attacked from the air, but played no part in the ensuing campaign except, to a small extent, as a coaling station for transports on the return trip from Aandalsnes.

The 148th Infantry Brigade (Territorials), consisting of the 1/5th Royal Leicestershire Regiment and 1/8th Sherwood Foresters, under the command of Brigadier H. de R. Morgan, had been in readiness on 7th April to proceed to Stavanger.[2] After their hurried disembarkation they were selected for Namsos, and were embarked together with the 168th Light Anti-Aircraft Battery at Rosyth on the 14th April. They were to go in the cruisers *Galatea* and *Arethusa* and a large transport, which last lay below the Forth Bridge and had to be loaded from lighters; hence stores were not tactically disposed, though this seemed to matter less as the holds were ample. The troops did not, however, sail for another two and a half days, during which new orders reached Brigadier Morgan—making in all four new sets of orders before he started on his expedition—and it was decided not to risk the large transport in the fiords, but to trans-ship instead to the two cruisers, the anti-aircraft cruisers *Carlisle* and *Curacoa*, and two destroyers. The new orders substituting Aandalsnes for Namsos

---

[1] See Clarke, Brigadier Dudley: *Seven Assignments*, p. 98.
[2] See p. 25

Aandalsnes and the mouth of the Romsdal

K. Harstad

rendered any information the Brigadier and his staff may have gathered for Namsos useless. The brigade suffered from two other disadvantages: owing to the fact that the transfer was made in the black-out, important stores were left behind, including brigade headquarters equipment, with the wireless transmitter, predictors for the anti-aircraft guns, and all the Foresters' mortar ammunition; and, secondly, one half of the Leicestershire battalion was relegated to the second flight for lack of accommodation in the warships.

The final orders were dated the evening of the 16th and delivered to Brigadier Morgan just before the expedition sailed at 7 a.m. next morning. While emphasising the fact that he would later be placed in subordination to the general commanding the final operations for the capture of Trondheim, these instructions defined his immediate duty quite clearly: 'Your role to land Aandalsnes area, secure Dombaas, then operate northwards and take offensive action against Germans in Trondheim area.'[1] But while he was still at sea, Brigadier Morgan received a further message from the Chief of the Imperial General Staff suggesting that he might be able to get to Dombaas very rapidly, as serious German opposition before that point was improbable, and imposing two further duties: 'When you have secured Dombaas you are to prevent Germans using railway to reinforce Trondheim: am sending small demolition party.' Secondly, 'You should make touch with Norwegian G.H.Q., believed to be in area Lillehammer, and avoid isolating Norwegian forces operating towards Oslo.' In other words, he was expected to face south as well as north. For these expanding operations, Brigadier Morgan had with him a first flight of almost exactly 1,000 men from the two Territorial battalions with one troop of the light anti-aircraft battery; only two officers apart from the Brigadier himself had any previous experience of active service. The second flight of 600 men, with all the motor transport of the Brigade and the second half of its anti-aircraft guns, was due to follow two days later.

The voyage across the North Sea was shadowed by enemy aircraft, which attempted one attack and were driven off; but there being no transport with the warships, the Germans did not detect the nature of the force. In order to reduce the risk of air attack during the landing, about one-third of it was landed at Molde, enabling disembarkation there and at Aandalsnes to be completed before daylight on the 19th. But there was an immediate complication. About 6.30 p.m. on 14th April, German paratroops had landed on the high mountains in the neighbourhood of Dombaas railway station, the junction between the Oslo-Trondheim and Romsdal lines. Their losses in landing were not inconsiderable, and the Norwegian battalion on guard in the

---

[1] See Appendix A (3), p. 250.

district was prompt to take up the challenge. These Germans were now only about sixty strong, but there was the implied threat that more might land at any place and moment, and those who had landed had put up a stubborn resistance which closed the road and rail route from Dombaas southwards. Brigadier Morgan therefore, in accordance with his instructions for a rapid advance on Dombaas, sent two companies forward at once on the night of the landing in a troop-train which was standing ready. The German paratroops had by this time been surrounded by the Norwegians in a farmhouse five miles south of Dombaas, and by 10 a.m. on the 19th a part of the Brigadier's force was reconnoitring the position. They were not, however, brought into action, as a naval gun from Colonel Simpson's party opened fire in support of the Norwegian ski troops who were preparing an attack, and the Germans then decided to surrender. During the day, our troops who had been landed at Molde were moved to Aandalsnes, and more of the troops in Aandalsnes were brought by rail to Dombaas.

Sickleforce had secured its position at Dombaas, from which it could turn north against the Germans in Trondheim, but a second and more decisive complication now intervened—the claims of the Norwegian army and its commander, which were at that time little known or regarded in London.

One of the last measures taken by the Norwegian Government in the crisis of 9th/10th April had been to require the retirement on grounds of age of their Commander-in-Chief, and to replace him by a younger and more energetic man, Colonel Otto Ruge, their Inspector-General of Infantry, who had vehemently urged the propriety of continued resistance and helped to organise the stand at Elverum on the night of 9th/10th April.[1] But in view of the German successes at the principal ports, it was then already too late for a general mobilisation to be effective. The divisional and regimental headquarters had in many cases been overrun, and not only the equipment but the actual mobilisation lists were in German hands. About 50,000 men reported eventually for service with the army or navy out of the very modest total of 120,000 (four per cent. of the population) provided by the latest pre-war mobilisation scheme; but even this took time.

On 12th April, Norwegian Headquarters was moved back to Öyer in the Gudbrandsdal, where it remained throughout the first phase of the operations. General Ruge had advised the Government at the outset that it was only worth while to offer further resistance in

---

[1] See p. 38.

so far as Norway could rely upon assurances of prompt and powerful Allied support. His plan of operations, therefore, had as its first object to keep resistance alive for an intervening ten days at most, and secondly to do what he could to safeguard the landing of the Allies and to enable their troops, when landed, to be deployed as advantageously as possible. He would try to retain sufficient ground in south-east Norway, clear of the central mountain range, to give an Allied army the means of recapturing the whole. But he was at the same time determined to avoid such severe losses to his troops, who were now rallying to the colours in circumstances of great confusion and discouragement, as might render them incapable of playing an effective part in joint operations later on. Orders were given on the 13th for delaying-actions to be fought on this basis, with systematic withdrawals and systematic demolitions.

The orders of the High Command were sent to the Trondheim area by air, but the message never arrived. On the south side of the city, however, General Ruge was in touch with a small improvised force which had blocked the road and rail routes twenty miles out against any German advance. Although Bergen likewise was in German hands, the division based on this area had its mobilisation centre about fifty miles away in the mountains at Voss, with the result that its commander, General Steffens, alone of the five divisional generals in South Norway, succeeded in setting up a complete field brigade according to plan. He was able to repulse the first German advance along the railway from Bergen.

Farther to the south, the results of the first few days were less satisfactory. A small force in the mountains behind Stavanger kept up the fight until 23rd April, but was too isolated for its efforts to have any effect on the general situation. More important, both numerically and because of their geographical position, were the troops who had fallen back with the loss of their equipment from Kristiansand up the great South Norway valley of the Setesdal. Determined resistance in this area might have provided a serious distraction to the main German effort, but on 14th April the Divisional Commander decided to capitulate, virtually in defiance of General Ruge's orders. A rather similar débacle had already occurred in the Telemark, where a surprise German attack on Kongsberg, the seat of a small-arms factory, produced the surrender of the whole regimental area. The only other point at which the main German advance might have been distracted was the Östfold, the district east of the Oslofiord, but in this area the River Glomma was the one important natural obstacle, and when this was crossed the Germans could drive their opponents over the Swedish frontier. About 3,000 of the small Norwegian Army were in fact disposed of in this way, also on 14th April.

General Ruge's task had therefore reduced itself with alarming rapidity to the defence of the agricultural area between Oslo and the high mountains, in which the most important natural features were the two great lakes, Mjösa and the Randsfiord. Mobilisation in this area was fairly effective, and four groups of the 2nd Division had fought a series of delaying-actions from Sollihögda, which is almost in the Oslo suburbs, to the shores of the two lakes. But the discouraging circumstances described above were made worse by the speed of the build-up of the German forces. In particular, the tanks, first thrown into the struggle on 16th April, were a weapon to which the Norwegians had no reply. It seems possible that General Ruge originally shared with the British public the illusion that no reinforcements could reach Oslo from Germany except by air, and that the effect of the air lift would be inconsiderable. But as the enemy's build-up through the Norwegian capital developed, so the provision of an equivalent base for an Allied counter-attack in Norway became an urgent question, and General Ruge (as we have seen)[1] came rapidly to the view that the first Allied objective must be Trondheim.

This did not, however, alter the nature of the campaign pending the arrival of the Allies. After a week of war, the Germans were pushing northwards in four small columns, which they manipulated with characteristic skill so as to outflank the Norwegian positions in turn. Casualties on both sides had been inconsiderable, and no engagement had amounted to more than a skirmish, but the Norwegians, suffering all the disadvantages of improvisation, were about equally short of men, equipment, rest, and encouragement. The easternmost of the German columns after throwing out a detachment to the Swedish frontier had made its way up the Glomma valley as far as Elverum, which fell on the 18th. What was probably the largest column took Hamar, half way up the eastern shore of lake Mjösa, the same day. On the west side of the lake the Germans were in an approximately corresponding position below Gjövik, where they also threatened the one remaining munitions factory (Raufoss). Still farther west they were advancing along the east bank of the Randsfiord, from where they might ultimately outflank the whole defence of Mjösa. To meet this situation General Ruge on 18th April threw in what we may call his strategic reserve. The troops belonging to the Bergen division would have wished to move forward from Voss for the recapture of the city, though it was perhaps a forlorn hope in the absence of British naval support there, on which Ruge had been told that he could not count. Instead, this 4th Brigade of nearly 5,000 men was ordered out of its home district right over the watershed into East Norway to check the advance along the

---

[1] P. 71.

Randsfiord up into Valdres, and to provide the Norwegians with the possibility of outflanking the Germans in their turn. It was at this stage that the first of the British troops, on which General Ruge had been counting, arrived on the scene.

Accordingly, in the early afternoon of 19th April Lieut.-Colonel E. J. King-Salter, the British Military Attaché, sent Morgan an urgent telephone message in guarded language; together with his French colleague, he joined the Brigadier at Dombaas in the evening. At their conference the British Military Attaché urged the need for the diversion of the 148th Brigade to operations south of Dombaas. Coming from General Ruge's Headquarters, he was in a position to explain that, unless some help was made available now, Norwegian resistance would almost certainly collapse and, with the Germans advancing up the valley of the Gudbrandsdal towards Trondheim, the position would be quite untenable. Brigadier Morgan's view was that his orders envisaged no movement south from Dombaas, and it might be considered a fair presumption that the quality and quantity of troops allotted to him were designed for a minor part, developing slowly, in siege operations against Trondheim. But Colonel King-Salter clinched the argument by informing him that a War Office telegram had been received at Norwegian Headquarters giving General Ruge a call on the 148th Brigade, which made mandatory the instructions he brought from General Ruge that the British should proceed at once to reinforce the Norwegians at the mouth of the valley. Ruge had indeed asked for the support of three British infantry battalions (as well as field artillery and tanks), and offered to provide lorries for first-line transport. The telegram cited by King-Salter accepted the offer of transport for Morgan's two battalions, but ignored the proposal for their employment far beyond Dombaas, which was originally attached to it. While referring back to the War Office for further instructions, the Brigadier prepared to meet the Norwegian demand by ordering the rest of his thousand men to move from Aandalsnes to Dombaas. Meanwhile he himself accompanied the Military Attaché to General Ruge's Headquarters at Öyer, about a dozen miles north of the town of Lillehammer: there the Gudbrandsdal terminates at the head of the great lake Mjösa, up whose shores the Germans were advancing.

At Öyer he described the British plan for the recapture of Trondheim. General Ruge received it rather coolly, although it had partly originated in Norwegian official circles, and did not conceal his regret that the British authorities had so far kept him in the dark about their intentions. Incensed by rumours of a British scheme to blow up the railway through Gudbrandsdal (which would have blocked his own retreat as well as the enemy's advance) he insisted in principle that, as he was Commander-in-Chief under the Norwegian Government, whose territory was to be defended, operations must conform to his strategy. The recapture of Trondheim could wait, and bad weather might help us by stopping the German air-lift. But the front south of Lillehammer, he argued, was of paramount importance, since, so long as it held firm, Allied forces would be able some day to deploy into the more level districts of eastern Norway, in which manœuvre was possible. He therefore insisted that British troops should at once be used to reinforce the Norwegian 2nd Division, which had two infantry battalions and a battery of artillery on the east side of the lake under the direct command of the Divisional General Hvinden Haug, and another group on the west side under Colonel Dahl. Brigadier Morgan agreed, though with considerable misgivings, and General Ruge received his agreement with enthusiasm.

British troops were thereupon hurried south by train from Dombaas down the Gudbrandsdal, so that by the time the earliest reinforcements reached Aandalsnes not only the base but even the advanced position at Dombaas had been stripped of our men, all of whom had been concentrated at or beyond the mouth of the valley. The lines of communication were now about 140 miles long. Meanwhile, at dawn on 20th April the Norwegian General, whose responsibilities and disappointments in the preceding ten days had been enormous, and whose lack of sleep was evident, was on the station to welcome the first British companies as they completed the journey down the valley. But Brigadier Morgan soon found that, instead of acting as a stiffening in one part of the line, his men were being widely dissipated and, instead of acting as a partial relief to a mainly Norwegian force, they were being left to hold hastily improvised positions without support of any kind.

In view of the almost inevitable sequel, there was some consolation in the fact that on the morning of the 20th Brigadier Morgan received a telegram from General Ironside, cancelling the original instruction to move north from Dombaas (which the abandonment of 'Hammer' had just rendered less urgent),[1] and therefore endorsing the line of conduct which Morgan had been driven by circumstances to adopt.

> You know situation of Norwegians in Lillehammer area. Clearly necessary to prevent German advance from south-east in order to secure Dombaas. Although you remain independent command under the War Office, you should, if you can spare troops, co-operate with Norwegian Commander-in-Chief while making use of Dombaas. Now probable that you will be reinforced by another brigade. Tell Norwegians.

Brigadier Morgan's telegram to the War Office had in fact coincided

---
[1] See p. 75.

with an independent suggestion from Mr Churchill as Chairman of the Military Co-ordination Committee, proposing to the Chiefs of Staff that half a battalion be sent south to enable General Ruge 'to sell ground more dearly and more slowly'.

The War Office telegram to Brigadier Morgan did not alter the position as regards the chain of command. This question was raised at a further conference called by General Ruge at Öyer at midday on the 20th, at which he put forward a written declaration to the effect that British detachments must comply with the wishes of the Commander-in-Chief or else he would resign. The atmosphere of the conference was not helped by the fact that General Ruge bitterly resented a (mistaken) suggestion that there might be a leakage of information at his General Headquarters. In this difficult situation the Military Attaché took upon himself responsibility for delaying delivery of a message decoded at 10.15 a.m. that day, in which the Chief of the Imperial General Staff explicitly informed General Ruge that Brigadier Morgan had instructions to co-operate with him but would not come under his orders. Colonel King-Salter's report of the conference also refrained from putting General Ruge's ultimatum in its categorical form, though, together with the French Military Attaché, he continued to press for General Paget on his arrival to be placed under Norwegian command. Brigadier Morgan contrived a satisfactory ending to the conference. General Ruge said he would endeavour to hold the Lillehammer front until Trondheim had fallen, but thought it involved risks. He added that he would feel confident with one British division at Trondheim and Brigadier Morgan's force co-operating with his force on the Lillehammer front.

In the course of this day, 20th April, the British troops were deployed to positions under Norwegian command. Brigade Headquarters was situated at Lillehammer but had no operational control. First to move were two companies and half the headquarters company of the Sherwood Foresters, who detrained at Faaberg and were sent along the west bank of Lake Mjösa to Biri and thence up a side valley to the village of Nykirke, about thirty-five miles from Lillehammer. They arrived at 2 a.m. and were quartered in the parish church—the only large building which could be heated sufficiently in the bitter cold—while a telegram was sent to the Norwegian High Command reporting that British soldiers had taken up their first position in Norway. Their function was to protect the right flank of the Norwegian forces operating west of Mjösa—the improvised formation known as Dahl Group from the name of the Colonel command ing it—againsta possible flank attack by the Germans, who had now come up against the Norwegian 4th Brigade in the region of the Randsfjord farther west.[1] But in the afternoon of the same day they were brought back to the neighbourhood of Biri, in rear of the Norwegians' position at Braastad bridge on the lakeside just north of Gjövik, on which the Germans were converging from several directions. They constructed a new position, by which one company slept rough in the open, but they did not come into action there, owing to the course of events on the opposite shore.

The other two and a half companies of the Foresters were placed at Bröttum, a village about eight miles south of Lillehammer near the east shore of the lake, where they formed a reserve for a Norwegian battalion of some 500 men which was in action that day (the 20th) at Lundehögda, the foremost of two ridges flanking the main Oslo-Trondheim road by the lakeside. The Leicestershire, with a strength of two companies (plus half the headquarters company), having arrived at the mouth of the valley last, were sent south-east of Lillehammer along a by-road to support a Norwegian dragoon regiment. This unit, consisting of about 1,000 men, unmounted but carried in civilian motor transport, was fighting in front of Aasmarka, a hamlet two or three miles east of Lundehögda. In both cases General Hvinden Haug, the Norwegian Divisional Commander, gave orders overnight for the British to relieve the forward troops at 2 p.m. on the 21st. But in the morning the Germans, who had been held satisfactorily in both positions the previous day, began a more determined attack, for which they had both the motive and the means. For the approach of British troops to the scene destroyed any idea that the operations against the Norwegian army might peter out without serious bloodshed; and Group Pellengahr for its advance up the east bank of Mjösa now disposed of two infantry battalions, a motorised machine-gun battalion, a battery of artillery and some smaller units —a total of something like 4,000 men. The Foresters' mortar section was sent forward to an isolated spur between Lundehögda and the lake; but German guns were brought to bear and it quickly ceased fire. The rest of the Foresters saw no fighting at Lundehögda, but were moved east to Slagbrenna, in the rear of the Aasmarka position, so as to leave the Lundehögda-Lillehammer route clear for an already impending Norwegian retreat. Meanwhile the Leicestershire, who were attacked from the air as they went forward (though the weather later in the day was fortunately cloudy), arrived about 3 p.m. at the positions where they were to relieve the Norwegian dragoons. The moment is not without significance. The Germans in Trondheim had launched their counter-attack towards Namsos earlier the same day, and here too, after nearly eight months of war, British troops at last stood face to face with the Germans on an active front.

Unfortunately, the Leicestershire were plunged at once into the

---

[1] See p. 103.

difficulties of terrain which were to characterise the whole campaign. The Norwegian posts were on a freezing hillside about 1,200 feet above sea-level, based on a few small farm-buildings, but stretching indeterminately into the woods on either side, and covered in about three feet of snow. The Germans had brought up artillery to protect their advance against the hill, on to which they were firing at a range of about 3,000 yards. The arrival of the two British companies was also followed by an immediate increase in the rate of mortar fire and by attacks through the woods on both flanks. The British mortar section came into action, but otherwise our troops were virtually immobilised by their inability to operate elsewhere than on the road —the only place where the snow was firm under foot. The Norwegian dragoons, whom the Leicestershire were intended to replace, continued perforce to engage the enemy and were gradually driven in from the flanks by superior weight of fire, so that after an hour the Norwegian colonel, who was directing operations, was clear that the position must be abandoned. The British established a new line just behind Aasmarka, where the road could be held in depth and the rough woodland at the sides would not lend itself to a German flank attack, especially with the approach of evening. By about 8 p.m. the dragoons had withdrawn from both their front and reserve lines through the new British position and retired northwards, as planned. The Germans had not followed up, and in any case the Foresters were now placed in support at Slagbrenna, where their preparations caused the Norwegian colonel to pass a comment which fairly sums up the whole episode: 'A difficult job; in a strange land, in frost and snow, with dark, thick woods in all directions. It might be difficult enough for us—for them it was infinitely worse.'[1]

The first achievements of the British brothers-in-arms were a disappointment to the Norwegians, but they were not the prime cause of General Hvinden Haug's decision, taken before 5 p.m. at latest, to substitute a general withdrawal behind Lillehammer for the original proposal to send back only the most exhausted units. It was not in any case a catastrophic change of plan, since General Ruge himself had been in doubt, even before the unsuccessful operations at Lundehögda and Aasmarka, as to the advisability of making the main stand in front of, rather than just behind, Lillehammer town, where a shorter front might prove more easily defensible. But its success presupposed the execution of an orderly retreat, especially as regards the British units, which would have to provide the new line. The withdrawal of the Norwegian battalion from Lundehögda, beginning in the early evening, inevitably uncovered the main road to Lillehammer for a German advance. This in turn would have the double effect of endangering communications back from Biri on the

---
[1] Jensen, Colonel Jörgen: *Krigen paa Hedmark*, p. 128.

far side of the lake—with consequences that must be dealt with later on—and necessitating a definite time-limit (fixed for 1 a.m.) by which the troops retiring from Aasmarka must have passed through Lillehammer to escape being trapped. Unfortunately, the only motor transport available for the Leicestershire had first to convey the Norwegian dragoons to their rest quarters a dozen miles beyond the town. Their colonel stayed behind near Aasmarka to see to the arrangements, but his subordinates failed to insist that the civilian drivers should make a further journey down the valley to pick up the two British companies. Accordingly, after their first day in action these Territorials had to set out at midnight on a fourteen-mile march over hilly, snow-bound lanes to Lillehammer—an ordeal whose effects on morale would be heightened by suspicions of Norwegian honesty. A serious setback followed. In the approaches to the town, when it was already daylight, enough transport met the column to carry the majority of the troops through in the nick of time, but the Germans cut off a considerable party, including six officers, and also overran the stores which had been accumulated at the railway station. At the Balbergkamp, two miles north of Lillehammer, the Leicestershire, their numbers further reduced by some of the transport overrunning their destination, rejoined the two and a half companies of Foresters, whose withdrawal from the intended rearguard position at Slagbrenna had been delayed by the fact that the march from Aasmarka took an unexpected route. The total was now 650 officers and men.

The new position, covering the river bridge at Faaberg as well as the main road north, was to be defended by British forces alone, while the Norwegians recuperated and reorganised farther up the valley, an arrangement against which Brigadier Morgan, now in direct control of operations, appealed to the Norwegian Command without success. Some civilian labour had been employed to prepare the site and Norwegian officers were available to indicate its features; but the delays described above prevented the British from reconnoitring. Moreover, the troops arrived piecemeal in the small hours of the morning and had abandoned their signals and much other equipment for want of transport and petrol.

Our principal strength was used to line a farm lane and a row of farm buildings astride the main road, the right flank resting on the river, the left on the precipitous side of the Balbergkamp. About noon, incendiary bombs were dropped on the British position; this was followed by a 4-inch mortar bombardment. While this engaged attention towards the main road, over which we had secured a good field of fire, the Germans also began to work round our left flank.

THE ACTION AT THE BALBERGKAMP

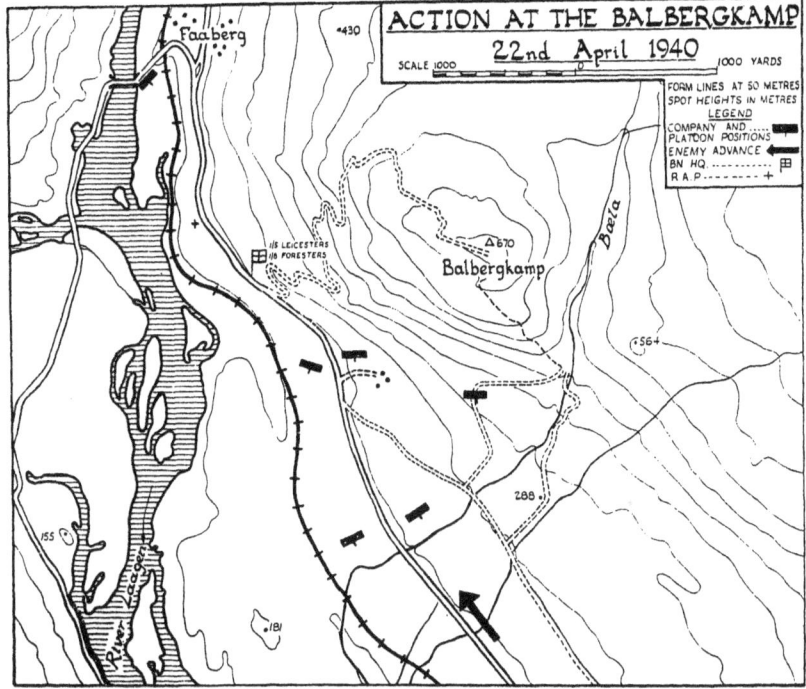

Our patrols defended the hill farms lying in that direction, from which a steep footpath gave access to the 2,000-foot summit of the mountain; but we had no protection against a wider movement to approach it from the farther side. By 3.30 p.m. small numbers of the enemy were in position behind and above our forces, and a ski patrol with machine guns even made a surprise attack on Brigade Headquarters some miles in the rear.

The result was a hasty withdrawal northwards up the road, rations and other stores being jettisoned so as to pack the available transport with men. The narrow, winding road, not for the last time, gave admirable opportunities for German air attack; troops on foot were overtaken or outflanked, and the Foresters lost a large part of their two companies which, it is believed, never received the orders to disengage. A new position was taken up south of Öyer with the support of one of the two additional companies of the Leicestershire, which had arrived at Aandalsnes on the 21st and been sent forward at once, the other fresh company being held in reserve. This position likewise came under heavy fire and was abandoned about 7 p.m., when another intermediate position was taken up at the hamlet of Tolstad. This had a clear field of fire down the main road and was held until noon next day, so as to make some reorganisation possible at Tretten.

The Norwegian Divisional Commander describes the loss of the

Faaberg-Balberg position as the 'first serious defeat of the war' and notes that 'it was to have catastrophic consequences for the Norwegian detachments'.[1] His comment invites the counter-comment that no Norwegian detachment was thrown in for its defence, in spite of repeated requests for help, and that they alone could have supplied ski patrols to remedy the situation on our left, where small numbers of Germans on skis manœuvred to such great effect along the heights. The Norwegians claimed that their men were utterly exhausted by the skirmishes which they had fought during the ten long days when they stood alone, whereas the British felt that theirs had been given no time to adapt themselves to the bewildering physical conditions of the fight. But these are imponderables between which we cannot judge; what is certain is that the Germans required no rest and made the deep snow and unfamiliar terrain their ally.

Meanwhile, the other two and a half companies of Foresters, whose help might have been invaluable at the Balbergkamp, were isolated on the west bank of the lake. The whole of the Dahl Group had necessarily to move back when the retreat began on the east bank—and thereby lose contact with the Norwegian 4th Brigade still farther west—because German artillery on the road between Lundehögda and Lillehammer could command the Biri-Lillehammer road, and the Germans could also have crossed the ice. The Dahl Group, like the 2nd Division, employed the British detachment as its rearguard. The latter withdrew northwards from Biri in the early morning of the 22nd, under cover of bridge demolitions carried out by Norwegian engineers, as far as Frydenlund, a road fork five miles south of Lillehammer. The big bridge over the lake at Lillehammer had by this time been blown up, but it was thought too hazardous to attempt to follow the road back to Faaberg. Having waited until nightfall to escape attack from the air, the troops set off again in their lorries on a long detour over hill roads to the next main river crossing at Tretten, where they arrived in two sections at 4 and 7 a.m. respectively.

It is possible to say that the ensuing engagement of 23rd April was lost before it began, since the British Territorial troops retreating up the valley had now for the most part been without both food and sleep for more than thirty-six hours and had had no real rest for a week; they had lost much of their equipment, and were in any case without supporting arms. The troops from the west bank of Lake Mjösa, who had just rejoined them, were in scarcely better plight after eleven hours' freezing travel in open trucks, the majority of them without greatcoats. Two fresh companies of the Leicestershire had also come in, as already noted, but the arrival of the second flight of the expedition at Aandalsnes on the 21st had been accom-

---
[1] Quoted by Jensen, p. 138.

panied by a further setback. For the motor transport of the Brigade, half the anti-aircraft guns, a quantity of urgently needed ammunition, demolition stores, and seventy-five tons of rations had been torpedoed off Aalesund in the transport *Cedarbank*—the only success obtained by German submarines against transports or storeships in the whole course of the April operation, but an important one. The three usable anti-aircraft guns were, however, ordered forward from Aandalsnes; but the troop was halted at Otta at 9.30 p.m. when the issue had already been decided lower down the valley.

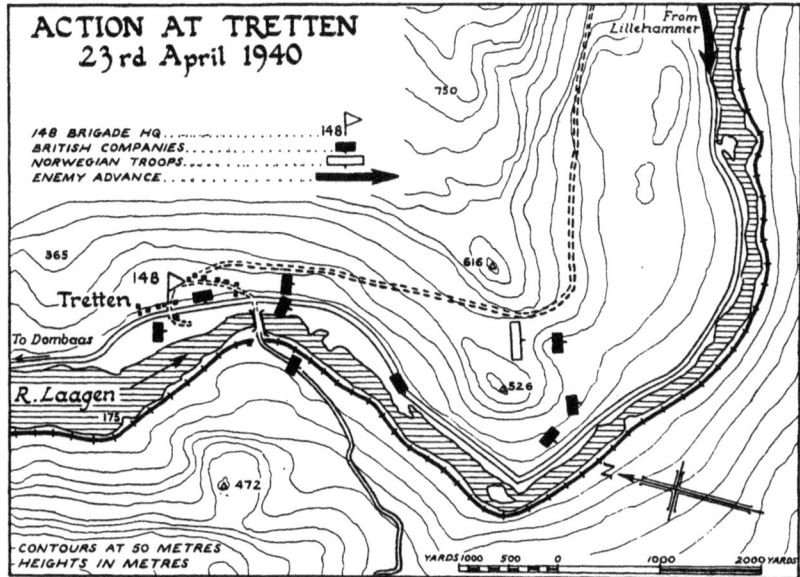

The possibilities of Tretten, which is the lowest of the points at which the Gudbrandsdal narrows to a gorge, had been in the mind of the Norwegian High Command for some days at least, and rudimentary machine-gun posts had been constructed with civilian labour on both sides of the river. The west bank of the River Laagen is here a precipice except for a narrow ledge carrying the railway, while the east bank leaves space only for the main road. This winds between the river and a mountain saddle about 1,200 feet high, which is crossed by a farm track running parallel with the road. The village itself stands about a mile and a half farther back, clustering round the bridge by which the British detachment from west of Mjösa had just rejoined; the defence of this bridge for at least one clear day was deemed essential by the Norwegian Commander-in-Chief, to enable Norwegian forces from the same direction under Colonel Dahl to rejoin. For this reason a stand had now to be made, whatever the cost, instead of a fighting withdrawal from point to point up the valley. The British expected the main German attack on their eastern flank, where the snow-covered mountain saddle was accessible and where the farm track also outflanked the road. Two companies of the Foresters were therefore set to control the main road on a three-quarter-mile frontage, with the one fresh company of the Leicestershire high up on their left flank. This flank was further strengthened by the remnants of three squadrons of Norwegian dragoons, with four medium machine guns and a mortar, whom Brigadier Morgan had induced General Ruge to place under his command; they were posted behind the Leicestershire on the plateau formed by the saddle. One company of the newly rejoined Foresters was left to guard the railway line on the other bank.

Fighting on the east bank of the river began about 1 p.m., and after an hour the threat to the main road caused the reserve company of Foresters to be moved forward. About this time three tanks began to force their way along the road into our forward positions, unchecked by the anti-tank rifles, which failed to penetrate. Some officers, including the Military Attaché (who was later severely wounded and taken prisoner), advanced from the village to reconnoitre and were overrun by the tanks at a bend in the road. The company of Foresters on the west bank was ordered on Norwegian advice to move some distance south, to prevent the enemy from working up along the railway to enfilade the main position; but it was quickly recalled in order that a part of it might be transferred to the east bank, where the engagement was being decided. The enemy tanks had broken through the main position along the road, so that all our advanced units were cut off, while the village itself came under heavy fire from 5·9-cm. close-support guns. Tretten and Tretten bridge were nevertheless held until early evening in the hope that troops from the forward area might filter past. Those on the west bank, reduced in number at an earlier stage, were fortunate and repelled an enemy party with good effect. Those on the east bank, though their small-arms fire could still be heard, had eventually to be left to their fate. The Norwegian dragoons, whose post on the saddle had not been seriously attacked, were able to get back to their transport along the farm track just before the final abandonment of Tretten, and a small proportion of British troops made their way through by the same route over the saddle. An improvised rear-guard defended a final position a mile north of the village until 9.30 p.m., after which what was left of the 148th Brigade dispersed, with the help of some buses mustered in the rear, to seek refuge forty-five miles back in the Heidal. In numbers, the brigade was now reduced to nine officers and three hundred men; as a fighting unit, the tale of events had reduced it for the time being to a lower figure. Such was the situation at the end of the first phase of the fighting in Gudbrandsdal.

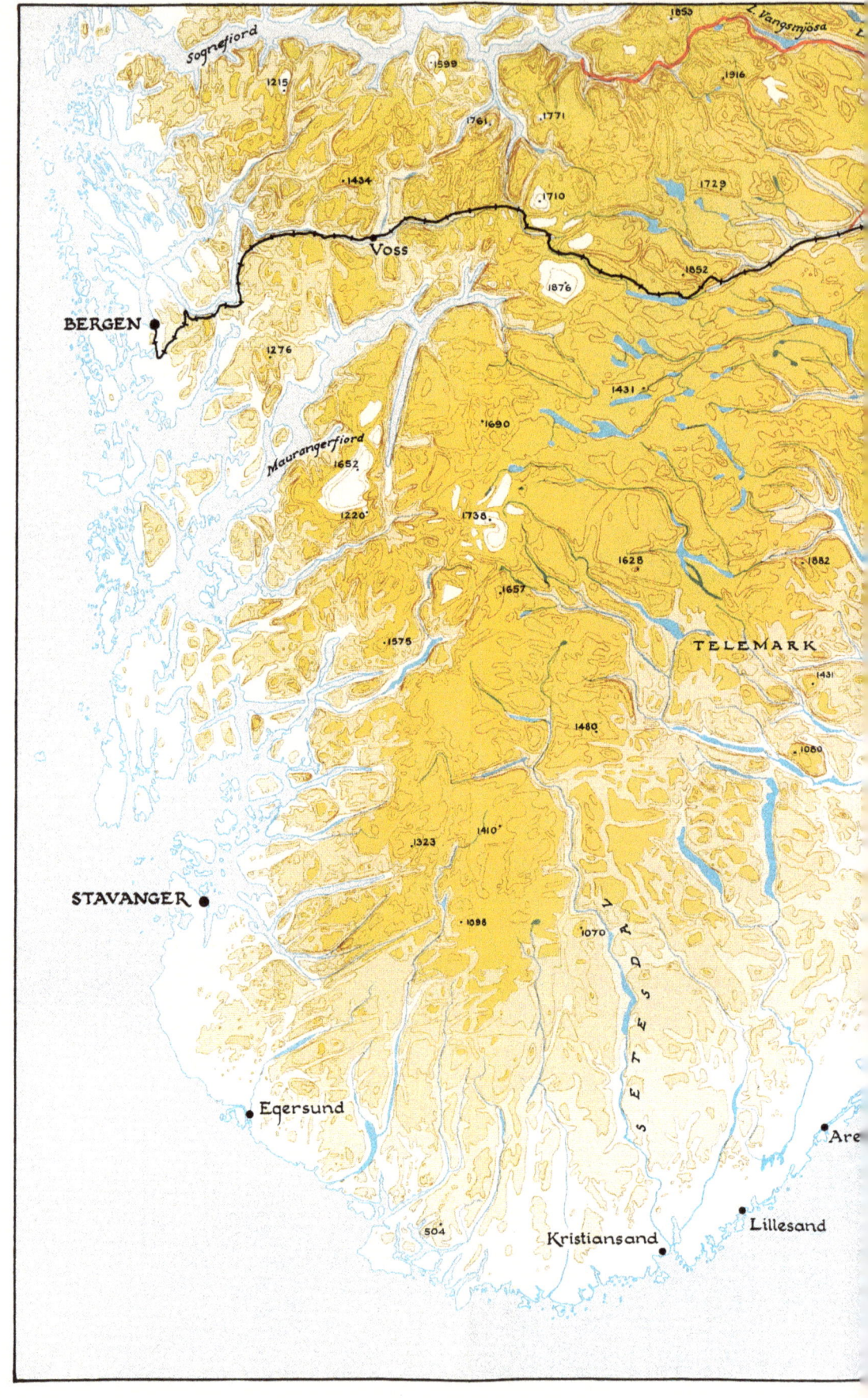

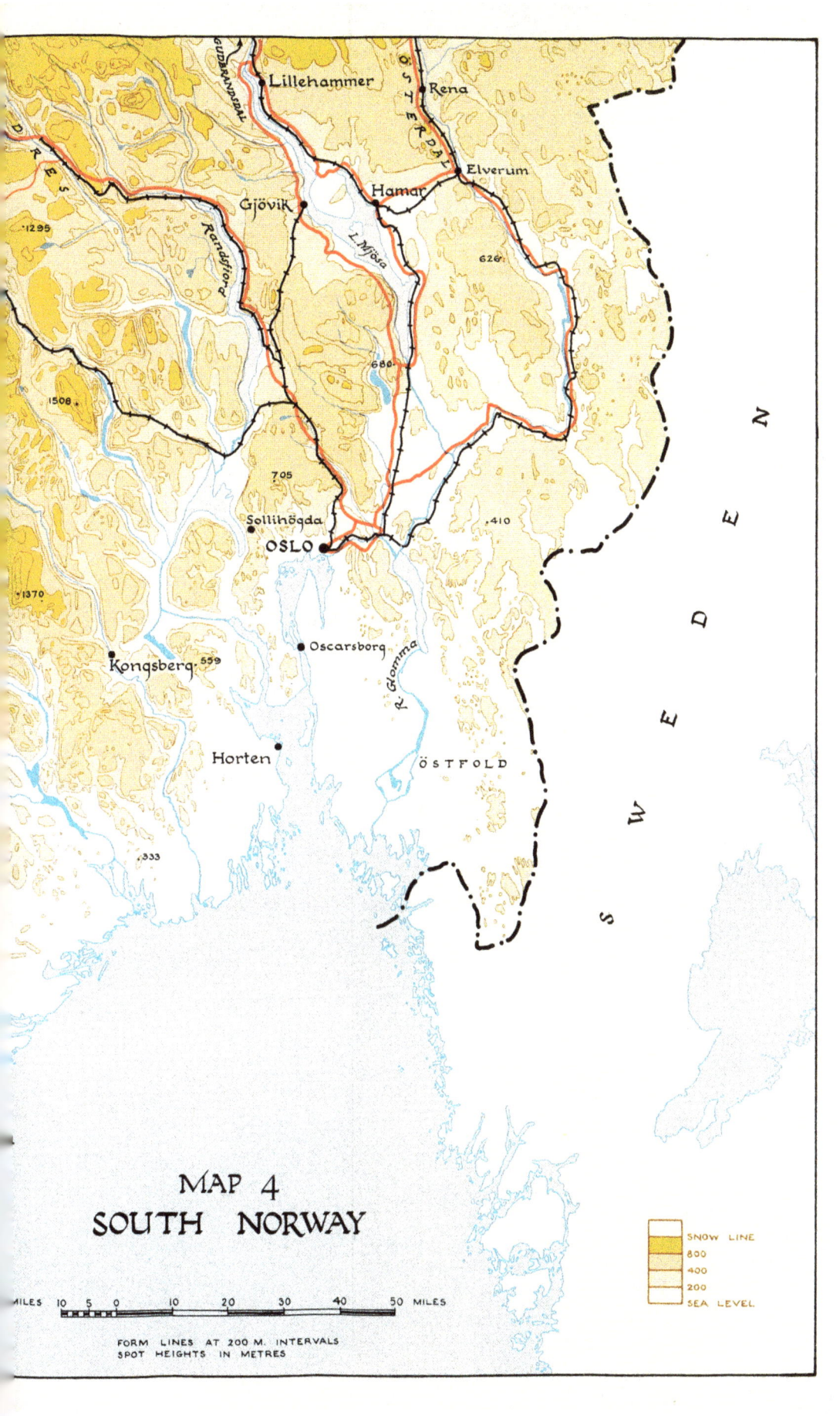

MAP 4
SOUTH NORWAY

CHAPTER VIII

GUDBRANDSDAL—THE SECOND PHASE

See Maps 7 (a) and (b), following page 144

BRIGADIER Morgan's operations, as we have seen, were planned to meet an unexpected emergency, and were planned on a temporary basis pending the arrival of a larger force. The very first message he received from the Chief of the Imperial General Staff after his arrival in Norway said that his reinforcement by another brigade was 'now probable',[1] and a War Office telegram on the morning of 21st April confirmed that the first 2,000 men of the 15th Infantry Brigade would arrive at Aandalsnes on the evening of the 23rd. Major-General B. G. T. Paget, a recent Commandant of the Staff College, who had been appointed to command Sickleforce in its expanded form on the 20th,[2] issued his first operational instruction from London on the same day, addressed to Brigadier H. E. F. Smyth, commanding the 15th Infantry Brigade. He at the same time advised Brigadier Morgan of his plan in briefer form, as follows:

> My intention: first, secure Aandalsnes, Dombaas, and lines of communication connecting them, against threats from air, Oslo, Trondheim; second, assist Norwegians Oslo direction by operating down Lillehammer and Österdalen valleys. My eventual plan that you in western, Smyth in eastern valleys. . . .

The first échelon of the 15th Infantry Brigade disembarked from cruisers and destroyers at Molde and Aandalsnes on the night of the 23rd, and General Paget himself with his Headquarters and the third battalion completing the brigade reached Aandalsnes from a similar convoy in the late evening of the 25th. Last-minute news received by the General at King's Cross station had shown that the Norwegians were giving ground fast in the Österdal, so that it would be difficult for us to take the offensive there; but in any case the disaster which had befallen the 148th Brigade at Tretten made the concentration of the British effort in the western valley, the Gudbrandsdal, inevitable.

Before leaving England General Paget, viewing the situation in the light of Brigadier Morgan's experience as reported to the War Office, had already taken what steps he could towards redressing the

---
[1] See p. 104.
[2] See Appendix A (6), p. 256.

balance. For, even before the disaster at Tretten, it was quite clear that the greatest of the handicaps under which the British troops were fighting was the almost complete lack of air protection. The base at Aandalsnes, though defended by a succession of anti-aircraft guardships and by some anti-aircraft guns ashore, was already experiencing daily air attacks, though on a small scale. Nearer the front German aircraft were free to scout and harass along road and railway as they pleased, and obvious targets such as the railway junction at Dombaas had been repeatedly hit. General Paget had therefore made representations on 21st April to General Massy, who had just assumed responsibility for all operations in central and southern Norway, as to the urgent need of air support, the need for more adequate anti-aircraft defence, and the desirability of establishing alternative bases and lines of communication. Arrangements were thereupon completed for at least one squadron of Gladiator fighters to operate from the ice on Lake Lesjaskog, lying at the head of the Romsdal and of the Gudbrandsdal, on the watershed from which the River Rauma flows north-westward to Aandalsnes and the Laagen south-eastward to Lillehammer and Lake Mjösa. Thus the prospect of turning failure into success depended upon a new arm as well as new troops. The Admiralty also undertook to supply carrier-borne aircraft for Central Norway, and the *Ark Royal* and the *Glorious* accordingly arrived off the coast (24th April) to try to protect the base and the troops,[1] as well as for the purpose of flying land-based aircraft to the Lesjaskog position. But before the effectiveness of this plan could be tested, the unremitting pressure of the Germans had already forced the 15th Brigade into action.

On 24th April, the day after the fighting at Tretten, 148th Brigade Headquarters were in the Heidal, formed by a tributary of the Laagen, the Sjoa, which joins the main valley of the Gudbrandsdal about forty-five miles above Tretten. Brigadier Morgan, even after the stragglers had come in, found himself with only about 450 men and not a single officer of the rank of Company Commander or above. After conferring with Brigadier Smyth (who was junior to him) he arranged to post the remnants of his brigade as a reserve defence in the main valley, but enemy air patrols apparently prevented their move. It was also agreed with the Norwegians that they should hold on lower down until the next night but one to enable the newly arrived British troops, which by this time had reached Otta, to take up a defensive position of some strength at Kvam; this was about twelve miles farther on, south of the junction of the Heidal with the Gudbrandsdal.

The situation developed unpromisingly during the day. There was

---

[1] See p. 95.

widespread enemy air activity, in which at least three enemy planes were shot down, but the strength of the enemy attack was such that all three of the anti-aircraft guns which had arrived at Otta the day before were temporarily put out of action. More serious was the inability of the Norwegian forces to hold out for the period required, though a fresh battalion had been brought from the Romsdal by train to bear the brunt of the attack, as the battalion which had fought at Lundehögda had already lost two-thirds of its strength. The Germans attacked in the early morning of this day, forcing their way through along the main road with tanks and armoured cars, and by evening the Norwegians from the Romsdal had fallen back well behind the British at Kvam. Meanwhile the last Norwegian battalion in this area had come down the valley from Dombaas (where it had been in action earlier against the German paratroops) and taken up a new position at Vinstra, south of Kvam, where it held out with difficulty overnight. That evening General Ruge despatched a pessimistic message to the Allied military authorities, stating that his troops were absolutely exhausted, that the situation had become critical, and that the front might be irretrievably broken: 'Unless immediate help is forthcoming, a débacle will occur'. The full weight of the campaign therefore fell immediately upon the 15th Infantry Brigade, whose object must be to prevent a further German advance while a larger force was built up on Aandalsnes and some approach to parity secured in the air. Fighting began at Kvam on the morning of the 25th and continued into the following day. The struggle for air power began about the same time and was more quickly concluded: it may therefore be considered first.

It had been intended at the outset to attach such units as could be spared from home defence and service in France to co-operate with our expeditionary forces in Norway. Squadron-Leader Whitney W. Straight was sent by the Air Staff on 17th April to find the most suitable landing ground to the south of Trondheim, an arduous task in one of the most mountainous areas in Norway. The choice lay between the ice of Lake Lesjaskog (already referred to) and that of Lake Vangsmjösa, which lies high up in Valdres, on another route from south-east to north-west parallel to the Gudbrandsdal-Romsdal route, and about sixty miles south-west of Kvam. His preference was for Lake Vangsmjösa because it was free of snow, could take two squadrons of any type of aircraft, and was connected by road to the inner reaches of the Sognefiord, where stores and equipment could be landed independently of the existing lines of communication. Lake Vangsmjösa was already being used as a sort of emergency base by a few Norwegian aircraft. The Air Staff decided otherwise, partly no doubt because they feared that the Norwegian forces in Valdres might not be able to prevent the Germans from overrunning the lake position but chiefly because it was too far away from the area of our operations. For what was sent would have to serve a double purpose—to help our troops in the front line and to protect their communications, including the base at Aandalsnes: clearly, the latter object would be most easily fulfilled if the airfield was close by. It was also decided that only a single squadron should be sent, although its eighteen aircraft could not possibly provide a constant patrol of six aircraft, which responsible opinion inside the Air Ministry apparently regarded as the minimum for safety.

Lake Lesjaskog is a long, narrow lake, about eight miles by a half-mile, bounded by woods. High and desolate mountains skirt the southern shore but there is easy access on the north from the road and railway connecting Dombaas and Aandalsnes, which lie almost within a stone's throw. The servicing flight arrived there in two parties on 23rd and 24th April, having experienced great difficulty in sorting their stores (which were neither listed nor labelled) and getting the essential items sent forward by the only two lorries which could still be found in Aandalsnes. A runway measuring about 800 by 75 yards had been prepared with local labour, which had also swept the snow from a track between the main road and the lake edge. Unfortunately, only one inadequate route had been swept from the edge to the runway; this was half a mile long and a foot deep in snow, and the stores had to be conveyed over it on three horse-drawn sledges, intermittently available. The village of Lesjaskog was two miles away, so that even the provision of forage for the horses involved difficulties. However by 5 p.m. (24th April), the servicing flight had laid out fuel and ammunition along the runway in small dumps and collected every possible tin, jug, or other container for refuelling. It had at once been perceived that the essential work of refuelling and starting machines would be difficult: only two refuelling troughs had been despatched, and the starter trolley could not be used as the batteries were uncharged and no acid had been sent with them. Moreover, the ground staff included only one trained armourer to maintain seventy-two Browning guns for the squadron. Two guns from a naval battery of Oerlikons, which was landed at the same time as the R.A.F. stores, had also arrived for anti-aircraft defence and a platoon of Marines to guard the petrol supply. Such was the position when No. 263 Squadron, commanded by Squadron-Leader J. W. Donaldson, took off from the deck of the *Glorious*, with four maps among eighteen pilots, none of whom had been in action previously, 180 miles from shore, in a snowstorm. Their aircraft were Gladiators—obsolescent biplanes which could operate from small landing-grounds. Escorted by two Skuas of the Fleet Air Arm, they descended on the lake at 6 p.m. without serious mishap, although the heaped-up snow at either side of the runway had melted during the day so that its ice surface was half covered by trickling water. Meanwhile, the Germans had flown high above the lake and reconnoitred it. Our aircraft were immediately refuelled and one section placed at instant readiness, but the enemy did not return that evening.

The night (not surprisingly) was bitterly cold. When daylight came, carburettors and aircraft controls were frozen stiff, and in the absence of batteries the engines were difficult to start. It was nearly two hours after first light when the first aircraft took off to protect the landing ground against an attack;[1] one Heinkel was shot down but the enemy succeeded in dropping some bombs on the lake. At 7 a.m. two aircraft were sent to patrol the battle area, but the servicing party was still struggling to get more engines started when the main enemy onslaught began an hour and a half later. This was clearly timed to coincide with the opening of the land operations at Kvam, in which it was one main function of our own aircraft to give much-needed support. Heinkel bombers approached in threes, which broke formation as they came up to the target to bomb and machine-gun the lake from various heights. At least five Gladiators were destroyed before they could get into the air, but two rose to meet the first big attack and accumulators then helped up others. But many of the ground staff, who were strangers to the unit and unfamiliar with their aircraft, took shelter in the trees, from which they did not emerge, although the naval contingent dauntlessly fought their guns (including some borrowed Lewis guns) and although they could see their own officers and sergeants at their tasks of starting engines and refuelling and rearming aircraft. In these circumstances, it took between one and one-and-a-half hours to refuel and rearm a single machine. Consequently most of the Gladiators were bombed and set alight or disabled by blast while awaiting fuel and ammunition on the ground.

Two sections of three aircraft took off during the forenoon, of which one renewed the patrol of the battle area at Kvam and gave encouragement to British and Norwegian forces alike, while the other sought to protect the landing ground. Altogether, forty fighter sorties were carried out during the day, in which the pilots engaged thirty-seven separate enemy planes and shot down at least six. But there could be only one ending to a situation in which the enemy could attack our sole landing ground with numerically superior forces and almost without intermission, bringing up more dangerous aircraft (Junkers 88s) as the day wore on, and could safely surmise that we had no reinforcements within reach. In the afternoon the lake was fast becoming unusable as the bombs broke up the runway (132 craters were counted in the immediate vicinity of the lake); the belted

---

[1] See MacClure, V.: *Gladiators in Norway*, p. 105.

ammunition was exhausted; and unarmed pilots were taking off in the brave but forlorn hope of turning enemy machines off their course and distracting their bomb-aimers by what could only be feint attacks.

An alternative landing place had been notified to the British at Setnesmoen, a Norwegian peace-time army camp just outside Aandalsnes, with a parade ground which was considered capable of forming a tolerable one-way landing ground. The necessary work had been put in hand at midday on the 23rd. The Squadron-Leader therefore flew to this position and sent back a message that the rest of the squadron were to transfer from Lesjaskog, where all aircraft no longer serviceable were to be wrecked and burned. The serviceable aircraft (apart from his own), by this time numbering only four, were moved accordingly, and at midnight the ground staff followed, bringing with them petrol and ammunition and leaving thirteen wrecked aircraft behind. The next day (26th April) it was decided that three aircraft should patrol the area of the landing ground and Aandalsnes, but they merely drove the enemy bombers to operate at heights to which the lack of oxygen equipment forbade our pilots to follow. The fourth aircraft acted as a scout in the Dombaas-Otta area, reporting troop movements to Force Headquarters, while the fifth was sent to examine Sunndal, where a German landing had been reported. Its engine failed completely, so that the pilot was obliged to descend by parachute, and by nightfall three others were unserviceable on account of damage which there was no means of repairing.

The one Gladiator left was not flown again. Instead, hopes were pinned on concealing Setnesmoen from the enemy until the arrival of No. 46 Squadron (Hurricanes), whose commanding officer landed on the evening of the 27th. He urged the Air Ministry to send his squadron at once, accompanied by key ground staff and servicing equipment in flying boats. But the Ministry ruled against this reinforcement: evacuation had now been decided upon, and in any case Hurricanes were not lightly to be expended. There remained the possibility of using No. 254 Squadron (Blenheim Fighters), which had been moved to Hatston in the Orkneys, and from there had succeeded in flying two one-hour patrols by three aircraft over Aandalsnes on the 25th, when they shot one Heinkel into the sea. On the 29th these patrols were renewed and plans made to increase their duration by refuelling the aircraft at Setnesmoen. But the Germans bombed Setnesmoen the same day, so the patrols found themselves unable to land.

Our attempt to base much-needed fighters in Central Norway was therefore abandoned after a trial of strength lasting forty-eight hours. The resulting situation was the more grave for our land forces as the

Air Ministry was unable to accede to General Paget's requests for heavy-bomber attacks, whether against the enemy's guns massed at Kvam or against his lines of communication down to Lillehammer or against his airfield, on the ground that the targets were out of range.

The 15th Infantry Brigade comprised the 1st King's Own Yorkshire Light Infantry (who had an extra company made up from the ex-drivers, carrier platoon, and battle patrol), 1st York and Lancaster Regiment, and the 1st Green Howards. Of these troops, only the K.O.Y.L.I. and the brigade anti-tank company, with five 25-mm. (French Hotchkiss) guns available and three more in support, plus some engineers had reached the position at Kvam by the morning of the 25th.

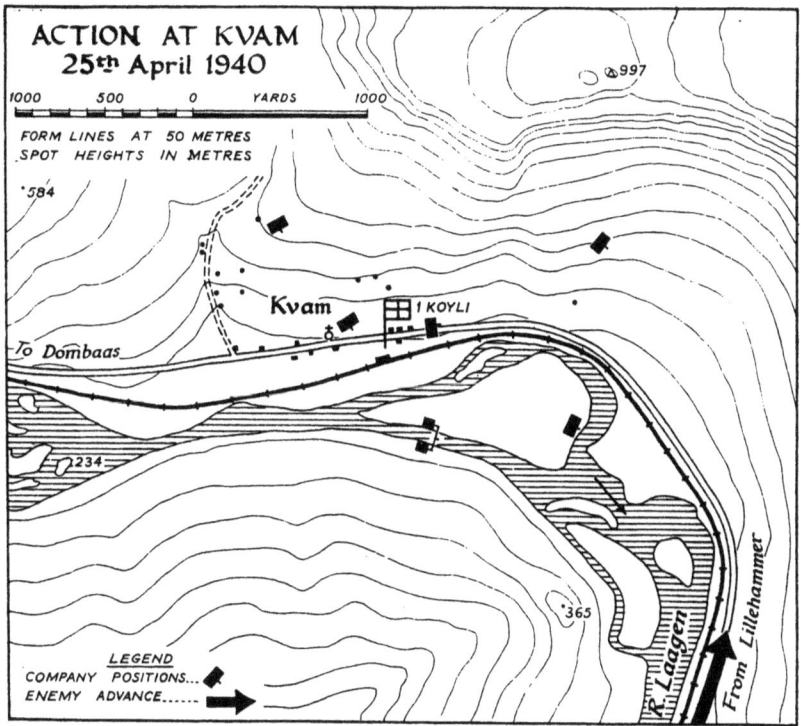

The railway and the road up which the Germans would be advancing here follow the left bank of the river round an abrupt right-angled bend from north to west—Kvam 'Knee'—beyond which the road runs dead straight for nearly a mile into and through the village. The lower slopes of the mountain on this side are dotted with farms; the far side is almost precipitous. The valley floor between is occupied by a flat pear-shaped island, easily accessible from the road over ice and shallow water but separated from the far side by a deep and swiftly running channel. Brigadier Smyth placed his Headquarters at the centre of the village, some distance in front of the church (in whose shadow now rests the largest single group of soldiers who died that year in the defence of Norway), and disposed his two forward companies to cover the road, one from the front edge of the island, where bushes gave some cover, the other on the hillside to the north. There they awaited the German forces which had already disposed of the 148th Brigade, including the troop of tanks first used at Tretten, and their presumed reinforcements. In actual fact their numbers were at least doubled by the troops which General Falkenhorst had allotted to Group Pellengahr from the operations now virtually concluded on the west side of Lake Mjösa: the Germans had seven infantry battalions, including one of mountain troops, and two batteries of artillery available, as well as the motorised machine-gun battalion and smaller units. But the narrowness of the road, broken bridges, and weakening ice were obstacles which caused the force to be strung out down the valley to Ringebu and even beyond, so that its spearhead may have been very small for a force of about 8,400 men, though certainly very large in comparison with our own.

An enemy column, headed by a medium tank, a light tank, and an armoured car, approached without warning at 11.30 a.m.; but an anti-tank gun on the island opened fire and presumably scored a hit, for both tanks stopped and the armoured car retired round the bend. Enemy infantry at once deployed on both sides of the road, and their 5·9-cm. close-support guns were brought into action, causing considerable casualties, especially to our advance position on the island. By 4 p.m. the advanced company, having lost four officers and eighty-five other ranks, was forced to fall back about half a mile to the western end of the island, where a second company was posted. The enemy tried also to outflank the other forward position: but our troops, who were well dug in there, did considerable execution and at about 5.30 p.m. the arrival of a company of York and Lancaster enabled this flank to be extended up the hillside in the rear of our original position. A second enemy medium tank was put quickly out of action, and a final attempt to turn our right flank by an advance along the river bed was stopped from the island position, to which a third company was brought up from the village. When night fell, the battalion was holding all its original positions except the eastern part of the island.

The enemy, in accordance with his usual practice, made no movement during the night. The British line was straightened by withdrawal from the forward position on the northern slope of the valley. This necessitated the abandonment of two out of the five anti-tank

Kvam, seen from a point north of the church

guns, but two others were brought up from reserve. The few hours of darkness were also used to make ready for house-to-house fighting inside the village. Brigadier Smyth had been wounded in the first hour of the engagement, so it fell to the Acting Brigade-Commander, Lieut.-Colonel A. L. Kent-Lemon, to arrange that the York and Lancaster should form a temporary position in the rear, through which the troops engaged at Kvam could withdraw if they succeeded in holding the enemy for a second day. As the Germans would then be approaching the mouth of the Heidal, this decision involved the 148th Brigade as well. They now received General Ruge's permission (refused twenty-four hours earlier on the score of air attacks) to move to Dombaas, using buses for the first few miles to Otta, whence they could be taken on by train. Two-thirds of them arrived at Dombaas that night, the rest on the night following.

The fighting at Kvam was renewed early next morning with a heavy artillery barrage; then at 6.30 a.m. the enemy attacked on the left flank in battalion strength. At the third attempt our flank position was enfiladed, the Germans having climbed up to the high plateau by a farm track out of sight beyond the 'knee'. By 11 a.m. the same enemy force had worked their way past the forward company and were on the flank of a second British company, posted on the hillside about three-quarters of a mile further back and slightly behind our headquarters in the village itself. A platoon was therefore detached from our forward company to protect its rear, while the second company was also heavily engaged. At this stage, enemy aircraft took up the attack with low-level machine-gun fire and bombs, and an additional group of enemy artillery was brought into action. This enabled the German infantry to close in on our positions and to establish machine-gun posts at short range. About midday, a thrust developed in the centre; it was held after heavy fighting, but not before the enemy had established a machine gun to fire directly up the road into the village. At two o'clock a tank succeeded in advancing up the road towards the village under cover of the screen established for our own protection against the machine gun. But after a volunteer had removed the screen under fire, an anti-tank gun engaging at a thousand yards burnt out both this and a second tank, though the gun was itself destroyed by an enemy shell only a few minutes later.

The position was now becoming precarious, as enemy infiltrations occurring at various points threatened to cut off the companies from each other. On our left flank in particular, they advanced down a side road, which meets the main road at right angles about half a mile behind the village; but the platoon guarding the rear of the forward company on our flank restored the situation about four o'clock, inflicting a number of casualties. The enemy in this area were also harassed in the rear by a small party of volunteer ski troops sent by the Norwegian 2nd Division. At about 5 p.m. General Paget issued orders for the withdrawal of the K.O.Y.L.I. (plus one company of the York and Lancaster) to take place at 11 p.m. through the position established by the rest of the York and Lancaster battalion and one company from the Green Howards at Kjörem, about three miles further up the valley. At this juncture, however, the enemy succeeded in setting fire to the woods, so that our lines had to be abandoned some hours earlier than was intended. But the Germans did not interfere seriously with the withdrawal, even though two companies on the exposed left flank which did not receive the instruction had to make their escape by long detours over the hills.

The orders which General Paget had given to the battalion at Kvam were founded on wider considerations besides the difficulties of their immediate position. After his first conference with Brigadier Morgan he had reported home at once through a liaison officer that the general situation was unsatisfactory. He based this to some extent on the fact that Morgan's Brigade, as he put it, 'had had a dusting' and that the Norwegian forces were 'unreliable and variable in different units', while he estimated that the Germans might have up to two or three divisions with good artillery to oppose the 15th Infantry Brigade and such reinforcements as might reach it. But his main emphasis was placed upon the situation in the air: the Germans, General Paget reported, had what amounted to complete air superiority, which they were using to strafe our forward troops, to spot for artillery, and to bomb communications, headquarters, and the base. Yet the following day brought him a telegram from General Massy emphasising the importance of securing a bridgehead to include Dombaas and the next forty miles farther north on the road to Trondheim as far as Opdal, so that a second base might be developed at the head of the Sunndalsfiord, north of the Romsdal. This was to provide for a build-up of strong forces, including the French, with a view to an ultimate advance down both the Gudbrandsdal and the Österdal, the alternative route by which the Germans might make contact with their troops in Trondheim. The failure to establish the fighter squadron on Lake Lesjaskog was not then known in England.

While the action at Kvam was being fought, General Paget's position had been clarified by his meeting with the Norwegian Commander-in-Chief in the early morning of the 26th, the results of which were recorded in a Norwegian Order of the Day issued on the 27th. It will be recalled that Brigadier Morgan's troops had for a time been placed under the command of the Norwegian 2nd Division. This arrangement terminated on 22nd April at 4 p.m., but the 148th Brigade, and the 15th Brigade on its arrival, remained subject to the orders of the Norwegian High Command, an arrangement which had been accepted in deference to General Ruge's wishes on the 20th. But by the time of General Paget's arrival at Norwegian Headquarters organised Norwegian resistance in the Gudbrandsdal was virtually at an end, and General Ruge was prompt to draw the obvious conclusion. His Order of the Day therefore gave General Paget command of the Gudbrandsdal from Dombaas, or strictly speaking from Lesjaskog, southwards. This included such Norwegian troops as were left in the fighting area behind Kvam and disposal of the Norwegian supply and transport system which was under General Hvinden Haug. The English, but not the Norwegian, version of the Order of the Day also placed under his command the small Norwegian detachments strung out north of Dombaas to Opdal and Stören. These detachments would in any case be replaced as British troops became available, except for small parties of ski troops which General Paget might require to secure his flank. Meanwhile, the other Norwegian troops were to be moved back into the Romsdal for reorganisation.

Thus the order to withdraw from Kvam was based upon the following considerations. A withdrawal up the valley was regarded as inevitable pending the arrival of artillery (25-pounders to deal with the German 5·9s) and the all-important air support. General Paget had telegraphed to the War Office on the afternoon of the 26th asking for both of these, for anti-aircraft artillery, and for the despatch of a third infantry brigade. For the time being, he considered that no one position could be held for more than forty-eight hours. There were particular reasons for standing as long as possible at Kjörem and Otta, the next points up the valley, as the Norwegian force of 1,200 men under Colonel Dahl, cut off to the west since the fight at Tretten, could still regain the main valley here but no farther up.[1] In general, however, the object was to hold the near approaches to Dombaas, thus protecting the southern side of the bridgehead leading from the west coast, while attempting to clear up the situation between Dombaas and Opdal and in the approaches to the Österdal, so as to maintain the northern side of the bridgehead.

General Massy's telegram from London, received early on the 26th, described the Germans as having advanced up the Österdal to Tynset and Röros and southwards from Trondheim as far as Stören. Röros, which in fact changed hands more than once, lies on a great bend eastwards of the railway, which turns west again to the junction at Stören, but from Tynset there was a road north-westward leading out on to the Dombaas-Stören route about fifteen miles north of Opdal. On the 27th, further information was made available which showed that the Germans had also sent a force up another side valley

---

[1] See p. 111.

by which they might cut the Dombaas-Opdal route at Hjerkinn, only nineteen miles north of Dombaas on the same route to Stören. They were already reported at a point about twenty miles short of Hjerkinn, and there was believed to be a German mountain regiment in the area which could operate on skis, and also a parachute group. As regards numbers the estimate was not far wrong. There were three battalions of infantry, and although this Group Fischer did not include any paratroops, it had more tanks than Group Pellengahr and, on a reckoning of all arms together, about two-thirds of its size and strength.

General Paget, therefore, while his troops still faced down the Gudbrandsdal, had also to look over his left shoulder, as it were, to protect the Dombaas-Opdal line if he could, and in any case the flank approach to Dombaas where his forces could be completely cut off. Information about the operations of the Norwegians in the Österdal area was very scanty but, in view of events in the Gudbrandsdal, General Paget was not likely to over-estimate the resistance that they could offer to German forces advancing with armour and some artillery along roads. Arrangements had been made to send a major of the Royal Engineers with a supply of explosives into the Österdal, in the belief that demolitions, to which the Norwegians were reluctant to resort, might prove a sovereign remedy; but nothing effective came of the venture. On the 27th, accordingly, General Paget himself set out by car to reconnoitre the Dombaas-Opdal road as far as Hjerkinn, but he failed to get through the deep snow. A reconnaissance was made on the following day, which brought news from the Norwegians that there had been no contact with enemy troops in that area. Meanwhile the action broken off by the British troops at Kvam had been renewed at Kjörem. General Paget did not think that the position there could be held for more than a day, so the Green Howards were ordered to prepare a second position at Otta, and Brigadier Morgan, on the afternoon of the 27th, was sent to reconnoitre a third in front of Dombaas itself, to provide for the possibility of a hurried withdrawal. General Paget's object, however, was 'to hang on at Otta if we possibly could, pending the arrival of the reinforcements I had asked for'.

At Kjörem the road and railway still run westwards along the left bank of the Laagen, but the valley floor is rather narrower. The position of the York and Lancaster battalion astride the road had been well dug in and troops were deployed in advance of it on both banks of the river, with standing patrols at a considerable height among the woods, broken ground, and occasional farms of the hillside. The enemy came up the road about 8.15 a.m. (27th April) and were engaged with some success from across the river. They then brought forward machine guns and mortars, not only along the road but also

THE ACTION AT KJÖREM

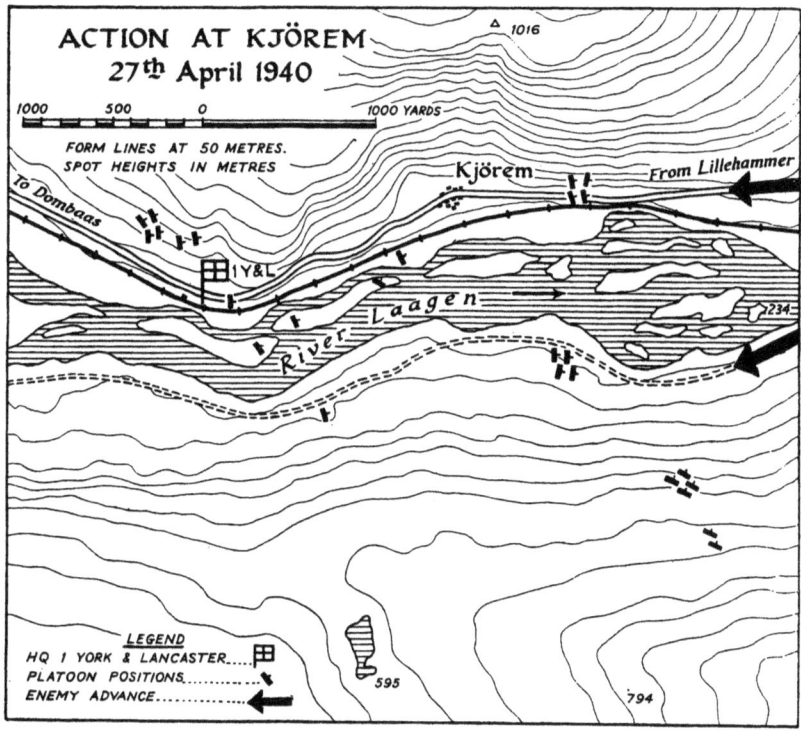

on the right bank of the river (where there was a farm track), by which means they were able to subject both flanks of the British position to cross-fire. Our forward position abreast the road and railway was protected by a wood, which the enemy succeeded in firing with mortar bombs. On this occasion we also had a 3-inch mortar in action, but it was employed to less effect. The fire caused one British company to withdraw, and when they counter-attacked the enemy had already secured the position with tanks and machine guns; but a new line was established a short distance west of the hamlet of Kjörem and held until nightfall. Our troops on the right bank, however, were now exposed to enfilade fire at relatively close quarters; and although the enemy advance along that bank met with little success, by six o'clock the cross-fire had compelled a withdrawal from our advanced positions and at 10 p.m. the last troops on the right bank went back to cross the river higher up. At 11 withdrawal began on the left bank as well, complicated by the fact that the enemy had come right over the hilltop behind our men. This enabled them to re-establish a roadblock in our rear, which had been found and dealt with by a battle patrol earlier in the evening, and from it they now opened fire with heavy machine guns at short range. At Otta next morning the strength of the battalion had fallen to 13 officers and 300 men. The equivalent of one more company from the right bank, having missed the river-crossing and wandered into the Heidal, arrived at Dombaas twenty-four hours later after a march over the snowfields. The York and Lancaster were therefore allotted a reserve role in the rear of the new front.

It was now the turn of the 1st Battalion Green Howards. They were short of one company, which was with Brigadier Morgan's troops protecting Dombaas; a second company, which had served on the right flank of the York and Lancaster the previous day, sustained serious losses while forming the rear-guard in the small hours and did not reach Otta until 7 a.m.

Otta, which looks not unlike some little North Riding market town, stands about ten miles up the valley from Kjörem on a tongue of land, where the river of the same name flows into the Laagen from the north-west. The main road follows the left bank of the Laagen, with a side-turning across a bridge into the town, while the railway and a subsidiary road follow the right bank. Two steeply rising spurs on the hillside, one on the left bank about one and a half miles in front of the town, the other on the right much nearer in, with sheltered access from the side valley, gave scope for effective cross-fire and would be very hard to storm. Each spur was held by one company; the rest of our troops were posted in and behind the town, where the five surviving anti-tank guns were also carefully sited.

An enemy air reconnaissance at 7 a.m. (28th April) was followed by an air attack which did little damage. At about half past ten, 150 enemy infantry with tanks and artillery advanced against our right flank along the track beside the railway. Heavy casualties were inflicted on them, whereupon they resorted to their usual tactics—a wide deployment to both flanks, artillery action against whatever targets could be located, and the incessant harassing of our forward companies by low-flying aircraft. Tanks were employed again later on both banks, but on the right bank they had very little room to manœuvre and on the left, where they came along the main road, a single anti-tank gun knocked out three in succession. Another party of the enemy was surprised while crossing the river in rubber boats to attack our forward position on the left bank. A series of attacks on our other forward position was equally unsuccessful. Even the enemy's usual outflanking manœuvre this time failed of success. Several small actions were fought by the company protecting the more distant spur, in one of which some thirty members of a German officers' conference were surprised and disposed of, and by evening the company, having shortened its lines, occupied a post higher up the hillside backing on to the foot of a precipice: from there it pinned down enemy detachments almost twice its own strength.

Withdrawal, in accordance with General Paget's orders, was timed

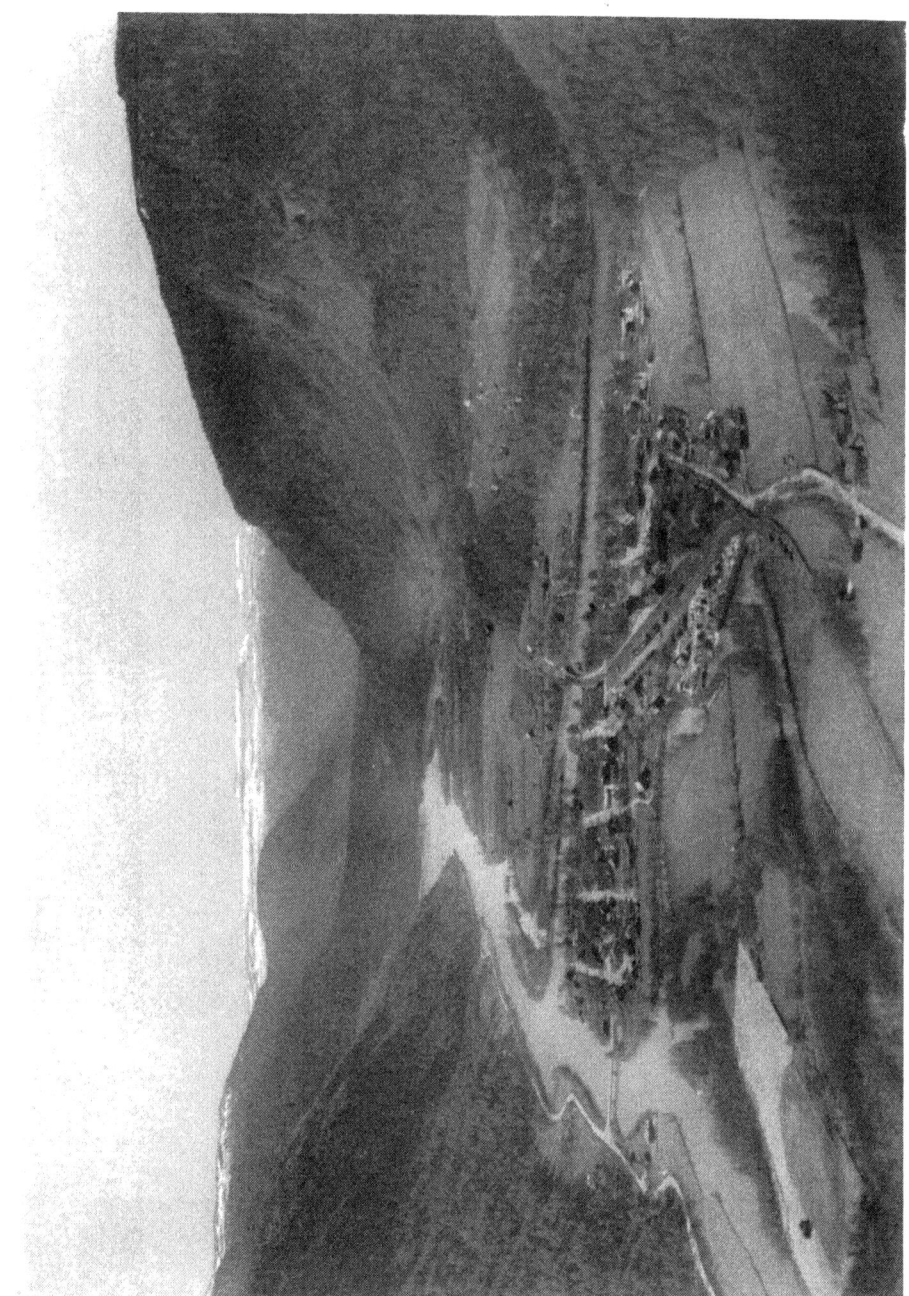

View of Otta from the north, showing the two spurs

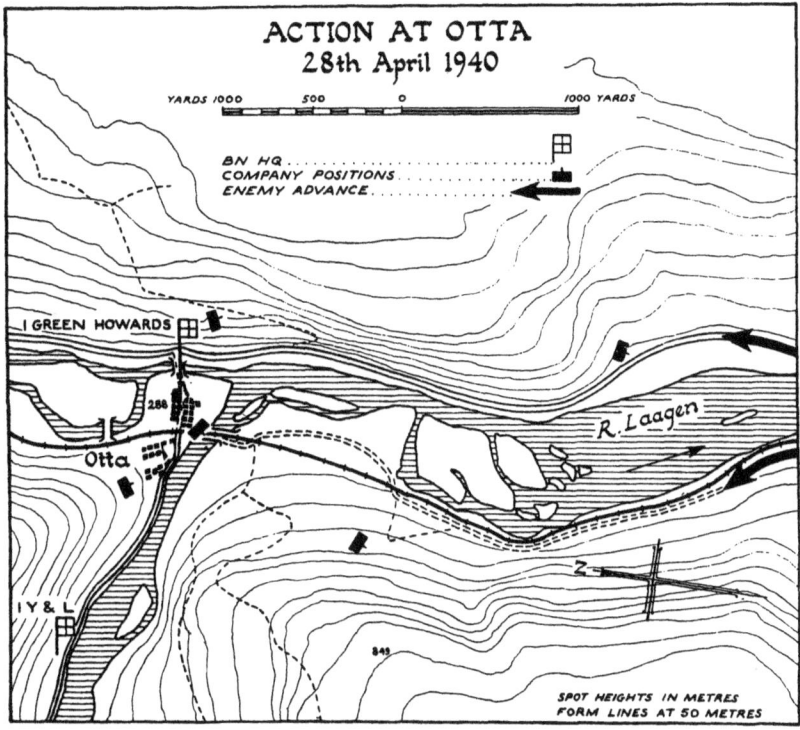

to begin at 10 p.m., when the forward company from the right bank crossed the River Otta by a ford after the railway bridge leading into the town had been partly blown up. Heavy fire was at the same time opened by the other companies upon the area which we had abandoned; and a general retirement from the town, after the disablement of our remaining anti-tank guns, was carried out successfully by the Green Howards and by the York and Lancaster in the rear. The advanced company in its strong but isolated position on the left bank did not receive the orders for withdrawal, but at half past ten drove off a superior force of the enemy with heavy loss. It then divided into four parties, which moved back in silence and for the most part on hands and knees at a height of a thousand feet or more above the valley floor along a precipitous slope—already famous in Norwegian story for the massacre of a force of Scottish mercenaries in 1612, when the peasantry rolled boulders down on them—and entered the village at 6 a.m. to find that the battalion had left. The company was still complete in numbers and arms and, though fired on by enemy snipers in Otta, suffered no loss as it set out on the thirty-mile march up the valley to Dombaas.

The break-away this time had been complete, and the enemy made no immediate attempt to follow. The German army reported 'bitter fighting for Otta', and General Paget was able to record that 'The Green Howards on the Otta position fought splendidly ... the enemy suffered many casualties in this battle, and his subsequent actions showed little desire or ability to press home an attack'.[1] The event was of importance in view of a complete change in the character of General Paget's campaign. Owing to a complex of circumstances described in the next chapter, his task was no longer to defend a bridgehead with a view to a subsequent advance. His task was to extricate his force along a narrow valley-route which the enemy might at any time outflank, through a base which lay already in ruins, under conditions imposing a severe strain upon British, much more upon Norwegian, morale.

---

[1] Cited in despatch by Lieut.-General H. R. S. Massy, Part III, Sec. 47.

MAP 5
THE APPROACHES TO TRONDHEIM
MILES 10 5 0 10 20 30 40 50 MILES
FORM LINES AT 400 M. INTERVALS
SPOT HEIGHTS IN METRES
Kristiansund
Bud
Sunndalsfiord
Molde
Aandalsnes
Aalesund
1696
Stadland
1824
1702
Geiranger
1513

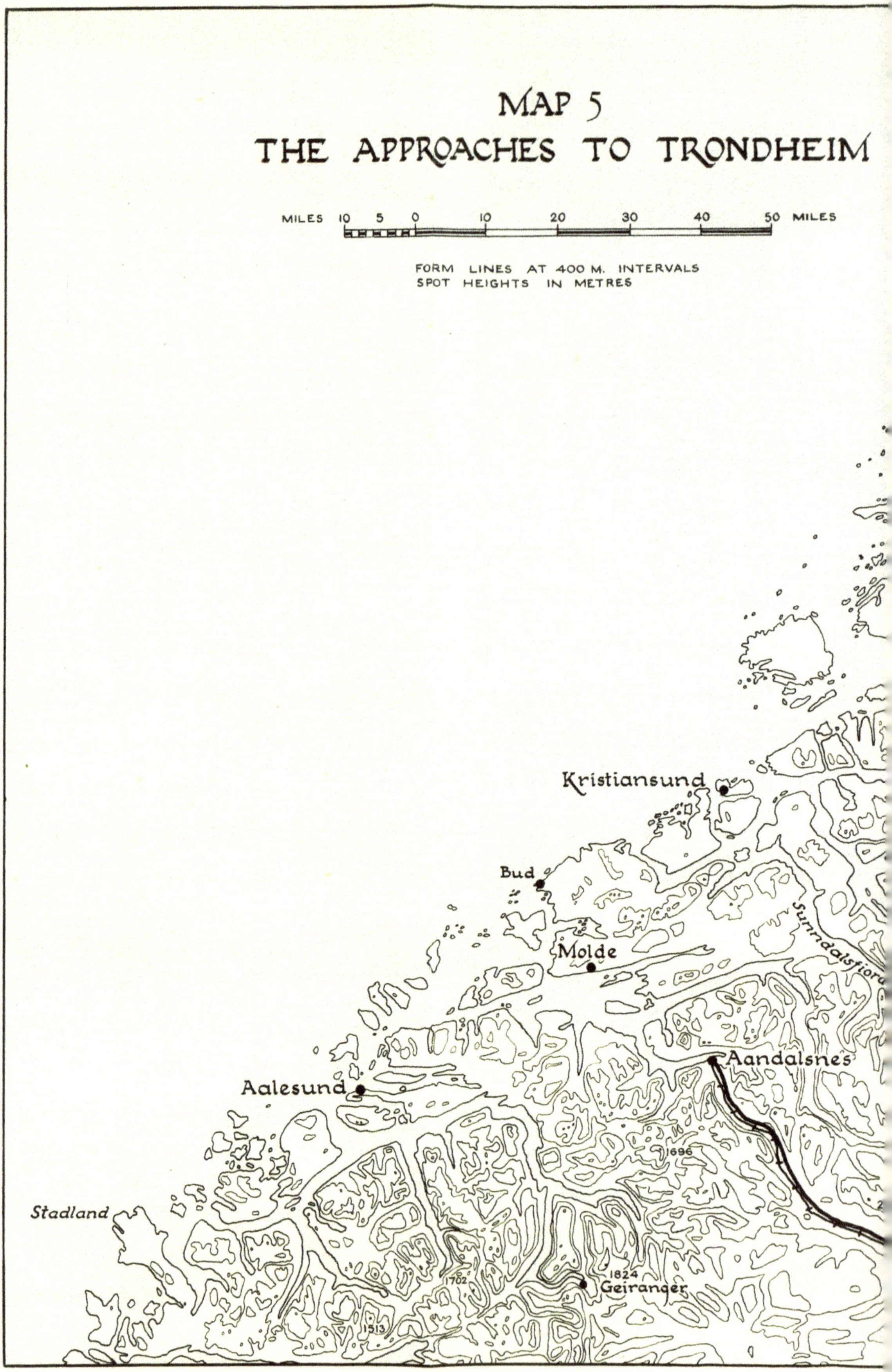

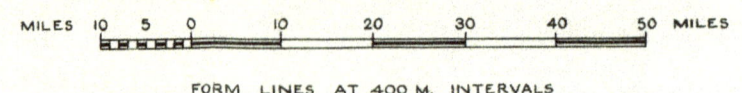

CHAPTER IX

THE EVACUATION OF CENTRAL NORWAY

THE expedition designed originally for the capture of Trondheim had fallen apart at an early stage into two expeditions under separate control, based respectively on Namsos and Aandalsnes. Both expeditions had met with serious and partly unexpected military reverses. Both had been discouraged by enemy air supremacy in the battle area; both lost all chance of recovery when that same enemy air supremacy destroyed their bases and imperilled their lines of communication. So far as the Government was concerned, the evacuation of the two forces was a single problem requiring a single decision. The engagement at Vist had been fought and lost on 21st and 22nd April; the defeat of Brigadier Morgan's Territorials had been completed at Tretten on the 23rd; the Gladiator squadron was destroyed and the position at Kvam abandoned on the 25th and 26th. On 25th April—the day when 'Hammer 2' was under consideration[1]—the Chiefs of Staff instructed the inter-Services planning organisation to collaborate with General Massy's subordinates in preparing plans for evacuation. On the 27th, General Massy's appreciation of the situation was considered by the Military Co-ordination Committee and final instructions for him to evacuate the two forces were approved by the Committee and issued over Sir Edmund Ironside's signature. The order to evacuate was telegraphed to both bases in the early afternoon, so that it reached General Carton de Wiart that night and General Paget in the forward area early next morning.

The two evacuations constitute a single naval and military operation of a very difficult kind, which was completed with unexpectedly small losses. But the positions of the two forces, geographically, tactically, and politically, were so different that it will be convenient to treat first the evacuation from Aandalsnes up to its completion in the early hours of the morning of 2nd May, and then separately the evacuation from Namsos which was completed a little more than twenty-four hours later, leaving the features common to both evacuations for some brief consideration at the end of the chapter.

General Paget and the 15th Brigade had been accompanied to Norway by an advance party of V Corps Headquarters under Brigadier D. Hogg, to take over responsibility for the base at

---

[1] See p. 80.

Aandalsnes from Headquarters Sickleforce. This skeleton Corps Headquarters had instructions to organise the base and its anti-aircraft defence, and also to reconnoitre subsidiary bases at Geiranger, which proved to be snowbound, and, as already mentioned, on the Sunndalsfiord. These subordinate tasks never had any practical importance owing to the unfavourable development of the campaign. The laying out of the main base had, however, been planned on 24th April by a reconnaissance group from Sickleforce Headquarters, and the siting of stores was begun accordingly on the 26th. But at this juncture Aandalsnes, as could be expected, suffered the fate that had already befallen Namsos.

There had been air attacks and ensuing damage every day except the first and one other. A number of small ships had also been sunk in the fiord, including six anti-submarine trawlers and the Norwegian torpedo boat *Trygg*. But it was not until the afternoon of the 26th that persistent raids succeeded in firing the wooden quay, much ammunition, and most of the lower part of the town. The harbour area was rendered useless except in the short night hours, as officers and men had to take cover outside the town, while the moral effect was greatly increased by the fact that the Germans had now begun to bomb from heights beyond the range of our anti-aircraft artillery. The situation was made worse by the fact that on 26th April Molde also had its first serious attack; this destroyed the electric power supply, so that we could no longer use the Norwegian wireless transmitter by which the expedition had communicated with England. One immediate result of the heavy bombing was the disappearance of the local boats, used hitherto to carry supplies between Molde and Aandalsnes; another was a decline in the working capacity of members of the Services subjected to the heavy strain of air bombardment, causing the naval officer-in-charge (Captain M. M. Denny) to report that it was only a question of time for the port activities to diminish to such an extent that the lines of communication could not be maintained. Aandalsnes had four more raids the following day between 11 a.m. and 4.30 p.m., in which rations, demolition stores, and explosives were lost, and two of the few railway engines available were immobilised by bomb craters outside the engine shed. That afternoon a supply convoy entered the fiord, but it left again at 2 a.m. on the 28th under strengthened escort, with the greater part of a heavy anti-aircraft battery, the first to reach Norway, still on board.

Shortly after midnight of 26th/27th April, while Captain Denny was at Molde, his representative in Aandalsnes made a warning signal to the Admiralty that evacuation might be necessary. Twelve hours later, after consultation with Captain Denny and all naval and military staff officers at base, Brigadier Hogg sent a message to the War Office, stating that, in the absence of proper communications with the front, he intended planning to evacuate from Aandalsnes in the first ten days of May. This proposal had, indeed, been foreshadowed to some extent in General Paget's first telegram to General Massy, despatched from Aandalsnes in the early morning of the 26th, which said, 'In view of the rate of the enemy advance, arrangements to evacuate should be prepared if aerial supremacy is not ensured forthwith'. Nevertheless, General Paget's reaction to Brigadier Hogg's message, which reached him the same evening—that is to say, before any official order to evacuate came through—was to send an immediate message to the War Office in the opposite sense, urging the need for effective action to deal with enemy aircraft and for artillery support. Given these, he could not agree that the situation at the front rendered evacuation necessary.

The day of the 28th, while the 15th Brigade was resisting the Germans so sturdily at Otta, brought the decisive change in the situation, in the shape of two messages from General Massy which reached General Paget from the base in the early morning. The effect of these was that evacuation had been decided upon in principle: ships would be available on the night of 30th April/1st May, the maximum use was to be made of Molde in preference to Aandalsnes, and evacuation from Molde might possibly be continued on the night of 1st/2nd May. Men were to be got away without regard to loss of equipment. General Paget still maintained the view that he could hold the Dombaas area for a time if further landings were planned and if air and artillery support were provided at once. But assuming the decision to be final, his chief concern was the reaction of the Norwegians, since their Commander-in-Chief had so often asked to know, not when the British were leaving but when more of them were coming. The formal arrangement with General Ruge, by which he had accepted complete command in the Gudbrandsdal, put upon General Paget an obligation of honour to adopt no measure for the evacuation of his own troops that was inconsistent with the safety and welfare of Norwegian troops behind the British front. Moreover, the hazards of a withdrawal would be so much increased as to make it a military impossibility if the Norwegians were to throw us over in disgust and come to terms with the Germans.

Accompanied by his principal staff officer, Lieut.-Colonel C. G. C. Nicholson, General Paget broke the news to General Ruge and his Chief of Staff at their headquarters, a remote farm a dozen miles south of Dombaas, on the morning of the 28th. The interview was inevitably difficult for both parties, and the Norwegian Commander-in-Chief declined at first to accept the decision, though General Paget suggests that he had, as a matter of fact, anticipated it. He despatched a telegram of remonstrance addressed to the Chief of the Imperial General Staff, pointing out that the recapture of Trondheim if postponed would become 'a great and serious affair' and referring to the promises of Allied operations, on the strength of which alone he had been able 'to keep his tired-out troops fighting continuously for these three weeks'. General Paget telegraphed at the same time, emphasising that evacuation was 'most hazardous' and making the suggestion referred to above about holding Dombaas. The replies received through General Massy made it clear that the evacuation must take place, basing the decision squarely on the inability to give adequate air support. Meanwhile the harsh necessities of the situation were emphasised by almost continuous air attacks on Aandalsnes. These completed the ruin of the town (and caused the troops to be put on half rations) in spite of temporary relief through the efforts of the anti-aircraft cruisers and sloops: the *Black Swan*, for example, fired 2,000 rounds of 4-inch and 4,000 of pom-pom ammunition in two days and then left again for Scapa with a 3-foot bomb-hole below the waterline. The subsidiary base at Molde was likewise subjected to increasingly severe attack and, what is more remarkable, the Germans at the same time inflicted even more complete devastation on the port of Kristiansund, north of Molde, which contained no military objective but a camp of German prisoners of war.

The problem of the withdrawal was governed, in General Paget's view, by four main factors. The first was his obligation to cover the retirement of the four thousand Norwegian troops in the area, as already agreed in outline in his interview with General Ruge. The second was the quantity of shipping that would be available on the nights of 29th/30th April, 30th April/1st May, and 1st/2nd May respectively. This part of the plan depended upon the Admiralty's judgement of the situation, and remained fluid, both as to the number of nights for the evacuation and as to the distribution of the task between Aandalsnes and Molde. The third factor was the dependence of his withdrawal upon a single railway line and road for a distance of a hundred miles. This was an even greater problem than it sounds. The road was throughout too narrow for lorries, especially the 3-tonners supplied belatedly by the War Office, to pass without careful manœuvring; the railway was a single-track line; road and railway, even on the mountain plateau round Dombaas, sometimes ran so close together as to afford virtually a single target to enemy bombers; and the precipitous gorge through which the Rauma makes its course from the watershed at Lesjaskog down to Aandalsnes restricts the area of movement so narrowly that the survival of road and railway was already something of a miracle. The fourth factor, in the General's phrase, was 'the physical endurance of the troops'.[1] A series of delaying actions had by now brought the 15th Brigade as

---

[1] Despatch by Lieut.-General Massy, Part III, Sec. 46.

far as Otta, where they were fighting hard throughout the day on which these difficult decisions were being taken.

A further factor, not specifically mentioned by the General, was the almost complete breakdown of communications between his headquarters and the base. The Norwegians claimed that the situation, already impaired by the bombing, was made worse by the British action in taking away what was left of the telephone-service staff at Aandalsnes. The Norwegian Army was still able to organise the details of its own retirement by a roundabout use of the civil telephone, passing its messages to Aalesund, from which town there were still wires available to the neighbourhood of Dombaas. But the British were left in the last stages dependent entirely on motor-cycle despatch riders, using the single road crammed with refugees and supply traffic and bombed faster than it could be repaired. Thus, for example, on the 29th Lieut.-Colonel D. W. Clarke, R.A., bringing a direct message from the Chief of the Imperial General Staff to General Ruge, took the best part of a day to cover the hundred miles. In the early morning of that day, Brigadier Hogg despatched a further telegram to the War Office about the evacuation, supposing that it would cover two not three nights, and stating his general intention of forming a defensive line in the neighbourhood of the base, behind which to evacuate non-fighting troops 'and General Paget's if they returned to base'. His ignorance of the General's precise intentions was due partly to the imminence of battle in the forward area but partly also to his dependence for liaison upon a single staff officer.

One aspect of the evacuation problem, which affected equally the forward area, the lines of communication, and the base, was the need for air support. As we have already seen,[1] the request that enemy communications south of Kvam should be bombed had not been met. Direct assistance was limited to the one-hour patrols over the Aandalsnes base by makeshift long-range fighters (Blenheims), which were supplemented by Hudson bombers to give partial protection to the evacuation convoys after they had left Aandalsnes for home. Namsos was entirely out of range. Accordingly, the Royal Air Force aimed at giving the maximum of indirect assistance to the operations from Aandalsnes and Namsos by a series of light bombing attacks upon Stavanger, Fornebu (Oslo), and Aalborg (North Jutland), which were to be stepped up to full strength one day before evacuation was due to begin. It was hoped that this would seriously reduce activity at the three airfields from which the Germans were believed to be operating. Accordingly, on the night of 30th April and during the following day thirty-one aircraft attacked Stavanger, and on the night of 30th April fourteen also attacked Fornebu. On the night of

---

[1] P. 119.

1st/2nd May Stavanger was again attacked by fifteen aircraft and Fornebu by six, while five aircraft also attacked Aalborg. All that could be noted at the time was a reduced scale of enemy air attack at Aandalsnes on 1st May and at Namsos on 1st and 2nd May, which might be attributable to the German belief that their bombing had reached saturation point and, in the case of Namsos, to unfavourable weather. But post-war disclosures show that Stavanger airfield was put temporarily out of action except for emergency landing.

Help was also planned from the Fleet Air Arm. The carriers *Ark Royal* and *Glorious*, accompanied by two cruisers and six destroyers, under the command of Vice-Admiral L. V. Wells, had reached the Norwegian coast from training work in the Mediterranean on 24th April, when the Gladiators were flown off the *Glorious*. Vaernes had then been attacked by thirty-four aircraft from both carriers on the 25th and by eighteen from the *Ark Royal*—her consort having gone home—on the 28th. The French considered that these attacks, delivered at a time when the thaw impeded repair, were effective, even though reports from Trondheim also told of 800 civilian workers being conscripted at once to restore the surface of the airfield. The Fleet Air Arm had also flown small daily patrols from positions about 120 miles to seaward over both Aandalsnes and Namsos. On 30th April the *Ark Royal*, which had moved farther out to sea to rest her airmen after five days' action and serious losses, came in to the coast again, followed by the *Glorious* the next morning with new aircraft brought from home. The intention was that the Fleet Air Arm should cover Aandalsnes on 1st May and Namsos on the 2nd and 3rd; but sustained enemy air attack on his ships caused Admiral Wells to withdraw the squadron (with a total loss of fifteen aircraft) at the end of the first day, as being unable to 'maintain a position from which aircraft could give support to our forces'. They had destroyed at least twenty of the enemy; but it must be admitted that German air supremacy was not seriously affected at any time during these operations, and that failure to press home the advantage was due primarily to weather conditions and to the fog of war.

Once evacuation had been decided upon, General Paget's first task was to break contact with the enemy. At 6 p.m. on the 28th, he ordered the K.O.Y.L.I. to occupy a position south of Dombaas railjunction and about twenty-five miles up the valley from the scene of the fighting still in progress at Otta. His troops were by this time tired but had the great satisfaction of feeling that they had latterly inflicted more damage than they received. In addition, General Paget had obtained from the Norwegians small but valuable detachments of ski troops for his flanks, as well as four field guns and the use of such transport as was available. A train was assembled at Dombaas and run forward to Rudi, on a stretch of the railway which follows the right bank of the Laagen, about four miles up the valley from Otta. Available motor transport was assembled at an almost exactly parallel position on the road, which here follows the left bank. Fighting slackened after dusk, as we have seen, and a successful withdrawal began about 11 p.m. By daylight, the troops from the front line were in Dombaas, covered by the K.O.Y.L.I. As the British forces made their withdrawal, a section of Royal Engineers exploded demolition charges in the wild Rosti gorge, where the road-bridge crosses on to the right bank of the river, and at a railway-bridge farther back towards Dombaas. The Rosti road-block was thought to be secure against a forward move by wheeled vehicles, including tanks and guns, for at least forty-eight hours.

Apart from the problem of escape along a route known to the enemy and exposed to air bombing throughout, there were two special problems to be faced. One was the responsibility for an additional Norwegian detachment which, as explained above, had had the task of delaying any advance upon Dombaas from the north along the Trondheim-Dombaas route which the enemy were fast approaching from the Österdal.[1] General Ruge made it known that this detachment could not reach Dombaas from the direction of Hjerkinn until the following night, which meant that—a daylight withdrawal being obviously impracticable—the British withdrawal beyond Dombaas must be postponed until the night of the 30th. In other words, Dombaas must be held for forty-eight hours. The other problem was the protection of the line of retreat against paratroops. The main body of the Norwegians was now being withdrawn as quickly as possible from the Romsdal to escape air attack, leaving the valley unprotected. The task was therefore entrusted to the remnants of the 148th Brigade, but these failed to reach their positions next day, apparently through a misunderstanding, so that the neighbourhood of Lesjaskog was left unguarded except for the anti-tank company—minus the anti-tank guns. It was a fortunate chance that the Germans (perhaps on account of Göring's lack of interest in the campaign) did not again resort to the technique that had caused serious trouble in the same area a week before.

The day of the 29th passed at Dombaas according to plan, with the troops resting in positions well hidden from German air observation. The last Norwegian detachment duly passed through from Hjerkinn and the 1st York and Lancaster left by rail for Aandalsnes at 10 p.m. But on the afternoon of the 30th the K.O.Y.L.I., from their position three miles south of the village, saw the enemy coming up the road.

---

[1] See p. 123.

They were on foot—having apparently circumvented the principal demolition in the Rosti gorge by moving up the railway on the right bank of the river, the tunnels of which were left intact—and were using hand-carts to carry mortars, etc. A single aircraft dropped stores for them. The enemy were doubly taken by surprise, for not only were our positions extremely well hidden in a series of dips and by a railway tunnel, but also the four Norwegian field guns on the hillside behind Dombaas opened up in support. The Germans suffered heavy initial casualties, and when the aircraft bombed our positions it was fortunately disposed of by small-arms fire. Even after the surprise had been exhausted, the engagement went well for us, and as the river guarding our right flank was now swollen by the thaw the Germans could only attempt the crossing in rubber boats, all of which were destroyed by a company of the Green Howards brought forward from Dombaas.

It is significant that on this occasion, when the enemy had no artillery or air support—the Luftwaffe was concentrating its attentions on Aandalsnes—our troops were able to hold them and, as Brigadier Kent-Lemon reported at 6 p.m., could even adopt 'an aggressive attitude'.[1] An hour later successive companies began to fall back on the station, from which they were due to depart at dusk. The enemy followed close on the heels of the last company but were held in check by the Green Howards, who had been guarding the approach to Dombaas from Hjerkinn and now provided the rearguard covering the village. The train had been backed into the station by the Norwegian railway staff from its hiding place in a convenient tunnel and, though pursued by desultory rifle-fire, it steamed safely away about 11.30 p.m. for Aandalsnes. The two rear companies followed in trucks half an hour later under cover of demolitions of the bridges where the road and rail routes cross the River Jora, a tributary of the Laagen, about a mile and a half north of Dombaas railway station.

Everything now turned upon the condition of the railway, which had been subjected to so much bombing and, with the completion of the Norwegian withdrawal and that of the 148th Brigade, no longer had troops to combine its protection with its repair. The train which carried the York and Lancaster on the night of 29th/30th April had been stopped by a break in the rails at Lesjaskog, the village at the west end of the lake, obliging the battalion to continue its journey by route march with some small assistance from trucks. Nevertheless, the line had been reported to be in working order at 5 p.m. the next day, and no special precautions appear to have been taken against the sort of accident which followed. At 1.15 a.m., after the train had

---

[1] Despatch by Lieut.-General Massy, Part III, Sec. 53.

picked up at a point well west of Dombaas the anti-tank company and the 280 Norwegian ski troops who had guarded our flanks, both engines overturned and the front coach was telescoped at a bomb-crater east of Lesjaskog. There were eight fatal and thirty other serious casualties. No relief train could reach the scene of the accident because the line was blocked above Verma, some seventeen miles nearer Aandalsnes. The whole area was deep in snow—Lesjaskog is nearly 2,000 feet above sea-level—and provided no cover from air attack or other facilities for defence. The troops therefore set out to march through to Verma, while vehicles were brought forward for the injured. They were attacked by enemy reconnaissance planes on the way, the first part of their journey lying over an almost treeless plateau, but reached safety about 9 a.m., very tired but without loss of heart, or even of their equipment.

A railway tunnel 481 yards long which adjoins Verma station provided perfect air cover though far from perfect air (the interior being neither lined nor ventilated) for the resting troops, who were crowded up with an ammunition train and the troop-train in which they were due to complete their journey at dusk. German aircraft tried in vain to block the exits. Meanwhile a party of the Royal Marines, who occupied a post near Verma to safeguard the electric power supply for Aandalsnes, had been hurried forward to hold the scene of the accident until 10 a.m. and then the head of the Rauma gorge, so as to protect the troops on the march from being overrun by an enemy advance from Dombaas. The Marines were joined by Norwegians belonging to a training detachment, left behind for lack of transport in the withdrawal of the 2nd Division. In the afternoon, however, they had a brush with enemy patrols—their main body being apparently held up by our demolition of bridges—and some of the Marines fell back hurriedly upon Verma. They arrived just as the troops had been smoked out of the tunnel by the raising of steam for their train. A company of Green Howards was thereupon deployed about three miles up the road, but about 6 p.m. a small Lewis-gun detachment of the Marines came through intact: this party had remained behind and delayed the enemy advance. It was then decided to risk the final stage of the journey by daylight. The train left at 8.30 p.m., carrying the main body of troops; rather more than one company of Green Howards, with a few Marines forming the last rear-guard, followed in seven trucks.

Meanwhile, preparations for evacuation had been completed at the base, in so far as the impairment of communications, both to the front-line troops and back to England, made co-ordination feasible. As previously related,[1] Brigadier Hogg had sent a telegram to the

---

[1] See p. 133.

War Office early on the 29th; in this he asked that the evacuation should begin at 9 p.m. the following evening and should be completed the next night. The base area was now divided into three sectors under the respective commands of Lieut.-Colonel Simpson, R.M., Brigadier Morgan, and Brigadier A. H. Hopwood; however, the rear-guard action fought by General Paget's troops rendered any last stand unnecessary. Enemy air attacks on Aandalsnes continued, and were for the first time prolonged into the night with fresh incendiary bombs amid woods and buildings already burning. At the last moment messages were received from General Massy to the effect that the evacuation could not begin for a further twenty-four-hour period. The cruiser *Glasgow* did indeed put in at Molde, where the want of ferrying-craft (sunk or scared away by bombs) prevented any concentration of troops, but this was for the special purpose of evacuating King Haakon and the Crown Prince of Norway, the members of the Government, and the Allied legations, along with bullion which had been brought overland from the Bank of Norway in Oslo. The town was on fire and night raids were in progress when the cruiser arrived. She came alongside with fire-hoses playing, but her errand was successfully completed, the passengers being transferred to a Norwegian vessel at a point just south of Tromsö, which a Cabinet vote taken on the voyage chose finally as their destination. The situation at Aandalsnes was almost equally serious. No less than 340 troops were evacuated in the sloop *Fleetwood*, which had replaced the *Black Swan* and went home on the morning of the 30th because she was out of ammunition; but a large part of the thousand men whom it had been planned to evacuate that night remained ashore, dispersed in the woods outside the bombed area.

Admiral Edward-Collins arrived from Scapa at 10.30 p.m. on the 30th with four cruisers, six destroyers, and a small transport. The *Galatea* and the *Arethusa* went in succession alongside the concrete quay which was the only proper embarkation place that had survived the air raids, and a small ship carried other troops to the *Sheffield*, which had anchored off the town. Altogether these three cruisers embarked about 1,800 men, described as 'dead-beat and ravenously hungry'. Other smaller parties were picked up by the *Southampton* and the lesser ships from positions just west and to the north of Aandalsnes, including a further small party from Molde, where General Ruge and his staff alone were, at their own insistence, left behind. There was no enemy opposition until the ships were leaving the outer fiords at first light next morning, when a few bombs were dropped near them without effect.

There remained the more hazardous task of bringing away the troops who had been last in contact with the enemy, as they came down to Aandalsnes by train and truck in the late evening of 1st

Map 6

ROMSDAL & GUDBRANDSDAL

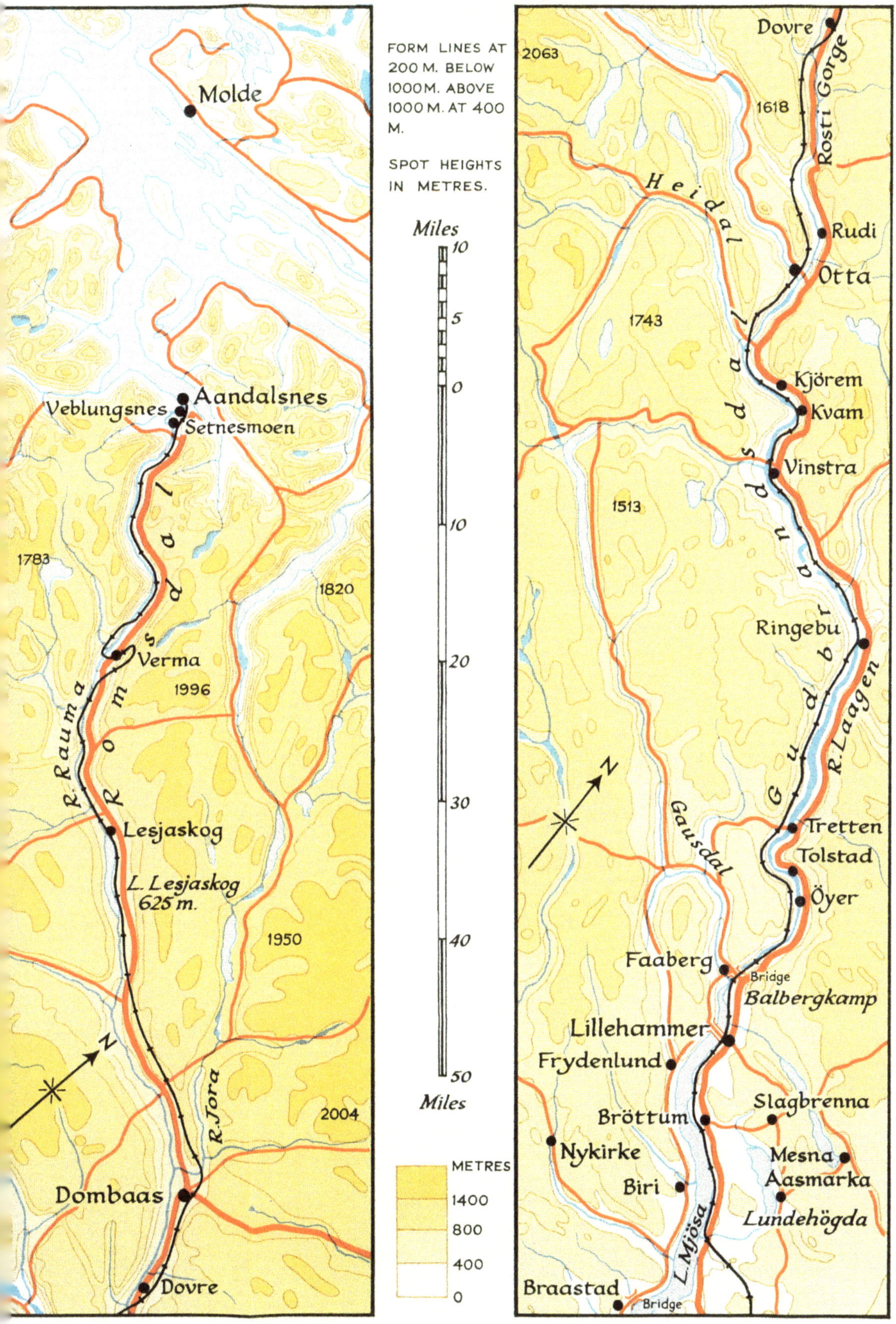
Molde
Aandalsnes
Veblungsnes
Setnesmoen
Romsdal
1783
1820
Verma
1996
R. Rauma
Lesjaskog
L. Lesjaskog
625 m.
1950
N
R. Jora
2004
Dombaas
Dovre
FORM LINES AT
200 M. BELOW
1000 M. ABOVE
1000 M. AT 400
M.
SPOT HEIGHTS
IN METRES.
Miles
10
5
0
10
20
30
40
50
Miles
METRES
1400
800
400
0
Dovre
2063
1618
Rosti Gorge
Heidal
Rudi
Otta
1743
Kjörem
Kvam
Vinstra
1513
Gudbrandsdal
Ringebu
R. Laagen
N
Gausdal
Tretten
Tolstad
Öyer
Faaberg
Bridge
Balbergkamp
Lillehammer
Frydenlund
Slagbrenna
Bröttum
Nykirke
Mesna
Aasmarka
Biri
Lundehögda
L. Mjösa
Braastad
Bridge

May. Aandalsnes was bombed again during the day, though intermittently, no doubt because there was little left to bomb. During the afternoon the two anti-aircraft ships in the harbour were forced by the weight of attack to put to sea pending the night's operations, and about seven o'clock a single raider dropped incendiaries on the outlying hamlet of Veblungsnes. This lies opposite Aandalsnes on the south bank of the Rauma, but the height of the intervening headland fortunately prevented the fires from lighting up the quay. Admiral Layton, with two cruisers and five destroyers, suffered several attacks on the way in. One destroyer was detached to collect the party that had been landed at Aalesund and a second put in at Molde to carry General Ruge, who had finally decided to follow in the wake of his king. The rest of the force reached Aandalsnes a little before 11 p.m., and by midnight two of the destroyers had ferried nearly 1,300 men to the two cruisers. In the belief that only the rear-guard had still to be accounted for, the Admiral ordered his ships out as quickly as possible. Of the two anti-aircraft ships left behind, one found accommodation for a strength of 755, made up of parties that had been overlooked in the confusion of departure; the other took the true rear-guard of 240 men, who were embarked in seven minutes. By 2 a.m. the quay was deserted and the Gudbrandsdal campaign at an end.

The evacuation from Namsos was, in all except the final stage, a relatively simple operation, for the farthest advance had been only half as far as in Gudbrandsdal and our withdrawal after the first engagement with the enemy had been immediate. The final stage was, as we shall see, complicated by the fact that it took place twenty-four hours after the completion of the evacuation from Aandalsnes. In other words, it was an evacuation of which notice had been given, whereas the ease of the departure from Aandalsnes means probably that the Germans remained uncertain of our intentions up to the last. In the Namsos sector British troops had made no further contact with the enemy by land after the withdrawal which followed the unsuccessful engagement at Vist. A counter-attack had, however, been planned by General Audet, in which the British were to have played a minor part, and, as already noted,[1] one of the problems of the evacuation was how to explain away the postponement of this attack without disclosing the secret of our ultimate intentions to the Norwegian forces which were to have taken part in it.

General Massy's telegram, announcing that evacuation was decided upon in principle, reached General Carton de Wiart late on 27th April, and movement began the next evening; two French

---
[1] See p. 96.

store-ships after they had completed their unloading embarked the 53rd Battalion of Chasseurs Alpins, who were easily withdrawn from their posts along the railway. But the Admiralty plan provided for the main embarkation to be in two halves, on 1st/2nd and 2nd/3rd May respectively. A general withdrawal had now to be organised as unobtrusively as possible having regard to the small and shattered base. For Namsos was heavily attacked from the air on the 28th and again with dive-bombers on the 30th. The sloop *Bittern* was disabled and had to be abandoned, as were three out of eight anti-submarine trawlers, though the trawler *Arab* (whose commander, Lieut. R. B. Stannard, received the Victoria Cross) crowned a series of exploits in fire fighting and rescue work during these attacks by sinking a German bomber single-handed on her way home. Moreover, it was an essential part of the General's plan to get the French force away first. He therefore decided to bring both the British and French troops back by a series of leap-frog movements.

The 13th Chasseurs Alpins lay nearest to the enemy, a little more than half-way from Namsos to Steinkjer. Much closer to Namsos were the positions held in succession by the K.O.Y.L.I., the Hallamshire, and the 67th Chasseurs Alpins; the Lincolnshire were nine miles up the railway to the east. The first stage of evacuation was to be the withdrawal of the 13th Chasseurs Alpins in driblets, which might escape enemy attention, leaving their sections of skiers as a rear-guard. The K.O.Y.L.I. would withdraw after them. It was intended that these two battalions should go round by sea from Bangsund to Namsos but they eventually moved back by road, so that the Hallamshire in their turn provided the rear-guard, with orders to hold the bridge at Bangsund at least until 9.30 p.m. on 2nd May. This would give time for the two battalions previously mentioned to get back to Namsos. In the same way, the 67th Chasseurs Alpins withdrew into Namsos, followed by the 4th Lincolnshire who covered the road from the east, along which a German advance was less likely. The Lincolnshire's rear-guard would eventually be relieved at the south end of the big bridge into Namsos by the rear-guard of the Hallamshire, who would move back into the town itself at the very last moment, accompanied by the French ski-ing sections. By the late evening of 1st May the plan was in full operation and the two battalions of Chasseurs Alpins were in the neighbourhood of the quay.

Admiral Cunningham had sailed from Scapa on 29th April, planning to bring off half the expedition in three big French transports on the first night, and the other half in the British cruisers *Devonshire* and *York* and the French cruiser *Montcalm* on the second night. There was an air attack on the afternoon of 1st May, when the *Devonshire* and a transport were nearly hit. Then in the evening the Admiral ran into thick and widespread fog forty miles short of his rendezvous, the Kya Light, which in turn was forty miles short of Namsos. The operation for that night (1st/2nd May) was therefore cancelled by a message which reached Force Headquarters at 9.30 p.m. This meant the re-dispersal of the assembled troops, who just got back into position by daybreak. To make the situation more disheartening, there was clear sky over Namsos itself, as was found by four destroyers which groped their way in through the fog. They were forced to put to sea again without embarking any troops, because the good weather facilitated the renewal of the German air attack; one destroyer suffered twenty-three casualties from a near miss as she hid in a fog-bank which was just too low to cover the masthead.

The situation now became critical. As we have already seen, the full relief from bombing which the R.A.F. had hoped to achieve during the evacuation period of the two expeditions had not been achieved. It could not be long before the Germans grasped the situation and applied a pressure which might put the whole force at their mercy; in point of fact the German air command at Trondheim had already detected and reported the start of the evacuation. The attitude of the Norwegians, from whom our intentions could not be concealed indefinitely, might also create serious complications, and the smoothness of our co-operation with the French might be impaired inasmuch as they would regard the re-embarkation as a British responsibility. Two other factors, unknown to Force Headquarters, made the situation still more precarious. The two aircraft carriers had left Norwegian waters earlier that evening, and the political situation prevented the Prime Minister from any further postponement of a statement on the progress of the war in Norway, which would announce the completion of the Aandalsnes evacuation and by implication direct the attention of the Germans to the similar move impending at Namsos. The Prime Minister's statement was made on the afternoon of 2nd May and broadcast, much to the discomfiture of Mauriceforce. It was General Carton de Wiart's opinion that the shortness of the hours of darkness made the completion of the evacuation in one night as impracticable as it was clearly desirable. But Admiral Cunningham had been warned by the Commander-in-Chief, Home Fleet, at the outset, that the work might have to be done in one lift, and he had prepared and announced an alternative plan on 30th April, when he knew that one battalion of French had been got away in the storeships on the 29th. There were about 5,400 men to be provided for: three transports could embark 1,700 men each at the stone pier, and the balance could be taken by the cruiser *York*, receiving them from trawlers a couple of miles off the town. Rear-Admiral J. G. P. Vivian, who had been in the port with the anti-aircraft cruiser *Carlisle*, shared General Carton de

Wiart's opinion; but Admiral Cunningham's transports were running short of fuel and he finally decided to make the attempt.

On the second night (2nd/3rd May) the squadron ran out of the fog forty miles from the Namsenfiord, where it divided. The Admiral with two cruisers and four destroyers waited off the Kya Light while the three French transports, the *York*, and five destroyers went straight in, arriving off Namsos itself about 10.30 p.m. Two transports loaded at the stone quay; the other two big ships were loaded from destroyers and trawlers, and the destroyer *Afridi* took the last parties on board at 2.20 a.m. It was touch and go at the end, as the Bangsund bridge was not exploded by the rear-guard until after midnight, leaving them with ten miles to cover to the embarkation area. At half past one, as General Carton de Wiart reports, 'the translucent twilight over the hills round the harbour became brighter, full daylight was fast approaching': but the trucks arrived soon after. The shelling of the massed motor transport on the quay by the *Afridi* on her departure emphasised the haste of the escape.

As it was, the Germans had received enough notice to make this voyage, which began at a point far beyond the range of British fighter escort, much more hazardous than that from Aandalsnes on the previous two nights. The sun cleared the fog early enough for the regular enemy air reconnaissance at 4.30 a.m. to spot the later groups in the convoy—two big French transports each escorted by one of Admiral Cunningham's cruisers and by destroyers. They were attacked on five occasions between 8.45 and 3.30 p.m.—by which time the first air escort of one Sunderland was approaching the head of the convoy—at distances ranging from 140 to 220 miles off the German-occupied airfield of Vaernes. Steep dive-bombing was for the first time systematically employed. Anti-aircraft fire from the warships and from the French transports under Rear-Admiral Cadart destroyed two or three aircraft out of the fifty or so that came in against us, and the ships were eventually formed for mutual support in single line ahead, with the anti-aircraft cruiser *Carlisle* last astern. But the third attack set on fire the French destroyer *Bison*, which was sunk by our destroyers after they had taken aboard the survivors of its crew. This caused some delay to the destroyers concerned, one of which—the *Afridi*—was hit by two bombs at 2 p.m. while returning to the squadron. She eventually capsized with the loss of about 100 killed, including fourteen men of the Hallamshire battalion which had formed the rear-guard.

The pursuit of Admiral Cunningham's ships by German aircraft so far from the Norwegian coast underlines the essential fact governing the failure of the two expeditions south and north of Trondheim, namely the virtually unchallenged supremacy of the enemy in the air, which rendered our bases, their sea approaches, and the lines of communication forward quite untenable. This from our point of view was amply sufficient reason for a sudden reversal of policy, to withhold intended reinforcement and cut our losses while they were still relatively small—from Sickleforce 1,402 men (of whom a number had been taken prisoner) and from Mauriceforce 157 all told. But the Norwegians could not be expected to see it in this light. General Paget had carried out his immediate obligation to them as comrades in arms in covering, at serious cost to himself, their withdrawal in advance of our troops to the Aandalsnes area. General Ruge's original intention was to take some part of the 2nd Division with him to North Norway in British ships, but the troops were too discouraged by the turn of events; so the only practical result of General Paget's action was that the division was able to prepare for demobilisation before signing the inevitable armistice with the Germans. In the Namsos area there was nothing like this to soften the blow: General Ruge had, indeed, been warned verbally on 29th April, but he was not in touch with the operations. The initial retirement of the French was covered by the suggestion that they were being re-formed for a direct attack on the Agdenes forts outside Trondheim. About half past ten on the night of 2nd May, while the ships were loading, the Norwegian Brigade Headquarters received a letter from General Carton de Wiart in his capacity as Commander-in-Chief, enclosed with a more elaborate letter from General Audet, who assured them that he was 'a victim of the necessities of war and could do no other than obey'.[1] Both letters, however, conveyed the bleak fact of the evacuation. The Norwegians found themselves deserted; left even without information as to the prospects of a German advance on the open flank; consoled only by references to material placed at their disposal—but in the inevitable confusion and haste of the embarkation this too was largely destroyed or disappeared.

The Norwegian forces south of Trondheim under General Hvinden Haug signed a capitulation at 5 a.m. on 3rd May; their forces north of Trondheim under Colonel Getz on the same day, with effect from 2 p.m. on the 4th. Resistance by the isolated Norwegian detachments in the Österdal and in the mountains west of Gudbrandsdal (Dahl Group) had ceased on 29th April, the day before the junction of the German forces south of Stören established the relief of Trondheim. The 4th Brigade, which had been pressed back in a series of strongly contested actions through Valdres towards the west, capitulated on the 30th, and its example was followed piecemeal by the other, much smaller, units based on West Norway. Except for scattered

---

[1] Getz, p. 150.

parties which 'took to the heather' and often made for North Norway by sea or across Sweden, the end came when, at 5.15 a.m. on 5th May, the white flag was hoisted by the virgin fortress of Hegra.

The total collapse of the attempt to recapture Trondheim, while felt most bitterly by the Norwegians, had wide repercussions outside Norway. At home, it was to lead directly to the fall of the Chamberlain Government, and even the fine feat of arms, by which General Paget had extricated his troops through the narrow valleys with all the odds against him, received little recognition in the prevailing mood of disappointment. Among the neutral powers, from friendly America to unfriendly Italy, what had happened seriously strengthened the view which had already grown up during the so-called 'phoney war', that neither our war planning nor the execution of the plans bore any comparison with the German in vigour or efficiency. Among our enemies, any lurking suspicion of the trickery upon which the invasion originally depended gave place to a romantic delight in German feats of arms in a romanticised Northland. But in order to see the full difficulties of our position less than four weeks after the opening of the campaign, we must now turn back to consider the initial phases of the struggle for Narvik. The Prime Minister's speech of 2nd May emphasised, 'It is far too soon to strike the Norwegian balance-sheet yet, for the campaign has merely concluded a single phase.'[1] He pointed out in another passage that 'the considerable supplies of ore which Germany was formerly obtaining from Narvik had been indefinitely suspended'.[2] In fine, the siege of Narvik, so remote from German air power, and economically of such cardinal importance, might be regarded as the main show, to which our efforts against Trondheim were altogether subordinate.

---

[1] H. of C. Deb., Vol. 360, Col. 912.
[2] *Ibid.*, Col. 911.

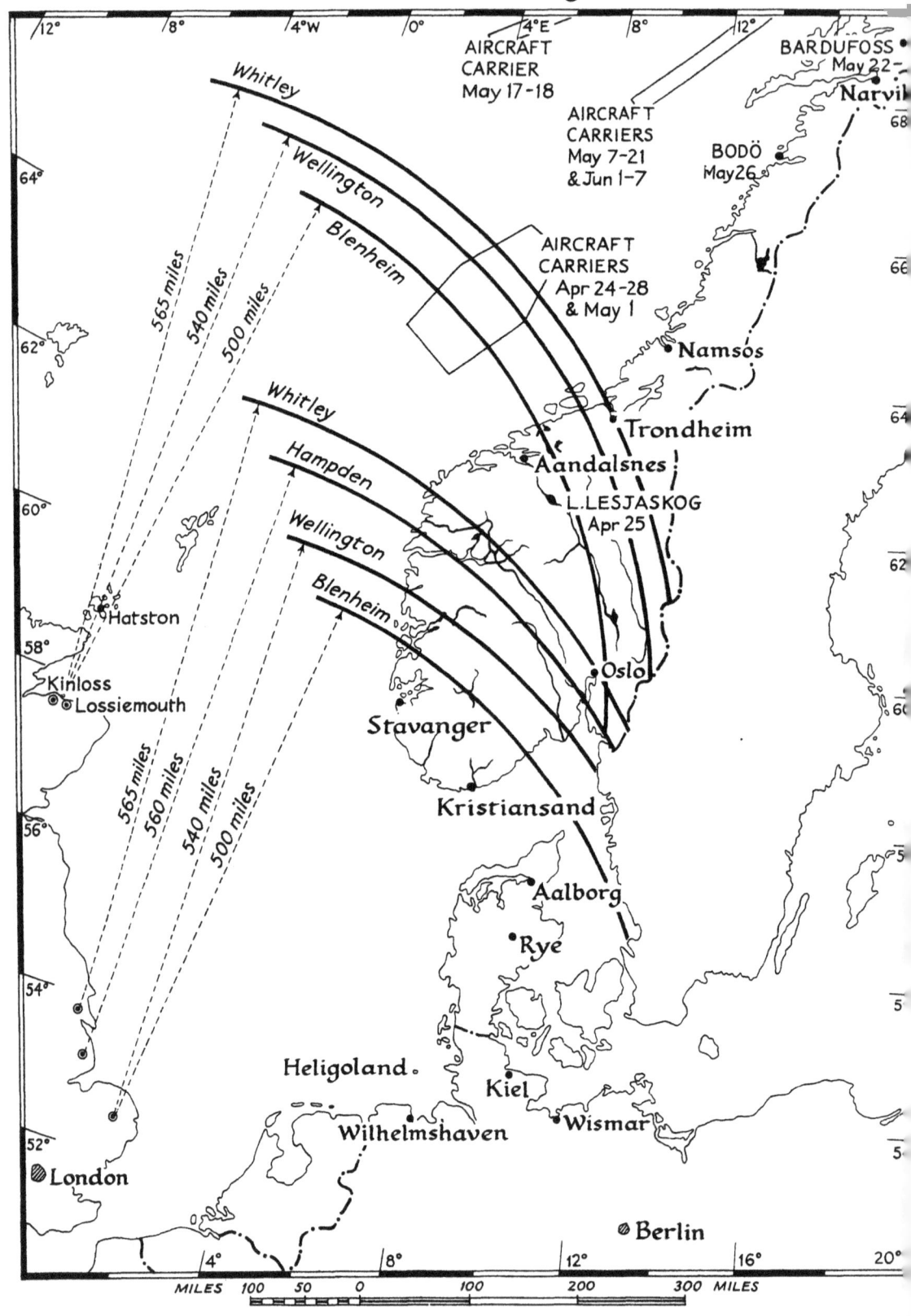

Map 7 (a) BRITISH AIR OPERATIONS IN NORWAY
Bomber Limits & Fighter Bases

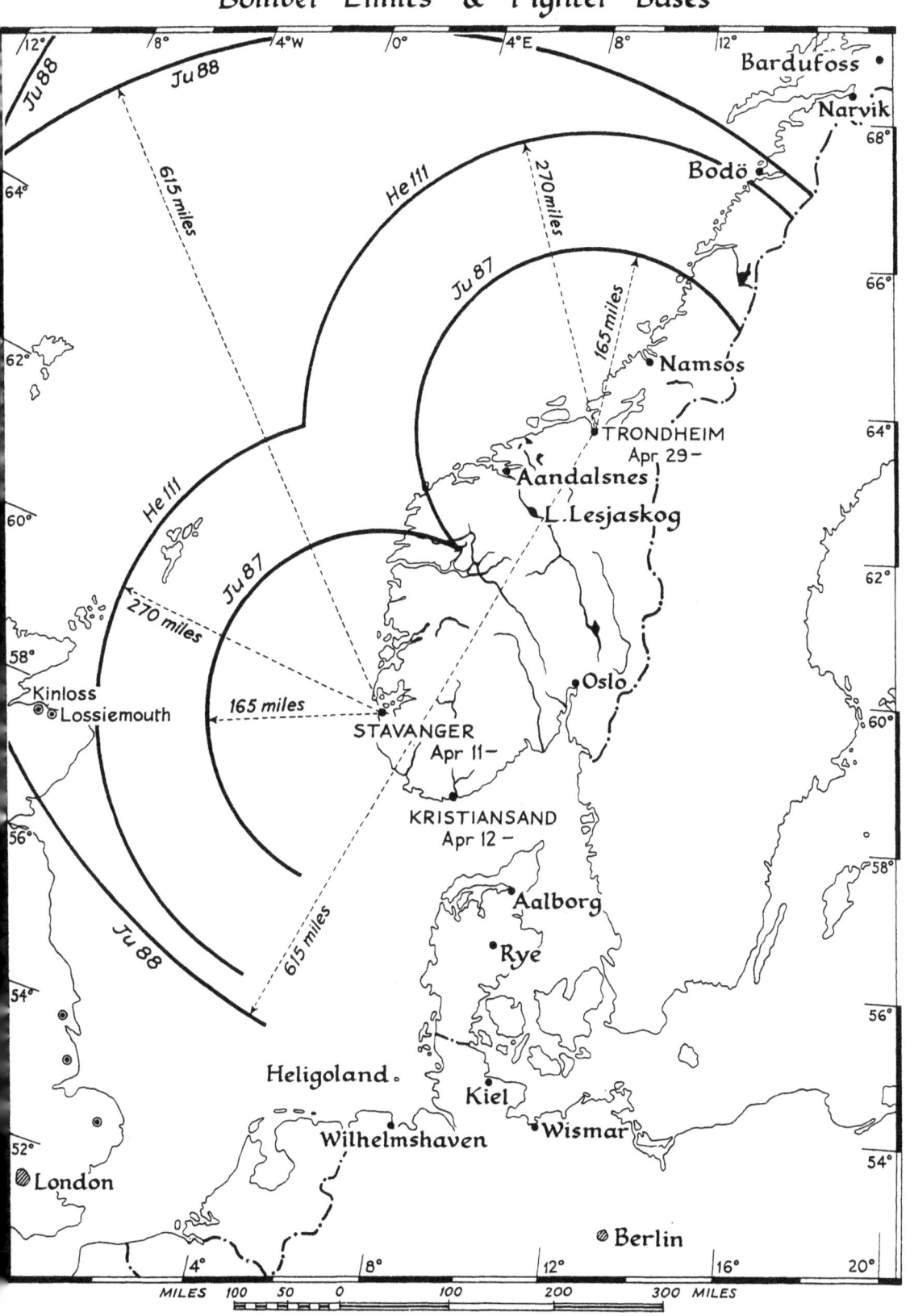

CHAPTER X

NARVIK—THE FIRST LANDINGS

See Map 10, facing page 220

A RETURN must now be made to the first week in April, when a military expedition under the code-name 'Avonmouth' was ready to carry out a landing at Narvik, for which German reactions to the laying of mines (Operation Wilfred) were expected to provide the justifying circumstance.[1] The Commander was Major-General P. J. Mackesy, G.O.C. 49th Division, who had served with distinction in the military mission in South Russia (1919–20) and commanded an infantry brigade in Palestine two years before the war. His present force had as its first échelon the 24th (Guards) Brigade, consisting of the 1st Scots Guards, 1st Irish Guards, and 2nd South Wales Borderers, under Brigadier the Hon. W. Fraser, to be followed by a second échelon consisting of Chasseurs Alpins and other French and Polish troops. The original instructions, dated 5th April, said that the object of the expedition would be 'to secure the port of Narvik and the line of communications inland as far as the Norwegian-Swedish frontier.' At a later stage, an advance on Gällivare was contemplated, as was an eventual withdrawal, to be preceded by demolition of the ore port. Two general conditions attached to the conduct of the expedition were that it would not land in face of serious Norwegian opposition, and that it would obey approved instructions designed to obviate the bombing of civilians in the course of land, sea, or air operations. The Scots Guards were already embarked in a transport in the Clyde, where a second transport contained the Hallamshire battalion of the 146th Brigade, intended for Trondheim, when, as we have already seen,[2] the news of the German ships at sea caused the sailing of the force to be cancelled.

Next day (9th April), when the first measures to meet the German invasion were hurriedly improvised, it was the Hallamshire battalion which was instructed to sail for Narvik, while General Mackesy and the Scots Guards were to be sent at the same time to secure an unnamed base 'after the port has been cleared of enemy vessels by the Royal Navy'. But before the two battalions, having shared their information and the mortar ammunition of which the Scots Guards were destitute, had got as far as Scapa, a third set of instructions had been signed in London. General Mackesy's object

---
[1] See p. 25.
[2] P. 26.

would now be 'to eject the Germans from the Narvik area and to establish control of Narvik itself', using the Norwegian military centre of Harstad as the first point of landing, if possible, but making no landing in face of serious opposition until 'sufficient troops' were available. These instructions, which were brought to Scapa from the War Office by the Deputy Director of Military Operations at midday on the 11th, were accompanied by a hand-written note from General Ironside which made the uncertain position little clearer. General Mackesy would have 'four battalions together, the whole arriving thirty hours after the arrival of two battalions', and 'the other two battalions' at a further interval of a week. The enemy in Narvik were estimated at 3,000 men and 'must have been knocked about by naval action', and it was supposed that the General might be able to 'work up' the local Norwegians round Harstad. But the vital point in the message was near the end, where Sir Edmund Ironside wrote: 'You may have a chance of taking advantage of naval action and you should do so if you can. Boldness is required.'[1]

Accordingly, General Mackesy with an advance party of two companies of Scots Guards and some staff, including the naval Chief of Staff, Captain L. E. H. Maund, transferred to the cruiser *Southampton*, which sailed for Harstad at 1 p.m. on 12th April, about twenty-four hours after the receipt of the final orders at Scapa. As we have just seen, he had reason to expect that he would be followed by the other half of the Scots Guards battalion and the Hallamshire, by four more battalions arriving very quickly, and by two more a week later. What actually happened was, that the two and a half battalions completing the 24th (Guards) Brigade, and the Hallamshire and two other battalions constituting the 146th Brigade, all left home waters for North Norway the same day as the General. Travelling in transports and therefore more slowly, they were about 130 miles from their destination when, at 8 p.m. on the 14th, the naval escort under Vice-Admiral Layton received orders to divert the whole of the 146th Brigade to Namsos.[2]

Meanwhile, at about the same time as General Mackesy left Scapa for North Norway in the *Southampton*, the Naval Commander of the expedition, Admiral of the Fleet the Earl of Cork and Orrery, set sail from Rosyth in the *Aurora*. He out-ranked the Commander-in-Chief, Home Fleet, whose post he had held from 1933 to 1935, and had been brought back to the Admiralty in September 1939 by Mr Churchill to organise Plan 'Catherine', his scheme for forcing an entry to the Baltic.[3] By general repute quick to act, Lord Cork had been given no written instructions for Norway, but had been orally

---

[1] See Appendix A (1), p. 249.
[2] See p. 69.
[3] Churchill, Vol. I, p. 364.

briefed on 10th and 11th April with varying degrees of informality by the First Sea Lord, by a meeting of the Military Co-ordination Committee, and by Mr Churchill in his car travelling from the Admiralty to the House.[1] Seven cruisers were assigned to his command, two of them only until the convoy had been discharged, one net-layer, also for temporary duty, and five destroyers. As the Admiral approached the Norwegian coast on the 14th, he received the signal previously mentioned[2] from the naval force which had fought at Narvik, in which Admiral Whitworth, while citing a Norwegian estimate that there were 1,500–2,000 enemy troops in the town, had stated his conviction that it could be taken by direct assault by a small landing-force without fear of serious opposition, given naval support of the strength which had been used there the previous day.[3] Lord Cork thereupon ordered the *Southampton* to meet him that night in Skejfiord, with a view to a landing at Narvik on the morning of the 15th by 350 Scots Guards carried in the cruiser and a party of 200 seamen and Marines from the ships present. But the difficulties of wireless transmission in North Norway (due to the iron in the mountains as well as to weather conditions) prevented the *Southampton* from receiving this or a second message, conveying the proposal direct to the General, until the troops on board had already been landed elsewhere. General Mackesy, in his reply to the Admiral, expressed doubts as to the feasibility of the scheme, but said that troops could be supplied from the transports following his advance party, which were due on the 15th. On top of this, there came an Admiralty telegram to Lord Cork, saying: 'We think it imperative that you and the General should be together and act together and that *no* attack should be made except in concert.'[4] The first proposal was therefore abandoned, and the *Aurora* went round during the night of 14th/15th April from the north side of the Vestfiord to the waters off Harstad.

Narvik itself, the object of the expedition, has already been briefly described,[5] but the land operations for its recapture cover a much wider area. The north shore of the Vestfiord, which runs in a generally north-easterly direction towards Narvik, consists of the long chain of the Lofoten-Vesteraalen Islands with Skjelfiord near their outermost extremity. The innermost of the larger islands, Hinnöy, with the small port of Harstad on its eastern coast facing the mainland, provided the nearest point to Narvik with facilities for a base, even on the smallest

---

[1] Lord Cork and Orrery: *My Naval Life* (Hutchinson, 1942), p. 192.
[2] See p. 51.
[3] This signal was made at 10.27 a.m. to the Admiralty and repeated to Commander-in-Chief, Home Fleet, H.M.S. *Aurora*, and H.M.S. *Southampton*: see Admiral Whitworth's Despatch, Sec. 66.
[4] Despatch by Lord Cork, Sec. I (6).
[5] See p. 3.

scale. From Harstad to Narvik is about thirty-five miles as the crow flies, but the shortest sea approach is through the narrow channel of the Tjeldsund, running south-west of Harstad into the mouth of the Ofotfiord, so that the journey involves two sides of an equilateral triangle, while the third side gives the distance direct. North of Harstad the Vaagsfiord leads into the Andfiord, which in turn leads to the open sea at the north-eastern extremity of the chain of islands. Finally, east of Harstad the mainland on the opposite side of the Vaagsfiord is indented by the Salangen, Gratangen, and a third small fiord, the heads of which give access to the main road running north from the Narvik-Öyjord[1] ferry.

Accordingly, General Mackesy, having reached the Vaagsfiord in the early morning of the 14th, hid his soldiers between decks while he made immediate but circumspect contact with the civil authorities at Harstad. He established that there were no Germans in the area and that our forces would be well received by the local population, and initiated arrangements for a base. Then, in the light of the information acquired, he crossed to the mainland, and by 2 p.m. the two companies of Scots Guards carried in the *Southampton* had been disembarked a few miles west of Sjövegan, at the entrance to an inner reach of the Salangenfiord, called the Sagfiord. This placed them about twenty miles from Fossbakken, a point on the main road north where Norwegian patrols were stationed to hold in check the German advance from Narvik, which was aimed at Bardufoss airfield and the nearby regimental depot for the Tromsö area. General Mackesy in his official report says that the early contact with our troops 'had an important effect upon the spirit and determination of the Norwegian forces.'[2] The bearing and discipline of the Guardsmen, who in all their long history had never before been brought within the Arctic Circle, were much admired, though their unfamiliarity with winter warfare was equally apparent.

Three big transports, escorted by the battleship *Valiant* and nine destroyers, arrived off Harstad on the morning of 15th April. The 1st Irish Guards, 1st Scots Guards (less the two companies referred to above), and Brigade Headquarters landed the same day, as did the 3rd Light Anti-Aircraft Battery, R.A., but without its guns. The 2nd South Wales Borderers landed on the 16th. The size of the force was doubled, however, by the number of divisional, base, and lines-of-communication troops, including a railway construction company intended for use at Narvik. Unloading of the transports and clearing of the quays were completed by the 17th and 18th respectively, but the confusion of the start had its counterpart in a more complete confusion in the arrival. The convoy had not been loaded

---

[1] Pronounced 'uy-you're'.
[2] Despatch by Lord Cork, Appendix A, Sec. 7.

tactically, so that every cargo had to be sorted on landing and some items even re-despatched to Namsos. In addition, the troops had three kit-bags per man, to carry their seventeen items of special clothing, thirty-five pieces in all—scale of issue as for winter garrison in Tientsin plus items got ready for Finland. No motor transport had accompanied the first flight of the expedition, originally designed for Narvik and the railway, and local hirings could not meet the need for road movement as the troops went farther afield. The Irish Guards received their trucks in time to push them into the sea, unused, for want of cargo space at the final evacuation. On 21st April the general congestion was still so great that the men of a large labour force, which was included in 1,141 new arrivals, were by General Mackesy's orders sent home in the ship which had just brought them. These administrative difficulties could be, and were, surmounted by time and trouble. More serious, because more lasting, were the physical disadvantages of the base.

Harstad had a population of less than 4,000, with transport and storage facilities roughly in correspondence with its size. The British landings inevitably attracted the attention of enemy aircraft operating from Trondheim, and the first slight casualties from this cause occurred while the landings were still in progress. Relations with the inhabitants were not helped by the fact that our anti-aircraft provision could not at first protect the town: a full week elapsed before the first pair of guns was landed. The three ship quays at Harstad were all designed for the coastal traffic, including coal bunkering: only one of them had cranes and there was anchorage for about half a dozen vessels. Most of the sheltered-water area was unfortunately far too deep to anchor in. Our larger ships had therefore, in any case, to depend upon a ferry service between ship and shore. In addition, there was the risk of air attack in fine weather and the hazard of coming too close inshore during the frequent snow blizzards. Consequently, disembarkation and unloading of convoys involved on each occasion a serious temporary strain on local water transport. Further, whatever was brought to the base was liable to require redistribution by water, since we were using an island military base for a mainland operation. A fleet of about 120 Norwegian fishing craft equipped with paraffin engines, popularly known as Puffers, was therefore assembled—a rather cumbersome device which involved all the difficulties of employing civilians under conditions of military service.

The naval base was developed off Skaanland, a tiny village on the mainland fifteen miles south of Harstad, in the angle where the principal channel of the Tjeldsund turns west, providing extensive anchorage for even the biggest ships. A Royal Marine Fortress Unit prepared sites for coast defence guns, but the campaign ended before the completion of this work or of the carefully planned anti-submarine defences by net and mine. Defence therefore depended upon the patrol vessels which were stationed from the outset at either end of the anchorage and base area. A German submarine had been located and destroyed, and its list of North Sea submarine dispositions captured, as the expedition was first approaching Harstad on 15th April, but there were no further submarine attacks upon the base. This was chiefly attributable to the assiduous work of the destroyers and other escort vessels (including about thirty trawlers), which in the first week sank one submarine and harried a second out of the Ofotfiord, while the *Warspite's* aircraft sank a third. But it was due in part to natural difficulties, such as the lightness of the nights, and also to serious technical defects in the enemy's torpedoes. Another uncovenanted mercy was the failure of the Germans to make more than a single attempt to mine the Tjeldsund from the air. For in other respects they made much use of their air supremacy to harass our ships, sparing some bombers to fly over from Vaernes even before the collapse of the Aandalsnes and Namsos expeditions freed their main force to operate in this area. The two Bofors guns already mentioned were transferred from Harstad at the end of April, more being added a week later, but it was not until 8th May that the first heavy anti-aircraft artillery was put ashore by motor landing-craft. Two anti-aircraft cruisers and two sloops were also sent out to operate in this area. Nevertheless, light nights, clear skies, and windless air later on made bombing possible from very great heights, and ships became unable to anchor. Powerfully defended cruisers might be attacked five times in a day; destroyers could never feel safe; and of the little trawlers no less than half were sunk outright. Harstad shared the fortunes of Skaanland with 140 air raids in eight weeks, though it suffered relatively slight damage, there being no objectives on land comparable with the nearby shipping.

Lord Cork, after his initial proposal to try to seize Narvik by an immediate *coup de main* on 15th April had proved inacceptable, still hoped for a direct assault to be launched at the next earliest moment. This assault, if successful, could be expected to solve the base problem while gaining for us far more important advantages as regards our prestige and the whole strategic position in Scandinavia. Lord Cork was sure that the implied directive for the operation was to capture Narvik by the quickest, rather than the most economical, means. Narvik harbour and the Rombaksfiord beyond were reconnoitred by two of Admiral Whitworth's destroyers, which on the night of the 15th signalled the opinion that a landing on the far side of the town, to advance on Narvik from the north-east, would not be opposed by fixed defences and might be covered by destroyers' guns. During the same day, however, the Admiral and the General had met for the first time, to make the discovery that they had left the United Kingdom with 'diametrically opposite views as to what was required'.[1]

In General Mackesy's view the tenor of his instructions, which had not envisaged any immediate landing whether at Harstad or elsewhere if he were faced with enemy opposition, was that he should contact the Norwegians (as he had done) and then prepare a careful plan of operations. His message to Lord Cork on 14th April[2] shows, indeed, that he did not interpret his orders as forbidding him in all circumstances to consider a *coup de main* against Narvik; but at best they provided a very serious practical obstacle, since they were the reason why the force had not been organised for an opposed landing. It was now in process of getting ashore at Harstad; it must sort its material before it could fight; and it had arrived with no artillery, 'practically no mortar ammunition', and no landing craft of any kind.

Moreover, the terrain of the Narvik peninsula outside the actual harbour front, where wreckage precluded landing, offered special difficulties. The shore line is of rocks interspersed with some small beaches, ideal for the siting of machine guns. The ground behind rises quickly to a low crest, which severely limits the effectiveness of fire from ships' guns. Across narrow waters, at Ankenes to the southwest and at Öyjord to the north-east, there are dominant heights from which enemy machine guns could take the landing areas in reverse. All these hazards were made worse by the weather, as the General testifies in his official report:

> Although nobody without personal experience of Arctic winter conditions can possibly picture the climatic difficulties we experienced in the early days, a word or two of description may not be out of place. The country was covered by snow up to 4 feet or more in depth. Even at sea-level there were several feet of snow. Blizzards, heavy snowstorms, bitter winds and very low night temperatures were normal. Indeed until the middle of May even those magnificent mountain soldiers, the French Chasseurs Alpins, suffered severely from frostbite and snow blindness. Troops who were not equipped with and skilled in the use of skis or snowshoes were absolutely incapable of operating tactically at all. I had no such troops at my disposal when I first landed. Shelter from the weather was of vital importance.[3]

General Mackesy's objections also depended in part upon the prevailing uncertainty as to the true situation of the Germans in

---

[1] Despatch by Lord Cork, I, Sec. 10.
[2] See p. 147.
[3] Despatch by Lord Cork, Appendix A, Sec. 6.

Narvik. Had the two naval actions really demoralised them? How numerous were they? What allowances ought to be made for the addition of destroyer crews to the original military force and the subtraction of such units as had been moved forward against the Norwegians? What was the value of the defences constructed by the Norwegians at Narvik, which were known to include some trenches as well as the pill boxes, and to what extent would the Germans have improved upon them already? The answer to the question about morale is still conjectural: the Mayor of Narvik claims to have observed a complete collapse on 13th April and a quick recovery next day, though he also noted that General Dietl's headquarters was withdrawn up the railway the following week and did not return.[1] As for numbers, they were more than doubled from the crews of sunk destroyers, for whom there was an ample supply of machine guns and rifles captured at Elvegaard, but General Dietl valued these men more as technicians than as soldiers—514 of them were apparently sent home through Sweden after the first week[2]—and used them chiefly to guard the remoter parts of the railway. Regarding defences, it is clear that the operations of the garrison were greatly hampered by the non-arrival of all three of the expected supply ships and one out of two tankers, though thirty-four goods trucks with 350 tons of provisions were accepted in south Sweden on 19th April for transit to Narvik. Moreover, the mountain artillery had been washed overboard from the destroyer decks on the rough voyage; guns dismantled from ships made at best an unhandy substitute. Ten aircraft were wrecked on the ice of Lake Hartvigvatn when four mountain guns were flown in on the 14th, and the experiment was not repeated. We may also notice that Hitler himself in the week following the second naval battle was strongly though fitfully inclined to cut his losses by abandoning Narvik and that, as late as 23rd April, demolitions observable from the sea marked Dietl's receipt of instructions to get ready for evacuation 'if necessary'.

The British General, however, had to make up his mind on the very little information available to him, though it was a reasonable supposition that the enemy's difficulties were greater than could be seen. His judgement on 15th April and later was that for him to attempt an opposed landing in the circumstances outlined above was an entirely unwarranted course of action from any military standpoint and could only result in the 'snows of Narvik being turned into another version of the mud of Passchendaele'. He was supported by many of the senior officers on the spot, naval as well as military, and (as we have seen)[3] his policy did not surprise the Director of Military

---

[1] Broch, Theodor: *The Mountains Wait*, pp. 97–109.
[2] Sundell, p. 228. These may have been men from merchant ships.
[3] See p. 70.

Operations at the War Office. Nevertheless it must be left an open question whether Lord Cork's instinct for the offensive, while it involved grave risk of heavy loss, might not have justified itself in the event. Narvik is surrounded on three sides by salt water, which we controlled; the Navy was present in great strength; the Germans were on the defensive, considerably dispersed, on remote and unfamiliar ground among a hostile population. An improvised attack, such as Lord Cork wanted, could almost certainly have won Narvik for us on the evening of 13th April, if troops had been dispatched from home in time to make it. Thereafter its chance of success was daily growing less, which explains and perhaps justifies Lord Cork's impatience of delay. But General Mackesy, rather than reorganise his men, the first brigade of a larger force, in a desperate hurry for what might prove a desperate venture, planned to act more scientifically, surely, and slowly[1].

Accordingly, Lord Cork reported on the 16th that the attack proposed for that day had been abandoned. But on the following afternoon the two commanders received a reply from the Admiralty and War Office pressing for an immediate assault, on the basis that the *Warspite* would be available in support for only two or three more days, and that the Chasseurs Alpins (diverted to the needs of Central Norway) would not be sent to strengthen the force even if it waited. The project for an attack was then renewed by the Admiral, who suggested that they should 'gamble on the chance' that the enemy's morale could be broken by the overwhelming gunfire from a battleship, two cruisers, and eight destroyers; and at a further conference between the Admiral and the General on the 18th the latter agreed with evident misgivings to have troops ready for a landing if the result of a naval bombardment satisfied him that the task was feasible. The troops would then be put ashore under cover of a second bombardment. After this, General Mackesy set out upon a personal reconnaissance of Narvik in the *Aurora*, which was delayed by a false report of German reinforcements arriving in five destroyers.

On his return to Harstad on the 20th he informed the Chief of the Imperial General Staff of his opinion as follows:—

> Owing to the nature of the ground, flat trajectory of naval guns, and the impossibility of locating the concealed machine guns, I am convinced that the naval bombardment cannot be militarily effective, and that a landing from open boats in the above conditions must be ruled out absolutely. Any attempt of the sort would involve NOT the neutralisation but the destruction of the 24th (Guards) Brigade.

The General proceeded to argue with increased urgency that in the circumstances the only effective bombardment would be one which induced the enemy to surrender before the troops landed, as at

---
[1] See Maund, Rear-Admiral L. E. H.: *Assault from the Sea*, pp. 34, 52, 58.

Duala in the Cameroons in 1914, but this would require the inclusion of the town itself in the target area. He therefore formally raised the point that such action might ruin relations with the Norwegians and was in any case contrary to the instructions from the Cabinet,[1] which he considered, only a direct Cabinet order could waive. This difficulty was eventually met by the restriction of the bombardment area, agreed between Lord Cork and General Mackesy. Tromsö Radio was used to urge evacuation, and in the upshot the civilian loss of life throughout the siege operations was very small. We may also note that the blizzards which became frequent from the 20th onwards made it easy to agree with the General's contention that the snow was a really serious obstacle. The Admiral had tested the conditions in his own person and with a section of Marines and 'found it easy to sink to one's waist, and to make any progress was exhausting'.

Meanwhile, the three British battalions were disposed as follows. The Irish Guards were brought round by sea to occupy positions at the Bogen inlet on the north side of the Ofotfiord, about ten miles in a straight line from Narvik, but thirty miles distant by road and ferry. They were billeted in two or three small villages, the easternmost of which was laid open by the withdrawal of some Norwegian volunteers to a possible attack by German patrols operating across the snowbound road from Bjerkvik. But there was only one exchange of shots during the four weeks of the battalion's stay. The 2nd South Wales Borderers, who were brought to Skaanland, were about twice as far from Narvik on the same road; but both battalions having completed their moves on 19th April could easily be embarked from the positions they now occupied in the event of an assault on the town after naval bombardment. This left one half of the Scots Guards in reserve at the base, the other half being at Sjövegan.

The final decision, not to attempt an opposed landing at Narvik but to try to induce the enemy to surrender outright by a powerful naval bombardment, the troops going in only on display of the white flag ashore, was taken by Lord Cork on the 21st, on which day news had been received of the Government decision placing him in supreme command of the expedition. Heavy snow had begun to fall the previous day and continued without real break until the 24th, the date fixed for the attack and, as the Officer Commanding the Irish Guards observed, the twenty-fifth anniversary of the landings in Gallipoli. For the bombardment, Lord Cork had his flag in the cruiser *Effingham*, and the other ships in the attack were the battleship *Warspite*, which fired some 150 rounds of common shell from her 15-inch guns, the cruisers *Aurora* and *Enterprise*, and the destroyer *Zulu*. The weather prevented the Fleet Air Arm from giving support from the *Furious*,

---

[1] See p. 253 for copy of Instructions to Govern the Conduct of Bombardment.

but it also prevented any intervention by German aircraft. The main bombardment, which was directed exclusively against military objectives, lasted about three hours, but it appeared to be lacking in depth and a thick carpet of fresh snow obscured every target. An outlying pier was shelled by the *Effingham* and a vessel alongside it was sunk, the *Enterprise* shelled both sides of the harbour entrance, and some damage was done to railway rolling-stock. A part of the military stores remaining at Elvegaard was also destroyed. But the all-important machine-gun defences, which were the chief obstacle to a landing, remained invisible and, presumably, undisturbed. The embarkation of the Irish Guards for the hypothetical case of a German surrender or a chance to exploit an uncertain situation by a quick dash ashore, for which the Guards had also laid their plans, was countermanded by Lord Cork just after they had gone aboard the *Vindictive* at Bogen. The result of the bombardment disappointed both the Admiral and the General. The former reported that weather conditions, which had been tempestuous as well as snowy, were entirely against a landing, while the low visibility prevented any estimate of the effect achieved by the bombardment. A later conclusion was that 'nothing indicated any intention to surrender', though a Norwegian who escaped from Narvik three days after the bombardment claimed that enemy casualties had been considerable.

On the day of the bombardment the first important reinforcements for the expedition, the 27th Demi-Brigade of Chasseurs Alpins, no longer held in reserve for Mauriceforce,[1] had left Scapa for Norway; it therefore became possible to develop the plan of action which General Mackesy had always intended to substitute for the much-discussed frontal attack on Narvik. This was to organise an advance by land against the Narvik peninsula from all three sides, so as to take both Ankenes and Öyjord and cut the railway at Hundalen, only eight miles from the Swedish frontier, causing Narvik to fall into our hands eventually 'like a ripe plum'. The Norwegians naturally enough had from the outset pressed for joint operations by their forces and ours to push the Germans back down the road, advancing from the positions they already occupied north of Narvik. Their point of view, which the British did not altogether share, was that, if the present might be regarded as a period of operational difficulty due to the snow, it would certainly be followed within a week or two by a period of operational impossibility due to the thaw. General Mackesy objected on principle to depriving his troops of any prospect of naval co-operation, but he had allowed a very limited degree of participa-

---

[1] See pp. 77, 79.

tion by the Scots Guards in the first Norwegian counter-attack, which was also launched on the day of the bombardment.

There had been some slight skirmishes with the advancing Germans as the Norwegians withdrew to Fossbakken, already mentioned. General Dietl then turned his attention to clearing the railway; by a surprise attack near Björnfjell he overwhelmed the Norwegian garrison that had escaped from Narvik on the 9th and secured control of the line from the frontier, substantially undamaged. But the Norwegians were able to bring in fresh troops from farther north, including two convoys from Kirkenes, for which British cruisers under Admiral Cunningham provided escort. These were troops which had been employed in the so-called Neutrality Watch and others newly mobilised, but all of them accustomed to the climate and terrain. They were therefore preparing a counter-attack towards Gratangen, west-south-west of Fossbakken, for which they now disposed of four battalions. The Germans employed two out of their three infantry battalions on this side of Narvik, making very effective use of small machine-gun posts, though these were as much as half a mile apart. They were, however, handicapped by the close British naval control of the fiord waters, which was maintained by a detached squadron of two cruisers and five destroyers under Captain L. H. K. Hamilton (H.M.S. *Aurora*); this forced the Germans to employ a long and difficult line of communications from Björnfjell down to Bjerkvik across the mountains north of Hartvigvatn. The Norwegian plan provided for a frontal attack from the north-east against the German post at Lapphaug, which is at the highest point on the road from Fossbakken before it descends again to the fiord-level at Gratangen. While the main forces were sent in there, one battalion was to advance due south over the mountain from a base on an arm of the fiord further north, so as to cut the German line of retreat.

It was agreed that the two companies of Scots Guards should hold a rear position for the main force, but they were not to be employed offensively. They were fitted out with snowshoes and camouflage cloaks from Norwegian stores and duly moved into Fossbakken when the Norwegians went forward to the attack. A heavy snow storm began on the 23rd and continued the next day when the attack opened. Its severity was such that a Norwegian battalion native to the country and expert on skis, not cumbered with heavy equipment, took eight hours to move less than two miles with a rise in height of about 300 feet. By 7 p.m. the 150 Germans in their entrenched position had repulsed the attack: three feet of snow had fallen in twenty-four hours and there was consequently no prospect of artillery support. Unfortunately for the Norwegians, the other wing of their attack had achieved rapid progress, and the men made their way down to the road at Gratangen, where the battalion could get shelter for the night. A second battalion was sent forward from reserve to support this right flank, but when morning came there was still a gap between the two Norwegian battalions; and the Germans, successful at Lapphaug, were able to surround the battalion at Gratangen, and opened machine-gun fire upon their position in the village. A part broke through at a cost of about 100 killed and wounded (three company commanders being among the dead) and about 150 taken prisoner.[1] The Norwegians had largely sacrificed one of their most efficient battalions; but the action was not without result as the Germans, to economise their forces, abandoned both Lapphaug and Gratangen within a day or two.

The Gratangen area was chosen by General Mackesy for the starting-point of an advance overland on Bjerkvik by two out of his three new battalions of French Chasseurs Alpins, though Lord Cork would have preferred to place them nearer Narvik in readiness for a direct attack. They landed on 28th April in the neighbourhood of Sjövegan, where General Béthouart conferred with the Norwegian General Fleischer before handing over the direct command of the demi-brigade to Lieut.-Colonel Valentini. The 14th Battalion was left for the moment in reserve, while the 6th was taken round by water to Gratangen for an advance up Labergdal, where on 1st May they made their first contact with the enemy. The Norwegians at this time had reorganised their expanding forces into two brigades. The 6th Brigade on the left, composed of three battalions and one mountain battery under the command of Colonel Löken, continued its fight in isolation, pressing the German outposts slowly back in the wilderness of mountains along the Swedish frontier. The 7th Brigade, composed of two battalions, one mountain battery, and one motorised battery, and commanded by Colonel Faye, held the right flank and worked in close co-operation with the French, who supplied two companies and a mortar section for the main line of advance along the road from Elvenes towards Bjerkvik. The two companies of Scots Guards were withdrawn to Harstad on 1st May, but the French were not only a far more numerous replacement, they were by definition mountaineers.

They included, however, only 70 ski troops to each battalion, which restricted their scouting; were short of mules and snowshoes, which slowed up the movement of supplies; and were unaccustomed to bivouacking in soft, deep snow (the depth was five feet on level ground at the top of Labergdal), which cost them as many casualties from frostbite as from enemy action, air attack included. On 4th May a battery of French colonial artillery was landed for support, and a day or two later the 14th joined the 6th Battalion in the line. But the

---

[1] Munthe-Kaas, Colonel O.: *The Campaign in Northern Norway*, p. 18.

intended manœuvre, by which the French advance up Labergdal was to turn the German defences along the main Bjerkvik road, was held up. By 10th May the French ski detachment had secured the top of the 3,000-foot mountain forming the west side of the pass, while the Norwegians were deployed ahead of them in the mountains on the east side: but along the road itself the Germans could not be dislodged from their position on the crest. It had taken ten painful days to advance five miles towards Narvik.

The British advance, made in conjunction with the Fleet and in little apparent relation with the plans or movements of the Norwegians, derived more profit from the thaw, which cleared away the snow at and near sea-level in the first few days of May, but like the French advance was without much immediate effect on the main issue. On the north side of the Ofotfiord, where the Irish Guards had been landed again at the Bogen inlet, the road to Narvik via Bjerkvik ran inland through deep snow. On the south side the road from Ballangen, opposite Bogen, was cut half way by the Skjomenfiord. The southern approach was chosen, and between 26th and 28th April the South Wales Borderers were brought across from Skaanland to Ballangen, followed by Brigade Advanced Headquarters on the 29th. The same day the South Wales Borderers, reinforced with a ski troop of the newly arrived Chasseurs Alpins, made an unopposed landing beyond Skjomnes at a small jetty west of Haakvik, only four miles from Ankenes and within range of German patrols. From Haakvik the advance continued along the main road to where it rounds the corner one and a half miles short of Ankenes. German artillery then opened fire, but a track along the shore gave enough cover for the troops to establish their forward position at Baatberget, on the very corner of the peninsula. A series of posts was also established along the lane leading inland from Haakvik as far as Lake Storvatn, to secure our flank against attack from the high ridge which runs from Ankenes in a south-easterly direction along the entire side of the Beisfiord. Brigadier Fraser while making a personal reconnaissance towards Ankenes was slightly wounded, and command devolved upon Lieut.-Colonel T. B. Trappes Lomax, O.C. 1st Scots Guards.

To threaten Ankenes was almost to threaten Narvik, which might at least be brought under close observation from across the water. There was also the hope that, as the weather improved, we might work round the head of the Beisfiord to the road which leads along its farther shore from Beisfiord village direct to Narvik. But the Germans were also alive to these possibilities. They had only one battalion of infantry and the naval battalion (less a little more than one company which General Dietl reallocated about the end of the month to his northern front) to cover Narvik, the railway, and Ankenes. Moreover, these troops, which had at first drawn their supplies from the *Jan*

Wellem, were now dependent on what could be brought from Sweden down the railway, often under fire. But their guns in Narvik covered the direct approaches to Ankenes; machine-gun posts at Beisfiord were easy to supply by seaplane; and at the use of the mountain terrain in between they showed themselves here as elsewhere adept. On 1st May a German patrol came down the mountain side at the north end of the Storvatn, and the following day a similar party of about a hundred men made a more serious counter-attack along the road towards Haakvik. The guns of the *Aurora* inflicted considerable losses on the enemy, who were beaten off, but we made no further progress on that side, although two British field guns were landed and brought immediately into action along the coast road on the 4th. Meanwhile the 12th Battalion Chasseurs Alpins had been allocated to this area. Serving under command of the Guards Brigade, they gradually took over the operation, being better suited to it than the South Wales Borderers, who could not move at all in the snow. On 9th May two French companies on snowshoes, supported by the ski-ing detachment, succeeded in dislodging the enemy from three main heights on the ridge north of the Storvatn; they could now look down on the waters of the Beisfiord. But the approach to Ankenes by that route was clearly a task for weeks rather than days.

The operations described above proceeded concurrently with a renewed demand for a direct assault on Narvik. But as that demand resulted in a largely distinct series of operations, in which British troops were not engaged, it will be more convenient to interrupt our narrative of events in the Narvik area at this stage, in order to see how the general strategy of the campaign had been affected by the abandonment of our operations in Central Norway. Already on the night of 29th/30th April one company of Scots Guards had been despatched from Harstad by destroyer, at the orders of the War Office, to forestall a possible paratroop landing by the enemy at Bodö. It was the first sign of a cloud in the south 'as small as a man's hand'.

CHAPTER XI

LAND OPERATIONS: GENERAL STRATEGY (PART 2)

ALTHOUGH the decision to evacuate our troops from Central Norway was not taken until 26th–27th April,[1] it is really the assignment of the second demi-brigade of Chasseurs Alpins to the far north, made after much discussion on the evening of 23rd April, which marks the moment when opinion in London began to revert to its original emphasis on Narvik as the main objective in Norway. In particular, the exigencies of the time factor, to which much consideration had been given in the plans made during the winter, were again being stressed: the British Prime Minister calculated that we might not have more than a fortnight left, in which to secure Narvik and arrive in strength at the Swedish frontier beyond, before the Germans, anticipating the moment (about two weeks later) when the thaw would put Lulea at their mercy, might issue an ultimatum to Sweden and prepare to seize the orefields. Thus the evacuation, which monopolised attention in London at the end of the month, at once simplified the strategic problem and emphasised its gravity.

The naval arrangements for the evacuation worked, as we have seen, with remarkable smoothness and discredited the pessimists who had feared a holocaust. This was the more impressive as it had proved impossible to challenge the enemy control of the air over the points of embarkation by the best efforts which our shore- or carrier-based aircraft could put forth, and a planned naval diversion, in the shape of a Fleet bombardment of the forts at Agdenes, had been cancelled at the last moment. But although the period of the evacuation, from the taking of the decision on 26th April to the arrival of the last Namsos convoy at Scapa on 5th May, was one of intense activity crowned by intense relief, the authorities in London were at no time oblivious of the underlying difficulties of the position in which we now found ourselves. The First Lord of the Admiralty had stated only a few days earlier that our biggest interest in southern Norway was to acquire a *point d'appui* on the coast for the eastern extremity of our intended mine barrage. He appeared then to think that we should still hold on to some suitable area which could be rendered unapproachable from the land side. But nothing came of this. It was

---

[1] See p. 80.

also proposed to contain large numbers of Germans in southern Norway by harassing operations, in which small parties landed by destroyer or submarine would demolish key points in the scanty network of communications and help to keep native resistance alive. This was first discussed in terms of a possible dispersion of the troops at Aandalsnes into small parties or as a likely employment for the newly-formed Independent Companies. A paper on the subject, drawn up by General Massy, was considered by the Chiefs of Staff on 4th May: he argued that, although the Norwegians might be deterred from co-operating by German ruthlessness, the enemy could be kept in a state of alarm and 'real and lasting damage' done by demolitions. The use of submarines, it was thought, would obviate the difficulty of concealing the arrival and departure of such parties; but a bigger problem was presented by the remoteness of the most suitable objectives from the coast. In the end, nothing came of this either. On the contrary, the sudden and complete abandonment of any attempt to contest control of that part of Norway in which seven-eighths of the population lived imposed a threefold handicap upon our strategy in the rest of the country.

Firstly, the Germans could now concentrate their attention upon the far north. Forces would automatically be released from other operations, and Trondheim provided the natural point of departure for a thrust towards Narvik by air, sea or land. In addition, they were now in a favourable position if they chose to harass our own East Coast ports by air attack, and might be able to impede to some extent the flow of reinforcements northwards. Secondly, we were less sure of the wholehearted support of the Norwegians, who were tempted to regard the German occupation of their country as an established fact, since the three unoccupied counties of North Norway were at least as remote in the eyes of the majority as the Scottish Highlands to the average Englishman. Moreover, they were only human in attributing the disaster to everybody else's shortcomings rather than to their own. The British Government had therefore strongly encouraged General Paget's attempt to evacuate the Norwegian forces from the Aandalsnes area to fight elsewhere; as one Minister put it, the retention of a Norwegian army in being would have great political value. The Foreign Office was very active in asseverating the seriousness of our intention to capture Narvik and at least hold on to territory in North Norway, and was instructed to denounce as a 'malicious falsehood' an obviously dangerous rumour that we were advising Norway to surrender. For the rest, it was hoped that our actions at Narvik might speak louder than words. Thirdly, our situation *vis-à-vis* the Swedes had become more delicate than ever. Their own reaction to Norway's need for help had been something less than quixotic, but it had been easy for them to question from the outset the value and sincerity of the help which Britain gave, and the story of our failure to save Trondheim, of which Swedish journalists had witnessed occasional episodes, lost nothing in the telling. Moreover, the support which we could offer if the Germans invaded their country was now limited practically to what could be sent through Narvik if both the port and the railway were captured in a usable condition before, or contemporaneously with, the invasion—a rather big supposition. The Supreme War Council thought of meeting this difficulty, if the worst came to the worst, by offering to pay compensation for the destruction of the iron mines whether by Swedish or Allied agency. How likely Sweden would be to agree to this may be judged by the fact, which was finally established on 7th May, of a recent interchange of letters between King Gustaf of Sweden and the German Führer confirming her neutral status. The anxiety of the British Government to get Narvik quickly was reinforced by legitimate doubts as to the likelihood that Sweden would continue in any serious degree to resist German pressure, much less support Allied measures.

Nevertheless, the evacuation of Central Norway was not all loss. For one thing, the allotment of reinforcements became a relatively easy task, limited by lack of shipping and by administrative difficulties in the reception area at Harstad, but not by the difficulty of finding men. The two battalions of the Foreign Legion and the four battalions of the Polish Brigade were dispatched at once to the north, as were the first five of the British Independent Companies. The second French Light Division was now stationed in the Clyde, where it was joined by the Chasseurs Alpins returned from Namsos, whom it was intended to refit and send on again to the north. A third French Light Division remained poised at Brest awaiting transport, and on 1st May it was agreed in principle that the British 5th Division might also be brought from France as reinforcement. Meanwhile five more Independent Companies were in course of formation, and there was even a notion of transferring Gurkhas to northern Europe. At all events, it was decided to establish a Corps headquarters for a force of about 30,000 men, and its intended commander was told in advance that he 'must plan and prepare for big things'.

What had happened in Central Norway helped also by showing the paramount importance of air protection. To provide it was not an easy task, since our resources were at this time hopelessly inferior to those of the enemy: the aircraft of an entire fighter squadron had been lost at Lesjaskog; and our anti-aircraft artillery had been depleted by the abandonment in the stress of the evacuation of all four batteries of guns which had been sent to Central Norway. But from this time onwards there was a more obvious sense of urgency in the handling of this problem in London. As regards aircraft, two (or even three) fighter squadrons were earmarked for use as soon as airfields could be made available in North Norway, including the squadron which had gained the expensive experience at the frozen lake; and a reconnaissance party to prospect for airfield sites was sent to the Narvik area on 30th April. The Chiefs of Staff had already in anticipation instituted a daily situation report to be made by the Air Ministry showing the practical result in terms of aircraft based there. On 1st May the Chairman of the Military Co-ordination Committee called the attention of the Chiefs of Staff to the fact that these were critical days for Narvik, which must expect concentrated attack the moment the evacuation was completed. He therefore urged the transfer of at least one of the carriers then stationed in the Trondheim area to cover the gap until our land-based aircraft could operate. As regards anti-aircraft guns, which were also considered in the note to the Chiefs of Staff cited above, the original provision of one light battery had already been supplemented by 36 more Bofors guns and a heavy battery of eight 3·7s, though another dangerous week was to pass before they were landed on Norwegian soil. But the matter was now considered by the Vice-Chiefs of Staff—who no doubt had in mind the important effect of a similar calculation regarding Trondheim, when the figure arrived at was only one-half as large—to see what we should have to provide as anti-aircraft defence for Narvik itself and for a naval anchorage, two airfields, and other key points in the area. Their estimate totalled 144 heavy and 144 light anti-aircraft guns, as against the figures of 48 and 60 actually allocated (including guns still mobilising in the United Kingdom). No further withdrawals could be made from our forces in France, which had about half as many guns as they required. To take the additional number of heavy guns from the air defence of Great Britain was judged possible: there were 900 guns to take from, though this represented only forty per cent. of authorised scale. To take the additional number of light guns for Narvik was, however, quite impossible, as home defence possessed no more than 166 guns (of which only 36 were mobile) or in terms of the scale a nine per cent. provision. Granted that an authorised scale for home defence may be expected to include a margin for accidents and argument, the figures offer a remarkable commentary upon our power at this time to undertake new oversea commitments within range of the German air force.

In other respects besides the measurement of artillery resources the evacuation coincided with a tightening-up of machinery for the conduct of the war, which might be expected in any case to follow what Mr Churchill called 'the first main clinch'[1] but which was probably expedited and intensified by the shock of its result. On 1st May the Prime Minister (Mr Neville Chamberlain), in order 'to obtain a

---

[1] Vol. I, p. 475.

greater concentration of the direction of the war',[1] reorganised the Military Co-ordination Committee so as to give an increased power of control to its chairman—a position which, it will be remembered, was held by Mr Churchill in his capacity as senior Service Minister except when the Prime Minister himself was present. The Chiefs of Staff Committee, while retaining its primary responsibility to the War Cabinet, was now to receive certain additional guidance. The Chairman of the Military Co-ordination Committee was made responsible for giving directions to the Chiefs of Staff Committee, which he might 'summon for personal consultation at any time'; he would in particular give directions for them to prepare plans, which would normally be submitted to the Military Co-ordination Committee before or instead of the War Cabinet; and he was to be provided with a 'suitable central staff' for this work—in practice the Military Wing of the War Cabinet Secretariat—the head of which was to serve as an additional full member of the Chiefs of Staff Committee. Major-General Ismay accordingly joined the Chiefs of Staff on 2nd May, and the new scheme may be assumed to have come fully into force with the next meeting of the Military Co-ordination Committee, which was held on 6th May. The fact that the latter committee came to an end with the change of Prime Minister four days later makes it impossible to pass judgement on the efficiency of the scheme; but it is not without importance for the strategy of the North Norway operations that the scheme was in operation just at this juncture.

Other minor structural changes were made at this time. One was the institution of a Narvik Committee, which met under the chairmanship of the Civil Lord of the Admiralty, to ensure that the administrative requirements for the defence of Narvik were handled expeditiously by all Departments concerned. This acted mainly as a clearing-house, the planning of the defence being expressly reserved as 'the responsibility of the Chiefs of Staff through the normal interservice machinery', but the arrangement shows a sense of urgency which had been less evident in the preceding month. On 8th May, as a natural sequel to the admission of Norwegian representatives to a part of the meeting of the Supreme War Council, it was agreed by the Prime Minister that Norway should be represented on the Allied Military Committee in London. Tentative arrangements were made by the Chiefs of Staff for Norwegian officers to serve in a liaison capacity in each of the Service Departments; they would then be in a position to attend meetings of the Committee when necessary. If the general military situation had developed more favourably in the next few weeks, this belated arrangement might have solved many liaison difficulties, especially regarding the provision of a necessary minimum

---

[1] Churchill, Vol. I, p. 506.

of material for the Norwegian forces, for which their Legation in London had made numerous ineffectual requests. As it was, the main result was to give a useful precedent for the immediate attachment of Belgian and Dutch officers when their countries were invaded on 10th May.

In so far as the operations against Narvik could be considered in isolation, the strategic effect of the decision to abandon Central Norway was relatively straightforward. One additional objective could be stated—'To preserve a part of Norway as a seat of government for the Norwegian King and people'[1]—and a second, namely to offset the reverse sustained by Allied arms farther south, was self-evident. The need to act quickly, before the German air force came north in strength, before Sweden was overrun, before the Norwegians (to say nothing of our friends in neutral countries) finally lost heart, was also very obvious in London. Troops were now available sufficient to intensify the hopes of Mr Churchill, who on the night of 27th/28th April addressed Lord Cork as follows:

> It is upon Narvik and the Gällivare orefields that all efforts must now be centred.... Here it is we must fight and persevere on the largest scale possible.... Plan out your scheme for establishing a strongly defended base and ask for all you want. Of course no large-scale operations can be conducted unless the port and town of Narvik are in our hands.

This was the first and perhaps the least explicit of a series of messages in which the Government renewed the pressure for an assault on Narvik, postponed since the naval bombardment of the 24th on account of the heavy falls of snow. Meanwhile, the authorities at home could give the attack their single-minded though distant support.

But a further distraction interposed itself. The French, it will be recalled, had at first cherished the hope that the whole of their force at Namsos might be able to withdraw overland into the north. This in the face of German air power was an obvious impossibility, but it gave place to a smaller scheme, approved by the British Government, for a fighting rearguard to contest the ground from Grong towards Mosjöen so as to delay the Germans, who might otherwise press forward towards Narvik. The commanders on the spot for a variety of reasons deemed this to be impracticable, and never carried out the proposal; but while the controversy still raged a small initial force was taken round by sea from Namsos to Mosjöen, so that the troops retiring overland might have a *point d'appui* on which to fall back. From this unpromising start there developed an involved discussion

---

[1] See Appendix A (8), p. 259.

as to the strategy which it was appropriate for us to adopt in relation to the whole of the long coastal strip separating the triumphant enemy garrison of Trondheim, with its outpost at Namsos, from the beleaguered enemy garrison at Narvik. The matter was not finally settled in principle until in practice the area was overrun by Germans. It involved the fundamental dilemma to which the inadequacy of our resources so often exposed us: we needed all our available air protection for the Narvik area, but by depriving our forces farther south of such protection we hastened *pro tanto* the speed of the German advance into the north, which in turn would render the air protection we were now zealously providing in the Narvik area either less effective or more expensive or both. The answer to the question about air protection would in turn settle the size of the ground forces to be employed, since it was now taken for granted that only small units widely dispersed could hope to escape or at least to survive the unhampered attentions of German aircraft. General Massy, who refused to dismiss the notion that we might be able not merely to stop but to throw back the Germans and renew our own advance south, wanted a considerable force to hold the Mo-Mosjöen area and pleaded for the establishment of a proper base there, with a reasonable equipment of anti-aircraft artillery and an airfield. In his opinion nothing else would make certain of holding up the Germans at a safe distance from Narvik. This view was shared by General Gamelin and the French Government, which continued to express anxiety about the security of Mosjöen as late as 9th May—the day before the Germans attacked it. The other view, which owed something to the recent advocacy of guerrilla warfare as a means of distracting large numbers of Germans in the south of Norway, supposed that no systematic regular defence would be called for. The Germans were to be stopped by demolitions along the road, by guerrilla activities on their flanks, by raising the countryside against them, and by preparing to deal firmly with whatever small parties they might land from the sea or the air. This was to be the work of the Independent Companies, which were so organised as to need air defence neither for themselves nor for their base.

Broadly speaking, it was the second point of view that won the day. Of the three coastal ports south of Narvik the nearest, Bodö, was given a garrison of one company from Lord Cork's forces; a small scale of anti-aircraft defence was intended, and the idea of constructing some kind of landing ground also actively pursued. But both Mo and Mosjöen were to be left unprotected from the air, as 'the only course open to us would be to attempt to deny these two places to the enemy for as long as possible by means of small easily-maintained forces, of the type which were being put ashore'. The War Office had shown foresight in deciding as early as April 18th to provide the Independent Companies to which the description refers, five of which (as previously noted) were ready to proceed overseas at the end of the month.

The strength of a Company was about 20 officers and 270 other ranks, all of them volunteers, and all drawn from the Territorial Army except the officers, who included a small number of Indian Army and other Regulars. Scissorsforce—the official name derived from the intended function of the five companies—was placed under the command of Acting-Colonel C. McV. Gubbins, with a staff approximating to that of an infantry brigade.[1] Each Company was divided into three platoons consisting of three sections each commanded by an officer, and the war establishment included sappers, signals, a support section of four Bren guns, and, last but not least, some Norwegian interpreters. For the essential feature of the Independent Company was its ability to operate throughout as a self-contained unit based on the country in which it found itself. They had no transport of their own, though the intention had been to allocate some trawlers and drifters to their exclusive use. Equipment included Alpine rucksacks, snowshoes, Arctic boots, sheepskin coats, and a five-day mountain ration of pemmican. It also included £4,000 to each Company in hard cash. The Independent Companies were not, however, trained or equipped to bear the brunt of a determined enemy attack, and in this respect were made the victims of a twofold miscalculation. On the one hand they had been designed for guerrilla warfare in which the local population would be playing a large part. A historically minded Minister put it to the Military Co-ordination Committee, with the Prime Minister's approval, that they should aim at making Norway a 'running sore' to the Germans in the manner of the Peninsular War. But the previous meeting of the same Committee had recognised that this result would be largely dependent on Norwegian co-operation, 'of which, so far, there had been little sign.' This might be disputed in detail; what cannot be disputed is that in the area of the fighting in which the Companies took part the population was in any case too small and too scattered for serious co-operation. On the other hand, the vigour of the German drive forward along a difficult route exceeded all expectations, even after allowing for the effects of our failure to establish the rear-guard from Namsos. On 8th May the nearest enemy was believed to be 100 miles from Mosjöen; on the 11th he was there.

General Massy's plan having been rejected, mainly on the ground that we must concentrate our resources in the area nearest Narvik, it was a natural sequel that responsibility for the forces concerned, being regarded as an appendage to the Narvik operations, should be trans-

---

[1] See Appendix A (7), p. 257.

ferred to Lord Cork. The policy was formulated for him, at his request, on 5th May; twenty-four hours later the Independent Companies were placed under his command. The Instruction makes no mention of any corresponding increase in his naval responsibilities, which is perhaps remarkable, as one of General Massy's arguments for the establishment of a base in the Bodö-Mo-Mosjöen area was his belief that otherwise German air power would enable enemy forces to be moved up the coast by sea. On 1st May, after the Chiefs of Staff had considered a Note by the Chairman of the Military Co-ordination Committee, the Chief of the Naval Staff undertook to ensure such dispositions as would prevent German sea-borne expeditions from landing at Mosjöen, Mo, or Bodö. This was to some extent modified on the 5th, when the Chiefs of Staff agreed 'that as regards naval patrols, Bodö should take precedence over Mosjöen and Mo'. On 10th May, as the story will show, the enemy made his descent from the sea, between Mosjöen and Mo, unimpeded by any special precautionary patrol.

Meanwhile, the full attention of the home authorities had reverted —for the last time, as it proved—to that most intractable of problems, the assault on Narvik. The London end of the story is quickly told. On 28th April, when it first became clear that the size of force might justify the employment of a corps commander, it was resolved to send out Lieutenant-General C. J. E. Auchinleck at once, in the belief that the change might lead to the immediate capture which the Government desired. But time was allowed to pass while a corps headquarters was collected, and, six days later, the Chiefs of Staff, in re-drafting the object of Operation Rupert at Lord Cork's request, noted that the definition would be useful for the Instructions to be issued to the General, 'who would be leaving for Narvik [sic] within the next few days'. On 30th April General Gamelin had sent the Chief of the Imperial General Staff a reminder of the time factor: '*Il faut faire vite pour ne pas être devancés*',[1] a point which was put even more forcibly to Lord Cork by Mr Churchill as : 'Every day that Narvik remains untaken, even at severe cost, imperils the whole enterprise'. On 3rd May Lord Cork gave orders to prepare for the assault, only to report on the night of 5th/6th May a series of military objections which 'with great reluctance' he referred to the judgement of His Majesty's Government.

The Chiefs of Staff proposed to send a reply which, while refusing on principle to advise on tactics, would probably have been read as encouraging Lord Cork to proceed. But the War Cabinet preferred to ask for his personal appreciation first; the same telegram mentioned that General Auchinleck would be joining him on 12th May. Lord

---

[1] Gamelin, t. III, p. 372.

Cork's appreciation next day showed that he himself favoured action —he did not consider success certain, but 'It is quite certain that by not trying no success can be gained'—but had now decided to await the new general. The Chiefs of Staff then sent a further reply, approved by the War Cabinet, to the effect that they would welcome vigorous action, that he would be supported in taking risks, and that Auchinleck's coming should be left out of his calculations. But the chance, if chance it was, was allowed to pass. Lord Cork's next telegram announced that he was now committed to other preliminary operations, for which he selected the French troops, and he shortly afterwards asked approval for the transfer of the whole of the British brigade to Bodö and Mo. Neither he nor General Mackesy believed that the tide of German advance which had just set in from that direction could be stemmed by Independent Companies. His proposal was accordingly accepted, subject to the two conditions that it must not lengthen the delay in taking Narvik and must not lead to any additional demands for anti-aircraft guns.

Thus the situation a month after the German invasion of Norway, on the eve of their other advances into more vital areas which were to distract the attention of the Allied authorities from any more brooding over lost opportunities in the far north, could be summarised as slightly qualified disappointment. Although all southern Norway was lost to us and no kind of operations seemed likely to be renewed there, Sweden had not been invaded nor coerced into any serious breach of her neutrality. We knew that we could not hold the intermediate zone south of Bodö against prolonged and determined attack, but five Independent Companies were in position and a brigade of Regulars would be moving south to form a stronger line. Our failure hitherto to take Narvik appeared inexplicable in London, but there were nine battalions of French and Polish troops investing it as well as two Norwegian brigades, and high hopes were entertained of General Auchinleck. How we should exploit the victory when won was a little uncertain. We proposed to extend our forces as far as Kirkenes, where the arrival of a battalion as a token force might help the Norwegians to hold the Russian frontier. Soviet intentions were still uncertain: there were persistent rumours of the presence of German troops at Murmansk. The King of Norway would be securely established, though in a limited area, and we should have redeemed a promise—which was not without value for world opinion as well as for the retention of the Norwegian mercantile marine under our control. Narvik itself on closer inspection was no longer coveted by the Navy to make a 'Gibraltar of the North', if only on account of the distance from the open sea, but we hoped to establish it as a place of arms, well protected from air attack, which the Germans would make repeated, costly, and ineffectual efforts to recapture. It was assumed that the ore port and the ore railway, in so far as they were still intact, would be destroyed by the Germans in their retreat to the Swedish frontier. As a long-term policy we were prepared to undertake big repairs to restart the flow of ore for our own use. The more immediate problem, so often discussed, was that of anticipating the Germans at the orefields. From Narvik to the frontier might have to be traversed on foot, all heavy equipment being discarded, with a view to using the railway beyond, in neutral territory, to Kiruna as soon as German action against Sweden gave us the occasion; alternatively, there were thoughts of improvising a light brigade to move across country with sledges. In any case the establishment of two airfields in the Narvik area should mean that, so long as we could afford the wastage of aircraft involved in their use (about which doubts had already been expressed) we should be in a position, if the worst came to the worst, either to bomb the orefields themselves or to stop up the outlet by mining Lulea harbour.

From 10th May onwards the launching of the great German offensive in the West reduced Norway to the status of a minor concern for Ministers in London, to say nothing of Paris, where two members of the Norwegian Government had just been conferring with the French authorities and found that they saw eye to eye about the military shortcomings of the British.[1] The formation of the Churchill Government and ancillary changes, such as the creation of the office of Defence Minister as an attribute, or rather a potent instrument, of the premiership, or the replacement of the Military Co-ordination Committee by the Defence Committee, though resulting so largely from the earlier events of the Norway campaign, would need to be considered in a wider context than that of the remaining events in the Scandinavian story. That story, though less regarded than before, was scarcely less disappointing, for it was on 10th May that a German seaborne attack between Mosjöen and Mo ruined our hopes of 'selling ground slowly and dearly' to the south of Narvik and gave a fresh shock to Norwegian confidence in us, which was not to be offset by the general reassurances given to their Ministers as they passed through London that day homeward bound. But apart from refusing any special provision to meet this crisis, such as direct convoys from home to the intermediate area, the home authorities did not interfere appreciably with the dispositions made by Lord Cork (or General Auchinleck) to stem the advance which in little more than a fortnight was to threaten Bodö. On 14th May, indeed, the new Prime Minister telegraphed to Lord Cork, 'I hope you will get Narvik cleaned up as soon as possible, and then work southwards

---
[1] Koht, Dr Halvdan: *Fraa Skanse til Skanse*, pp. 118–120.

with increasing force'; but a study of the map would suggest that the operative part of the message is at the beginning. The capture of Narvik was still urgently desired, and the success with which the French on the 13th carried out an opposed landing at Bjerkvik to secure the coastline facing the town only strengthened the demand from London for the final assault. Local reasons caused delay and postponement, while a number of telegrams from the Chiefs of Staff and the Prime Minister himself expressed impatience and dissatisfaction. As late as the 20th Mr Churchill still found time to telegraph that delay was costing more men and ships than vigorous action, and the issue of a direct order for the assault was considered by the Cabinet but postponed.

The delay was not due primarily to the denial at this stage of needed reinforcements. In spite of the grave shortage of anti-aircraft artillery in this country, the Chiefs of Staff, meeting at 10.30 p.m. on 10th May, resolved to let a further regiment sail, which had then completed loading for North Norway. It is true that no more was spared—notwithstanding a report which claimed that the topography of North Norway rendered any given quantity of anti-aircraft guns only one-half as effective as elsewhere—but the total already sent was very considerable. On the 12th, after a crisis in which the 2nd French Light Division, after being held up for some time in the Clyde, was nearly diverted to garrison 'Fortress Holland', Lord Cork was asked if he required more troops; and the French troops were in fact retained in Scotland for three more days. Even then the three battalions of the Chasseurs Alpins from Namsos, which had been re-equipped after their return, and five more Independent Companies were kept at his disposal; the former had had valuable experience already, the latter were to complete training at Harstad. They would have sailed on 22nd May, but Lord Cork was for administrative reasons unable to accept the French before the 30th—by which time the game was up. The question of fighter aircraft, which became urgent as airfields in North Norway at last became available (21st May), was appallingly difficult in view of the demands made for reinforcement in France; but one squadron of Hurricanes, of which the diversion to French soil had been authorised as early as 8 a.m. on 10th May, was eventually allowed to go north. No bombers were sent, but the Chief of the Air Staff maintained that the use for which they were in the end requested, namely to protect the rear-guard, was in no way a proper function for a bomber squadron.

The policy of continuing our efforts in North Norway is partly attributable to the momentum which a campaign gathers, making it hard for psychological as well as practical reasons to order its abandonment. Its success would, as the French Prime Minister observed, do something to offset the bad news from other quarters. We retained a hope, though a sadly diminished one, of influencing or coercing the Swedes in the matter of iron ore, and Mr Churchill in particular wanted to bottle up Lulea; although he at one time contemplated the use as minelayers of aircraft based in south-east England, an airfield in North Norway would be far more convenient. But the main objective in this penultimate phase of the campaign was that disproportionate diversion of German resources to a distant and almost inaccessible theatre of war which had been one of the attractions when we first thought of challenging the Germans in Scandinavia. That it was something more than making the best of a bad job is shown by the strength of the Prime Minister's reaction to the Mowinckel Plan, which seemed at this moment to offer us a strategic alternative.

It was very natural that a project for neutralising the Narvik area should have originated among the Swedes, since for them the area had a special economic interest to distinguish it from the rest of Norway; they were also painfully aware that the continuance of the military struggle for its control might sooner or later drag them in. A private Swedish kite, flown in mid-April, attracted little attention, but about the end of the month, when Allied prospects looked dark, the former Norwegian Prime Minister Mowinckel, who had rejoined the Cabinet since the invasion, in a conversation with the Swedish Foreign Minister in Stockholm, suggested as 'a passing thought'[1] the possibility of securing the neutralisation of North Norway. The Swedes took the idea up, adding the not very welcome corollary that Swedish troops should be left in occupation of Narvik. The Norwegian Government, who did not wish to lay themselves open to a charge of defeatism or desertion, and who disliked the way in which the project had arisen, were reluctant to commit themselves. The Swedes, however, becoming more apprehensive as the predicament of the Germans in North Norway became more acute, continued to press the Norwegians, and finally, on the day Narvik fell, put their suggestion forward in Berlin. Meanwhile, it had been reported by our diplomatic representatives in Sweden and Norway and was brought to the attention of the War Cabinet, nine days before the entry into Narvik, as a 'proposal apparently of German origin' which showed the strain on the enemy. The Foreign Office, which was anxious for the Norwegian Government to remain established in North Norway, even at the cost of reasserting a neutral status, had been disposed to welcome the scheme; after all, the presence of Swedish forces in Narvik might mean that, though neither side got any ore from the port at the moment, a German quarrel with Sweden would subsequently deliver the port, the ore, and the orefields into our hands

---

[1] *Norwegian Parliamentary Report*, Appendices, Vol. II, p. 301.

intact. But the Prime Minister was adamant. 'The main remaining value of our forces in Norway', he told the Foreign Secretary, 'is to entice and retain largely superior German forces in that area away from the main decision. Norway is paying a good dividend now and must be held down to the job'.

This bold argument was advanced as late as 19th May, when the situation was such that the War Cabinet was awaiting a report on the consequences which would follow the fall of Paris or the withdrawal of the British forces from France. The possibility that the United Kingdom would be exposed to a direct threat of invasion drew attention to the value of every destroyer and every fighter aircraft, while the ordeal through which France and Belgium were passing emphasised the need for anti-aircraft artillery to be shipped home. Moreover, once the idea of leaving North Norway was considered, the timing was seen to be a crucial factor. Since the assault on Narvik was now at long last on the very verge of execution, the arguments which the Inter-Services Planning Staff formulated for the Chiefs of Staff fell on willing ears. The capture of the town still had some prestige value, although the eyes of the world were riveted elsewhere; it would enable us to complete the demolition of the port and railway; and by driving the enemy inland in confusion it would enable our forces to disengage. But once Narvik was captured, the sooner the area was evacuated the better, in order that no part of our naval resources or of such men and material as could be extricated from the north should be still on passage home—and therefore out of service—if and when the country had to meet the supreme test of an attempted invasion.

Accordingly, on the evening of 20th May the Prime Minister, who had pressed so vehemently and recently for Narvik to be taken, opened to the new Defence Committee his arguments for its subsequent abandonment. They were three in number. As the Germans were now strong enough to insist on passing troops through Sweden, we could no longer contemplate any advance from Narvik to the orefields. To hold Narvik would be a drain on our resources. And Narvik was not essential to us as a naval base. Three days later the War Cabinet was considering an appreciation drawn up by the Chiefs of Staff to show the military implications of a complete withdrawal from Norway. The Chiefs of Staff doubted the importance of maintaining a centre of resistance in Norway because 'the Norwegians have neither the numbers, the material, nor the heart to offer a firm core on which to build'. They were on surer ground in pointing out that we could spare no more aircraft, had only one and a half divisions in Norway to face eleven divisions of Germans,[1] and

---

[1] The Germans actually moved seven divisions (107,000 men) into Norway up to 15th June.

were using up temporarily in Norway—pending the passage of two big convoys to Narvik—no less than half the destroyer strength available for meeting invasion. The Chiefs of Staff therefore proposed that Narvik should be abandoned after capture, though the Prime Minister still preferred to leave the matter at the stage of planning. But at a meeting of the Defence Committee next day (24th May) the situation appeared still more dangerous—evacuation would take twenty-eight days from the first order to the last landing, and 'if an invasion of the United Kingdom began during the process of evacuation it would probably be necessary to withdraw all naval forces immediately'. Accordingly, a telegram ordering the evacuation was handed to the First Sea Lord's Secretary for despatch that evening. The order was confirmed by the War Cabinet next day and by the Supreme War Council at its meeting on 31st May.

Difficulties arose from the conflict between the need for absolute secrecy in relation to an operation so vulnerable to attack and the obligation to inform the Norwegians of our intentions, but the British Government would not permit anything to be divulged before 1st June. More agreeable to relate is the intervention of the Chiefs of Staff to require in view of the plight of France that as far as possible British troops should be the last to come away. But in general the urgency of the situation caused the Admiralty to be left to conduct the evacuation as they chose; by the 27th the Chiefs of Staff were even considering instead what use the Germans might make of Norway to invade Britain. But the reluctance with which the decision was taken may be judged from the fact that it was three times challenged in the Cabinet during the next few days—on 27th May, when it was argued on behalf of the Admiralty that the Narvik operation was draining the enemy's forces more than ours; on the 30th, when a paper from the Ministry of Economic Warfare was considered; and finally on 2nd June, when the build-up of our home forces made possible by the success of the Dunkirk evacuation prompted the Prime Minister himself to throw out the suggestion of maintaining a garrison at Narvik for some weeks on a self-contained basis.

As the decision taken on 24th May proved final, it only remains to notice our abortive attempts to salvage something from the wreck of our policy. The neutralisation plan, turned down so recently, had received a sympathetic hearing on 22nd May from the Chiefs of Staff, but it was not until after its reconsideration by the Cabinet nine days later that the Foreign Secretary could let the Swedish and Norwegian Governments know that we now supported it. The Norwegians asked for, and obtained, a twenty-four-hour delay in the evacuation programme, so that the Norwegian might meet the Swedish Foreign Minister at Lulea. But the Germans had now lost whatever interest they may have had in such an agreement; the only practical result, which might have had the direst consequences, was that Dr Koht told the Swede that the Allies had decided to evacuate.[1]

No greater success attended the revival of the notion of guerrilla warfare. There was a scheme for leaving troops behind in the Narvik area. But the French were judged the most suitable and they were the most needed elsewhere; besides, what could a small force without any air protection achieve in the unfamiliar wilderness? If there was to be guerrilla warfare, it would have to be waged by the Norwegians, who had complained on 1st June that they needed 20,000 rifles and had been given only 1,000. Nevertheless, the last effective orders told Lord Cork to bring home all small arms and ammunition; a counter-order for leaving 4,500 rifles and up to two million rounds of ammunition behind as an encouragement arrived some hours after he had put to sea.

Finally, although the abandonment of Narvik had set the orefields out of our grasp, there remained the possibility of blocking Lulea harbour, which could be reached from aircraft carriers in lieu of airfields, as soon as their tasks in covering the withdrawal from Norway were at an end. On 8th June, the day on which the evacuation of the Narvik area was completed, we knew that at long last the north Baltic port was about to be declared ice-free, and the Commander-in-Chief, Home Fleet, received preparatory orders for minelaying and torpedo attacks on ore ships to be attempted. But it was agreed that the likely political repercussions must first be examined; they were found to be serious; and our iron-ore strategy was then finally abandoned.

---

[1] Koht, p. 168.

CHAPTER XII

NARVIK—DELAYING OPERATIONS TO THE SOUTHWARD

See Maps 8 (a), facing page 186, and 8 (b), facing page 192

Towards the end of April the second stage in the Norwegian campaign, which we have just traced in outline, opened with the first movement of British troops into the region south of Narvik. By the time they came into action there on 10th May, the siege of Narvik was also moving towards its dénouement; but it will be convenient to treat first the contemporaneous operations farther south. The distances along the North Norwegian coast are very great: from Trondheim to Narvik is about 360 miles in a straight line, a form of measurement which has meaning only for air transport. The only town of any size along the route is Bodö, with a population of 5,000, though Mo i Rana,[1] connected by a poor quality road with Sweden, was nearly chosen by the Norwegian Government for its temporary seat instead of Tromsö.[2] Otherwise it was a region of mountains and fiords, attracting little population or traffic other than the coastal traffic through the Leads, its railway not yet functioning past Grong (the junction for Namsos), the single highroad to the north interrupted by several ferries south of Bodö, and beyond Bodö non-existent until the approaches to Narvik were reached. But, as we have already seen, the withdrawal of the Allied forces from the Trondheim area meant that the Germans might be expected to advance northwards up the coast until their air bases, if not their actual troops, could turn the besiegers of Narvik into the besieged.

As early as 21st April, a trawler had been sent to report on facilities at Mosjöen, a tiny port at the head of the Vefsenfiord about ninety miles north of Namsos (150 miles by road), and five days later the Commander-in-Chief, Home Fleet, mentioned it again, apparently thinking that it would be feasible to relieve pressure at Namsos if a suitable landing place could be found there or elsewhere in the same direction. But it was not until the decision had been taken to leave Namsos altogether that operations north of that town became urgently necessary. On 27th April General Carton de Wiart's headquarters passed on to the War Office information received from

---

[1] The full name, used to distinguish it from a smaller 'Mo' farther south, which, however, plays no part in this history.
[2] See p. 138.

their Norwegian allies that the enemy intended to occupy Mosjöen. Two days later a message from General Massy stated that it was essential to deny Mosjöen to the enemy. His plan was that one detachment should be sent from Mauriceforce direct to Mosjöen by sea, and a second detachment, with the available transport, left as a rear-guard at Grong, east of Namsos, to hold up the enemy along the road north. This second detachment might, if necessary, be composed of skiers only. General Carton de Wiart and General Audet were, however, equally opposed to providing the rear-guard.[1] The ski troops were not sufficiently numerous to achieve much and would be at the mercy of air attack; reconnaissance had shown the road to be impassable during the thaw for the motor transport required to supply them; and in any case the skiers were needed in their present positions to cover the evacuation. The matter remained under discussion as late as 2nd May, when there was a further conference between General Carton de Wiart and General Audet because direct instructions for a French detachment to be posted at Grong had been received by the latter from General Gamelin. But the original view that such a rear-guard could not be set up because it could not withdraw by road to Mosjöen was maintained.

As to the practicability of a retirement by road at the date given, enquiry from the Norwegians would perhaps have been pertinent. According to Colonel Getz, the line of the uncompleted railway had been cleared of snow by the 19th; by the 26th the supplies for his brigade were being brought overland from Mosjöen, and on 1st May he was advising the Norwegian Legation in London, who were purchasing stores for him, of the good connections available between Mosjöen and Grong.[2] A Norwegian battalion based on Mosjöen had been moved south to Grong on 21st April; it moved back with no great difficulty along the same route in the first week of May—130 miles by rail and 35 miles, on high ground in the middle where a railway bridge awaited completion, by a shuttle service of lorries.

The other half of the plan put to General Carton de Wiart was carried out, though on a reduced scale. A party of a hundred Chasseurs Alpins and a two-gun section of a British light anti-aircraft battery were sent by sea from Namsos in the only available transport, a destroyer, on the night of 30th April, arriving at Mosjöen late next day unobserved from the air. A week later the French were replaced by British troops, so that the defence of Mosjöen and the subsequent operations became exclusively a British-Norwegian venture. Meanwhile, as previously related,[3] the forces at Narvik under Lord Cork had received orders to safeguard the main inter-

---

[1] Despatch by Lieut.-General Massy, Part I, Sec. 8, Part II, Secs. 23, 28.
[2] Getz, pp. 60, 99, 133.
[3] See pp. 159, 167.

mediate point at Bodö and a company of Scots Guards was sent to that area, so that the delaying operations to the southward henceforth had Bodö to fall back upon as an outpost protecting our operations at Narvik.

The situation was difficult, since British naval control of the inshore routes, which might have been expected to make our successive positions along the coast more tenable, was much impaired by the threat of air attack in the narrow waters of the fiords. There was no proper landing ground known to us south of Narvik: a search for possible sites to be developed round Bodö, Mosjöen, and Mo—in that order of priority—was ordered by the Air Ministry on 30th April. Four days later the R.A.F. reconnaissance party came to Bodö in two flying boats chartered from Imperial Airways; bombs began to fall within half an hour of the arrival of the second aircraft and reduced them both to wreckage. Clearly there was no immediate prospect of providing air cover, and the needs of Narvik made it impossible to attempt any serious anti-aircraft defence. The Norwegian forces with which we were now to co-operate might indeed be expected to be apt for delaying operations, since they knew the country. Unfortunately, one battalion of the local regiment had been posted before 9th April to the Kirkenes area, leaving only a reserve battalion of uncertain value and the battalion referred to above, which was falling back on Mosjöen from Grong. This battalion was shaken, first by the Namsos capitulation, then by a railway accident, in which seven of its men were killed, and finally by a curious dispute as to the verification of orders received from the Norwegian High Command for the demolition of road and railway as they withdrew. One consequence of declining morale was that their demolitions proved to be quite ineffective. The brunt of any attack would clearly have to be borne by the British troops now beginning to arrive in the area from home, under orders to fight a series of delaying actions in circumstances of recognised inferiority to the enemy but without any definite prescribed time-table.

Scissorsforce was brought to Norway in three flights by single transports under destroyer escort. No. 1 Independent Company landed on 4th May at the head of the Ranfiord, at Mo, 54 miles north of Mosjöen by road. No. 3 Independent Company, to be joined later by No. 2 Company, landed much farther north at Bodö, and Scissorsforce headquarters was set up at the same time where the Scots Guards company had already established themselves, at the village of Hopen, eleven miles east of that town. The initial actions—apart from enemy air attacks, which began at Mo the day after No. 1 Company's arrival—were therefore the concern of the 4th and 5th Companies, these being the troops that replaced the French at Mosjöen on the night of 8th/9th May. No. 4 Company was disposed so as to protect Mosjöen from the sea and to guard the first part of the road to Mo, while No. 5 Company moved south to link up with the Norwegians. Colonel Gubbins, who had landed with them, learnt that the Norwegian battalion, after its attempted reorganisation in Mosjöen, had gone forward again only 400 strong; indeed, the reports reaching the Norwegian High Command in the north were such that a staff officer was already on his way south to stiffen resistance. Colonel Gubbins found the Norwegians at Fellingfors, twenty-five miles south of Mosjöen; there a side road led to the snowbound Hattfjelldal airfield up the East Vefsna valley and the demolition of the river bridge gave a line of defence. These troops were driven in by the Germans on the 9th, only four days after the latter had started their advance from Grong. Our own position was then being established nearer Mosjöen, at a point where the Björnaa river forms a lake and a long stretch of road is exposed to fire from the steep hillsides shutting in the water. No. 5 Independent Company had a party of two platoons (100 strong) on one flank of the two Norwegian companies, while its third platoon defended the alternative approach along the line of the railway at the bridge over the Vefsna river, which was duly blown. In the early morning of 10th May the enemy vanguard, cycling incautiously down the road, was ambushed and destroyed to the number of about fifty men. But a little after midday German pressure along both road and rail routes drove our forces back towards Mosjöen, which was some ten miles distant. Colonel Gubbins had hopes of taking up a new position on the outskirts of the town, but there is no natural line of defence and both the British and the Norwegian commander concluded that a further withdrawal beyond Mosjöen would be necessary. Colonel Gubbins thereupon sent orders to No. 1 Company at Mo to safeguard the line of the Ranfiord, which he would reach about half-way along the route of his retreat. It was of course intended that the British-Norwegian withdrawal should be made as slow, and the German advance as costly, as possible. This seemed a reasonable proposition, since the German force had advanced overland from Grong over the long route which we had believed to be impracticable at this season, and would presumably have to use that same route as its line of communications for any further progress.

But on this same day—10th May, the day on which the Germans broke into Holland and Belgium—they staged a further *coup* in Norway, which a Norwegian historian calls 'as audacious as the original invasion'.[1] A party of about 300 German troops had been embarked near Trondheim in the Norwegian coastal steamer *Nord-Norge*, which had a crew drawn from the German destroyers. After a twenty-four-

---

[1] Roscher Nielsen, Major-General R.: *Norges Krig*, p. 427.

hour delay due to a submarine alarm, this vessel left Trondheimsfiord under escort of two aircraft, and set its course north towards the scene of the present operations. The movement was observed by the Norwegian coast watch in the early morning and reported to British Naval Headquarters at Harstad. The first definite news was received there at 10.15, but it was not until 11.55 that orders were sent to the only ships available—the anti-aircraft cruiser *Calcutta*, which was with a convoy fifty miles west of Skomvaer Light, and the destroyer *Zulu* at Skjelfiord. The *Calcutta*, had she proceeded at once, alone, and on the right course, might have intercepted the enemy; but more than two hours elapsed before a second signal gave Mo as the possible destination, and in any case the *Zulu* could not meet the cruiser earlier than 5 p.m., off the Myken Light. The two ships were then about forty miles north of the Ranfiord, which they entered behind the enemy.

But by seven o'clock the Germans had completed their voyage, for their intended landing-place was nearer than we supposed—at Hemnesberget, fifteen miles west of Mo on the seaward edge of the Hemnes peninsula, from which the route between Mosjöen and Mo could be effectively cut. The arrival of the steamer was preceded by that of two Dornier seaplanes, which put ashore about forty men with mortars and machine guns west of the town and then dropped bombs on it. A platoon from No. 1 Independent Company was still remembered there nine years later as having fought with determination through the streets, but they could not hope to hold the quay and were forced eventually to make their escape as best they could by boat to Mo or to the neck of the peninsula at Finneid, where they were joined that night by the rest of No. 1 Company and by about 120 Norwegian troops with four heavy machine guns. Meanwhile the two British ships had come on the scene about one and a half hours behind the Germans, and had sunk their ship, but not before two mountain guns had been landed as well as all the men. Next day a small fleet of seaplanes was at work bringing in stores which would help to replace lost cargo.

Colonel Gubbins had already withdrawn No. 5 Company through No. 4 Company to a position north of Mosjöen. But a move in that direction was now blocked farther on, so Mosjöen and district had to be abandoned forthwith, leaving the Germans free to improvise a forward air base in this area if they could. No. 4 Company were embarked in a small Norwegian steamer the same evening at and near Mosjöen, No. 5 the next morning at a point farther down the fiord; the Light Anti-Aircraft section which had originally accompanied the French to Mosjöen was also embarked, but had to destroy its guns. They landed at Sandnessjöen on the north side of the large island at the mouth of the Vefsenfiord, where two destroyers made touch with them in the early morning of the 12th, and were brought on to Bodö partly by destroyers and partly by a local steamer under destroyer escort. By 4 a.m. on 11th May Mosjöen was already in German hands. As for the Norwegians, their reserve detachments collected at Mosjöen had already been despatched to Mo by sea, but the battalion with which our Independent Companies were co-operating went back overland from Mosjöen to Elsfjord, half-way to Mo, where the road was interrupted by a ferry route terminating at Hemnesberget. That terminus being no longer available, they had to leave the ferry at a point farther down, on the road north from Korgen, which would bring them past the neck of the Hemnes peninsula—the position at Finneid—to Mo. But their heavy equipment was all abandoned and their military value more than proportionately diminished.

Even before the catastrophe at Hemnesberget, Colonel Gubbins's initial report from Mosjöen had aroused serious misgivings at headquarters at Harstad, where General Ruge's liaison officer also had instructions to give a daily reminder about the importance of stemming the German advance from the south. Lord Cork's proposal that the southern front be reinforced, made on 9th May, was welcomed by General Mackesy, who that evening put the Scots and Irish Guards at short notice to move to Mo. Brigadier Fraser, who had now returned to duty, was given command of all British troops in the area, and three companies of Scots Guards, with four 25-pounders and four light anti-aircraft guns, landed at Mo in the early morning of the 12th. The ships conveying them fired on the wharf at Hemnesberget on their way. But although they included an anti-aircraft cruiser and a sloop, the weight of air attack, both at Mo itself and in the approaches through some forty miles of narrow waters, was such that an agreed report was sent back, saying that large ships other than anti-aircraft cruisers ought not to enter the fiord. Two further attempts were made to harass the enemy on the Hemnes peninsula by naval bombardment, but it was not deemed possible to meet the Army's request for ships to be kept in the area so as to hamper any German advance across or alongside the water.

An attack from Finneid against Hemnesberget had been made by the Norwegians on the 11th. They penetrated about half-way along the road between the two places but were then driven back by German gunfire. The recapture of Hemnesberget was considered again next day when the Scots Guards had arrived, but Colonel Trappes-Lomax decided to await further reinforcements, establishing in the meantime a defence position at Stien, on the road which skirts the fiord between Finneid and Mo. The other possibility, that the

Germans might cross from Hemnesberget to the north side of the Ranfiord to attack Mo from the west, was covered by the Norwegian reserve troops evacuated earlier from Mosjöen. Next day, the Germans had pushed so far across the peninsula that their mortars and heavy machine guns commanded the road to Finneid, along which the Norwegians who had made the detour from Elsfiord would have to pass. A counter-attack was therefore launched which enabled the Norwegians to pass through, but on the 14th the Germans pressed forward again, and that evening, after some serious fighting, No. 1 Independent Company and the Norwegians abandoned Finneid and retired through the position at Stien.

By this time Brigadier Fraser, who received instructions from General Mackesy's successor, General Auchinleck,[1] to maintain an advanced detachment at Mo as long as possible, was on his way down to view the situation. Having conferred with Lieut.-Colonel Trappes-Lomax and the newly appointed Norwegian area commander, Lieut.-Colonel R. Roscher Nielsen, he formed the view that the position in the Mo area was untenable. In the first place, the Navy could not maintain an adequate flow of reinforcements and supplies because of the air threat. Then there was no good alternative route of communication overland, since the road north from Mo to Bodö was a mountain road climbing well above the snow line; this could be dominated by the German air force, which was already reaching as far afield as Bodö. Moreover, Colonel Trappes-Lomax said that in any case he required another battalion if he was to hold Mo against serious attack. The Germans, on the other hand, were increasing their strength daily. Hemnesberget was being reinforced and supplied by seaplane. A German battalion was already using horse-drawn transport to make the difficult mountain crossing (which the thaw might soon render temporarily impassable) to Korgen from a point near Elsfiord, where the ferry and possible substitutes had been withdrawn to delay them. Other German columns were reported north of Mosjöen. They had not yet been identified as troops of the 2nd Mountain Division under General Feurstein, which had been diverted from the impending attack in Western Europe and shipped to Trondheim as an additional division by the Führer's orders with a special mission to penetrate at top speed towards Narvik; they now totalled five mountain infantry battalions and at least three troops of mountain artillery. The German progress, however, gave sufficient indication that we had more than scouting parties to contend with.

But the importance of holding on was evident both to Lord Cork and to General Auchinleck, while at the same time the Norwegian Commander-in-Chief, General Ruge, and the Divisional General

---

[1] See p. 201.

Fleischer were renewing their representations that a further withdrawal would be disastrous. Particular importance was attached to the existence of a partly developed airfield site at Rösvik, ten miles north-east of Mo, though the Germans did not in the sequel appear to use this site (or Hattfjelldal) for the current operations. Thus on the very day (15th May) on which Brigadier Fraser reported that to continue to hold Mo was militarily unsound, Lord Cork was informing the Admiralty of his feeling that we must hold on and fight at Mo, since otherwise the whole Narvik situation would become precarious. There was also, no doubt, the unvoiced consideration of British prestige at stake. As Mr Churchill had minuted about the position at Mosjöen, many miles farther south, only eleven days earlier: 'It would be a disgrace if the Germans made themselves masters of the whole of this stretch of the Norwegian coast with practically no opposition from us and in the course of the next few weeks or even days.'

The position at Mo, already difficult, was fated to be made worse by two disasters occurring in quick succession at sea. It was decided on the 14th that the Irish Guards, who sailed that day for Bodö, should be followed by our one remaining battalion, the 2nd South Wales Borderers. But shortly after midnight of 14th/15th May the Polish liner *Chrobry*, with Brigade Headquarters, 1st Irish Guards, and some other troops on board, was attacked from the air as she left the seaward extremity of the Lofoten Islands to steer across the Vestfiord. The Guards colonel, all three majors, and two junior officers were killed or mortally injured by the bombs as they slept. Fire broke out immediately amidships and most of the men were isolated in the fore-part where they could not lower the boats. While stacked ammunition ignited and the fire spread, so that the final explosion could be expected at any moment, the Irish Guards formed up on deck, with arms and kit, as on parade. Search parties dragged the injured from the blazing wreckage; the rest waited in their lines in the cold twilight; their chaplain began to recite the Rosary. The commander of the escorting destroyer *Wolverine*, which hastened to the rescue, while the sloop *Stork* warded off further attack, compares their discipline, which enabled him to trans-ship 694 men in sixteen minutes, to the conduct of the soldiers in the *Birkenhead*. The troops had, however, to return to Harstad to refit, and for the rest of the campaign their Commanding Officer was a captain.[1] Much of the equipment lost was irreplaceable: it included three light tanks belonging to the 3rd Hussars, which were the only British tanks landed in Norway and had originally been destined for Mosjöen. Then on the evening of the 17th the cruiser *Effingham*, carrying

---

[1] Fitzgerald, Major D. J. L.: *History of the Irish Guards in the Second World War*, Chapter IV.

Brigade Headquarters and the South Wales Borderers to the same destination, after taking an unusual route outside the Leads to lessen the risk of air attack, together with a destroyer ran aground at twenty knots on the Faksen shoal within a dozen miles of Bodö. One of the escorting anti-aircraft cruisers brought the troops back to the Harstad area, but there was again a serious loss of stores, including machine-gun carriers. Attempts to refloat the *Effingham* failed. The expected attack on Mo had begun six hours before; our reinforcements would now be belated and under-equipped.

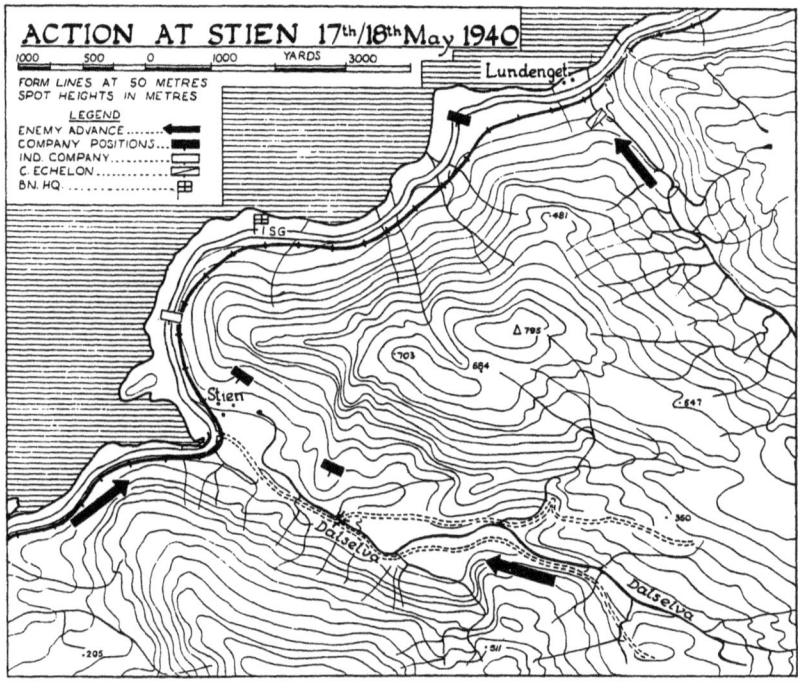

On the afternoon of 17th May, the Germans moved forward from Finneid, where they had built up a force of about 1,750 men, against the Scots Guards' positions. The latter had two companies at Stien itself, where the small river Dalselva debouches into the fiord, and their third company and the Independent Company (which was under their command) placed farther back on the road towards Mo. The four 25-pounders were also sited in the rear, but had little effect owing to the destruction of their communications which ran along the road. Serious fighting began about 6.30 p.m., and although the enemy brought a field gun into action from the high ground across the river and also covered the forward slopes of our position with machine-gun fire, the frontal assault along the road, which is fully exposed as it turns inward to the river-bridge, was firmly held. The

Germans suffered a good many casualties at the bridge itself, which they tried to restore with planks, but they made their main thrust down the river valley, which they had approached over the snow-bound mountains from a point south of Finneid, collecting skis from farms as they went. Our forces had not been posted on the heights, in spite of warning, and three small Norwegian ski detachments which were supposed to watch the flank did little. The Germans also dropped paratroops on the mountainside nearer Mo, who developed a subsidiary flank attack at Lundenget. Along the Dalselva valley the fight continued through the short twilit night, with the Germans making full use of their tommy guns as they pressed along the north side of the valley towards the road, until at about 2 a.m. the Scots Guards were forced to fall back through the reserve position near Lundenget, where their third company still guarded the road to Mo.

Brigadier Gubbins had arrived on the scene during the night, having been appointed with acting rank to command the troops in the Bodö-Mo area in place of Brigadier Fraser, who had returned to Harstad to report and was then invalided home.[1] After a telephone conversation with General Auchinleck the new commander gave orders for the retirement to continue to the north of Mo. The information was conveyed to the Norwegians by Colonel Trappes-Lomax, who said that he had been outflanked by superior German forces and had lost two companies. This had reference to the fact that, in addition to some seventy casualties suffered during the fighting of the previous day, there was a presumed loss of the entire rear company, which by morning held the point on the road nearest to the oncoming enemy, and was cut off before the instruction to retire farther came through. Brigadier Gubbins's orders provided opportunity for the Norwegians to withdraw first, using nearly all the available civilian transport, and their Divisional Headquarters agreed. At 3 p.m. the two bridges over the River Rana at the north side of the town were blown. Within the next half-hour the enemy entered into possession of Mo i Rana, marking the second main stage in their advance towards Bodö.

The geographical conditions of the area between Mo and Bodö made serious delaying actions—to say nothing of a counter-offensive—very difficult in face of enemy air power. Unfortunately, too, the decrease in the distance separating our forward troops from the base at Bodö did not mean a proportionate increase in the ease of reinforcement—though Bodö was at any rate a sizeable county town, provided with a concrete steamship-quay and four substantial wharves. As already related, a company of Scots Guards had been

---

[1] See p. 158.

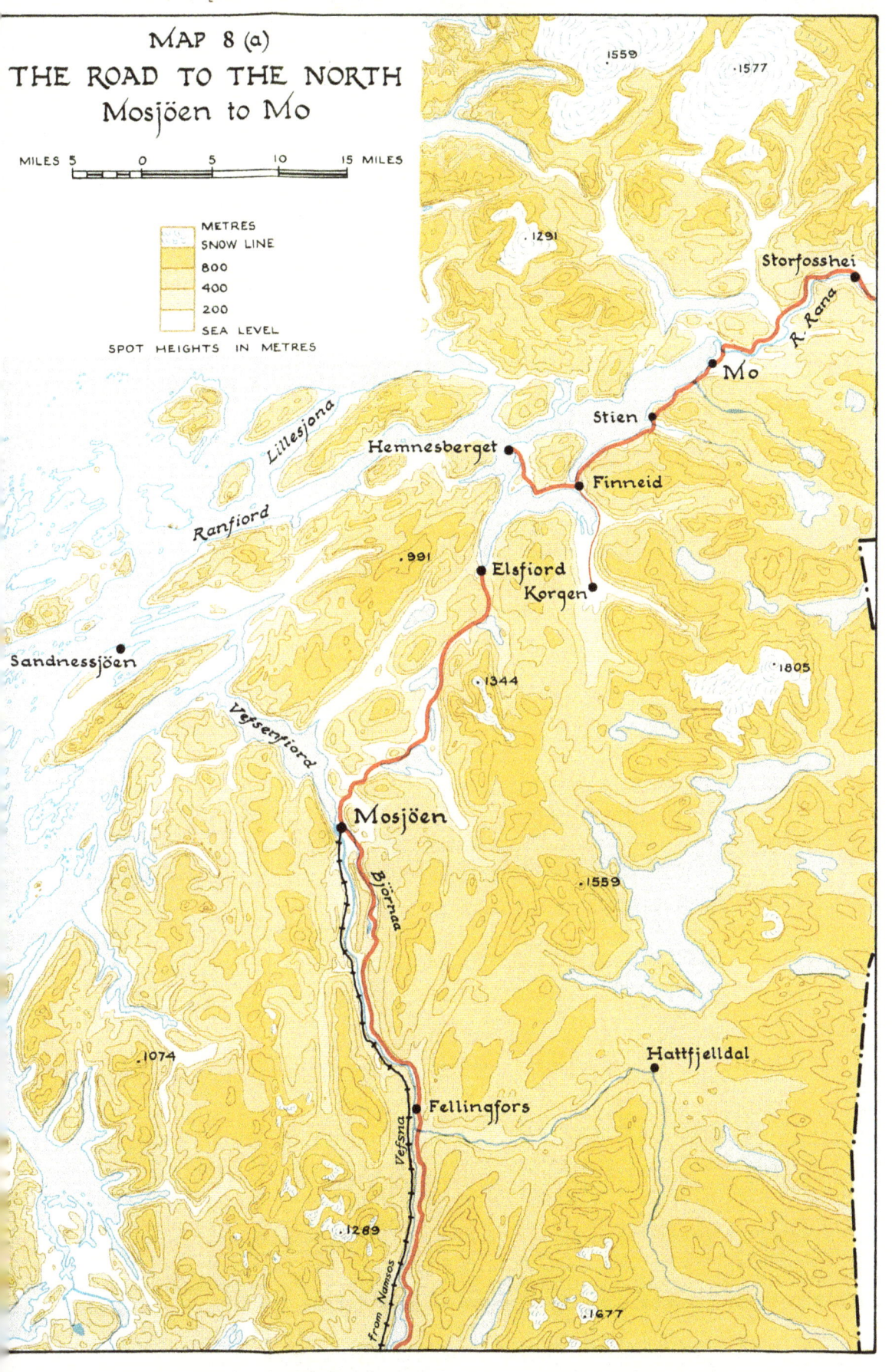

sent there on 30th April, followed at intervals by two Independent Companies direct from home and the two that were evacuated from Mosjöen. Early on 10th May, just before that evacuation, an Admiralty telegram advised Lord Cork, only three days after all operations to the southward had been placed under the Narvik command, that it was essential to hold Bodö pending a full examination of the problem involved, and that, if necessary, the garrison must be reinforced from the resources at his disposal. Hence the diversion of all British troops from the Narvik area to serve under Brigadier Fraser and the orders which were given him, to hold Mo if he could but to 'deny the area Bodö-Saltdal permanently to the enemy'.

The double misfortune which befell the transportation to Bodö has already been related. The result was that both the South Wales Borderers and the Irish Guards reached the Bodö area by detachments in destroyers and Puffers and they were not beginning to arrive there until the 20th. Therefore, although the Bodö Command, as we shall see, sent what it could, the withdrawal north of Mo must be considered substantially as a self-contained operation. A Norwegian machine-gun company and other very small Norwegian units accompanied the force, which was joined in the course of the first day by a fresh company of the Scots Guards, brought forward by motor transport across the mountain plateau from its position east of Bodö, and next afternoon by the missing company. After being encircled south of Mo, they had extricated themselves by an arduous cross-country march over hills deep in snow to Storfosshei on the River Rana and had lost only four men in doing it.

The first part of the long route to be traversed follows the valley of the Rana in a generally north-easterly direction for fifty-five miles. It then descends again by a second valley system in a more northerly direction to where the Saltdal debouches into the fiords leading out to Bodö. The distance from the watershed to Rognan on the Saltdalsfiord is about forty-five miles, making about a hundred miles in all. Population is very thin even in the lowest reaches of the respective valleys; the barrenness of the mountain plateau between may be imagined from the fact that it lies within the Arctic Circle and includes a belt of perpetual snow. The German advance was not, at first, pressed hard: the demolition of the bridges imposed a serious obstacle, and the speed with which Mo had come into their hands had probably something of the effect of a windfall. Thus the British force (less the Independent Company, which was carried straight through to Rognan) was able to spend the second day after its withdrawal from Mo resting about thirty-two miles from the town in a position covered by the freshly arrived company at Messingsletten bridge. At this juncture Colonel Trappes-Lomax received orders from General Auchinleck, saying: 'You have now reached good position for defence. Essential to stand and fight . . . I rely on Scots Guards to stop the enemy'. The Colonel maintained, however, that it would be throwing away the only battalion available for immediate defence if a major stand were attempted before his men were safely across the vulnerable area of the snow belt, beginning about twenty miles up the valley. After reference to General Headquarters by telephone, Brigadier Gubbins issued modified instructions for 'hitting hard' and withdrawing only if there was 'serious danger to the safety' of the force.

By midnight three defence lines had been manned, where the wide and rather featureless floor of the upland valley seemed most suitable. The enemy did not attack in earnest until the evening of the next day (21st May), when they outflanked our first line and followed up as far as the main position at Krokstrand, where the road crosses the river and a demolished bridge was defensible from good cover on the far side. But this likewise was held only for a few hours, until the Germans were able to enfilade it from higher ground on their side of the river, while it was also being machine-gunned from the air. It took the enemy (whose force included two bridging columns) one day to build a new bridge here in the wilds, and the British troops were not seriously pressed in their withdrawal to their third position, from which they moved in small parties that evening across the plateau, where the road for twenty-three miles ran between steep walls of snow. Three Bren carriers which had been salvaged from H.M.S. *Effingham* successfully screened the embussing. Thus the attempt to stop the enemy in what General Auchinleck called 'the narrow defile north of Mo'[1] had been abandoned. As in so many other instances, German air supremacy played a large part—not so much in the actual assault on our positions, but in providing unhampered reconnaissance of our movements and in restricting within the narrowest limits the use of our lines of communication back to Bodö.

In the early hours of 23rd May a new position was taken up at Viskiskoia, where the road crosses to the east bank of the river, as it descends towards the Saltdal. The Scots Guards were deployed to cover the demolished bridge, while No. 3 Independent Company, which had marched up from Rognan, supported by a few Norwegian ski troops, was posted on the far side, high up and well in front, to deter the enemy from a flank advance. The German ground forces came up the following afternoon, supported by low-flying attacks from a single aircraft and by mortar fire. Two of our Bofors guns were out of action; the Scots Guards had only one 3-inch mortar left (which did some damage); and the field guns could give only very limited support on account of the loss of their signalling equip-

---
[1] Despatch by Lord Cork: Appendix B, Sec. 32.

ment. By 4 p.m. the Independent Company had been driven back, so that our main position was enfiladed. At 6, Brigadier Gubbins gave the order for another retirement to Major Graham, Scots Guards, who had succeeded to the command of the battalion on the sudden recall of their lieutenant-colonel to Harstad. Five miles farther on there was another bridge at Storjord, where it was planned to fight an action with much the same dispositions as at Viskiskoia. However, the Germans did not make contact until the evening of the 24th, when orders had just been received for the force to withdraw without further delaying actions, as fresh troops had now taken up position fourteen miles in their rear. Accordingly, the Scots Guards and other units continued down the valley, and in the course of the next morning they reached the Bodö area by boat from Rognan, where a flotilla of Puffers had just been assembled under British naval command.

The situation as viewed by General Auchinleck was that the Germans now had about 4,000 men with tanks and artillery in the Mo-Mosjöen area. He also knew that the vigour of their advance was enormously aided by control of the air, which we had as yet been unable to challenge. The policy therefore was to strengthen our ground forces for the defence of Bodö by all means within our power —it was even intended to add a battalion of French Chasseurs Alpins besides three more Independent Companies from England. Help was also sought from the Fleet Air Arm, while the landing ground at Bodö was being hurriedly prepared for aircraft to be transferred from Bardufoss. Already available in the Bodö area were the 1st Irish Guards, 2nd South Wales Borderers, less two companies, and four of the Independent Companies. The new position at Pothus was, therefore, manned in considerable strength, though Brigadier Gubbins, hampered by lack of transport, kept about half his troops strung out along the lines of communication to Bodö in anticipation of a turning movement from the sea or air. The action at Pothus was intended at least to give time to complete our preparations to repel the Germans finally at the approaches to the Bodö peninsula.

The hamlet of Pothus is only ten miles from the mouth of the Saltdal, and stands on both banks of the river, which by this point reaches a considerable size. As a defensive position, its leading features were the two bridges, a substantial girder bridge which carried the main road from the east to the west bank and a smaller structure crossing a tributary that flows into the Saltdal from the east a few hundred yards farther down-stream. A platoon (fifty-five men) of No. 2 Independent Company was concentrated here first. The battalion of Irish Guards and No. 3 Independent Company followed them and had completed their dispositions by midnight on 24th May, at which time the Scots Guards marched wearily through and went

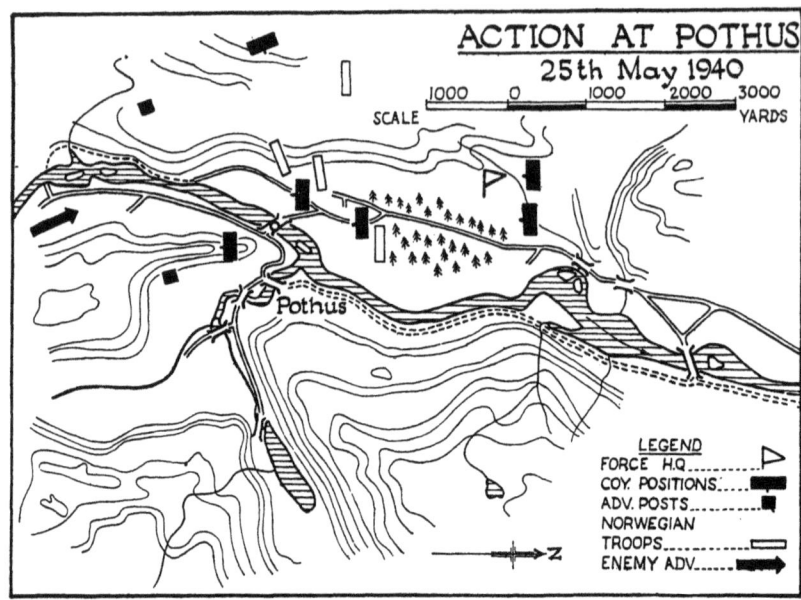

out of the line. The Norwegians had sent forward two mortars and some patrol troops additional to their machine-gun company already posted with the rear-guard. There was now a clear sky by day and virtually no night, so that enemy air activity reaped the fullest benefit in reconnaissance and in attack—a fact which must be weighed against the natural strength of the new position. The platoon and the support section (with a 3-inch mortar) belonging to No. 2 Independent Company held outpost positions on the west and east sides of the Saltdal respectively. The Irish Guards had their No. 1 Company strongly placed on a steep ridge beside the main road on the east side a little in front of the girder bridge (which was blown up prematurely and imperfectly in the small hours of the morning). Their No. 4 Company covered the bridge from the west side, with No. 3 behind them covering the main road and the river banks below the bridge. A reserve position, rather more than a mile back, was occupied by the last company of the Irish Guards and No. 3 Independent Company, and had the prospect of further reinforcement from the remainder of No. 2 Independent Company coming south towards the scene of action. The Norwegians were used in support of the British, with their mortar detachment placed on the high ground to the west of the British positions in rear of the road bridge, while the main road was further covered by our own single troop of artillery, which had been in the withdrawal from Mo. The headquarters of Stockforce—from now on the field operations in the Bodö area were commanded under Brigadier Gubbins by Lieut.-Colonel H. C.

Stockwell, formerly O.C. No. 2 Independent Company—were near the reserve position, hidden in a wood to the west of the road.

Enemy cyclists made contact with the outpost position along the main road on the east side of the Saltdal at 8 a.m. on 25th May. By 11 a.m. the support section had been driven in on the principal position protecting the girder bridge, where the Guards in slit trenches held the ridge firmly with the help of cross-fire from the field guns and the Norwegian mortars on the other bank. In the early afternoon, while five Heinkel aircraft were machine-gunning to create a diversion on the far side, the Germans tried to storm the ridge. They were driven back, but then proceeded gradually to outflank the position, by which means they eventually forced its defenders to withdraw. The last platoon to move back found that the bridge on the flooded side-river had been blown up and had to cross under fire by a hand-line improvised from rifle slings. The men from the ridge then made their way along a track down the Saltdal to a hanging foot-bridge about a mile below our reserve position on the other side. Meanwhile No. 4 Company, Irish Guards, posted immediately behind the main road bridge came under heavy fire, but with the help of Norwegian troops prevented any enemy advance across the river on to the west bank and inflicted considerable casualties. Headquarters, which had been burnt out by incendiary bullets in one of the air attacks, learnt of our reverse on the east bank about 6 p.m. and sent the reserves—No. 2 Company, Irish Guards, and No. 3 Independent Company—across the river to hold positions on and near a high shelf protected by cliffs at the northern angle of the river junction. These were occupied by 4.30 a.m. on the 26th and made the situation on our left flank reasonably secure.

During the night, however, the enemy had built a floating bridge a little higher up the river, so as to transfer the weight of the attack to the other flank. Our outpost on the hillside was forced to fall back towards the position still held by the Guards, preventing access to the wrecked girder bridge; and thereupon our only remaining reserve, a portion of No. 2 Independent Company, was sent up on to the hill in the forlorn hope of stemming the advance there and preventing our prospective encirclement. By 11.30 the enemy were already pressing hard, and shortly afterwards Brigadier Gubbins at Rognan gave orders for a withdrawal; but it was not until mid-afternoon that Colonel Stockwell was able to concert this with his officers and it actually began at 7 p.m. No. 2 Independent Company was accordingly concentrated near the foot-bridge, where it occupied a covering position and engaged the enemy until 10.30 p.m. It was intended that the forces which had been posted to the east bank overnight should also withdraw to the foot-bridge, so as to occupy a rearguard position almost abreast of No. 2 Independent Company. The order never reached No. 2 Company, Irish Guards. No. 3 Independent Company, whose position was more accessible, received the order but could not comply quickly enough. Instead of crossing by the foot-bridge, they continued their retreat down the east side of the Saltdal to its mouth, followed by the Guards company, when the latter heard of the withdrawal through a Norwegian liaison officer late in the evening. Meanwhile, No. 4 Company, Irish Guards, across the wrecked girder bridge, seized their chance to disengage when a Gladiator fighter appeared out of the blue and machine-gunned their astonished opponents. The withdrawal down the road to the mouth of the valley at Rognan then proceeded according to plan, except for a party from Battalion Headquarters, who had been kept back to load the reserve ammunition on the last of the motor transport and were ambushed from a roadside farm afterwards as they marched. By this time the Germans were working their way down on to the road at many points. But at Rognan boats were available to ferry the force across the end of the Saltdalsfiord—a six-mile gap in the road which would hold up the advance of the enemy. This provided for the main body of troops which had been brought back down the road, and No. 3 Independent Company after its journey down the east bank made its way across the river to join them in time for the embarkation. But No. 2 Company, Irish Guards, unable to cross the river into Rognan, extricated themselves by means of a forced march of twenty arduous miles across steep and pathless mountains, arriving ultimately at Langset, where the road resumed at the other end of the ferry journey.

The only encouraging feature of the withdrawal was the presence (already referred to) of British aircraft, three Gladiators which had been sent from the newly-established air base at Bardufoss on the 26th. One of them unfortunately crashed on taking off from an improvised runway of wire-covered grass sods outside Bodö, but even two fighters patrolling by turns had a value quite beyond their immediate score of two German aircraft brought down and two more damaged. How far this new factor might have altered the whole trend of the campaign so far as the defence of Bodö is concerned it is impossible to calculate, since the remaining operations were governed by factors which had nothing to do with local conditions. On 25th May a destroyer from Harstad, carrying the last company of South Wales Borderers southwards, carried also a senior staff officer to concert plans for retirement with Brigadier Gubbins, who had already been warned by telephone of the Government's decision to evacuate North Norway. This decision, difficult enough in relation to the situation at Bodö, involved still harder problems farther north in relation to what had been achieved or was on the verge of achievement at Narvik.

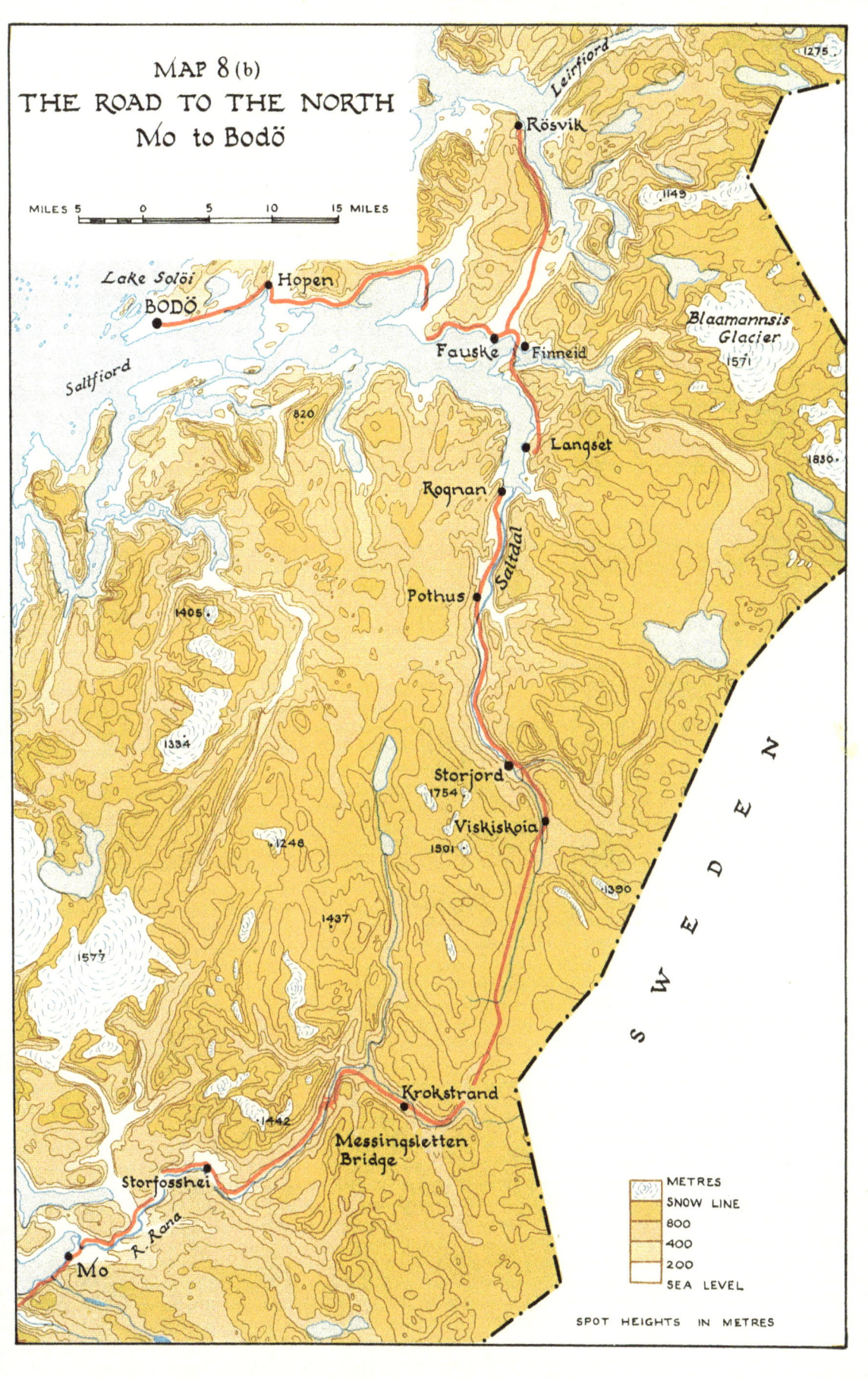

CHAPTER XIII

THE CAPTURE OF NARVIK

See Map 9, facing page 212

IT will be recalled that the proposals for a direct assault on Narvik had died down temporarily after the naval bombardment of 24th April. But the first reliable signs of the long-awaited thaw encouraged Lord Cork, to quote the language of his official despatch, to 'look forward to the conduct of operations without the tremendous handicap of snow'.[1] Accordingly, he had already made a further reconnaissance of Narvik in his flagship (1st May) when he received on the 3rd the imperative message from the First Lord of the Admiralty pressing for action 'even at severe cost'.[2]

The build-up of the Allied force was still in progress. The arrival of the Chasseurs Alpins was followed on 6th May by that of two battalions of the Foreign Legion, which had been formed in February in North Africa, where they were destined to serve again as a 'Free French' unit in 1942. Then, on the 9th, a Polish brigade of four battalions arrived, styled *Chasseurs de Montagne*. Their fighting qualities were still to be tested—a Pole who was in the brigade records that 'only a few of them had ever seen mountains at all'[3]—but their officers and non-commissioned officers had for the most part served in the Polish campaign and then escaped from Poland to raise the flag in France. The force had been created originally to utilise Polish anti-Russian feeling in connection with the abortive Allied expedition to Finland and had now been directed first to Tromsö; but the Norwegian authorities there were bitterly opposed to any suggestion that the Poles might help to garrison the extreme north of Norway, where the Russian attitude was thought to be uncertain. Allied artillery in the Narvik area now totalled 24 guns—a French group of 75's, which accompanied the Chasseurs Alpins, and twelve British 25-pounders. The gunners of 203 Field Battery, R.A., had arrived on 22nd April, the first of their guns with the landing craft a whole week later. Four of these were assault landing craft for infantry (A.L.C.s), the other four, shortly afterwards increased to six, were motor landing craft for material (M.L.C.s); the signal asking for them had been sent before General Mackesy left Scapa on 12th April. As for anti-aircraft artillery, although a week of May had passed before the first

---

[1] Sec. II (5).
[2] See p. 169.
[3] Zbyszewski, Karl: *The Fight for Narvik*, p. 3.

heavy battery was landed, the position at the beginning of the month was that three light batteries were also actually on the way to Norway, making a total of one heavy and four light batteries in all, and five more heavy and one more light battery were due to follow.

The naval force at Lord Cork's disposal had been increased after his arrival in Norwegian waters not only by a battleship (H.M.S. *Resolution* had now replaced *Warspite* in this role) but by the aircraft carrier *Furious*, which was likewise left behind when the Home Fleet returned to Scapa on 15th April. She worked in and out of the fiords as far north as Tromsö throughout the latter part of April, until she had only eight aircraft serviceable and her engines damaged by a near miss. Her place was, however, taken by the *Ark Royal*, and on 6th May the Scots Guards described her Skua fighters flying high over Harstad base as 'the first British aircraft that had been seen since our arrival in Norway—a very welcome sight'. The number of cruisers was indeed reduced, particularly by the needs of the Aandalsnes and Namsos evacuations, but until the middle of May there were usually as many as fifteen destroyers available, indefatigable and ubiquitous. Thus German air attacks, though they sank the Polish destroyer *Grom* and did other damage, could not prevent the Navy from exercising a steady pressure against their forces in and around Narvik by its constant patrolling of the fiords.

The size and condition of the German force defending Narvik remained an open question. General Dietl's Mountain Division, which had been brought in by destroyers, could be estimated fairly accurately at 2,000 men, presumably doubled from the destroyer crews, but we did not know what losses they had sustained from the hard conditions as well as from naval bombardment and other fighting on an extended front. It was guessed at the time that a trickle of reinforcements, chiefly technical troops, was being brought in to Narvik by the railway from Sweden—it was scarcely within the power of the Swedes to refuse facilities for civilians, alleged Red Cross workers, etc., analogous to the facilities they had granted to volunteers for the Finnish war. What quantities of supplies were also being brought in by the same route was uncertain. The main consideration, however, was the air lift. Seaplanes were eventually ousted from the Rombaksfiord, but they could alight in Narvik harbour and the Beisfiord at will; and pending the establishment of our own fighter aircraft we could not interfere at all with parachute deliveries, which were to be observed first near Bjerkvik and then high up on Björnfjell as a daily operation whenever the weather permitted. The cessation of hostilities in Central Norway, which was clearly seen to portend a big development in the enemy bomber offensive in the North, was expected also to make it relatively easy for the Germans to build up their infantry strength by air at Narvik.

The arrangements which they actually made at this juncture were as follows. On the termination of the campaign in the south, Army Group XXI was instructed to send one division home to Germany—this move apparently was not even started—and at the same time received back direct control of General Dietl's force, which had been placed under the Supreme Command (O.K.W.) since 15th April. The directive now given to Group XXI was that 'In co-operation with Air Fleet 5 every available means are to be used to get supplies to it [*sc*. Dietl's force] as quickly as possible'. A further order, emphasising the importance of supporting the troops at Narvik, was issued by Hitler himself direct to the new air command formed for Norway under Colonel-General Stumpff, who had taken up his post in Oslo about the beginning of the month. There was a big increase in bomber attacks from a force of nearly 200 bomber aircraft now based on Trondheim. Paratroops and mountain infantry were dropped on Björnfjell, with heavy and light machine guns, and on 20th May provision of men was given a temporary priority over ammunition. But the Germans experienced many difficulties. Although their resources of aircraft at this time seemed limitless in comparison with our own, they had not enough of the long-range Junkers 52s, which could carry only a ton at a time and were wanted also to supply the overland advance from the Trondheim area, quite apart from large-scale withdrawals for the forthcoming invasion of the Low Countries. There were questions of organisation and management which caused considerable friction among the enemy even in the later stages, when the air lift was being controlled from Oslo by telephone through Sweden: Air Force objections, for example, to the dropping of mountain infantry not trained as paratroops. Lastly, they were hampered by the weather—poor visibility restricting operations and the thaw complicating them, because supplies had to be dropped close to widely scattered troop positions so as to minimise portage through melting mountain snow.

The German supply arrangements were therefore on a hand-to-mouth basis throughout: not until mid-May did they even have enough pairs of skis to equip their transport columns. The scale of reinforcement was likewise modest. When his troops were first cut off, Hitler proposed to send essential supplies and possibly key men into Narvik by submarine, but nothing came of this: during the first month of the siege the total of arrivals, which were by parachute, seaplane, and railway, was only about 300 men, the railway handling chiefly supplies. The air lift began in earnest on 14th May, and between that date and the end of the campaign there were a further 1,100 arrivals, rather more than half of which were of paratroops, the rest being of mountain infantry with a few artillerymen and other specialists. But the besiegers had no means of estimating with any exactness the effects of the air lift; and in any case the use made of this new and formidable technique might have been stepped up at any moment, which constituted an additional reason for aiming at the speedy liquidation of the German defence of Narvik.

In all the circumstances it does not seem surprising that Lord Cork issued orders on 3rd May for an attack on the 8th, to be launched from the sea or across Rombaksfiord 'as judged best'. But General Mackesy had in effect rejected the latter alternative as regards the immediate future only five days before, when the newly arrived General Béthouart after a preliminary reconnaissance with Lord Cork had proposed to land on the Öyjord peninsula forthwith, so as to take Bjerkvik in the rear and then with the help of artillery cross the Rombaksfiord to Narvik. As we have seen,[1] the Chasseurs Alpins were employed in the northern sector for an overland advance instead. General Mackesy accordingly now prepared an outline plan to land two British battalions direct from the sea on the north shore some three miles from the town. But the senior British Army officers other than the General, who could not be wholly unaware that he had been subordinated to the Admiral to secure a more aggressive policy *coûte que coûte*, made representations to Lord Cork against the proposed attack. Their main objections were the following: the shortage of A.L.C.s for the first landing; the need to supplement the available M.L.C.s by local craft and trawlers, which would restrict the area of attack to steeply shelving beaches—only three in number, small, and bordered by high rocks; the impossibility of effecting a surprise in perpetual daylight and without smoke shells; and the prospect of enemy air attack against men in open boats or ashore and unable to dig in. Some senior naval officers, including Lord Cork's principal staff officer, Captain L. E. H. Maund, concurred with the Army in desiring that the attack should be put off pending further preparation. On the night of 5th/6th May Lord Cork forwarded the military representations to London for consideration, but before the final reply of the Chiefs of Staff had reached him,[2] he decided to postpone this operation until a new general arrived on the scene, adopting in the meantime a course of action proposed by General Mackesy. It is an interesting coincidence that on 6th May Dietl himself had for the first time independently contemplated evacuating his forces from Narvik.

The alternative British plan was to invest Narvik more closely by landing on the shore of the Herjangsfiord north-east of the town, so as to mount artillery at Öyjord and move farther inland to cut the

---

[1] P. 157.
[2] See p. 170.

railway near the frontier. This step in the campaign had been projected as early as 29th April to fit in with the British push towards Ankenes as well as the Norwegian-French advance in the Gratangen area; but it was not until 7th May that General Mackesy, though pressed (as we have seen) by the French command, decided that the time was ripe. A careful reconnaissance from the sea on the night of 7th/8th May disclosed no sign of life on the part of the enemy, and the terrain near Bjerkvik at the head of the fiord appeared not unsuitable for the operation. From this village it should be feasible to move southwards about eight miles along the fiord on to the tip of the peninsula at Öyjord.

The landing operation, in which the British Navy was to convey and give close support to a French force, was to be combined with a further attempt by the Norwegians and the French to press overland towards Bjerkvik from the Gratangen area. It was agreed that there should be a simultaneous advance by the Norwegian left wing up in the mountains. But the main operation was postponed by Lord Cork from the night of the 11th/12th until the following night, with the result that the Norwegian 6th Brigade on the left flank, unable to make a last-minute postponement, moved forward first. They had the support of a few miscellaneous Norwegian aircraft functioning as bombers, and succeeded in occupying a succession of heights which brought them forward in the course of two days' fighting to the north edge of the Kuberg plateau; this mountain massif, rising (at the Kobberfjell) to nearly 3,000 feet, is the dominant feature in the country east of the Bjerkvik-Öyjord shore line, from which it is about seven miles distant. One battalion of Germans was thus driven back or otherwise accounted for by the Norwegians, the tactical gain being considerable and the more meritorious because of the conditions under which the 6th Brigade operated. The depth of the snow on the mountains had been up to 6-9 feet, and on the extreme left the supply-line had a stretch of about ten miles over which no cart traffic was possible throughout the period of snow and thaw. Their brigade staff officer describes the nature of the advance as follows:

> Our push forward right until Kuberg was taken had to be made through narrow valley passages between mountain tops of up to 3,000 feet. These tops dominated the valleys. The Germans made use of this, climbed up and established themselves on the summits, and in order to go forward we had to climb up after them and get at them there on top.[1]

The naval force for the landing assembled on the 12th near Ballangen, where it picked up the two battalions of the Foreign Legion, having already embarked five of the ten small tanks which

---
[1] *Norges Krig*, p. 404.

the French had brought with them. They sailed about 9 p.m., General Béthouart accompanying Lord Cork in the *Effingham*. The battleship *Resolution* and a second cruiser, the *Aurora*, would give weight to the bombardment. There were also five destroyers, one of which (the *Havelock*) had mounted a French mortar battery on the forecastle. The foremost landing party of 120 men made the twenty-mile passage to Bjerkvik in the four assault landing craft; the rest of the 1,500 infantry mainly in the two cruisers, each of which drew a ready-made-up 'tow', consisting of a power boat and two pulling boats, behind her. The tanks were carried in the battleship, together with two motor landing craft for putting them ashore; a third, which was of a more modern type, went under its own steam. The whole was to be covered by aircraft from the *Ark Royal*. The original plan had provided that there should be no preliminary bombardment if there was a possibility of surprise, but in the end the leading destroyers had orders to open fire as soon as they reached their stations off Bjerkvik.

This bombardment began punctually at midnight—broad day in the latitude of Narvik but dark enough at Trondheim, it was hoped, to impede the German air force from flying to the rescue. It was timed to last a quarter of an hour, during which houses were set ablaze and ammunition stores exploded; but as the Germans kept up machine-gun fire a general bombardment followed, with the particular object of knocking out enemy machine-gun posts on the foreshore, in houses, and in the woods behind. At one o'clock, when the landing commenced, the ships moved their barrage of fire inland. At two o'clock it ceased temporarily, but was reopened an hour or so later to fire overhead in order to cover the second landing. This completed the naval operations in the main, the big ships departing as the last troops left them, though some of the destroyers remained off Bjerkvik to give any further help. Such help was now less likely to be needed, as the aircraft of the *Ark Royal*, at first grounded by low cloud, began their fighter patrol for the landing about 2 a.m. and were later available to bomb objectives on the railway. No German aircraft put in an appearance. As for the main task of the naval force during the landing, it is difficult to estimate the precise effect of the bombardment: some part of an uncertain number of enemy machine-gun posts remained in action, but the troops at no time found opposition really heavy. British field ambulances helped to bring the French wounded to an improvised hospital ship.

The intended order of landing was: tanks—the first party of 120 men from A.L.C.s—other men from ships' boats. But the hoisting-out from the *Resolution* took so long that the more modern M.L.C. put her tank ashore independently, and this gave the signal to the men in the A.L.C.s. Two more tanks struggled ashore at the same time as the 'tows' were bringing in the rest of the first battalion; the two remaining tanks came in with the second battalion. Nevertheless, it was the tanks which silenced the enemy machine guns. An officer of the Legion describes them as 'frisking about like young puppies, firing all the time, in the midst of fields which were here free from snow'.[1] The first battalion had to land half a mile to the west of the village, but the tanks enabled it to make its way eastwards quite rapidly, and to advance from the village up the road north towards Gratangen. Meanwhile the other battalion had found the opposition from machine-guns in the Elvegaard direction too strong for a landing, so came ashore on the south-east side of the village about three furlongs from it. They were landing on the road to Öyjord, and their nearer objective, the former regimental depot at Elvegaard, was on the same side of Bjerkvik. Supported by their tanks, the French stormed Elvegaard building by building and captured a hundred machine guns and other material. Nevertheless, General Béthouart during the assault sent for two companies of the 2nd Polish Battalion as reinforcements. Destroyers went to fetch them from the Bogen inlet; but the battalion, whose orders were to press against the German patrols in that area, had set out overnight with no transport through the snow, and marched fifteen miles to the scene of action. When they arrived, victory was already complete. In the course of the morning the motor-cyclist section of the Foreign Legion arrived in Öyjord, where they found no enemy but their general and his staff, who had landed from the *Havelock*, which was supporting the patrol from the fiord. So ended, with only 36 casualties, the first of the opposed landings on which Allied fortunes in the later war years were so largely to depend and our first experiment in war with the landing craft which proved to be one of the main instruments of victory.

Unfortunately, however, it was not until 1.45 p.m. on the following day (14th May) that the troops from Bjerkvik were able to make contact with the right wing of the advance from the north, where the Chasseurs Alpins were due to clear the line of the Gratangen-Bjerkvik road. These now had the support of a battery of British anti-aircraft guns as well as of their own field artillery, and the 14th Battalion by the end of the day had reached a position commanding the first steep descent towards Bjerkvik. But the 6th Battalion, who had to move forward from mountain to mountain on the east of the road, stuck fast on the exposed slope between Roasme and Örnefjell and were unable to link up with the Norwegians on their left, so the enemy managed to withdraw to the south-east before the trap closed. Thus the Germans on the northern side of Narvik, though their position was greatly worsened by the successful landing, still held two fronts meeting in a right angle at the Hartvigvatn—a northern front against

---

[1] Lapie, Captain B. O.: *With the Foreign Legion at Narvik*, p. 34.

the Norwegians up in the mountains, and a western front inland from the Bjerkvik–Öyjord road. The key to the position was the Kuberg plateau.

South of Narvik, the fighting had continued in the Ankenes peninsula, where the Officer Commanding 2nd South Wales Borderers was now operating with his own battalion and a battalion of Chasseurs Alpins, plus one company of Irish Guards in the rear at Haakvik.[1] The French held about two-thirds of the line, including the snow-bound ridge to the east, the British the area nearest Ankenes, from which our field guns could fire across the Beisfiord. But on the 14th, to complete the general policy of moving British troops to the Bodö area, arrangements were made to bring the South Wales Borderers away from the Ankenes peninsula, from which the company of Irish Guards and Brigade Advanced Headquarters had already been withdrawn. When this relief was carried out by the 2nd Polish Battalion, ferried over from Öyjord at 11 a.m. on the 16th, British soldiers (apart from the artillery, especially anti-aircraft artillery, and ancillary services) ceased to play any direct part in the siege of Narvik.

These arrangements to hold up the Germans in the south were instituted, under the general authority of Lord Cork, by Major-General Mackesy, but carried out by his successor, Lieut.-General C. J. E. Auchinleck. General Mackesy's last operational instruction placed all British troops except the South Wales Borderers under command of Brigadier Fraser for operations in the Mo area. This was issued on 11th May, after Lord Cork had left in the *Effingham* for the scene of action at Bjerkvik; General Auchinleck arrived from England, had a brief meeting with Major-General Mackesy, and joined Lord Cork on board the flagship the same day. He then accompanied the Admiral on a preliminary reconnaissance of Narvik, where he noted that 'information as to the enemy strength and dispositions is practically non-existent and appears unobtainable', and witnessed the events of the landing at Bjerkvik. His instructions from the Secretary of State for War had been signed on 5th May, by which date his coming was known to both commanders in the field.[2] He was appointed as General Officer Commanding-in-Chief Designate, to take independent command of the land forces and air component when Lord Cork's existing plans—meaning presumably his proposals for the assault on Narvik—had been either executed or abandoned. In the meantime General Auchinleck was to prepare a report on the needs of the situation. However, on the afternoon of the 13th, when

---
[1] See p. 159.
[2] See Appendix A (8), p. 259.

the Admiral and General returned to Harstad, a conference was held, of which the upshot was that General Auchinleck, exercising discretionary powers given him by the Chief of the Imperial General Staff, assumed immediate command, under Lord Cork, of the land and air forces, to which the name of North-Western Expeditionary Force was now given. At a further conference with General Béthouart at 10 o'clock next morning, General Auchinleck took the final decision to employ all the British land forces in the struggle farther south —these were the forces which defended the Mo-Bodö area as described in the last chapter—and to place General Béthouart in command of all land forces in the Narvik area. His recent success at Bjerkvik had underlined the fact that the Frenchman was an expert in both mountain and winter warfare, who (like Dietl) had served a course in Norway before the war. Thus the assault on Narvik would be the direct concern of the French and Poles, in co-operation with the Norwegians, who readily agreed to transfer to General Béthouart's command for the period of the operation their most appropriate battalion, one largely recruited from the Narvik area. The plans were then prepared in concert with the British naval staff.

Meanwhile General Auchinleck had orders from the Chiefs of Staff to report in conjunction with Lord Cork as to the area to be held in North Norway and the means required to hold it. Collaboration was made easier by the transfer of the Admiral's headquarters to shore on 16th May, the date on which the General sent home the agreed report. He took as his starting-point the assumption that our first object, the denial to Germany of an iron-ore supply shipped through Narvik, had already been achieved by the destruction of the port facilities through our naval operations and the German demolitions. General Auchinleck further assumed that our position *vis-à-vis* the Swedes rendered any attempt to interfere with the iron-ore route through Lulea impracticable. Therefore he had only to plan for the maintenance of the integrity of North Norway. The General concluded that Bodö must be held permanently to defend Narvik: hence the troop movements already described. Secondly, a tentative project for a military base at Skaanland was found impracticable, and Tromsö selected as an additional base and a hospital base (for 1,200 beds). The headquarters of the Norwegian Government was already located there. The Tromsö project was to involve an additional demand for anti-aircraft defences to secure the assent of the Norwegian authorities, who were particularly apprehensive about air attacks because of the nearness of Russian territory, from which they thought the Germans might operate. An advance base party left Harstad for Tromsö on 23rd May, and four anti-aircraft guns were duly set up there, marking incidentally the farthest northward stretch of our military power in Europe.

As regards the defence requirements of the area as a whole, General Auchinleck's report proposed a nucleus of four cruisers and six destroyers for naval defence, a military force based on seventeen infantry battalions, 200 anti-aircraft guns (thirteen heavy and eight light batteries), seven batteries of field artillery and howitzers, some armoured troops, and an air force of four squadrons. But the details thus set out read ironically in view of the desperate position already taking shape in northern France. On the 17th the Chiefs of Staff telegraphed, stating that the size of the force must be severely limited and asking for the General's views as to the retention of Narvik under the new conditions. General Auchinleck on the 21st returned a reasoned answer, pointing out, for example, that in the case of anti-aircraft artillery he was being asked to make do with less than one-half of his estimate of his needs, which in turn was only two-thirds of the estimate prepared by the War Office before he left London. He concluded as follows:

> The inevitability of the evacuation of Northern Norway in the circumstances envisaged in your telegram is, in my opinion, entirely dependent on the enemy's will to avail himself of his undoubted ability to attack. Should he attack I cannot, with the reduced forces suggested by you, hold myself responsible for the safety of this Force, nor will I pretend that there is any reasonable certainty of my being able to achieve the object given to me in my Instructions. If, in spite of this, larger considerations lead His Majesty's Government to decide that Northern Norway must continue to be held with the diminished resources laid down by them, I cannot answer for the consequences, but you may rest assured that every effort will be made to do what is possible with the resources at my disposal.

The inadequacy of the force at its disposal, actual and prospective, was not the only difficulty confronting the British Supreme Command. General Auchinleck's arrival in North Norway had been closely followed by that of Colonel R. C. G. Pollock as head of a military mission to the Norwegian Government, which was intended to reduce friction and misunderstanding. Unfortunately, the situation was too unmanageable. The King and Government, to whose respective seats in Maalselvdal (north-east of Bardufoss) and round Tromsö Lord Cork paid formal visits on 23rd May, had transferred executive responsibility for defence to General Ruge as head of a Supreme Defence Command, situated in Maalselvdal and staffed mainly from the entourage which had accompanied him as a Supreme Military Headquarters from Gudbrandsdal. It was, for instance, General Ruge who initialled the agreement for a British base of severely circumscribed extent at Tromsö, and the intention was gradually to transfer all such negotiations to his charge, leaving General Fleischer free to devote himself entirely to the operations of his Division. This might have made for more harmonious relations with the Allies in the long run, but the short run was beset with difficulties, and General Ruge continued to press for the appointment of a new military attaché in place of Lieut.-Colonel King-Salter,[1] so as to have a separate channel of communication with the British military authorities at home. One of General Auchinleck's first actions was to arrange a conference with Generals Ruge and Fleischer at Harstad, when he found them 'both anxious to help apparently'; but the clouds of suspicion were not dispelled.

The Norwegian generals tended naturally enough to interpret every British action in the light of the recent abandonment of Central Norway and the current retreat on Bodö. They were also extremely sensitive to any interference with civilian liberties or property in the battle area, such control being their prerogative even if they did not choose to exercise it. Our reticence regarding operational movements again provided many unintentional slights. But what was perhaps most hampering to good mutual relations was the silent argument with which they were presented by the spectacle of our delays and apparent hesitations: ought there not to be a unified command in the hands of a general who understood the climate and the terrain? On 11th May General Ruge had proposed to Lord Cork that Lieut.-Colonel Roscher Nielsen[2] should command the British troops in the Mo area 'in this present crisis'; he and his principal subordinates would have welcomed a similar solution in larger areas. And in the background there was always the natural fear of divergent strategic interests, which made the Norwegian military leaders concerned even at this stage that they and not the Allies should provide the garrison of Narvik and the troops which would subsequently seize the key position on the Swedish frontier.

But Narvik could not be garrisoned before it was recaptured, a task which had from the outset presupposed the assertion of British maritime power and was seen increasingly to require also the establishment of our air power. To this we must now turn.

The reconnaissance of the Narvik area had been carried out by Wing-Commander R. L. R. Atcherley at the end of April while the proposed air component, two fighter squadrons and one bomber squadron under the command of Group Captain M. Moore, was still being made ready. Banak, at the head of the Porsangerfiord, proved to be the only possible base for bombers. It had the advantage that it was not snow-bound, but the disadvantage that it lay two hundred miles north-east of Narvik. The distance might not prove

---

[1] See p. 112.
[2] See p. 183.

an insuperable obstacle to the operations of the aircraft concerned, but it involved a heavy drain on naval resources, which would have had to be stretched to protect seaborne communications round the North Cape. Banak was in fact never used, though Lord Cork and General Auchinleck urged persistently that without the help of at least one bomber squadron we could make no effective reply to the German offensive. One of the fighter squadrons was to be based on Bardufoss, fifty miles north of Narvik—a small Norwegian military airfield equipped with two short runways. The nearest point on the fiord for landing supplies was the little wooden jetty at Sörreisa, seventeen and a half miles away by a narrow lane requiring immediate reconstruction. The other squadron was to be based on Skaanland, south of Harstad, where a stretch of level ground was found which had been partially drained. In addition it was intended from the outset to develop a forward landing ground on a conveniently placed site just outside the town of Bodö.

The physical obstacles were enormous. The reconnaissance party found Bardufoss under four and a half feet of snow and Skaanland under two feet, though at sea-level; beneath this there was a layer of ice; beneath the ice a further penetration of frost deep into the soil. Snow clearance, blasting of ice, drainage of the site, and surface rolling had all to be taken in hand, while the spring thaw hindered as much as it helped because the melting heaps of snow flooded back on to the cleared area. There were also other obstacles raised, to begin with, by the Norwegian General Fleischer, who demanded a written promise from the R.A.F. that there would be no sudden withdrawal as from Aandalsnes and (more effectually) resisted the introduction of British or French troops at Bardufoss to clear the snow. Nevertheless, work began forthwith. At Bardufoss there was help from Norwegian airmen familiar with the site, from a local labour supply providing two ten-hour shifts of about 300 men each, and from a reserve battalion of General Fleischer's troops sent primarily for guard duties. A bulldozer was fortunately available, and the R.A.F. even stooped to conquer with a baggage train of two hundred mules. Bardufoss was eventually equipped with one runway, having a usable length of rather more than 800 yards and up to twenty camouflaged blastproof shelters for aircraft in the surrounding woodland, with convergent taxi-ing lanes which suggested the nickname of the Clock Golf Course. The second runway was cleared but its surface could not be made satisfactory, so work was begun on an extension of the first runway to 1,400 yards. A rudimentary operations room was constructed underground, and an extensive system of air-raid shelters was also gradually developed, which, together with the safe dispersal of aircraft, should go far to avert such a disaster as had befallen the Gladiators at Lesjaskog.

ESTABLISHMENT OF AIR BASE AT BARDUFOSS

At Skaanland, however, in spite of a similar expenditure of effort the airfield never became fit for use and has since reverted to farm land. As for Bodö, the site there was crossed by two large ditches and a network of power and telephone lines; 176,000 grass sods had also to be cut to cover a section which had been ploughed; but there was no snow and plenty of labour in the neighbouring town. The Norwegian authorities had the field prepared in ten days in spite of air raids, which were probably precipitated by a broadcast appeal from the Chief of Police for five hundred men to report on the site. As we have already seen,[1] it came into service on 26th May, and after the first trial the runway was relaid in fourteen hours with 900 feet of snowboards. But Bodö was then given up so quickly that the forward landing ground there plays little more part than Skaanland in the general story.

Bardufoss, therefore, had to be used without any alternative being available in the event of heavy attack; but it was not without defences. The field was equipped with eight heavy and twelve light anti-aircraft guns; and two lines of Observer Posts had been set up, which were all the more important because it was not found possible to establish radar stations in North Norway without further experiment. One such line was in the south from Bodö east to Fauske; the other covered the western approach through the Lofoten Islands. Unfortunately the pack wireless set supplied was far too weak to send messages across the high iron-bound mountains. It was still more unfortunate that our initial preparations were made in ignorance of the fact that the Norwegians had their own chain of Observer Posts, operated chiefly by women volunteers, which stretched down into enemy-held territory along the coast to a point south of Mosjöen. Nor did it make for smooth working that a force of six officers and 269 men (R.A.F. and Army combined) had been sent out on a task involving wide dispersion with no transport and no prearranged billets. However, by the time the first squadron arrived at Bardufoss the two observer screens between them were reporting enemy movements to Headquarters at Harstad with a delay of between two and ten minutes. Thus the air base got general warnings, but they depended upon the eyes and ears of the watchers and the efficiency of the telephone by which they were transmitted, and it was impossible to dispense with standing patrols all round the clock. Finally, there was a company of Chasseurs Alpins at the airfield to guard it against attack by paratroops.

As we have noticed, there had been a lull in German air activity the day of the Bjerkvik landing, but it was afterwards renewed more fiercely. In spite of the work of the Fleet Air Arm, which operated

---

[1] P. 192.

some fighters from the *Ark Royal* until the 21st, more than a dozen ships were bombed within a fortnight; the most important were the battleship *Resolution*, which was sent home for safety on the 18th after a bomb had pierced three decks, the transport *Chrobry* (already referred to), and the anti-aircraft cruiser *Curlew*, lost with many of her crew on the 26th after innumerable attacks while protecting the construction of the Skaanland airfield. The headquarters of the French units had also been bombed on several occasions, and the 6th Chasseurs Alpins suffered serious losses on the 21st while moving into a reserve area. Thus it was clear that the further progress of the campaign must depend upon the provision of land-based fighter aircraft, the first of which took off for Bardufoss from the carrier *Furious* at 6 a.m. on May 21st, the day that she replaced the *Ark Royal* on the station.

They were the same Gladiator squadron, No. 263, which had made the ill-fated flight to Lesjaskog nearly a month earlier. The weather was again thick and foul, with the result that two aircraft were wrecked on the mountain side, but from the following morning patrols were maintained over the base and the fleet anchorage. The final assault on Narvik was timed for 28th May, to allow of a further strengthening of our position in the air by the arrival of the Hurricanes of No. 46 Squadron. They flew off from the *Glorious* on the 26th for the Skaanland airfield, which had that day been passed as fit for use, but three out of eleven aircraft tipped on to their noses on landing as a result of the soft surface of the runway. The Hurricane squadron had therefore to be diverted to Bardufoss, which meant that the Bodö area was at extreme range for them, and Gladiators (as already noted) went to Bodö in their stead. However, the air component had now reached its final strength, which may be computed at rather less than two-thirds of what had been requested: for there was no bomber squadron and the slower Gladiators had been substituted for one of the two squadrons of Hurricane fighters specified in the original Air Ministry project. The force also included a squadron of six naval Walrus amphibians, which arrived at Harstad on 18th May, but they were used more for transport than patrol work.

From 22nd May to 7th June there was no day without important activity in the air; the lowest total of sorties in twenty-four hours being ten in appalling weather, and the highest, flown on the day that Narvik fell, reaching ninety-five. The task set for the R.A.F. was not an easy one. The enemy's advance northwards made it increasingly possible for him to employ short-range aircraft, such as dive-bombers (fitted with extra petrol tanks) and twin-engined Messerschmitt fighters, whereas our own Gladiator fighters were actually slower than the regular Heinkel bombers. Moreover, our standing patrols—relays of aircraft continuously at work in all flying weather—

were exposed to heavy strain by the unusual terrain, as the mountains cut them off from communication with the ground and the narrow fiord valleys threw up dangerous air currents. Nevertheless, the Gladiator squadron claimed to have destroyed twenty-six enemy aircraft, the Hurricane eleven. This was a rate of loss which—even when we add in the 'bag' of the anti-aircraft batteries, computed to be twenty-three—the Germans at this stage in the war could easily accept, but our losses in action were less than one-third of theirs and the important fact is that the R.A.F. acquired a sufficient ascendancy to preserve the base areas and lines of communication from sharing the fate of Namsos and Aandalsnes. Otherwise, Narvik would have been much harder to take and impossible to hold.

The situation of the troops on the eve of the final assault—postponed by stages from 21st to 27th May, for reasons which included waiting for the M.L.C.s (busy with the transport of guns and stores for the airfields) and later for the Hurricanes—was as follows. The Norwegian 6th Brigade, continuing its separate struggle in the high mountains, had made two attacks against the German posts in the region of the Kuberg plateau, the second of which (on 22nd May) had been successful. Thus the Germans had been pressed back from any position which might threaten Allied control of the Öyjord peninsula. Moreover, the 14th Chasseurs Alpins, closely supported by warships, had been working eastwards along the shore of the Rombaksfiord and up on to the heights behind, where they joined hands with a part of the Norwegian 7th Brigade. The French were now based on Lilleberg and controlled the greater part of the road leading from there to the narrows at Straumen. Only the width of the Rombaksfiord separated them from the defenders of Narvik and the railway line, about 800 strong (including one new infantry company dropped by parachute and some sailors), with their headquarters in the northern outskirts of the town. On the south side of Narvik, beyond the Beisfiord, there had been a brisk German counter-attack with strong mortar support on the morning of 17th May, a few hours before the Chasseurs Alpins were due to be relieved by the Poles, who had the previous day relieved the British.[1] This had been repelled with the help of the British field guns, left behind under French command, and the operations in this area then passed into the charge of the Polish General Bohusz-szyzko, with the 1st, 2nd, and 4th Polish battalions and a detachment of French ski troops. The Poles held most of the long ridge beside the Beisfiord, but at its bottom end German patrols of about 100 infantry and the pick of the sailors were

---

[1] See p. 200.

still ensconced in the mountains and threatened to outflank them at the Storvatn. At the other end of the Polish line, however, the western part of Ankenes village as far as the church was reported on the 24th to be clear of the enemy, though beyond this point (as we now know) they had about 200 men with mortars and machine guns deployed on a front of two miles.

Accordingly, the final plan of attack envisaged an assault landing from Öyjord straight across the Rombaksfiord, a distance of about one mile, to a stony beach, behind which the side of the Taraldsvik-fjell rose so steeply that every possible machine-gun post except one railway tunnel lay open to bombardment beforehand from the sea. Once established ashore, the troops were to move over the shoulder of the mountain south-westwards into Narvik. This operation would be synchronised with a double thrust by the Poles—against Ankenes and to the head of the Beisfiord. Meanwhile the French and Norwegians on the northern flank would keep up the pressure on the far side of the Rombaksfiord, leaving the Germans with only one way of retreat, namely the route along the railway through Sildvik towards the Swedish frontier. At that stage, if all went well, General Béthouart hoped to administer the *coup de grâce* by sending one company of the 3rd Polish Battalion (held in reserve at Ballangen) and the skiers of the Chasseurs Alpins across the mountains from the head of the Skjomenfiord[1] to seize the railway in the Germans' rear.

The forces to be brought across the Rombaksfiord comprised the two battalions of the Foreign Legion, a Norwegian battalion as arranged, and a section of tanks. Only three assault and two motor landing craft remained, which automatically limited the first flight to 290 men. The next flight could not be brought across until three-quarters of an hour later, so there would be a critical interval. Naval support available was much less powerful than it would have been had Narvik been attacked earlier. There was no capital ship, and only one ship with 6-inch guns, but a full table of objectives was arranged for a preliminary bombardment, to be directed particularly against the mouths of the railway tunnels and supposed machine-gun posts; this was timed to start twenty minutes before the first landing. Four destroyers were to bombard from the Rombaksfiord, while the anti-aircraft cruisers *Cairo* (the flagship) and *Coventry* with the destroyer *Firedrake* bombarded from the Ofotfiord. The *Southampton* with her 6-inch guns stood farther out, and had for additional targets the east end of Ankenes village and German embarkation points opposite. The sloop *Stork* was to protect the landing craft from air attack if necessary, but both our fighter squadrons were due to patrol the area throughout the operation.

---

[1] Pronounced 'Showmenfure'.

ARRANGEMENTS FOR THE ASSAULT

The naval bombardment began at twenty minutes before midnight of 27th/28th May, and covered a wide enough area to conceal our intentions, while two batteries of French 75's and one Norwegian motorised battery posted behind Öyjord concentrated their fire upon the landing zone. Described in General Auchinleck's report as 'heavy and accurate'[1] and by the Mayor from inside the town as 'one continuous explosion',[2] the bombardment does not appear to have had much lasting effect upon German morale or armament. But under cover of it the landing was made punctually at midnight without loss or detection, and the Germans missed their chance in the first three-quarters of an hour when the only support available came from the guns, which operated under the greatest difficulties, as the troops advanced through broken ground where the prearranged system of signalling by naval officers proved almost impossible to carry out.

In order to preserve surprise, the first flight had been embarked, in the three assault landing craft and two motor landing craft still surviving, from a position in Herjangsfiord which could not be observed from Narvik. The second flight was due to embark at Öyjord itself, which came under fire from a German field gun or mortar, so that it was necessary to bring the remoter position into use again. This not only delayed embarkation but reduced numbers from four sections to three, because the water there was too shallow for the use of Puffers in place of the M.L.C.s, which were now transporting the tanks. These last, two in number, were intended to lead the infantry advance towards the town, but they were bogged down on the landing beach (where one of them could still be seen in 1949). Nevertheless, by 4 a.m. the first battalion of the Foreign Legion and the Norwegian battalion were both ashore. The Foreign Legionaries had then established their position on the lower slopes, through which the Norwegians began to clamber up, with the shoulder of the Taraldsvikfjell as their first objective. Once this was gained they could dominate the approach to Narvik, which lay to the west of them. To the east, along the line of the railway, they were protected by the naval bombardment of the railway station at Straumsnes and of the intervening tunnels.

The situation at this point was altered greatly to our disadvantage by a sea fog, reaching Bardufoss airfield about 4.15 a.m., which grounded our aircraft for some two hours but left the fiords farther south unfortunately clear. German dive-bombers then appeared on the scene. Two bombs hit the flagship, which lost thirty men killed and wounded, and the need to take constant evasive action reduced support of the troops on shore by naval gunfire to very little. General Béthouart, however, at this stage requested the assistance of only two destroyers, so about 6.30 a.m. the Admiral withdrew,

---
[1] Despatch by Lord Cork: Appendix B, Sec. 63.
[2] Broch, p. 135.

P

leaving the *Coventry* with the necessary destroyers to complete the Navy's task. Only one small craft, a Puffer loaded with ammunition, was lost to the landing forces through the bombing; but it had the important effect of delaying the arrival of the second battalion of the Foreign Legion, which did not complete the crossing until 11 a.m. German aircraft intervened again later in the morning against the Poles advancing on Ankenes, and there was yet a third attack on troops in the evening, when they nearly hit the *Coventry*; but after the fog cleared from Bardufoss continuous protection was provided by the R.A.F., which kept three aircraft patrolling over the battle area, made ninety-five sorties and fought three engagements during the day.

Meanwhile, the Germans made a determined counter-attack; this may have been encouraged by the factors mentioned above, but was probably based primarily on the possession of the higher ground along the Taraldsvikfjell. The Norwegians had reached but not secured a declivity which runs along the side of the hill about 900 feet up, making ambush possible, when the counter-attack came, delivered by a well-hidden party armed with hand grenades and some light mortars. The Norwegians and French were at first driven back across the railway down the steep hillside towards the beaches, one of which came under machine-gun fire, so that a new landing point had to be found for the second battalion of the Foreign Legion farther west. General Béthouart's Chief of Staff was among those killed on the beach. But with the help of a destroyer and the field guns firing from across the fiord, the officers rallied their troops and the situation was restored after a critical half-hour. The last enemy gun in a railway tunnel to the east was eventually silenced by the French manhandling one of their own small pieces up the precipitous slope from the shore. No further threat to the Allied landing developed, but the wilderness of rocks and scrub through which the Germans now withdrew along the railway lent itself to defence, so it was not until late afternoon that the Norwegians and the Legionaries of the 1st Battalion had finished clearing the hillside. Meanwhile, the 2nd Battalion on the right flank occupied a knoll north-west of Narvik railway station, where General Fleischer, who had accompanied his own troops in the landing, now joined the French. The German garrison, having finally dwindled to a lieutenant and a hundred men, had escaped from the town about midday along the Beisfiord road.

This result depended partly upon the operations on the south side of the Beisfiord, where the Poles, with two battalions in the line, one in reserve, and the fourth protecting the rear at Ballangen, likewise launched their attack against Ankenes at midnight. Two French light tanks had been put ashore for their assistance, but were stopped by mines. With the help of the naval bombardment and the British 25-pounders one company penetrated the village at the first onset, but in so doing exposed the right flank, against which the Germans at about 7 a.m. launched a serious counter-attack. Positions held since the first days of the landing in this area were forfeited for a time, but about noon the enemy began slowly to give way, as Polish pressure farther inland threatened to cut their line of retreat. The Poles secured the heights above Ankenes in time to sink the last boatload of sixty Germans escaping across the harbour, but more got away down the road on the north side of the Beisfiord. Meanwhile the other wing of the Polish force also met with stubborn resistance on the heights, but by early evening they were pushing across towards Beisfiord village at the head of the fiord, where they made contact with the motor-cyclist section of the Foreign Legion advancing by road from Narvik the same night.

Narvik itself, thanks to a characteristic act of courtesy on the part of the French, was entered first by the Norwegian battalion, who were followed under General Fleischer's instructions by a detachment of Norwegian military police. They went in at 5 p.m., the tiny vanguard of all the armies of European liberation; and the capture of the town and the Narvik promontory was officially reported by General Béthouart at ten that evening. The operation had resulted in a casualty list of about 150, of which the Norwegian losses were sixty; between 300 and 400 prisoners had been taken. Neither French nor Polish troops were billeted in Narvik, where heavy air raids were not unreasonably expected, and the fighting moved away to the east towards Sildvik, a distance from which the Germans could not easily launch a counter-attack. It had been decided at an earlier stage not to use Narvik as a base for military or naval purposes, and the ore traffic which had made it a centre of the world's interest for so many months seemed to be in any case at an end. After careful examination of the harbour, where twenty wrecks was 'a conservative estimate', the burnt-out ore quays, destroyed ore-handling plant, and battered railway, the Chief Engineer of the Allied forces reported that ore could not be exported again in appreciable quantities within a period of less than a year. But none of these considerations was primarily responsible for the paradoxical situation that Narvik, once in our possession, had ceased to count.

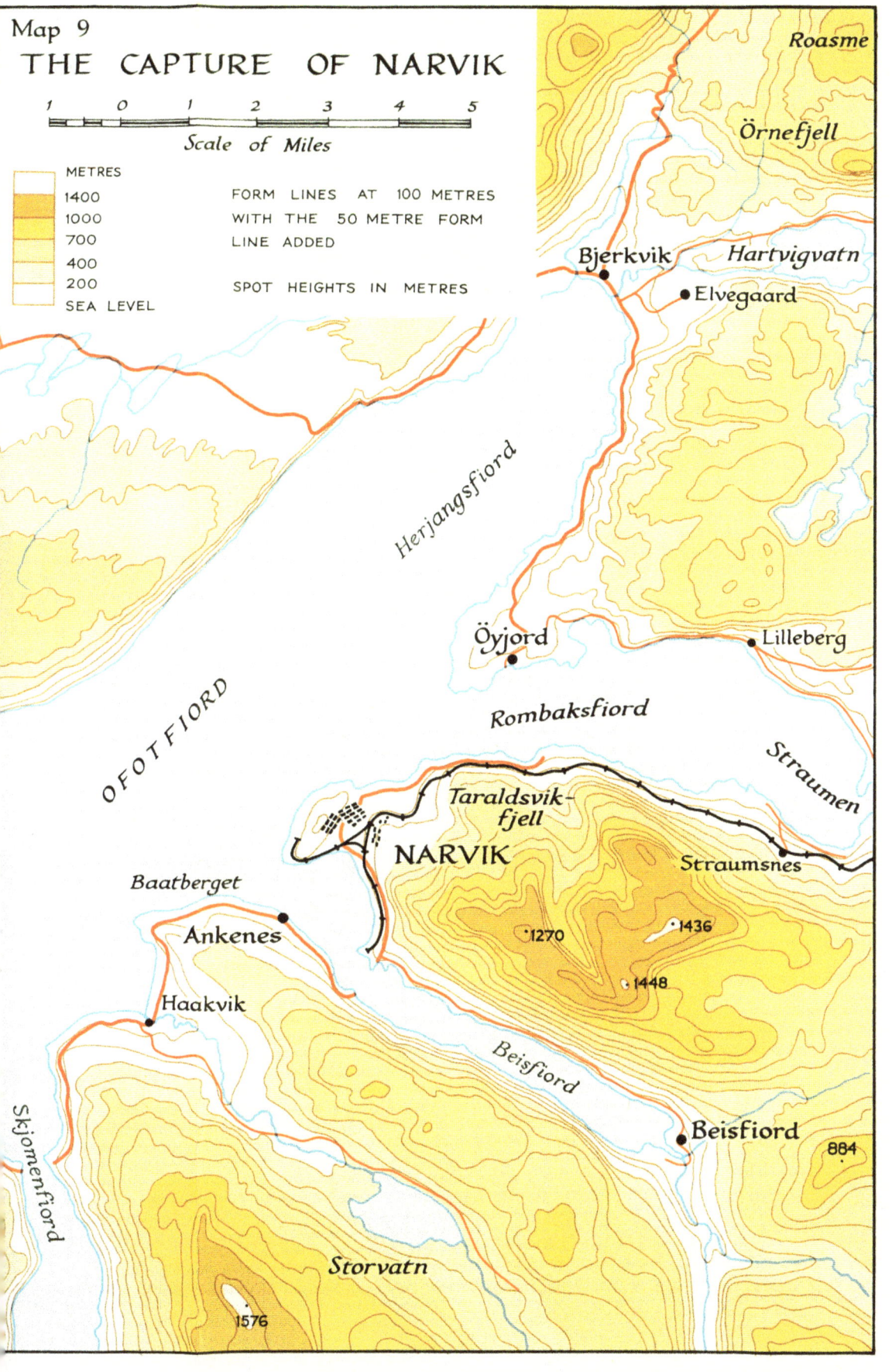

CHAPTER XIV

THE EVACUATION OF NORTH NORWAY

See Map 11, facing page 228

THE telegram ordering the evacuation of his forces was received by Lord Cork on the night of 24th/25th May, nearly three days before the attack on Narvik. It ranked the destruction of the railway and Narvik port facilities as objects which made the capture highly desirable, and noted that evacuation operations would be made easier by the destruction or capture of enemy forces. Nevertheless the telegram, which envisaged the sacrifice of most of the equipment, emphasised that 'speed of evacuation, once begun, should be of primary consideration'. General Béthouart, for whom the news from France made the dilemma even more painful than it was for the British commanders, was brought into consultation, and after he had reflected for a brief half-hour he agreed with them that the attack on Narvik should be continued, even though it kept French troops far from their own country in its hour of need. It was important to make sure that the means of shipping iron ore had in fact been destroyed. A successful attack would do much to conceal the intention of, and preparations for, withdrawal. To these General Béthouart adds in retrospect a third consideration, the importance of a victory from the standpoint of Allied morale. The secret was closely guarded, not least from the Norwegians, and the capture of Narvik duly followed.

One problem of the evacuation, however, the disentanglement of our forces in front of Bodö, had no need to wait, and steps had already been taken to inform Brigadier Gubbins of the changed situation by 26th May, the day our troops made the withdrawal from Pothus over the headwaters of the fiord.[1] Their new position was at Finneid, at the south-eastern extremity of the Bodö peninsula, where it was at first intended to establish a firm defence line with the help of the reinforcements which had been accumulating round Bodö, some forty-two miles west by road but with easier communications along the fiord. At Finneid the road north crosses a bridge (which was duly blown) over the outlet from the lowest of a chain of lakes about a dozen miles in length, beyond which a great glacier, Blaamannsis,

---

[1] See p. 192.

effectively bars the way. But on account of the new turn of events the British line was suddenly moved back behind Finneid on to the Fauske isthmus, the name given to the flat, ten-mile wide neck of the Bodö peninsula, which was palpably less defensible but closer and handier for a withdrawal on Bodö.

The Norwegians, who had only recently transferred a battalion to this area from Bardufoss to reinforce the remnants withdrawn from Mo, found the decision quite inexplicable and therefore sinister. They did not, however, feel strong enough to fight at Finneid on their own, so they joined under bitter protest in the withdrawal to the isthmus, which was divided into two sectors, the Norwegians defending the northern half. At the same time they were almost equally distressed and alarmed by the failure to bring forward reinforcements from Bodö, the more so as we had recently had Gladiators operating from there to give air cover. These local difficulties were cleared up to some extent when news of our intention to evacuate Bodö came through from Norwegian Divisional Headquarters to their local commander. The reason for this evacuation was still unknown to any Norwegian, and it naturally seemed madness to them because of the resulting threat to Narvik. All that their representations could achieve, however, was a promise that our evacuation would not take place for three days. This would enable them to withdraw their own troops from the northern half of the Fauske isthmus to Rösvik, which was then the terminus of the main road north, and to arrange for their evacuation in fishing boats to the Lofoten Islands. Unfortunately the movement of the British troops westwards into the Bodö peninsula, which necessarily preceded our evacuation but of which the timetable had been kept secret, at once exposed the Norwegians to attack. They lost a small number of prisoners in consequence, but their rearguard succeeded in holding up the Germans, a motor-cycle detachment, ten miles short of Rösvik. In the end they got away safely except for one company, which had been posted on the extreme left wing of the abortive Finneid position and made a brave but belated march back across the Blaamannsis.

The move to the west, referred to above, was achieved by one long day's march along the narrow coast road, under the protection of a small rear-guard and the demolition of bridges, after which the troops could be transferred to Puffers. When the Irish Guards and Independent Companies left the Fauske isthmus in the early morning of 29th May, an enemy force, estimated to be 1,200 strong, was within twelve miles. But they passed unmolested through to Bodö, making no contact with the enemy until the evening of the 30th, when a company of Scots Guards at Hopen, eleven miles from Bodö, blew up the bridge as cyclist troops entered the village. The Hopen position, which seemed a strong one, was believed to have been turned during the night, but its defenders were able to fall back on the main line south of Lake Solöi, which was occupied by the rest of their own battalion and by the South Wales Borderers. It is described by the Scots Guards as 'the first really good defensive position which the battalion has occupied and on which the Germans could have been held'. However, there was no further clash with the enemy, though local tradition affirms that the twenty-eight cyclists to whom Bodö was surrendered were coming into sight when our last troops withdrew to the quay.

The main enemy threat to the evacuation came instead from the air. The Gladiator pilots sent to the Bodö landing ground on 26th May had begun to give cover to our troops by engaging the enemy in the air. This brought relief to the fighting line, but the Germans switched their effort to Bodö itself. At 8 a.m. next day they took the two surviving Gladiators by surprise with superior numbers, wounded both pilots, and disposed of both aircraft. The runway escaped serious damage on that occasion, but on the same evening the enemy resumed the attack with a force of more than a hundred bombers, which laid most of the town in ashes, put the Bofors guns out of action, and wrecked the runway beyond repair. In these circumstances the evacuation was a precarious operation, which Lord Cork based upon the use of his destroyers rather than await the aircraft carriers and four fast liners promised for 2nd June. Two destroyers brought away troops on three successive nights—on the first to the *Vindictive* lying in the offing, and on the others to the Harstad area. On the third night an extra destroyer was sent to cover the withdrawal of the Norwegians farther north, though this was in fact completed before the destroyer arrived. The advancing Germans, as we have already seen, made no serious attack, and we were able to destroy all our guns and the motor transport as well as the oil installations in the port. It is more remarkable that German bombing had missed the embarkation quay and failed to injure the troops embarking or embarked. Two Gladiators and two Hurricanes were maintaining a patrol over the town in the final stages, and the Gladiators originally based on Bodö had taken some toll of the Germans; this may have induced caution. Two of the Independent Companies went in the *Vindictive* direct to Scapa. The rest of the forces from Bodö were disembarked at Borkenes, west of Harstad, to await the final evacuation. Our losses had amounted to 506 officers and men, including some small casualties in the Narvik area as well as what had been suffered in the long retreat.

Meanwhile, the German mountain troops had split into two groups, one for Bodö and the other for Rösvik, whence they proposed to proceed by boat to the head of the Leirfiord, so as to march across country through what a Norwegian historian terms 'one of the wildest mountain districts'[1] to the relief of General Dietl on Björnfjell. The route had been prospected by German 'scientists' before the war and a system of airborne supplies was carefully worked out. By 7th June the vanguard of the three nominal battalions had reached Tysfiord, which meant that they had another fortnight's march between them and their goal, though—under altered circumstances—two patrols accomplished the feat in seven and eight days respectively. They could only have enabled Dietl to stave off surrender if the Germans had proved able to follow up with another project, which envisaged the occupation of the Bardufoss area from the north by a glider attack on the airfield and a landing in Lyngenfiord from the big liners *Bremen* and *Europa*. But this project was still at the discussion stage as late as 4th June, though it figures in an Air Force order, dated the 5th, which emphasises the importance of interim measures for keeping General Dietl supplied and reinforced. In the meantime the Norwegians had observed the move across the fiord from Rösvik and, while assembling some troops to hold a line farther north, had asked for British help. The last vessel to leave Bodö was a small Norwegian passenger steamer, s.s. *Ranen* alias *Raven*; this had been taken into use as a British decoy ship, manned by a mixed party of naval ratings, Irish Guardsmen, and South Wales Borderers, and sent in search of information and chances of surprise attack as far south as Sandnessjöen. She returned to the Rösvik area on 3rd June, when her concealed armament of one Bofors, one Oerlikon, and numerous machine guns held up part of the German advance northwards across the fiord. The *Raven* was again employed north of Tysfiord to cut the telephone cables by which the Germans were believed to report progress to General Dietl.

The next problem was the more complicated one of disentanglement from the fighting east of Narvik. On the morning of 1st June our military mission at Tromsö reported that the Norwegian Government was so perturbed by the evacuation from Bodö that it might decide to ask for a separate armistice, irrespective of the military situation. The position was the more difficult because of the success with which the capture of Narvik had been exploited. General Dietl had indeed received orders to hold out to the bitter end in North Norway, since considerations of prestige had given Hitler a passionate interest in the event, and the Germans (as we have seen) did not altogether despair of effecting a relief. But in the days immediately following the fall of Narvik they could take the offensive only in the air.

---

[1] Major-General R. Roscher Nielsen: *Norges Krig*, p. 438.

The R.A.F. squadrons had their hands full. An operation instruction issued on 29th May required them to give maximum support to the French and Norwegian forces. On the following day a message from Norwegian Headquarters emphasised the need for preventing parachute landings to reinforce the German units in the mountains; the Germans did as a matter of fact plan to send in 2,000 men by this means, but they never arrived. The R.A.F. had also their primary task of defending our bases at Harstad and Skaanland. Shipping was heavily raided on 29th May. Three days later both base and anchorage were methodically assailed by successive groups of long-range bombers escorted by Messerschmitt 110s, but the R.A.F. fought them off in twenty-four actions involving seventy-five separate sorties. The enemy lost at least nine aircraft that day and achieved no substantial result against military objectives, though the high explosive and incendiaries which were rained down on Narvik (where there was no standing patrol) largely destroyed the business quarter of the town.

Nevertheless, the main fact was the retreat of the Germans, who were known to be physically exhausted and were running short of ammunition as well, into the mountains up against the Swedish frontier. They had withdrawn from Narvik along the line of the railway, demolishing the tunnels as they went, towards the head of the Rombaksfiord, with the Foreign Legion following up a little past the narrows at Straumen half-way along the fiord, where supporting destroyers could now penetrate past the minefield. At the same time the Poles, following other German remnants from the head of the Beisfiord, progressed north-eastwards towards the railway line. The two forces linked up on 2nd June. On this side the cancellation by General Béthouart of the encircling movement from the Skjomenfiord (which the Germans had in any case anticipated) left the Germans with one place of refuge, the Björnfjell mountain, south of which the railway passes to the frontier. They also held Rundfjell, which adjoins the frontier farther north, and the large bastion of the Haugfjell; this lies to the west of the other two mountains and overlooks the north shore of the Rombaksfiord. Here the Germans were hemmed in by the French forces based on Öyjord. To attack Rundfjell and the Haugfjell from the north was a task for which the Norwegians were eagerly preparing. Their positions on the Kuberg plateau were separated from the Germans by a chain of high lakes and morasses, Jernvatnene, which the thaw had now made into a formidable obstacle, and the Norwegian lines of communication were still long and precarious. Three battalions were grouped for a direct attack on Rundfjell, where the German positions had been softened by preliminary air bombing. Once Rundfjell was taken, it was thought that with artillery support a further attack could be made across the lakes and morasses against Haugfjell; the Germans there would in any case feel themselves trapped by the approach of the French and Poles to their remaining outlet into neutral territory at Björnfjell. Since 25th May, by arrangement between the German and Swedish Governments, four trains had been waiting on the other side of the frontier.

Meanwhile the preparations for evacuation had been conducted by senior British and French officers in closest secrecy and with elaborate and carefully worked out deception. Our naval resources being stretched to the uttermost, the paramount need was to exploit the capture of Narvik in such a way that the Germans might have no inkling of our intention to withdraw until the main convoys were well on the way home. Exaggerated ideas as to the number of quislings in Norway; the lack of discipline—as it seemed to us—among the population; some disagreeable experiences of unintentional leakages of information, one of which had made it necessary to postpone the date of the final assault on Narvik; and fear that natural disappointment might provoke a not unnatural retaliation—all these factors drove us to conceal our intentions from the Norwegians lest they should become known also to the enemy. Moreover, the means lay ready to hand. Lord Cork and General Auchinleck had been negotiating with the Norwegians since the middle of May about the formation of the new base farther north at Tromsö. The movement from Bodö and the intense activity at Harstad and Skaanland were therefore disguised as part of the transfer. To make the story more colourable, the Royal Marines' base organisation was actually despatched from Harstad for Tromsö, redirected on the way, and its members held *incommunicado* at Scapa. There being no airfield at Tromsö, the R.A.F. let it be understood that their fighter squadrons were removing to Skaanland, so as to free Bardufoss for Blenheim bombers. The deception was kept up even after the issue on 31st May of the detailed movement order for the withdrawal.

Four days before this, the British and French commanders referred home the question of our relations with the Norwegians. General Béthouart wrote: 'I am operating with Norwegian troops whom for reasons of national honour I will not abandon in difficulties on the battlefield'.[1] But on the 29th the Prime Minister stated at the meeting of the War Cabinet that there must still be a few days' delay in telling the Norwegians; Lord Cork was instructed accordingly and told to plan for the Norwegian forces either to be evacuated to this country or left in a satisfactory position of defence. The latter was the only real possibility, involving a very nice adjustment between the needs of the French and Poles, who must adhere to a time-table for evacuation, and those of the Norwegians, who must not be exposed in

---

[1] Sereau, p. 84.

a disadvantageous position to a sudden German onslaught. In the end, the decision to evacuate was communicated to the Norwegian Government late on 1st June, and on the following day to General Ruge.

As for the military operations in progress in the mountains, evacuation could not be delayed to await the final success which the Norwegians had so long hoped for and might possibly have achieved, had we allowed them to know the urgency of the situation. They now took over the main part of the French line north of the Rombaksfiord and pushed forward on their other flank, where they occupied the frontier post due east of Rundfjell. These efforts were inspired by the vain hope that time would somehow be given for them to make their final attack, which was fixed for 8th June. But it was not to be: all that was possible was to arrange a withdrawal which would enable the Norwegian forces to be demobilised in the back areas before the Germans overran them. This was successfully achieved by General Ruge, who stayed in Norway with his troops, while General Fleischer was to accompany the Government overseas; a preliminary armistice came into effect at midnight on 9th/10th June. All detachments reached demobilisation points the following day, and negotiations for a formal armistice were begun the next night. Meanwhile, nine watch-boats and other small surviving units of the Norwegian Navy were ordered by their Commander-in-Chief to the Shetlands and a handful of Norwegian aircraft made good their escape to Finland.

The withdrawal of 24,500 troops from an improvised base and a dozen smaller embarkation points presented many problems. The area to be covered stretched from Ballangen on the south side of the Ofotfiord as far north as Tromsö, where the cruiser *Devonshire* had the special mission of embarking the King of Norway and his Government as well as the advance party sent in connection with the base project. Fifteen troopships, of which two were left unused, were sent across in two groups to two rendezvous about 180 miles from the Norwegian coast, passing into the charge of Rear-Admiral Vivian in the *Coventry*. Thence they came in two at a time with anti-submarine protection to sheltered waters north of Harstad, where the troops were put on board from destroyers, which worked up and down the narrow channels unceasingly to collect the men from quays and Puffers; a couple of small cross-channel steamers alone shipped men and stores at Harstad itself. All this required exact co-ordination, which a small combined headquarters now set up at Harstad successfully achieved; even a 'bag' of some sixty captured airmen was not left behind. In addition, the instructions sent to Lord Cork emphasised the need to bring away guns and other material to the extent that was compatible with the necessary speed of evacuation, the order of priority being determined by the needs of defence at home. The evacuation of his men of course came first, then, successively, light anti-aircraft guns and ammunition, 25-pounders (of which we had in the area only six), heavy anti-aircraft guns and ammunition. In the event, a greater quantity of material was got away than had been contemplated, for it included aircraft.

Throughout the evacuation period, precautions were taken to watch for an enemy advance overland from Bodö, but the terrain was extremely difficult, and no threat developed from the south except for a dozen parachutists in the Ballangen area on the last night of evacuation. A second risk was that of a seaborne or airborne landing on Hinnöy to attack the base at Harstad, but the Germans did not try this. Another possibility was the mining of the fairway, which enemy aircraft attempted in the Tjeldsund once (29th May), but they were spotted and the mines promptly swept up. The biggest and most obvious danger, however, was from air bombing, which might have destroyed ships, quays and men during the period of embarkation—and it is to be remembered that there were twenty-four hours of daylight throughout the area concerned. The days of the final embarkation were to our great good fortune uniformly cloudy and overcast, but British counter-measures were also a very important factor.

In the first place arrangements were made to keep our anti-aircraft guns in action until the last, although this in many cases meant their abandonment. Second, and more important, the *Ark Royal* arrived off the coast on 2nd June: her aircraft bombed German troops and communications, not only in the mountains east of Narvik but farther south along their lines of communication beyond Bodö; Bodö airfield was also attacked. Third, and most important, there was the cumulative effect of the work done by the Gladiators and Hurricanes, which remained in action until the very end. Great care was taken to conceal our intention to evacuate Bardufoss, of which the demolition, by the making of 120 craters, was not begun until half an hour after midnight of the 7th/8th. On the previous day both squadrons had been in action from 4 a.m. until nearly midnight. Then, led by naval Swordfish, they flew to the carrier *Glorious*, which had accompanied the *Ark Royal* to Norway for their reception. Ten Gladiators and ten Hurricanes all landed successfully, every pilot in No. 46 Squadron having volunteered to run the risk, though Hurricanes had never alighted on deck before. But they were fated not to complete the journey so bravely begun.

The naval plans for the voyage home must be judged in relation to the catastrophic situation on the western front, to which the French troops from Norway were to be at once transferred. Naval escorts had

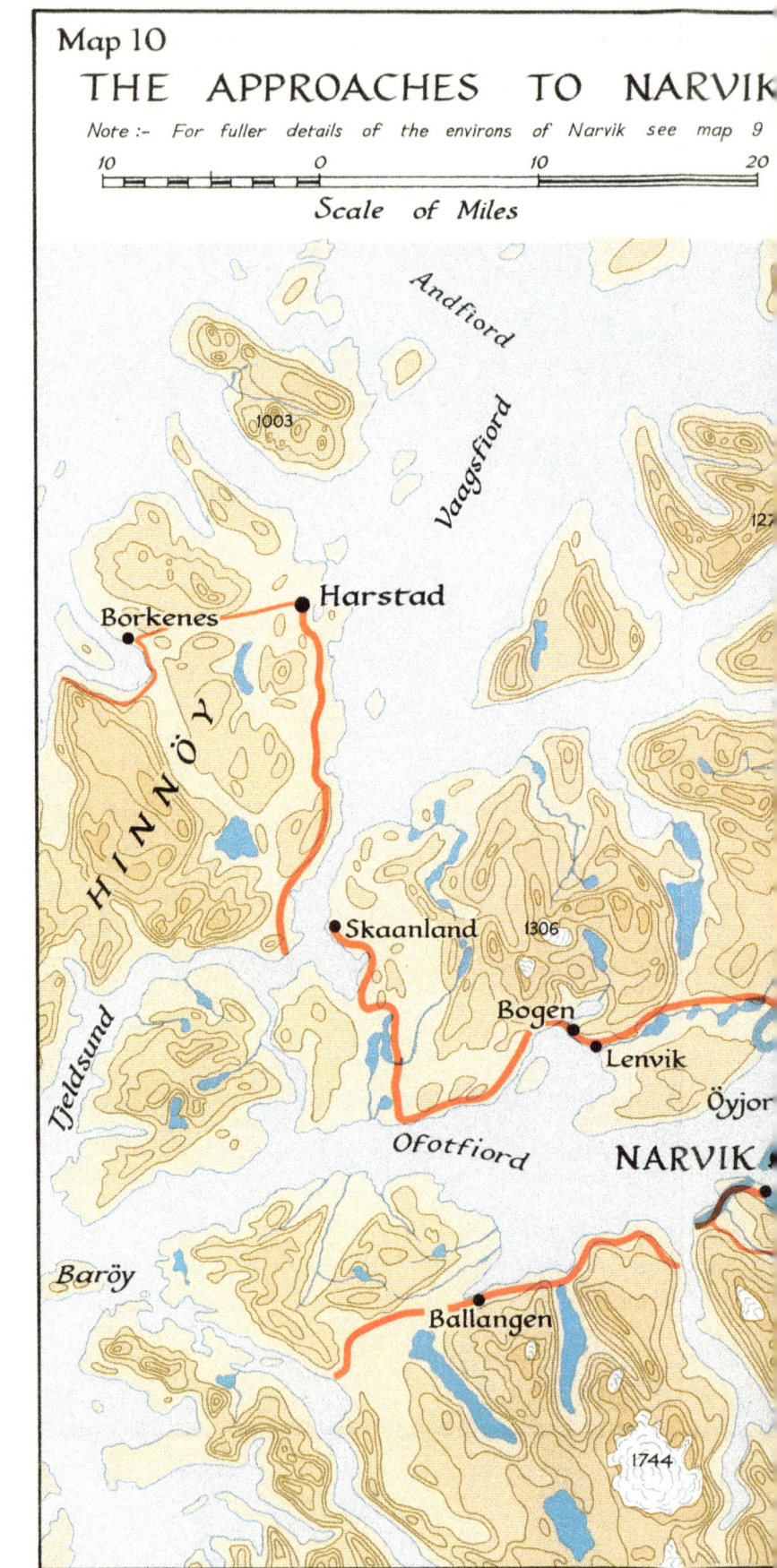

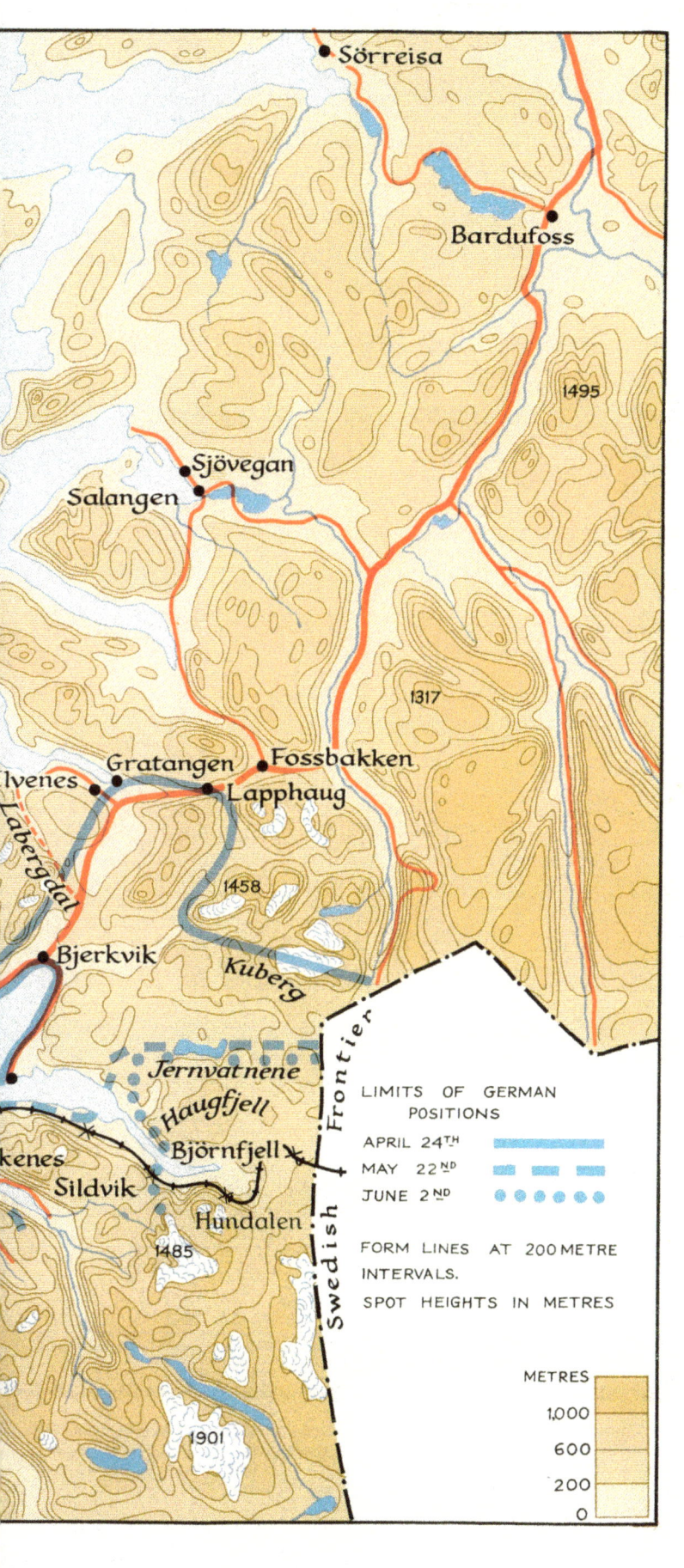

accordingly to be kept to the absolute minimum because of the paramount need then felt for ships to guard home waters against invasion. The Commander-in-Chief, Home Fleet, and Lord Cork may also have been influenced to some extent by the unbroken immunity from attack by surface vessels enjoyed by the Narvik convoys throughout the preceding seven weeks. As for air escorts, the route from Narvik was for the most part out of range. In any case, the Admiralty did not ask the help of Coastal Command; its commander-in-chief alone was informed of the evacuation in strictest secrecy, and the employment of his few long-range Sunderland flying boats was not suggested or, apparently, sought. The arrangements actually made were as follows.

Lord Cork organised a preliminary convoy from ships already under his control in Norway, with a trawler escort, so as to send home before the end of May a quantity of stores including some French tanks and guns. There was a second storeship convoy which was loaded at Harstad and left on the evening of 7th June, and a smaller detachment of storeships left simultaneously from Tromsö. These two slow convoys had some protection from trawlers but depended in the main upon destroyers, which would join them after completing their other duties. Lord Cork had asked for fifteen destroyers but had only eleven actually at his disposal. The first group of troopships, six large merchantmen and the *Vindictive*, having loaded nearly 15,000 men in the early mornings of 4th, 5th and 6th June, left the distant rendezvous early on the 7th for home. They were without escort for the first day's sailing, as Lord Cork's destroyers were all still in use for further embarkations. Group 2, four large and three small merchantmen, took up nearly 10,000 men on 7th and 8th June and left the rendezvous on the morning of the 9th, escorted by the *Southampton*, the *Coventry*, and five destroyers. This group also had the protection of the *Ark Royal*, with her aircraft patrolling, and her screen of three destroyers. The Chasseurs Alpins had provided the rearguard round Harstad, but the rear party at the quays consisted of Royal Engineers and Military Police. These were taken up at about 9 a.m. on the 8th, when the *Southampton* left the port, wearing the flag of Lord Cork and also carrying Generals Auchinleck and Béthouart. So far, the operation had proceeded according to plan, and a twenty-four-hour delay to help Norwegian diplomacy[1] had even enabled extra stores and equipment to be loaded; but the element of luck, never far distant from an operation of war, was now to play its part.

The success of our measures of concealment was such that the

---

[1] See p. 175.

Germans remained unaware of the evacuation project until it was virtually completed. Destroyers fired at German positions from the Rombaksfiord as late as 6th June. On the 7th the situation from the German point of view was still uncertain. It was only on 8th June, when the last of the Allied forces had already left the shore, that the winding-up of the campaign through the armistice negotiations entrusted by the Norwegian Government to its Commander-in-Chief showed what had happened. The same evening General Dietl reported the re-entry into Narvik. German attention had no doubt been concentrated upon the problem of relieving General Dietl's forces, and it must have seemed highly improbable that the Allies would let slip the chance of completing their success, if only for the sake of prestige. But in addition to the advance overland from Leirfiord and the possible seizure of Bardufoss the Germans had had a third plan, to make an attack with their two battle cruisers.

The naval operation known as 'Juno' achieved by luck a considerable success for which it was not designed. One result of the holocaust of German destroyers on 10th and 13th April had been to keep the *Gneisenau* (after repair) and the *Scharnhorst* inactive for a time for want of escort. But since 14th May the German naval staff had been preparing to act against British forces in the Narvik area, and since 16th May the plan had been extended by Hitler's orders to provide also for the conveyance of seaborne supplies through the Leads from Trondheim to Bodö. On the 27th the plan was further extended to include a more ambitious sortie by the battle-cruisers from Trondheim into North Norwegian waters, this final decision being encouraged by a wireless intercept which showed the organisation of the British naval patrol south of Iceland. On the 29th a directive was issued to the Commander-in-Chief, Admiral Marschall: his principal task was to attack warships, transports, and bases in the And and Vaags fiords (the Harstad area) or, if it proved to be more advantageous, in the Ofotfiord. The operation in the Leads was to be carried out either concurrently with the main task or as a second operation based on Trondheim, which for security reasons the ships were not to enter until the main operation had been completed. The force was to consist of the *Scharnhorst* and *Gneisenau* with the cruiser *Hipper* and four destroyers.

The Germans put to sea accordingly on 4th June at 7 a.m. On the evening of the 6th they had arrived safely in approximately the latitude of their objective, but to escape the attentions of the Royal Navy they were standing right out to sea about half-way between Norway and Iceland. Admiral Marschall then timed his attack on Harstad for the night of the 9th. Early the following morning (7th June) German air reconnaissance spotted a west-bound convoy, which the Germans decided were merely 'returned empties' to be ignored accordingly, and then a little after midday it found no less than three groups of warships in the Andfiord area. This was belatedly reported to the Commander-in-Chief by Group Command West, the naval headquarters which had given him his directive, at eight o'clock that evening, while he was discussing 'Operation Harstad' with his commanders on board the *Scharnhorst*. The Commander-in-Chief drew the correct inference 'that the noticeable westward movement may indicate a British evacuation of Norway, and that the westward-bound convoys will now offer valuable targets'; at 3 a.m. next morning he informed headquarters of his intention to attack the convoy. It is a striking fact that Group West in its reply wished to insist that the battle cruisers should still be directed to the Harstad-Narvik area, but the Chief of Naval Staff intervened to modify the instructions. For if Group West had had its way there would have been an attack on Harstad yielding nugatory results, and the British Navy would have been spared a serious loss.

It will be recalled that our naval programme for the evacuation required the protection of several distinct groups of ships. There was the slow convoy of storeships in two divisions, escorted by destroyers and trawlers. Then there was Group 1 of the troop transports; this had left the rendezvous 180 miles out with the *Vindictive* (which was only partly armed) early on the 7th and, under arrangements made between Admiral Forbes and Lord Cork, was being met by the *Valiant* and her screen of four large destroyers about 1 a.m. on the 8th. Finally, there was the second group of transports, some of whose protecting vessels had been spotted north of the Andfiord by German reconnaissance. This second group was due to meet the *Valiant* and her destroyers on the evening of the 9th, after the latter had handed over Group 1 to a detachment of five destroyers so that the battleship might turn north again. Thus the last convoy was well within reach of Admiral Marschall's force and, although it had the protection of the *Ark Royal*, our two cruisers and four destroyers would be heavily out-gunned by the *Scharnhorst* and *Gneisenau*. However, the Germans were fated to meet an easier prey.

An hour and a half after Admiral Marschall had announced his decision, he sighted the 5,000-ton tanker *Oil Pioneer* escorted by the trawler *Juniper*. They had sailed from the Tromsö area on the 6th. They were sunk at 7 a.m. without being able to signal their plight, and the search for the convoy continued with the help of aircraft launched from the *Hipper* and the *Scharnhorst*. A convoy consisting of a cruiser and a merchant ship was reported to the south, an armed merchant ship and a hospital ship to the north. The *Hipper* was thereupon ordered to sink the armed merchant ship, which proved to be the 20,000-ton transport *Orama*, carrying a hundred German prisoners. She had been sent home alone and unloaded the previous day because she had arrived without sufficient oil or water to await her group. The *Orama* was sunk just after eleven o'clock, 275 survivors being picked up. The *Gneisenau* had successfully jammed her S.O.S. signal, and the hospital ship *Atlantis* which was in company with her respected the obligation not to use her wireless, thus securing her privilege of immunity from attack.

Admiral Marschall had still failed in his search for the convoy. He therefore planned to attack the aircraft carriers north-west of the Andfiord, which had been identified several times by means of wireless intercepts as well as in the more general message received from Group West the previous evening. The *Hipper* and the destroyers were, however, detached to go to Trondheim for refuelling and for the minor operation of protecting German convoys through the Leads. The Admiral's luck held. At 3.45 p.m. he sighted a mast-head to the eastward, which proved to be that of the aircraft carrier *Glorious* with the customary escort of two destroyers, *Ardent* and *Acasta*. She was 200 miles ahead of Group 2, making the voyage independently because she was short of fuel. Furthermore, she was at a grave disadvantage because of the nature of the task in which she was engaged—her accommodation overcrowded with the Gladiators and Hurricanes that had been flown on board, her own complement of aircraft reduced for the occasion to one squadron of Skuas and a half-squadron of Swordfish, and her pilots exhausted by their share in the evacuation from Bardufoss. No reconnaissance aircraft were up (they were at ten minutes' notice), and wireless messages were almost completely jammed.

The *Glorious* made off at her top speed (which in theory exceeded that of the battle-cruisers) to the southward, and attempted to range her Swordfish: but it was too late. At 4.30 the *Scharnhorst* opened fire at a range of nearly 28,000 yards, at which our 4·7-inch guns were helpless. The forward upper hangar was hit at an early stage, starting a fire which destroyed the Hurricanes and prevented any torpedoes being got ready. A salvo hit the bridge about five o'clock, and a heavy shell, striking aft about a quarter of an hour later, virtually finished the action so far as the *Glorious* was concerned. The order to abandon ship came about 5.20 and in another twenty minutes she had sunk. Meanwhile the two destroyers were rendering a good account of themselves. The smoke screen which they laid from the beginning of the action had given the *Glorious* a short respite from the gunfire of the two battle-cruisers and made it difficult for the Germans to observe the fall of shot. The *Ardent* fired two four-tube salvoes of torpedoes at the enemy, who was several times forced to take avoiding action, but she was sunk shortly before the carrier. This left the *Acasta* alone against overwhelming odds. With her guns still firing, she steered south-east, got temporary shelter in her own smoke screen, and discharged a four-tube salvo, of which one torpedo struck the *Scharnhorst* aft at a range of about 13,000 yards: the German Naval Staff claimed afterwards that a better tactical conduct of the action could have avoided it. This torpedo-hit, which killed two officers and forty-six men, put the after-turret out of action, and a leak of water later made the centre and starboard main engines unusable. The damage done to the *Scharnhorst* caused both German ships to withdraw after the engagement to Trondheim, so that the second convoy of troopships passed through the wreckage-strewn waters next day unmolested. But first the enemy sank the *Acasta*, badly damaged and stopped with a list to port, by a final salvo at eight minutes past six; one Able Seaman lived to tell her story.

The loss of the *Glorious* was a threefold disaster. We had begun the war with only five large aircraft carriers and had lost one of these (the *Courageous*) in September 1939. The twenty fighter aircraft which went down in the ship would have been of value in the impending Battle of Britain, but much more serious was the loss of life. The crews of the carrier and both destroyers, together with the air pilots on board, were lost to the number of 1,515, the Germans having left the scene of action at once, as already noted. Thirty-nine survivors were eventually landed in the Faeroes from a small Norwegian vessel; two were picked up by a German seaplane; and four more were brought back to Norway by another small Norwegian vessel which found them in mid-ocean—they were all that was left of thirty-two men who had clambered on to a raft nearly twenty-four hours earlier. The Norwegians said that the area through which they were then passing contained many drifting bodies.

Our regular air reconnaissance had caught no glimpse of *Scharnhorst* and *Gneisenau* in their passage through the patrolled areas of the North Sea, and they cannot even be identified with two unknown vessels which the Q-ship *Prunella* had sighted hull-down on the horizon between Norway and Iceland on the morning of 5th June. From this insubstantial report, however, the Admiralty inferred that an invasion of Iceland or even Eire might be impending, so the Commander-in-Chief weakened the potential protection of the Norway convoys by sending his two battle cruisers *Renown* and *Repulse* with two cruisers and five destroyers to Iceland, the convoy duty for which they had previously been earmarked being assigned to the single battleship *Valiant*. As a result of the imperative needs of areas farther south, he had left with him at Scapa only the battleship *Rodney* and a very few destroyers. On the 8th the Admiralty ordered the *Renown* to return; meanwhile the Home Fleet remained in harbour. Thus no news of the German activities reached British units other than those which were attacked until the hospital ship *Atlantis* met the *Valiant* about 9 a.m. next morning (9th June). The latter ship was then on her way north to join the last convoy: she promptly worked up to full speed to close the distance of about 400 miles. Her signal relaying the hospital ship's account received confirmation an hour later from the *Devonshire*. This cruiser, with the King of Norway and his Government and some 400 other passengers on board, had been only a hundred miles west of the *Glorious* when the action began the previous afternoon, and she was the sole recipient of a very faulty message from the *Glorious* (whose wireless apparatus may have been badly hit) mentioning only a previous message (not received) and two pocket battleships. Admiral Cunningham in the *Devonshire* had decided not to break wireless silence owing to the nature of his mission.

The Commander-in-Chief took immediate steps to protect the convoys. The *Glorious*, of whose fate he was, of course, in ignorance, was ordered to join the *Valiant* if possible. The *Repulse*, with two cruisers and three destroyers, was ordered to join the convoys from the area south-east of Iceland. Finally the Commander-in-Chief himself with the *Rodney* and *Renown* and (initially) two destroyers—every ship which remained at his disposal—left Scapa shortly after midday (9th June) to complete the guard for the convoys. However, the only danger that day came from German aircraft. The *Valiant* was shadowed and attacked on her way to join the troopships, and there was a more serious attempt against the *Ark Royal* when night came, but her fire and that of the *Valiant* kept the Germans at arm's length and her aircraft shot down one of them. Farther north, the armed boarding vessel *Vandyck*, which had been sent empty to an inner rendezvous in case a substitute transport were needed during embarkation, had gone by mistake into the Harstad area, where she was bombed by aircraft, disabled, and abandoned. Two small Norwegian passenger steamers were also sunk from the air. British warships were now converging upon the convoys from two directions, but their situation was by this time less dangerous, for the troopships had set a course farther westward during the evening in order to keep a maximum distance from the enemy's air base at Trondheim. This manœuvre was the more effectual because his naval striking force too was now in the port.

On the morning of the 10th aircraft of Coastal Command reported an enemy force of four cruisers at Trondheim. They had found the raiders. The damage done to the *Scharnhorst* had caused Admiral Marschall to steer for Trondheim, where his ships arrived on the afternoon of the 9th, a few hours later than the *Hipper* and the destroyers, and he then received belated news of the evacuation of Narvik. The following morning, the 10th, the *Gneisenau* and *Hipper* put to sea again with a view to continuing operations against the convoys, which were now farther from their reach. Their movement was reported at 2 p.m. by the submarine *Clyde*, which was watching the northern approach to the port (and to such good purpose that she put the *Gneisenau* out of action for many months by torpedo next time she emerged, which was ten days later). The Commander-in-Chief, who had ordered the *Ark Royal* to join him with a view to a Swordfish attack in Trondheim harbour, therefore turned eastward for a search at sea. By 4 p.m. he had aircraft scouting ahead and was hoping for air action from the carrier, but he could not find the enemy, whose ships re-entered Trondheim early next morning, Admiral Marschall having now abandoned the operation on the ground that no worthwhile targets remained. The German naval staff would have liked him to persevere, but his conclusion was probably the correct one, since by the morning of the 11th the last convoy was well to the westward and had the protection of the main force under the Commander-in-Chief. Only the Tromsö store convoy and widely scattered trawlers and merchantmen, chiefly Norwegian, might still have been within reach.

Two further attacks were organised against the German ships in Trondheim. On the afternoon of 11th June, twelve R.A.F. aircraft claimed two hits with 250-lb. bombs, but were actually unsuccessful. It was then arranged that naval aircraft should attack and the fleet moved south, passing the store convoy from Tromsö on the morning of the 12th and then turning eastward for an attack in the small hours of the 13th. The fleet was shadowed by German aircraft, but fifteen Skuas armed with bombs left the carrier to attack at 2 a.m. The R.A.F. created a diversion by bombing Vaernes, and also provided some fighter protection for the Skuas, though their main effort was switched to Bergen, where ships were believed to be assembled for use in the invasion of Britain. The defence was on the alert and eight of our aircraft were lost, some of them in attempting to regain the fog-bound carrier, while the one 500-lb. bomb which hit the *Scharnhorst* glanced off and fell into the water without exploding. The *Ark Royal* brought the survivors back to Scapa on the 14th. Admiral of the Fleet Lord Cork and Orrery having struck his flag in the *Southampton* at midnight on 9th/10th June, the campaign was formally concluded when the Commander-in-Chief, with the *Rodney* and *Renown* and their destroyer screen, re-entered Scapa Flow on 15th June at 5 p.m.

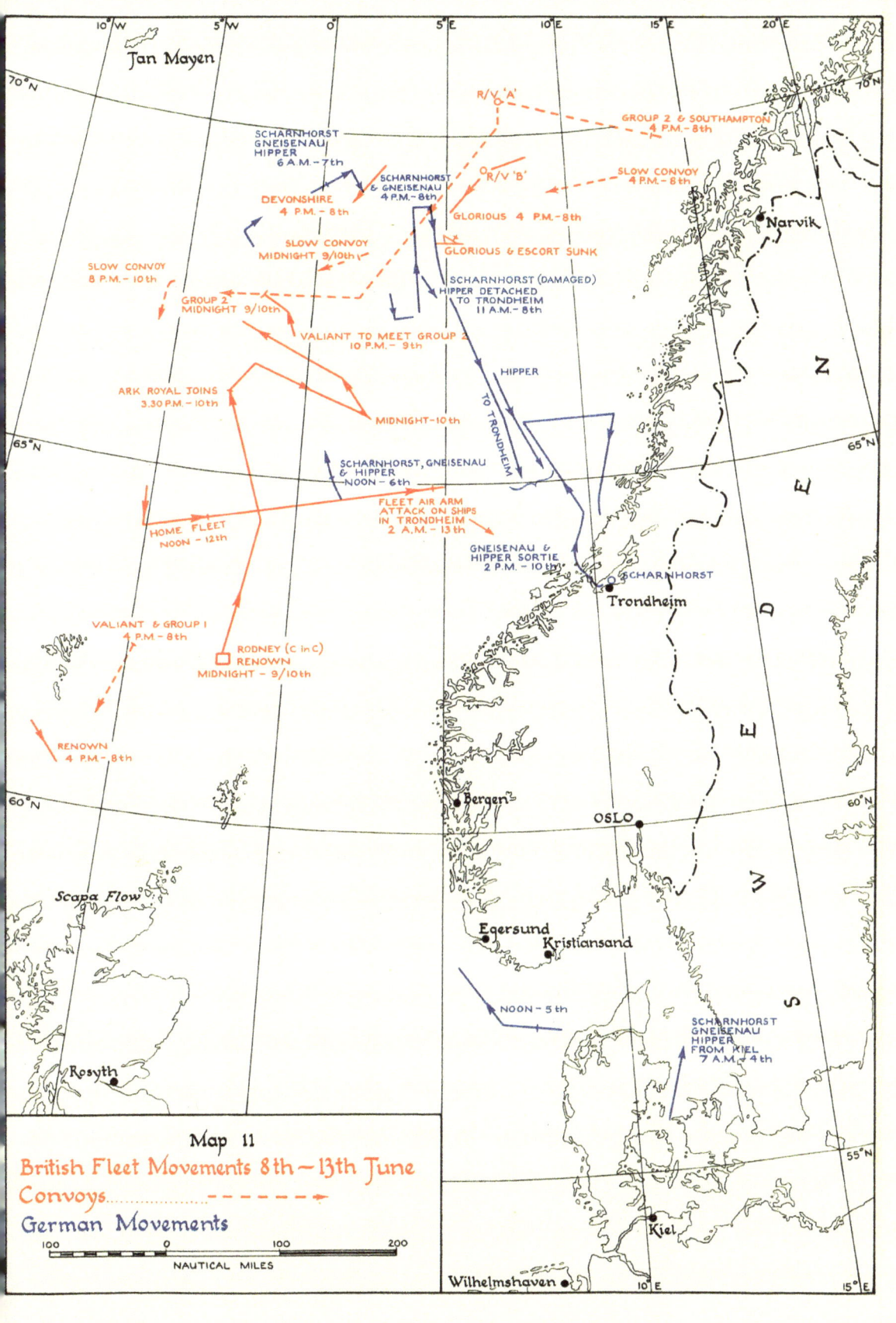

CHAPTER XV

THE CAMPAIGN IN RETROSPECT

GERMANY's strategic gains resulting from the occupation of Norway form no integral part of this campaign history; three main points only need be noted here. First and foremost there was the acquisition of naval and air bases flanking the British Isles. This added to the apparent danger of invasion and, long after that danger had receded, it complicated the problems of home defence and, most serious of all, weakened our control of the northern approaches to the Atlantic. Henceforth the route through and alongside the Norwegian Leads was carefully protected by German air power with the help of the development of coastal fortifications and other naval defences. At the same time the enemy's chances of raiding our commerce by a break-out with heavy ships into the open sea were very considerably increased; in particular, the North Norway fiords provided the bases for deadly attacks by aircraft, submarines, and surface ships against our Murmansk convoys in 1942. Submarines, which did not require the shelter of the Leads, also ranged freely from the elaborately constructed pens at Trondheim and Bergen.

The exploitation of the Norwegian economy in comparison proved to be of secondary importance. The mercantile marine which was the chief source of wealth had never been within Hitler's reach; the Norwegian Government requisitioned it by decrees of 22nd April and 18th May, which gave plenary powers to a Shipping Mission in London, but the private owners would have been most unlikely in any case to withdraw many ships from profitable Allied service. The time taken to reopen the bitterly contested iron-ore route proved, however, to be nearer six months than the twelve on which we had calculated. The first shipment was in January 1941 and, according to the Swedish iron company's records, altogether some 600,000 tons of ore left Narvik for Germany that year, rising to a rate of 1,800,000 tons *per annum* in the early months of 1943, after which exports fell off again until the end of the war.[1] Norway provided Germany with some iron ore of native origin, scarce metals like molybdenum and titanium, ferro-alloys, aluminium (from imported materials), and her timber, wood-pulp, and fish, the last of these being wanted for glycerine and vitamin A as well as for its general value as food. Heavy water was another Norwegian product of possibly crucial importance. But it is difficult to say how much of all this might have accrued to

---
[1] Buckley, C.: *Norway—The Commandos—Dieppe*, p. 152.

the Germans if Norwegian neutrality had never been assailed, and it is certain that the gains were to some minor extent offset by the need to provide Norway with a minimum of foodstuffs from German-controlled stocks elsewhere.

The result of the campaign meant in the third place an access of prestige to Germany in the eyes of neutrals, whose policy in practice was likely to be affected less by detestation of Germany's flagrant act of aggression than by admiration of her military skill and power of organisation and by fear that the Allies would show themselves unable to save a new victim from a like fate. This applied particularly to Sweden and Finland, which were now isolated from the West. But the campaign in the Low Countries and France provided similar arguments on a far larger scale and, with the entry of Italy into the war, German prestige was in any case rapidly approaching its zenith.

In the generally unpropitious situation in which we found ourselves at the close of the Norwegian campaign, some emphasis was laid upon the allegedly large German losses. The House of Commons, for instance, was frequently reminded that 'if we had losses, the Germans had far heavier losses in warships, in planes, in transport, and in men'.[1] To take first the loss of men, the casualties incurred by our own forces on land were small—1,869 British, and about 530 French and Polish, officers and men in the two months' fighting in Central and North Norway. The Norwegians do not compute separately the losses they incurred in joint operations with us but, not counting prisoners, their casualties in the entire campaign numbered 1,335. The official casualty list of the German General Staff, on the other hand, gives a figure of 5,296, including losses sustained in passage to Norway. Making allowance for naval and air force casualties, the former at least being larger on our own side, we must conclude that the total losses of the enemy in terms of human life were not significantly larger than they had inflicted, and were certainly small in relation to the results which the Germans achieved; even the campaign in the Balkans, involving no sea passage, cost them as much.

As regards material, the losses in military equipment on our side were necessarily much larger—in the absence, that is, of major battles —because our forces were three times evacuated, and each time under threat of air attack. Moreover, nearly all our equipment for Norway was taken from stocks which could otherwise have been used for our forces in France and the Middle East, where they were badly needed, or for home defence. The Germans, who lost much less, could at this stage in the war spare it far more easily. *Mutatis mutandis*, the same applies to the losses of the respective air forces,

---

[1] Mr Neville Chamberlain, 7th May: H. of C. Debs., Vol. 360, Col. 1075. See also speech by Sir Samuel Hoare, 8th May: *ibid.*, Col. 1268.

though our special handicap in this case was not the evacuations but the need to improvise airfields. One of the two R.A.F. squadrons which operated in Norway lost all its aircraft and equipment in the Lesjaskog venture; three Hurricanes were destroyed at the Skaanland airfield, which was never brought into use; and the operations at Bardufoss, in which the Hurricanes and the re-equipped Gladiator squadron each lost eight aircraft during a fortnight's operations, were also seriously impeded through lack of airfield facilities. The British also incurred some loss in attacks on German-held airfields in South Norway from British bases. The losses of the Luftwaffe amounted to 242, of which one-third were transport aircraft: this, though a far larger total, represents a smaller proportion of the number committed in Norway.

It is only in relation to her naval forces that Germany may be said to have incurred any disproportionate loss. The British Navy suffered one major casualty in the sinking of the *Glorious*. The cruiser *Effingham* was wrecked and the anti-aircraft cruiser *Curlew* sunk by bombing; three other cruisers were damaged. There was a reduction in destroyer strength by seven sinkings and eight cases of damage which we could very ill afford. We also lost one sloop, four submarines, and many smaller craft. The French and Poles lost one destroyer and one submarine each, and the French cruiser *Emile Bertin* was hit off Namsos. But the German loss was far more significant. Operation Juno resulted in the torpedoing of *Gneisenau* as well as *Scharnhorst*, and the loss in cruisers and destroyers was such that at the end of June Germany's naval forces in these categories were reduced to a total of one 8-inch cruiser, two light cruisers, and four destroyers. There was also a loss of merchant shipping which Hitler noted as an additional problem in relation to Operation Sealion. Mr Churchill in his book emphasises the point that the German Navy, by reason of the Norwegian operations, was 'no factor in the supreme issue of the invasion of Britain'.[1] We may also notice that the Germans had no surface craft available to help in the attack on the Low Countries in May or to hinder the evacuation from Dunkirk; conversely, our increased margin of superiority enabled us in the nick of time to reconstitute the Mediterranean fleet.[2] A German naval historian corroborates this, and points out that their 'very heavy losses were never made up'.[3]

In assessing Germany's losses through the Norway campaign, one is tempted also to include what the five years' occupation cost in man-power subsequently. Whether the military effort required to defend the long northern bastion of 'Fortress Europe' was worth

---

[1] Churchill, Vol. I, p. 519.
[2] Playfair, Major-General I.S.O.: *The War in the Mediterranean*, Vol. I, Chapter 5.
[3] Assmann, Kurt [ex-Vice-Admiral]: *Deutsche Schicksalsjahre*, p. 159.

while for the profits derived from its possession it is hard to say. Certainly a huge garrison was locked up in Norway during the later years of the war as a result of the obvious geographical factors favouring an Allied counter-attack and the less obvious war of nerves, by which we convinced Hitler at least that we were coming there. The Norwegians point also to the cost of police measures directed against the obdurate spirit of resistance in the people themselves, a spirit which had its roots in proud memories of the campaign: had not Norway held out twice as long as Poland, and, at Narvik, achieved Hitler's first defeat? If so, then we may fairly claim a share in the credit, since Norwegian resistance in April 1940 would scarcely have begun without Allied promises, and it would certainly not have continued without their partial fulfilment.

The scale of the Norwegian campaign, as compared with the later events of the war, was in any case extremely small. The profit and loss account therefore requires above all an estimate of the lessons taught and learnt for the later stages of a war in which combined operations were destined to play a dominant part. Indeed, those lessons may not be wholly irrelevant to the consideration of defence policy at large: for one high authority, reflecting on the events of 1939–45, makes the generalisation that it is the early campaigns of a war which, though quantitatively insignificant, provide 'the difficult problems . . . the practical problems which we and every democratic nation have to solve'.[1]

At the first impact the German campaign in Norway appeared to owe everything to surprise, where a less bold project would probably have been quickly scotched, and fortune continued to favour the bold. No German ship of war met superior surface forces on the high seas in the journey out or home, though the margin of time and space was often very narrow,[2] and out of four sporadic contacts[3] which were made by sea or air during the most critical period, from dawn to dawn of 8th/9th April, two positively helped us to misconstrue the general scope and shape of the German activities. It is true that audacity could not have sprung the surprise it did, had it not been allied to a ruthlessness which never shrank from shedding innocent blood. But a whole series of events, ever since the murder of Dollfuss nearly six years before, made it difficult to argue that the breaches of international law and contempt for human rights which the invasion of Denmark and Norway involved were too monstrous to be anticipated. Moreover, the development of the campaign showed that it had in

---

[1] Tedder, Marshal of the R.A.F. Lord: *Air Power in War*, p. 25.
[2] See pp. 31 (Bergen, Narvik) and 47 (Trondheim).
[3] See pp. 29 (the *Glowworm*), 30 (*Orzel*, the Sunderland flying-boat), and 32 (*Renown*).

fact been prepared over a considerable period of time and with the utmost thoroughness.

Therefore one obvious lesson was that deficiencies in our Intelligence work, including appreciation of intelligence, had cost us very dear. In general, it seems remarkable that, when forming the Allied plans of action for Scandinavia, we had not studied with more sense of reality the possibility that the Germans might forestall us there. The idea was indeed entertained as an intellectual hypothesis, but all our plans were based broadly upon the supposition that we should be making the first move and not the first countermove, a grave oversight which a more thorough examination of enemy intentions might have remedied. More particularly, the information about German ships and ports which accumulated during the first week of April,[1] though consistent with various alternative plans, might well have been so interpreted by us as to avoid the surprise at Narvik—to say nothing of the indication given by the sinking of the *Rio de Janeiro* 16 hours before the moment of invasion, which the Germans thought capable of giving the whole show away. Not only so, but the information about Norway available for our own use when the Germans were once inside the country was hopelessly inferior to the information which the Germans had collected for their invasion. Our leaders and their troops were again and again handicapped by their ignorance of climatic and geographical peculiarities, by the lack of detailed knowledge of harbours, landing grounds, and storage facilities, and even by ignorance of the general qualities and prejudices of the Norwegian people.

It is true that our total expenditure on intelligence purposes was normally small, and that the Scandinavian countries—in spite of their importance for us during the First World War—took a low place in our list of priorities for such expenditure. Allowance must also be made for the fact that in 1939-40 the Allies stood everywhere on the defensive, whereas in war the side which has the initiative can usually to a large extent keep its opponent guessing—a phenomenon which the Germans in their turn were to experience at the time of the Allied landings in North Africa, Sicily, and France. Nevertheless the special importance which Norway had assumed in the strategy of the Second World War since the invasion of Finland, more than four months before the events of 9th April, makes it very difficult to understand the lack of comprehensive and precise intelligence and the failure in evaluating what intelligence there was.

Intelligence might have enabled us to foresee much of what the enemy were going to attempt in Norway; but no degree of foresight

---

[1] See pp. 22, 28.

could at that time have prevented us from suffering the full effects of German air superiority. This was the most obvious lesson of the campaign—or in a sense no lesson at all, since the Air Staff, knowing the insignificant size of the air support which would be available for any Scandinavian expedition, had correctly appreciated in advance the peril to which our lines of communication would inevitably be exposed. An Air Ministry historian is even able to say, 'It is very rare in war that dangers that have been anticipated correspond so exactly to the dangers that eventuate'. But this is not the whole story. Pre-war discussions as to the possibly paramount importance of air power in given conditions had been regarded generally as inconclusive, and in the first winter of the war the fact that there were no serious air raids on British or French soil tended to drive into the background doctrines which the Polish campaign had largely vindicated. Moreover, since for the time being we had no option but to fight our enemy at a disadvantage however serious, there was a natural tendency to make light of it: hence perhaps a general optimism in our planning, which was not necessarily due to want of knowledge or imagination among the planners. This may also help to explain the excessive hopes which were based on the efficacy of anti-aircraft guns, ashore and afloat, and some exaggerated estimates of what our own small bomber force could achieve against enemy-occupied airfields. The Secretary of State for Air said in the House of Commnos on 8th May that 'Strong air power must be met by stronger air power'[1]—a truism, but one which by implication summed up the lesson of our discomfiture in the preceding month by land and sea.

As regards the Navy, this lesson, which had never clearly emerged before the war, was now increasingly realised, though it remained well hidden from the public gaze; the importance of the aircraft carrier waxed accordingly. Meanwhile, the striking-power of land-based bombers operating off south-west Norway, their efficiency once tested in the approaches to that coast, caused the Admiralty to decide that our heavy units should not be risked in the Skagerrak, much less in the Kattegat. Hence the ability of the Germans to reinforce their troops through Oslo, on which their securing of the hinterland of South and Central Norway chiefly depended—torpedo attacks by our submarines and all forms of mine-laying taken together accounted for only 1·57 per cent. of German sea reinforcements between 10th April and 13th May. It was the same threat from German air power, effective against smaller ships in the narrow waters of the Leads and fiords, which prevented our naval superiority from exercising its accustomed influence on the operations along the Norwegian coastline in the later stages of the campaign. The enemy retained con-

---

[1] H. of C. Deb., Vol. 360, Col. 1275.

siderable freedom to ferry troops in local boats and steamers; our own forces had to be moved chiefly by destroyer and even so were in constant danger of attack.

The close support which German aircraft gave to their army, and the constant pressure which they exerted against ours, were clearly shown in almost every phase of the campaign. They influenced the battle by reconnaissance activities, by bombing and machine-gunning, and even by the mere threat of their presence; our lines of communication were at their mercy; and they put two of our bases virtually out of action. A more novel employment of aircraft was their use to drop paratroops, though this was done only on a small scale in Norway; to land reinforcements on captured or improvised landing grounds or by seaplane on the fiords; and especially to supply food and munitions to troops in forward areas, notably the garrison of Narvik. Our reply to all this was largely ineffective. Our home-based bombers were too few to neutralise those enemy-occupied airfields in Norway and Denmark which were accessible to us.[1] We could not have spared an adequate fighter force to give 'cover' to our interests, even if the German seizure of every usable airfield had not confronted us with the problem of improvising airfields in the face of the enemy, which we were unable to solve except in the far north, where distance gave us some respite. The Fleet Air Arm was not designed to fill the gap: trained to operate with and for the fleet, their fighters slower than German bombers, the naval air squadrons were essaying a new (though important) role in their inshore operations along the Norwegian coast. Finally, there was the shortage of anti-aircraft artillery, which had to be supplemented both at Namsos and Aandalsnes by ships' guns and was still incomplete in the north after two months; even if there had been much more of it and a larger proportion had been heavy guns, the rate of loss inflicted on the enemy would scarcely have exceeded what he could at this time readily accept.

If the German achievement of surprise and the demonstration of the paramount importance of air superiority constitute two outstanding features of the Norwegian campaign, a third may be summed up as the comparative slowness and vacillation which appeared to characterise the British reaction to the German enterprise. We suffered under a great handicap. What has already been pointed out in connection with our Intelligence deficiencies applies to almost everything else: because the Germans then possessed the freedom of initiative, which we had as yet no means of wresting from them, we could be—and again and again were—forced into situations where confusion,

---

[1] See pp. 53–54, 133–34.

hasty planning, and unsatisfactory improvisation became inevitable. Nevertheless, the study of the origins of the campaign, showing that in this instance at least the Germans struck where we had long considered striking, must to some extent confirm the view so widely expressed at the time, that our reaction to the stroke was weaker than it need have been. It was the belief held by the public that our actions in Norway had been muddled and hesitant which provided the immediate occasion for the transfer of supreme responsibility from Chamberlain to Churchill. In the famous debate of 7th May the charge took many forms; but they may be summed up in the expression used by the then Leader of the Opposition (Mr C. R. Attlee), who said that the Government had lacked 'a settled plan for the vital objective'.[1] It is, however, more important for the present purpose to notice that commanders' opinions confirm this.

The two generals who fought in Central Norway make the same complaint that the operations they were respectively called upon to conduct had not been properly planned. Both maintained that background information was lacking and that the immediate situation was not correctly appreciated. The older commander, who writes witheringly that 'plans as such were concocted from hour to hour', implies in his report that the lessons learnt in Gallipoli, Salonika and Mesopotamia might have been applied to reduce the mistakes made in the emergency of April 1940. The younger, then a recent Commandant of the Staff College, points to a fundamental mistake in planning, in that a proper appreciation from available information or a preliminary reconnaissance would have shown that three infantry brigades could in no case be maintained through the port of Aandalsnes. He claims, in effect, that realistic planning was not attempted because of a basic assumption 'that what the General Staff consider to be politically or operationally desirable is administratively possible'. The argument that more foresight could reasonably have been expected was also applied in the controversy about the proposed naval attack on Trondheim. The details of an unopposed landing there and, much more definitely, at Narvik had been under consideration, as we have seen, for several months. The problems of a contested landing at either port were of course very different; but it is at least arguable that a reasonable degree of foresight should have rendered the adjustment of our plans to meet the new situation both prompter and more efficient. Whether the 'hammer' blow at Trondheim would have succeeded, if it had been done quickly, is matter for conjecture;[2] the effect of issuing incompatible instructions to two not wholly compatible commanders for Narvik unfortunately is not.[3]

---

[1] H. of C. Debates, Vol. 360, Col. 1090.
[2] See p. 77.
[3] See pp. 150–54, 196.

PLANNING OF THE CAMPAIGN CRITICISED

Confusion also marked the conduct of the campaign at lower levels. Weaknesses in the staff work among junior officers, for most of whom this was the first test of their organising capacity, may explain some of the troubles which were experienced in the unloading of ships, establishment of bases, and distribution of material. It is significant that General Paget urges the importance in 'a military gamble' of having headquarters units which had not been subjected to recent change, so as to make hurried team work possible. In fact, the build-up of our forces in France had not left us with any surplus of administrative experience. But in any case administrators on the spot were at the mercy of decisions taken far above their heads, which all too frequently seemed to make light of such considerations as completeness of training and equipment, or the tactical loading of transports: they had no control over the kaleidoscopic changes of plan. It was the Government which kept on varying the objective, with little regard to the havoc wrought at all lower levels, from the Joint Planning Sub-Committee, called upon to furnish new data and work out new conclusions almost every day, through all the ramifications of staff called upon to switch men and material from one destination to another, down to the man on the quay at Harstad, Namsos, or Aandalsnes grappling with unexpected arrivals (and non-arrivals), often under air attack.

Criticism may well be directed towards the system of command. There was, as we have seen,[1] much intervention by the Military Co-ordination Committee (and even by the War Cabinet) with the detailed conduct of the operations, intervention which was often disconcertingly sudden and sometimes seemingly impulsive. Apart from the interplay of personalities, this was encouraged by the close daily —and even hourly—contact with the execution of the military plans which arose from the fact that the Chiefs of Staff, who were in attendance at both the Committee and the Cabinet, were themselves in immediate control of what was being done in the field. Had the Scandinavian venture been entrusted at the outset to a single Supreme Commander or (more probably) to Commanders-in-Chief from the three Services, functioning through a Combined Headquarters, the situation would have been different. The collection of information, the preliminary appreciations and planning, and the administrative preparations would have been the direct concern of a single integrated staff—work done under the compelling knowledge that the responsibility for the success of the resulting action was also theirs; hence a much stronger resistance to changes of objective and consequential diversions of forces. Not only so, but the instructions for all three Services would have passed through the Combined Headquarters,

---

[1] Chapter V, *passim*.

where inconsistencies of aim and even incompatibilities of persons might have been noticed and adjusted; and the fact that operations were being conducted at a stage farther away from Ministers would have encouraged the restriction of their intervention to its proper field of grand strategy.

But if we ask why arrangements which became habitual later in the war were not made for Norway, the answer lies partly in the peculiar nature of the campaign for which the headquarters would have been preparing. It was to be a contingent and (as the Services hoped) very limited operation, of uncertain geographical scope, with no obvious location for a headquarters outside this country—the sort of venture to which it might have seemed improvident, in January or even in March 1940, to sidetrack any part of our very scanty supply of trained staff officers. The most significant reason, however, is the fact that combined operations were then 'a no man's land'.[1] The Inter-Service Training and Development Centre, which was formed in 1938 not long after the Japanese landing (made with several hundred landing craft) at Tientsin, had been closed as superfluous during the first months of the war, in spite of its plea that the possibility of combined operations could not be ruled out, at least as regards Norway and Greece. The entry into Scandinavia was thought of as the concern of the Army, to which the Navy contributed mainly a service of convoy protection and the Royal Air Force a token support which it could ill afford to spare. That in the sequel this proved to be the first campaign in European history requiring the full combination of all three Services took us by surprise.

After the fall of France the logic of events brought the study of combined operations inevitably to the fore, and the lesson that our system of command must be one which would contribute to the closest integration of effort throughout the Services was duly learnt —perhaps it was the most important lesson learnt in Norway. For the Norwegian campaign, small as it was, provided the first major clash of arms involving British forces since 1918. It therefore served as a testing-ground, in which all the elements of command, from the Chiefs of Staff organisation downwards, were given a trial run, revealing some inevitable weaknesses in a blueprint for the conduct of war drawn under peace-time limitations.

The campaign also posed another, special problem of command which was left undetermined, in the frequency of *ad hoc* interventions by the Admiralty in the conduct of the naval operations. As the appropriate volume of this History clearly shows,[2] the Admiralty was in duty bound to intervene occasionally in the dispositions made by Commanders-in-Chief, when intelligence newly received in London

---

[1] Lord Tedder: *Air Power in War*, p. 24.
[2] Roskill, Captain S. W.: *The War at Sea*, Vol. I, Chapter 10 *ad fin*.

rendered the policy and plans with which the fleet had sailed suddenly inapplicable and time or facilities were lacking for the intelligence to be appraised by the commander for himself. Moreover, whenever the flagship was preserving wireless silence for security reasons it would be impossible for a sudden change of orders to be signalled to the units composing the fleet except from the Admiralty. But at the start of the Norwegian campaign such Admiralty intervention took place no less than four times in four days—to modify the directions for the cruiser sweep on the fateful night of 8th/9th April, to cancel the attack on Bergen next morning, to allow Captain Warburton-Lee's destroyers to proceed without reinforcement to Narvik, and to specify the cruiser *Penelope* for the second Narvik venture.[1] In none of these instances does post-war information suggest that the Admiralty's orders produced results demonstrably better than would have been achieved by the independent actions of their commanders at sea, having the weather and much else under their immediate eye, and the very fact of intervention was bound to be in some measure disconcerting and even vexatious. In the case of the Bergen attack the First Sea Lord thought the risk to our cruisers excessive, and Mr Churchill, whose role in Admiralty affairs as First Lord went some distance beyond that of the conventional political head, says that he concurred and cancelled it. His own retrospective judgement, however, is that 'the Admiralty kept too close a control upon the Commander-in-Chief and . . . we should have confined ourselves to sending him information'.[2] What is true of the projected attack on Bergen, which might have altered the shape (though not the outcome) of the campaign, may not be wholly untrue of the other interventions.

Criticism of the way in which our forces were handled was often combined with criticism of their strength. In the Central Norway campaign the build-up never approached completion, so that the Norwegian complaint that the help we were sending them was inadequate refers logically only to the speed of its arrival. In North Norway General Auchinleck requested a scale of reinforcement which was denied him, although he put the general proposition that 'In every campaign there is a certain minimum of force which must be provided in fairness to the responsible commander and to the troops under him'. But this was after 10th May, when our inability to spare aircraft, artillery, or ships could be easily explained by reference to our needs nearer home than Narvik. Fundamentally the same answer,

---

[1] See pp. 31, 33, 44, and 46.
[2] Churchill, Vol. I, p. 470. The reason for Admiral Pound's decision is taken from the same source.

that from our small resources we could not send to Norway what was urgently needed elsewhere, applies as regards quantity throughout the campaign. As for the general scale of our operations in Norway, even before the main German assault in the west began, the lesson is of course the unpalatable one that our policies needed to be, but were not, strictly commensurate with the weakness of our armed forces and the gradualness of their expansion. The political history of the preceding six or seven years sufficiently explains the contrast between the German forces and our own. General Auchinleck's final report closes a long list of their advantages with the words: 'The enemy's thoroughness and foresight in providing everything required for fighting were extraordinary'.[1]

Nevertheless, the extent of our deficiencies in material must be included among the lessons of the campaign. At sea it was clear that the number of destroyers available could never be equal to the emergency demands on their services for protection and patrol. But in addition they were required to ferry troops and their equipment and to help maintain communications. This was partly because conditions in the fiords made the use of large vessels from our merchant navy, such as the converted luxury liners of the Namsos expedition, unsafe even if they were available; trawlers, again, fell an easy prey to German bombs; and there were, for much the same reason, difficulties in maintaining in use a steady supply of the small Norwegian fishing boats popularly known as 'Puffers'. This involved us in friction with the local inhabitants (about working during air raids) as well as serious delays and inefficiency, which could have been avoided if we had had an inland water transport organisation running suitable craft of our own provision, 'including fast motor boats for intercommunication and control, together with trained crews'.[2] Still greater importance attaches to the chronic shortage in the Narvik area of landing craft. This impeded the Bjerkvik attack and helped to cause the postponement of the final assault on Narvik, since motor landing craft were our only means of getting heavy anti-aircraft artillery ashore elsewhere in the area. Neither A.L.C.s nor M.L.C.s had been used for war in Europe before, but special tank carriers had been suggested in 1917 and actually planned in connection with the Zeebrugge raid. The key part which such craft played in the combined operations of later years seems to argue that their importance in a mechanical age might have been better foreseen.

In comparison with the enemy our land forces were almost entirely lacking in armour and artillery, and were frequently inferior in scale of automatic weapons; but however disastrous the consequences, there was no new lesson in this, since there were still some deficiencies

---

[1] Despatch by Lord Cork: Appendix B, Sec. 102.
[2] Despatch by Lord Cork, Appendix B, Sec. 103.

of equipment in the B.E.F. in France after eight months throughout which it had had first claim on the slowly expanding output of our war industries.[1] There was also a lack of mobility which handicapped us throughout the campaign—in marked contrast to our enemies, whose advance seemed never to be seriously impeded either by natural conditions or by our efforts to destroy bridges and roads as we retreated. Our 3-ton War Department lorries proved unmanœuvrable on the narrow roads of the Romsdal and Gudbrandsdal; the 146th Brigade at Namsos, issued with three kitbags of clothing per man, but not issued with the vehicles to convey them, are described as 'mechanised to immobility'; the Guards on their first arrival in the Arctic north found it impossible to operate without skis or snowshoes and the skill to use them. Other subjects of serious complaint were the deficiencies in signalling equipment and the chronic scarcity of maps, which hampered the activities both of the Army and of the Royal Air Force.

The campaign, though so small, was not without some influence upon our ideas of military training, which General Paget as Commander-in-Chief, Home Forces, was destined later to reshape. In the first place it must be conceded that, apart from the single battalion of experienced skiers, which was prematurely disbanded after the Finnish peace (12th March 1940), our troops were inevitably at a disadvantage, so far as training was concerned, when matched against the two German-Austrian Mountain Divisions. Field Service Regulations contained a section on Mountain Warfare, derived from experience on the North West Frontier, but the very different problem of operating at a high altitude (or in high latitudes) in snow was nowhere considered. The lesson was learned, in the sense that plans for a second Norwegian campaign envisaged the employment of forces properly trained in snow and winter warfare. Then there was the question of the effects of air bombing upon morale of troops, which up to that time had been much discussed but little experienced. The casualties from air action were far less than had been expected, though repeated and unchallenged air attacks were found to interfere seriously with the efficiency of those who worked under exposed conditions, as at the bases in Central Norway or by the briefly-held airstrip on Lake Lesjaskog. But a much wider problem was posed by General Auchinleck's report on *Operations in Northern Norway*, which was printed for the War Cabinet in March 1941. From his experience of less than a month, he concluded that the morale of British troops under his command had often been lower than that of other troops working under comparable conditions. While emphasising the effects of inferiority of equipment and, above all, of the absence of adequate

---

[1] See Ellis, Major L. F.: *The Campaign in France and Flanders, 1939–40.*

air support, the General (who had only recently returned from a long term of service in India) concluded that our existing methods of training lacked realism and did not do enough to inculcate habits of self-reliance. This judgement is weighty, though it is not of course to be applied with equal force to every phase of the campaign in the far north, much less transferred to Central Norway, where the later stages in the long retreat from the Gudbrandsdal were seen to bear ample testimony to 'the endurance, discipline and fighting quality of the troops engaged'.[1]

Lastly, we may notice that General Massy's report, which pleads for the establishment of a reserve force approximating to an army corps, ready 'to act swiftly and decisively at any point overseas',[2] states four essential requirements for effective campaigning, each of which was fulfilled in the later years of the war. There must be time to train in amphibious operations; a suitable training area must be set apart; there must be a proper provision of landing craft; and there must be a thorough study of air co-operation, particularly with both a fighter and bomber component. In other words, the weakness of our reaction to the German *coup* in April 1940 is the measure of our failure to prepare for action by applying to the age of mechanised and aerial warfare that technique of combined operations, which British sea power had in former wars established as a world-ranging instrument of conquest.

One remaining point of interest in the operations is the light they shed upon inter-Allied relations. Relations with the French and with the Polish contingent worked on the whole very smoothly. An interesting example in the medical sphere was the adoption of an international code already in use by the Foreign Legion to label casualties, so that treatment need never be delayed by language difficulties. There was inadequate provision for interpreters to the French at Namsos, where General Carton de Wiart considered that they were needed at the rate of one per battalion because French troops were frequently placed under British command, but the fact that our General was virtually bilingual prevented the possibility of serious misunderstanding at the top. In the Narvik campaign no serious friction arose in the execution of military operations either before or after their delegation to the French commander. At a higher level, however, Anglo-French relations showed some signs of the strain which is liable to occur when the forces of any sovereign Power fight a disappointing and unsuccessful campaign under alien command. The fact that these operations had been assigned in ad-

---

[1] Despatch by Lieut.-General Massy, Part III, Section 63.
[2] Despatch, Part IV, Section 71.

vance to British management was accepted by the French Cabinet with a rather bad grace at the outset, when they seemed anxious to make a scapegoat of Gamelin for our failure in the *course de vitesse*.[1] The French Government continued to be very critical of what they called the rhythm of our conduct of the campaign, by which they meant that the administrative plan should somehow have been stretched so as to speed up reinforcement, and General Gamelin eventually made clear his preference for an independent French command over the French contingent. The success with which the Allied Military Committee in London handled thorny questions of transporting and allocating French troops suggests that a widening of its functions might have helped to prevent friction.

The main problem, however, was that of our relations with the Norwegians, in whose native land we were fighting—a consideration to which they were so sensitive that General Fleischer formally protested against the inclusion of his forces under the heading 'The Allies'. Both the expeditions to Central Norway suffered from a lack of organised liaison. The liaison officer sent out to Namsos was not retained by the Force Commander; relations with the Norwegian forces under Colonel Getz suffered accordingly. General Paget in his report recommended that in future special attention should be paid to the provision of organised liaison in advance of disembarkation, designed to penetrate throughout both fighting and administrative units; the want of such liaison in his opinion had affected not only security but the availability of every kind of local resource in men or material, right down to telephones and lorries.

But in the peculiar circumstances of the Norwegian campaign, there was need for effective liaison in a much wider sense. The general cordiality of Anglo-Norwegian relations must not blind us to the fact that they were, at the outset of the campaign, inevitably clouded. The plans with which General Mackesy was sent to the North still owed something of their outlook to the earlier plans, in which we had envisaged that a British force might be crossing Norwegian territory on its way to Finland (via the orefields) with the acquiescence rather than the support of the Norwegians. This in turn derived some of its justification, or explanation, from our resentment at the way in which the Norwegian authorities, like those of other small neutral Powers, had shown themselves to be influenced more by fear of German ruthlessness than by recognition of the principles of international justice for which we were fighting. They wished us well, but not too loudly, and interpreted even well-meant advice that they should look to their defences as an attempt to drag them into the war. True that from 9th April onwards the Norwegians were actively resisting

---

[1] See Gamelin, t. III, p. 325, and Reynaud, t. II, pp. 29–32.

a German invasion, but the initial success of that invasion was erroneously believed by us to be mainly due to the strength of Major Quisling's pro-German faction. Conversely, the Norwegian attitude to Britain was one of some reserve founded on the supposition, to which the *Altmark* incident seemed to them to lend colour, that we had for a long time been manœuvring them towards participation in the war. The minelaying of course confirmed this attitude, though the German invasion followed it too quickly for it to take full effect. Reserve developed naturally into indignation when General Ruge and others found that the landing of our troops on Norwegian soil, which they believed us to have been covertly planning for so long, was slow and disorganised. The shortcomings of their own forces might be conspicuous, but their morale was not helped by an apparent lack of sympathy and even suspicion on our part. Their Commander-in-Chief goes so far as to say that an Allied and a Norwegian account of the campaign will never agree, and points to the misunderstandings which occurred between us at all levels—about security, about political objectives, about support in the field, on technical and administrative matters, and in the relations of the rank and file. 'It always takes time', adds General Ruge in extenuation, 'to get to know each other's good points as well'.[1] But the fact that only twelve months later the Joint Planners believed Norway to be the most fertile ground for subversive operations in the whole of German-occupied Europe, argues the feasibility in 1940 of some more effective appeal for the co-operation of the Norwegian people. So far from achieving this, we had not even achieved a unification of military command.[2]

Our forces in the Namsos area noted the existence of a further problem, namely the control of the civil population in the forward area, though the evacuation from Central Norway intervened before the problem became serious. In the north, liaison arrangements were extended, towards the end, from the appointment of military liaison officers to the provision of a liaison officer accredited to the civil government authorities at Tromsö. But General Auchinleck, who found the situation on his arrival 'Gilbertian' and considered that there were some thousands of the population who ought to be moved out of forward zones for their own safety as well as ours, put the case for a regular civil affairs organisation in the following propositions. The Norwegian civil authorities were by our standards unorganised and unrealistic. They imposed no restrictions upon civilian movements or civilian communications, thus unconsciously facilitating enemy intelligence work or sabotage. And thirdly, there were no civil resources to meet the difficulty of providing for civilian needs,

---

[1] Ruge, Major-General Otto: *Krigens Dagbok*, Vol. I, pp. 370–72.
[2] See pp. 58, 103–5, 122–23, 202–3.

ranging from food and light to sanitation and hospitals, if the base at Harstad were to suffer sustained air attack such as had laid our other Norwegian bases in ruins. A scheme to meet any such emergency was devised for the North Africa landings two and a half years later.

It is easy to be wise after the event. The Norwegian campaign was in many respects a novelty. None of the parallels adduced for it, not even the Gallipoli venture, was at all satisfactory. Hitler, as we now know, saw a useful precedent in von der Goltz's operations in Finland in 1918; the parallel activities of the British Army at Murmansk and Archangel were not apparently brought into account by us, although the Chief of the Imperial General Staff had commanded in them. As General Carton de Wiart concludes, this was 'a campaign for which the book does not cater'.

Moreover, we could at no stage consider the campaign in isolation. At the very outset our naval operations were governed more by the need to prevent German heavy units from breaking out into the Atlantic than by fear for the safety of Norwegian ports. The employment of bomber and fighter squadrons of the R.A.F. was always conditioned by the known inadequacy of the provision made, not only for the task of army co-operation in France, but for the needs of home defence. The air defence of Great Britain was not, in fact, tested seriously until the Norwegian campaign was over, but it was always the principal preoccupation of the Air Ministry. The employment of troops in Norway was, indeed, defended at the time on the uncertain ground that it caused a disproportionate diversion of German troops from the western front; but, although General Gamelin favoured such distractions, the western front was the main consideration throughout. Having regard to the immediate sequel, there was much wisdom in the warning Mr Chamberlain gave on 7th May, when he urged that because of the situation in Norway we must not be 'tempted into such a dispersal of our forces as might suit the purposes of the enemy'.[1]

In the third place we were not, at this stage in the war, free to work out any campaign without consideration for the position of neutrals. The supposed susceptibilities of American opinion helped to enforce the strict regard for international law which largely enabled the Germans to 'beat us to the draw'. The possibility that Russia might make her action in Poland a precedent for a share-out of North Norway added one more uncertainty to our actions at Narvik. The fear (which is now believed to have been exaggerated) that any new shock to our prestige might precipitate Italian intervention in the

[1] H. of C. Deb., Vol. 360, Col. 1082.

war made us hesitate to risk a battleship at Trondheim. Above all, there was the not unreasonable supposition that Germany was only awaiting a suitable moment to infringe the neutrality of Sweden, which might bring us new resources of manpower or the Germans a new route of supply; Swedish resistance was an uncertain quantity.

In the long run, we could not have defended Norway, though a better knowledge of Norwegian conditions and a more realistic approach to the problems involved might have made our piecemeal intervention there into something more coherent and in the short run more effective. But given the political situation of 1939–40 British intervention in some form was inevitable; and given the paucity of our then resources in men and arms, a more or less calamitous issue from it was likewise inevitable. Fortunately for civilisation, the events of 1940 were not final, and this same northern fastness, where the Germans seemed to have established themselves in triumphant security, was to be freed again five years later without a blow struck, as a consequence of overwhelming Allied victories elsewhere. So well were the lessons learnt, both of this small, ill-starred campaign and of a whole triennium of reverses—as it will be the more grateful task of later volumes in this History to show.

APPENDIX A

Instructions to Commanders

		Page
(1) April 10:	Major-General P. J. Mackesy	247
(2) April 14:	Major-General Carton De Wiart	249
(3) April 16:	Brigadier Morgan	250
(4) April 17:	Major-General Hotblack	251
(5) April 22:	Lieut.-General H. R. S. Massy	255
(6) April 22:	Major-General B. C. T. Paget	256
(7) May 2:	Lieut.-Colonel C. McV. Gubbins	257
(8) May 5:	Lieut.-General C. J. E. Auchinleck	259

(1)

INSTRUCTIONS TO
MAJOR-GENERAL P. J. MACKESY, C.B., D.S.O., M.C.

1. His Majesty's Government and the Government of the French Republic have decided to send a Field Force to initiate operations against Germany in Northern Norway.

2. The object of the force will be to eject the Germans from the Narvik area and to establish control of Narvik itself.

3. (a) You will command the troops including all units of the French Army and any R.A.F. component which may subsequently be added to the force. The force will consist in the first instance of all troops now on board the s.s. *Chrobry* and *Batory*.

(b) Should you become a casualty or otherwise be prevented from exercising command of the force, command will pass to the next senior British officer, who will exercise command and, in the event of a French General officer being with the force, assume the acting rank of Major-General until another British officer can be appointed.

4. No information is available as to the strength of the Norwegian forces in the area but it is known that Harstad is normally the Headquarters of a mixed brigade and it is supposed that some troops are there now. Their attitude is not known but it is believed that they will be ready to co-operate.

5. Your initial task will be to establish your force at Harstad, ensure the co-operation of Norwegian forces that may be there and obtain the information necessary to enable you to plan your further operations.

6. It is intended to reinforce you with a view to subsequent operations from such base as may be selected by you in consultation with the Senior Naval Officer. Salangen is the only neighbouring anchorage of which the Admiralty have full knowledge.

A timetable showing the time at which these reinforcements might be made available is attached as Appendix 'A'.

7. It is not intended that you should land in the face of opposition. You may, however, be faced with opposition owing to mistaken identity; you will therefore take such steps as are suitable to establish the nationality of your force before abandoning the attempt.

8. The decision whether to land or not will be taken by the Senior Naval Officer in consultation with you. If landing is impossible at Harstad some other suitable locality should be tried. A landing must be carried out when you have sufficient troops.

9. You will appreciate the importance of the destruction of the railway leading from Narvik to the Norwegian-Swedish frontier should you be able to engineer it. This is the only known means of communication from Narvik into Sweden.

10. Your force will constitute an independent command directly under the War Office. You will keep in constant communication with the War Office and report as regularly as is practicable as to the situation.

11. A duplicate of these instructions has been handed to Brigadier Phillips.

The War Office,
10th April 1940.

E. IRONSIDE,
General,
C.I.G.S.
for S. of S.

APPENDIX 'A'

	Arrival Date
(a) Remainder 24th Infantry Brigade (Regulars)	a.m. 16th April.
(b) Two T.A. Brigades (less two battalions)	p.m. 16th and 18th April.
(c) Transport for all above troops	p.m. 19th April.
(d) Remainder 49th Division	a.m. 27th April.
(e) Leading échelon Chasseurs Alpins	Between 21st and 25th April.
(f) British formations ordered from the B.E.F.	Twelve days between date of giving order for move and date of arrival of first brigade (without transport).

COPY OF A MESSAGE WRITTEN OUT IN MANUSCRIPT BY C.I.G.S. FOR GENERAL MACKESY 2330 HOURS 10TH APRIL, TAKEN BY BRIGADIER LUND

General Mackesy.

Brigadier Lund is bringing your instructions. Owing to naval difficulties in escorting, we have decided to send 4 Bns. together, the whole arriving 30 hrs after the arrival of 2 Bns. With a week's interval before the arrival of the other 2 Bns.

Latest information is that there are 3,000 Germans in Narvik. They must have been knocked about by naval action.

You will have sufficient troops to allow you to make preliminary preparations and reconnaissances. You yourself being some hours in front of your 4 Bns. with some men.

You may be able to work up the Norwegians, if they still exist in any formed body in or around Harstad. Tell them that a large force is coming.

There should be considerable numbers of ponies in the village and neighbouring ones. Let no question of paying trouble you. Issue payment vouchers and we will see that you get a paymaster as soon as possible. Don't allow any haggling over prices.

You may have a chance of taking advantage of naval action and you should do so if you can.

Boldness is required.

We will keep you informed of any action by the Germans giving them a chance of getting men in via Sweden. At the moment they cannot reinforce Narvik. Their first effort will be for reinforcing Bergen and Trondhjem.

Good luck to you. We know your responsibility and trust you.

Yours ever,
E. IRONSIDE,
General,
C.I.G.S.

(2)

INSTRUCTIONS TO MAJOR-GENERAL CARTON DE WIART COMMANDING FORCES SCHEDULED FOR 'MAURICE OPERATION'

1. His Majesty's Government and the Government of the French Republic have decided to land an expedition in Central Norway with the object of:

(*a*) Providing encouragement for the Norwegian Government.

(*b*) Forming a rallying point for the Norwegian Government and armed forces.

(*c*) Securing a base for any subsequent operations in Scandinavia.

This operation will be carried out concurrently with but independent of the operations already initiated in Northern Norway.

2. You are appointed to command the Allied forces which are being despatched to Central Norway.

3. Your role will be to secure the Trondheim area. Subsequently you should take such steps as are possible to secure the use to the Allies of the road and rail communications leading from Trondheim, especially to the east.

4. *Points of Landing.*

(i) It is suggested, but of this you, together with the Senior Naval Officer, must be the final judges, that the initial landing should be in the Namsos area, and should be carried out by Morgan's and Phillips' Brigades.

(ii) A second landing should be carried out about Trondheim preferably to the east of the town, and after the Navy has cleared the fjord of German vessels, by 147th Infantry Brigade and Chasseurs Alpins.

(iii) Administrative facilities should initially be developed about Namsos until Trondheim has been secured.

5. A forecast of the dates of arrival in the Trondheim-Namsos area of the elements of your force is as follows:—

(a) 146th Infantry Brigade, Brigadier Phillips, available on 15th April.

(b) One infantry brigade (less one battalion), under Brigadier Morgan, should be available about dawn 17th April.

(c) 147th Infantry Brigade, with artillery and ancillary troops, should be available on 20th or 21st April.

(d) Two battalions Chasseurs Alpins available (in the same area) 18th April.

6. Should you become a casualty or otherwise be prevented from exercising command of the force, command will pass to the next senior British officer, who will exercise command, and in the event of a French General officer being with the force, assume the acting rank of Major-General until another British officer can be appointed.

7. As soon as you are established ashore you will get in touch with any Norwegian forces in your vicinity, inform them of the impending arrival of further Allied forces and secure their co-operation in action against any German forces.

8. The Royal Navy are making preliminary landings in the Namsos area with landing parties about 300 strong in all and it is their intention to seize and hold any point in the Namsos area at which your disembarkation might take place.

9. Your force is not organised for landing in face of opposition, and it is not intended that you should undertake such an operation.

10. During the voyage and during landing operations, the Senior Naval Officer will be in command, and he will decide, in co-operation with you, where and when to land.

11. A note as to the strength of the Norwegian forces in the area, and of the strength of any German forces operating in the vicinity, is being given to you separately.

12. Your force will constitute an independent command directly under the War Office. You will keep a constant communication with the War Office and report as regularly as is practicable as to the situation.

(Sd.) EDMUND IRONSIDE,
C.I.G.S.

The War Office,
14th April 1940.

(3)

TO BRIGADIER MORGAN FROM THE WAR OFFICE

1. Your instructions as follows.
2. Festing will have told you role of Carton de Wiart and of Hotblack's

APPENDIX A

projected combined operation on Trondheim. Small force British guerrillas operating your right flank. About 600 sailors landing Aandalsnes night 17/18. Their role after landing will be communicated to you later.

3. Your role to land Aandalsnes area secure Dombaas then operate northwards and take offensive action against Germans in Trondheim area. Not intended that you should land in face of opposition. Second échelon your force will follow you in two days later. As you are without transport you should rely on Norwegian rolling stock and locally impressed transport. You will be kept informed of progress and timings of other British forces operating Trondheim area.

4. Your force independent command under War Office until receipt further orders. Intention later place you under Commander General Operations Trondheim area.

5. During the voyage and during landing operations Senior Naval Officer will be in command. He will decide in co-operation with you where and when to land.

6. Previous instructions *re* co-operation with Norwegians and reports to War Office unchanged.

The War Office,
  16th April 1940.

(4)

INSTRUCTIONS FOR MAJOR-GENERAL HOTBLACK

Object and Scope of Operations in Central Norway.

1. His Majesty's Government and the Government of the French Republic are agreed that the early capture of Trondheim is vital to the success of the further operations in Scandinavia.

2. The immediate object of the Allied operations in Central Norway is therefore the capture of Trondheim. With this end in view, operations as follows are projected and in process of execution:—

(*a*) Operation 'Maurice'—Commander, Lieut.-General Carton de Wiart. This comprises an advance southwards on Trondheim from the Namsos area by 146th Infantry Brigade (Brigadier Phillips) which is probably to be reinforced by the first échelon of the leading French light division (three battalions and attached troops).

(*b*) Operation 'Boots'—Commander, Major-General Hotblack. This comprises a combined operation by the Navy and Army, with an R.A.F. component to be added later, with the object of forcing the entry of Trondheim Fiord, capturing Trondheim, and destroying the German forces in that area.

(*c*) Operation 'Sickle'—Commander, Brigadier Morgan. This comprises a landing by 148th Infantry Brigade (two battalions) at Aandalsnes, with the role of securing Dombaas, preventing the Germans from using the railway to reinforce Trondheim, and possibly a subsequent demonstration northwards towards Trondheim.

3. You are appointed military commander of the land forces detailed for Operation 'Boots'.

The forces placed under your command are as follows:—
15th Infantry Brigade.
Two Canadian battalions under Brigadier Samson (Princess Patricia's Canadian Light Infantry and........................).
147th Infantry Brigade (Brigadier Lammie).

4. The system of command of the combined operations to be carried out by force 'Boots' will be that of 'Joint Command' by the naval, military and air commanders as laid down in Chapter IV, paras. 2–5 of the 'Manual of Combined Operations, 1938'.

The name of the naval commander appointed by the Admiralty is ....

5. In view of the paramount need for speed, the plan of operations has been prepared by you in co-operation with the Staffs of the War Office and the Admiralty, and is being communicated by you to the naval commander.

Should you and the naval commander desire to depart from this plan, you will bear in mind that any appreciable delay may have the most serious consequences on the course of operations in Scandinavia.

6. The organisation of command of the Allied military forces in Scandinavia is given in Appendix 'A'.

7. Should you become a casualty or otherwise be prevented from exercising command of the force, command will pass to the next senior British officer, who will exercise command, and, in the event of a French General officer being with the force, assume the acting rank of Major-General until another British officer can be appointed.

8. When your forces have successfully landed, it is important that good relations with the Norwegians should be fostered.

9. You will be guided by Appendix 'B' with regard to the conduct of all forms of bombardment.

10. You will be kept informed regularly by the War Office as to the latest situation.

11. You will keep a constant communication with the War Office, and report regularly as to the situation.

The War Office,
   17th April 1940.

Appendix 'A'

ORGANISATION OF COMMAND OF THE ALLIED MILITARY FORCES IN SCANDINAVIA

1. *First stage.*

Major-General Carton de Wiart assumes rank of Lieutenant-General (local unpaid), and commands British forces now operating from Namsos and 1st Echelon (three battalions and attached troops) Chasseurs Alpins under General de Division Audet (Operation 'Maurice'). Major-General Hotblack commands independently all land forces involved in sea-borne operation 'Boots' for capture of Trondheim.

APPENDIX A

2. *Second stage.*

Major-General Hotblack's force ('Boots') becomes subordinate command under Lieutenant-General Carton de Wiart at a time to be decided by the latter, which will not be before Major-General Hotblack has reported to Lieutenant-General Carton de Wiart that his force has been effectively established ashore.

3. *Third stage.*

When Lieutenant-General Carton de Wiart reports that he is in a position effectively to exercise direct command of components of Major-General Hotblack's force, Major-General Hotblack himself will be withdrawn under orders of the War Office.

4. Brigadier Morgan's force (Operation 'Sickle') remains independent under War Office until further orders. Lieutenant-General Carton de Wiart will report when communication has been established with Brigadier Morgan.

5. The movement of the 2nd Echelon Chasseurs Alpins (three battalions and attached troops) will be directed by the War Office in the first instance, but the intention is that as soon as the tactical situation permits, the whole French force should come under the command of General de Division Audet, subordinate to Lieutenant-General Carton de Wiart.

6. It is intended that once the Allies are in full control of the Trondheim area, a corps commander should be appointed to command all British, French and Norwegian forces in Scandinavia.

Appendix 'B'

INSTRUCTIONS BY HIS MAJESTY'S GOVERNMENT TO GOVERN THE CONDUCT OF ALL FORMS OF BOMBARDMENT

1. The following instruction will govern the conduct of all forms of bombardment until the restrictions therein contained are modified.

These restrictions, in the meantime, are not to be relaxed on any account pending further instructions, even in retaliation for indiscriminate action by an enemy.

2. The object of the instructions is not to define legitimate military objectives, but to lay down a course of action in accordance with the agreed policy, which it may be expedient to adopt at the outset of war. It will be observed that the effect will be to restrict bombardment more severely than is required by a reasonable interpretation of existing international law.

3. Only the following 'purely military objectives in the narrowest sense of the word' may be bombarded from the sea or air. Army Commanders will conform generally to the spirit of these instructions.

(*a*) Naval forces, i.e. warships, auxiliaries actually attendant on the Fleet, naval dockyards, barracks, and other establishments manned by naval personnel.

(*b*) Army units, fortifications, coast defence works, barracks, camps, billets, depots, dumps, and other establishments manned by military personnel.

(c) Air units, military aerodromes, depots, storage units, bomb stores and other establishments manned by air personnel.

(d) Troop transports (whether at sea or in harbour), roads, canals, and railways used for military communications, military road and inland water transport. Trains, road and inland water transport are not to be attacked unless they can reasonably be presumed to be of a military character.

(e) Accumulations of Navy, Army or Air Force stores. (This does not authorise attack on factories.)

(f) Naval, Army and Air Force fuel installations or dumps in the field or situated within the confines of the Naval, Army and Air Force establishments mentioned in sub-paragraphs (a) to (c) above.

(*Note.*—Bulk stocks of fuel not covered by the above definitions are not to be bombarded under these instructions.)

4. Action against objectives in paragraph 3 above will be subject to the following general principles:—

(a) The intentional bombardment of civil populations is illegal.

(b) It must be possible to distinguish and identify the objectives in question.

(c) Bombardment must be carried out in such a way that there is a reasonable expectation that damage will be confined to the objective and that civilian populations in the neighbourhood are not bombarded through negligence.

Thus it is clearly illegal to bombard a populated area in the hope of hitting a legitimate target which is known to be in the area, but which cannot be precisely located and identified.

5. Subject to the general policy set out above, Commanders must exercise their discretion, and orders for bombardment should be framed according to the spirit of that policy and not necessarily to the letter. In particular it must be borne in mind that the fact of an objective being unquestionably military does not necessarily or invariably justify bombardment of it. Thus an anti-aircraft or coast defence gun situated in the centre of a populous area could not be bombarded with reasonable expectation that damage would be confined to it. A small detachment of troops in billets in, or a convoy of transport passing through a town, or a troop transport lying alongside a commercial wharf, are unquestionably military objectives, but the bombardment of such objectives in a town might involve risks to the civil population out of all proportion to the military importance of the target at the time and might thus be unjustifiable. Justification for bombardment even of unquestionably military objectives must therefore depend on circumstances and must be decided by Commanders acting in the spirit of these instructions.

6. The necessary action is being taken to secure the adherence of our prospective Allies to this policy, and the necessary communications are being made to the Governments of the Dominions and of India.

7. Later it may be desirable to extend the scope of these instructions to the full extent allowed for by the following:—

Naval Bombardment—Hague Convention No. IX of 1907.

Air Force Bombardment—The Draft Hague Rules of Aerial

Warfare 1922/23 as interpreted in the Air Ministry instructions to be issued in the near future.

Until such times as further instructions are issued from London, however, the above will stand. They are, however, liable to be modified at the shortest notice.

8. The action of armies is well established by practice and is not in dispute. Commanders of military forces on the ground will use every reasonable precaution to avoid undue loss of civilian life by artillery bombardment.

(5)

INSTRUCTIONS FOR
LIEUTENANT-GENERAL H. R. S. MASSY, D.S.O., M.C.

1. His Majesty's Government have placed you in command of all British and French troops operating in Central Scandinavia, excluding any which may be operating in the Narvik area or based on Narvik. These latter will continue to be commanded by Major-General Mackesy under the orders of Lord Cork and Orrery.

2. Your object will be to establish, in co-operation with the Norwegians, Allied control of Central Norway. To enable this to be done it is essential that adequate ports of entry, including Trondheim, should be secured for the maintenance of your forces.

3. A list of the original instructions issued to Lieutenant-General Carton de Wiart is attached as Appendix B.

A copy of the original instructions issued to Brigadier Morgan and of messages subsequently amending these instructions is attached as Appendix C.

4. Certain measures of which you have been informed have already been taken to provide reinforcements for Maurice and Sickle. The forces which you may anticipate having at your disposal as further reinforcements are shown as Appendix D. These forces will only come under your orders when so ordered by the War Office.

5. An operation Scissors for guerilla operations by a number of independent companies is being organised. The first company is due to be dispatched immediately.

6. You will act in co-operation with, but not under the command of, the Commander-in-Chief, Norwegian forces. You are at liberty to place any part of your force under Norwegian command should you think fit.

7. Should the course of operations develop in such a manner as to necessitate unified command by a Headquarters in Scandinavia of all the Allied forces in Scandinavia further orders will be issued by the War Office.

8. Should you become a casualty or otherwise be prevented from exercising command of your force, command will pass to the next senior British officer, who will exercise command and, in the event of a French General Officer being with the force, assume the acting rank of Lieutenant-General until another British Officer can be appointed.

9. You will be guided by Appendix E with regard to the conduct of all forms of bombardment.

10. You will keep a constant communication with the War Office, and report regularly as to the situation.

The War Office,
? 22nd April 1940.

[*Appendices omitted.*]

(6)

EXPEDITIONARY FORCE INSTRUCTION No. 1

To Major-General B. C. T. Paget, d.s.o., m.c.

Sickle Force

1. (*a*) A German Army of about one Corps, based on Southern Norway, is operating against the Norwegian Army, which is believed to be fighting a delaying action on the approximate line Hamar-Elverum.

(*b*) The Germans have also landed about 3,000 men at Bergen; at Stavanger, where they have occupied the aerodrome; and at Trondheim, where they have between 3,500 and 5,000 men and at least two destroyers. The aerodrome at Vaernes, near Trondheim, is also in their hands.

(*c*) The German force in the Trondheim area is believed to be disposed as under, but the numbers may be increased by airborne reinforcements.

    (i) 1,500 in the area Levanger-Verdalen facing the British force based on Namsos.

    (ii) 500 protecting the coast defences at the entrance to the Trondheim Fjord about Agdenes.

    (iii) 200 at Stören (twenty-five miles south of Trondheim) operating in a southerly direction.

    (iv) 300 operating on the Trondheim-Ostersund railway to the east of Trondheim.

2. Allied forces, consisting of 146 Infantry Brigade and a demi-brigade of Chasseurs Alpins, both under the command of Major-General Carton de Wiart, are based on Namsos. If possible these forces are to be kept in being in order to maintain pressure against Trondheim from the north.

You have been informed separately of the composition of the British forces now operating south of Dombaas and of the forces to accompany you.

3. A force of Gladiators will, it is hoped, be ashore by the 25th April. In the meantime a Carrier with fighter aircraft will be off your base at Aandalsnes. Contact with these should be arranged through Brigadier Hogg at the Base.

4. An advance skeleton Corps Headquarters, under the orders of Brigadier Hogg (D.A. and Q.M.G.) is travelling with you and will be responsible for:—

(*a*) Organising the base at Aandalsnes and organising the anti-aircraft defence of that base.

(*b*) Reconnoitring a subsidiary base at Geiranger and arranging for its anti-aircraft defence and for the requisitioning of transport for employment on the road L. of C. from Geiranger to your forces south of Dombaas.

(c) Making similar arrangements at Sundalen.

(a), (b) and (c) above are in order of priority. Brigadier Hogg will be operationally under your orders.

5. On arrival in Norway you will assume command of all British troops in the country, other than those operating under the orders of Major-General Carton de Wiart based on Namsos and those in the Narvik area.

6. Your task will be to co-operate with the Norwegian Army in preventing the northward advance of the German Army based on Southern Norway.

7. It will be necessary for you to safeguard your left and rear against attack by the German forces in Trondheim and parachute-landed detachments on your L. of C.

8. You should make the earliest possible contact with the Commander-in-Chief, Norwegian Army, with a view to obtaining close co-operation towards the fulfilment of your task and the safeguarding of your forces and communications.

You will not be under the orders of the Commander-in-Chief, Norwegian Army.

9. You should report your situation and your requirements at frequent intervals and all information that you are able to obtain.

Your channels of communication are laid down in the Outline Plan and first Maintenance project (G.S. (P) No. 650).

(Sd.) H. R. S. MASSY,
Lieutenant-General,
Commander, 5th Corps.

Headquarters, 5th Corps,
22nd April 1940.

(7)

INSTRUCTIONS TO LIEUT-COLONEL C. McV. GUBBINS, M.C.

Information

1. Force Maurice has been instructed to send a detachment of 100 French Chasseurs Alpins to Mosjoen by sea to hold it until relieved by you. This detachment should have arrived there night 1st/2nd May.

2. A detachment from Force Rupert (one company Scots Guards) arrived Bodo area on 30th April and reported 'all well'.

3. No. 1 Independent Company sailed for Mo against any attempted landings by sea or air. Copy of instructions at Appendix A.

4. Nos. 3, 4 and 5 Independent Companies together with your Headquarters will be shipped from the Clyde probably on morning 4th May 1940.

Task

5. You will assume command of Nos. 1, 3, 4 and 5 Independent Companies and any further companies that may be subsequently placed under your orders.

6. You will send two companies to the Mosjoen area as soon as

possible, after which arrangements are to be made by this Headquarters for the shipment of the French detachment to the United Kingdom.

You will send one company to the Bodo area to relieve the company of the Scots Guards whose removal is being arranged by Rupertforce.

7. Your first task is to prevent the Germans occupying Bodo, Mo and Mosjoen. This they may try to do by small parties landed from the sea or dropped by parachutes. Later the Germans may be expected to advance northwards on Mosjoen from the Trondheim area via Grong. You will ensure that all possible steps are taken by demolition and harrying tactics to impede any German advance along this route. Your companies operating in this area should not attempt to offer prolonged frontal resistance but should endeavour to maintain themselves on the flanks of the German forces and continue harrying tactics against their lines of communications.

8. Similarly, should the Germans invade Sweden and attempt to reach the Mosjoen-Mo-Bodo area across the Swedish border, you will employ harrying tactics and demolitions in order to make their advance slow and costly.

Reinforcements

9. You will report as soon as possible whether you require additional independent companies sent to join you.

In addition, you can be reinforced at short notice by any of the following in small detachments:—

 (*a*) Light tanks.
 (*b*) Bren Carriers.
 (*c*) 3·7-inch howitzers or 3-inch mortars.
 (*d*) M/c combinations.

provided you can be sure of landing them, employing them to good purpose, concealing them from air attack and maintaining them.

Administration

10. An Independent Companies Administration Group is now in process of formation and will leave for Bodo about 7th May. It will be accompanied, or followed closely, by supplies and maintenance stores for the whole force for thirty days. Thereafter Bodo will be kept stocked with thirty days' supplies and maintenance stores by periodic shipments from the United Kingdom.

Each Independent Company leaving the United Kingdom has been, or will be, accompanied by thirty days' rations (plus a proportion of mountain ration) and its G.1098 equipment.

11. *Transport.* You will report as soon as possible what assistance you require in the way of small craft for sea transport. If considered necessary by you trawlers or other small ships can be made available.

Intercommunication

12. Signal instructions have been issued separately.

Special Reports

13. Report early on the possibility of any landing ground with 1,000 yards runway in the Bodo area.

Additional Officers .

14. Eight Indian Army Officers are allotted to you for employment as

you think fit. The fullest use should be made of their knowledge and experience of irregular warfare in mountainous country.

Brig., G.S.,
N.W.E.F.

Headquarters, N.W.E.F.,
   Nobel House,
     2 Buckingham Gate, S.W.1.
   2nd May 1940.

(8)

INSTRUCTIONS FROM THE SECRETARY OF STATE FOR WAR

INSTRUCTIONS FOR LIEUT.-GENERAL C. J. E. AUCHINLECK, C.B., C.S.I., D.S.O., O.B.E.

1. The object of His Majesty's Government in Northern Norway is to secure and maintain a base in Northern Norway from which we can:—
   (a) Deny iron ore supplies to Germany via Narvik.
   (b) Interfere so far as may be possible with ore supplies to Germany via Lulea.
   (c) Preserve a part of Norway as a seat of Government for the Norwegian King and people.

2. As a first stage in the achievement of this object, operations are now in progress for the capture of Narvik. The present forces assembled for this purpose are under the command of Admiral of the Fleet Lord Cork and Orrery; the Military Commander, Major-General Mackesy, being subordinate to him. A list of the Anglo-French troops at present under Major-General Mackesy is given at Annexure '1'.

3. It is the intention of His Majesty's Government that there should be no interference with the existing plans of Lord Cork and Orrery until they have either achieved success or been abandoned. At some future date, however, it will be necessary to revert to the normal system of command.

4. You are appointed G.O.C.-in-C. Designate of the Anglo-French Military Forces and the British Air Component in this area. His Majesty's Government will decide when the present system of unified command shall terminate. Thereafter you will be in independent command of the Anglo-French Military Forces and the British Air Component and will act in close co-operation with the Senior Naval Officer in the Narvik area.

5. You will proceed to the Narvik area with an officer detailed by the Chief of the Air Staff, and, in conjunction with Admiral of the Fleet Lord Cork and Orrery, report for the information of the Chiefs of Staff the forces required to attain the object in paragraph 1 above and the area which you recommend should be occupied. You should take into account the necessity for making arrangements to enable any iron ore now at Narvik to be despatched to the United Kingdom, and, if the situation permits, for resuming the supply of iron ore from the Swedish iron mines at Gallivare.

Your report should include recommendations as to the practicability and desirability of repairing the railway from Narvik to the Swedish frontier.

Scale of Enemy Attack up to October 1940

Naval

6. The scale of naval attack that may be expected against Narvik is:—

   (a) Raids by capital ships or cruisers which, although not very likely, are a possibility.

   (b) A heavy scale of submarine attack by both torpedo and mine.

   (c) Light craft and M.T.B. attack. Germany will probably take full advantage of such measure of control as she may be able to obtain over Norwegian waters to secure the approach of attacking light craft.

Land

The scale of land attack that may be expected is:—

   (a) Raids or attempted landings by parties carried in coastal vessels.

   (b) Sabotage, especially of the railway.

   (c) Parachute landings.

   (d) A German advance from Sweden following invasion of that country.

Air

The Narvik area is within reach of German bombers based on or re-fuelled in Southern or Central Norway. A daily weight of attack of 40 tons is possible from these bases from now onwards.

To this must be added a light scale of attack from seaplanes operating from fjords. The scale and frequency of this attack would be very seriously increased if the Germans succeed in establishing air bases in Sweden, such as Boden (near Lulea) and Ostersund, or further north in Norway.

To meet this scale the Chiefs of Staff estimate that two or three fighter squadrons, one bomber servicing unit and some Army co-operation aircraft are required.

7. When you have taken over command it is intended to withdraw Major-General Mackesy and the Staff of the 49th Divisional Headquarters, less such personnel as you may wish to retain.

8. The forces operating in Norway south of the Narvik area, at present under the command of Lieut-General Massy, may at an early date be placed under your command. The policy as regard operations in this area is described in the attached telegram which is being despatched to Lord Cork and is at Annexure '2'.

9. Should you become a casualty or otherwise be prevented from exercising command of your force, command of the Anglo-French land and air forces will pass to a British officer to be nominated by you until another British officer can be appointed. This officer will be given the acting rank of Lieut-General.

10. You will act in co-operation with the Norwegian Commander-in-Chief.

11. You will maintain constant communication with the War Office.

(Signed)   OLIVER STANLEY.

War Office,
5th May 1940.

[*Annexures omitted.*]

APPENDIX B
Lists of Forces Engaged

	Page
I. NAVAL OPERATIONS	261
II. COMBINED OPERATIONS	262

§1. General Note on Command.
§2. Operations Based on Namsos.
§3. Operations Based on Aandalsnes.
§4. Operations Based on Mosjöen, Mo, and Bodö.
§5. Operations Based on Harstad (Narvik Area).

III. AIR OPERATIONS 267

PART I
Naval Operations

§ 1. Engagements of 8th and 9th April
(8th April)
Destroyer   *Glowworm* (Lt-Cmdr G. Broadmead Roope).
(9th April)
Battle Cruiser   *Renown* (flagship of Vice-Admiral W. J. Whitworth, commanding Battle Cruiser Squadron; Captain C. E. B. Simeon).

§ 2. First Battle of Narvik (10th April)
2nd Destroyer Flotilla
    Hardy (flotilla leader, Captain B. A. W. Warburton-Lee).
    Hunter (Lt-Cmdr L. de Villiers).
    Hotspur (Cmdr H. F. H. Layman).
    Havock (Lt-Cmdr R. E. Courage).
    Hostile (Lt-Cmdr J. P. Wright).

§ 3. Second Battle of Narvik (13th April)
Battleship   *Warspite* (flagship of Vice-Admiral W. J. Whitworth, commanding Battle Cruiser Squadron; Captain V. A. C. Crutchley, V.C.).
Destroyers   *Bedouin* (Cmdr J. A. McCoy).
    Cossack (Cmdr R. St. V. Sherbrooke).
    Eskimo (Cmdr St. J. A. Micklethwait).
    Punjabi (Cmdr J. T. Lean).
    Hero (Cmdr H. W. Biggs).
    Icarus (Lt-Cmdr C. D. Maud).

                Kimberley (Lt-Cmdr R. G. K. Knowling).
                Forester (Lt-Cmdr E. B. Tancock).
                Foxhound (Lt-Cmdr G. H. Peters).
F.A.A.   striking force from Aircraft Carrier *Furious*.

§ 4. *Engagement of 8th June*

Aircraft Carrier *Glorious*   (Captain G. D'Oyly Hughes).
Destroyers   *Acasta*   (Cmdr C. E. Glasfurd).
           Ardent   (Lt-Cmdr J. E. Barker).

PART II
Combined Operations

§ 1. *General Note on Command*

1. Admiral of the Fleet the Earl of Cork and Orrery, who had been appointed Naval Commander of the Narvik Expedition on 10th April, was appointed on 21st April to command all forces committed to the task of capturing Narvik, and on 7th May the military forces in the Mosjöen-Bodö area were included in this command.

2. Lieut.-General H. R. S. Massy was appointed on 21st April to command the North-Western Expeditionary Force, consisting of all military forces engaged in Norway elsewhere than at Narvik. This command terminated on 7th May; the Narvik force took its name.

3. Naval operations, other than those of the Narvik expedition within 100 miles of Vaagsfiord, were included in the command of the Commander-in-Chief, Home Fleet, Admiral Sir Charles Forbes.

§ 2. *Operations Based on Namsos*

A. ROYAL NAVY

Naval escort to Norway:
    (*a*)[1] Cruisers *Manchester, Birmingham*.
        Anti-aircraft cruiser *Cairo*.
        Destroyers.
    (*b*)[2] Cruiser *Emile Bertin* (French).
        Destroyers (French).
Landing Party (Operation Henry):
    Seamen and Marines from H.M.S. *Glasgow, Sheffield*.
Anti-aircraft defence:
    Anti-aircraft cruisers *Cairo, Curlew, Carlisle*.
    Sloops *Auckland, Bittern*.
F.A.A.:
    Aircraft carriers[3] *Ark Royal, Glorious*.

---

[1] Under Vice-Admiral G. Layton, who sailed from Scapa on 12th April.
[2] Under the French Vice-Admiral Derrien.
[3] Sailed from Scapa 23rd April, under command of Vice-Admiral L. V. Wells.

Naval escort from Norway:
    Cruisers *Devonshire, York, Montcalm* (French).
    Anti-aircraft cruiser *Carlisle*.
    Destroyers (British and French).

B. ARMY (Mauriceforce)
          Major-General A. Carton de Wiart, V.C.

British

146th Infantry Brigade (Brigadier C. G. Phillips):
    1st/4th Battalion The Royal Lincolnshire Regiment (Lieut.-Colonel R. W. Newton).
    1st/4th Battalion The King's Own Yorkshire Light Infantry (Lieut.-Colonel W. S. Hibbert).
    The Hallamshire Battalion, The York and Lancaster Regiment (Lieut.-Colonel C. O. Robbins).
    One Section 55th Field Company Royal Engineers.

French
Général de Division Audet

5th Demi-Brigade Chasseurs Alpins (Général de Brigade Béthouart):
    13th Battalion Chasseurs Alpins.
    53rd Battalion Chasseurs Alpins.
    67th Battalion Chasseurs Alpins.
    Detachments, Anti-Aircraft and Anti-Tank Artillery.
    One Section Engineers.

§ 3. *Operations Based on Aandalsnes*

A. ROYAL NAVY

Naval escort to Norway:
    (*a*)[1] Cruisers *Galatea, Arethusa*.
        Anti-aircraft Cruisers *Carlisle, Curacoa*.
        Destroyers.
    (*b*)[2] Cruisers *Galatea, Sheffield, Glasgow*.
        Destroyers.
Landing Party (Operation Primrose):
    Seamen and Marines from H.M.S. *Hood, Nelson, Barham*.
    21st Light Anti-Aircraft Battery Royal Marines.
    Two detachments 11th Searchlight Regiment Royal Marines.
Anti-aircraft defence:
    Anti-aircraft Cruisers *Carlisle, Curacoa*.
    Sloops *Black Swan, Flamingo, Bittern*.
    Escort Vessel *Fleetwood*.
F.A.A.:
    Aircraft Carriers *Ark Royal, Glorious*.[3]

---

[1] Sailed from Rosyth on 17th April under command of Vice-Admiral G. F. B. Edward-Collins.

[2] Sailed from Rosyth on 22nd April under same command.

[3] See § 2 above.

Naval escort from Norway:
  (a)[1] Cruisers *Galatea, Arethusa, Sheffield, Southampton.*
    Destroyers.
  (b)[2] Cruisers *Manchester, Birmingham.*
    Anti-aircraft Cruiser *Calcutta.*
    Destroyers.

B. ARMY (Sickleforce)
            Major-General B. C. T. Paget.[3]
  148th Brigade (Brigadier H. de R. Morgan):
    1st/5th Battalion The Royal Leicestershire Regiment (Lieut.-Colonel G. J. German).
    1st/8th Battalion The Sherwood Foresters (Lieut.-Colonel T. A. Ford).
  15th Brigade (Brigadier H. E. F. Smyth):
    1st Battalion The Green Howards (Lieut.-Colonel A. E. Robinson).
    1st Battalion The King's Own Yorkshire Light Infantry (Acting Lieut.-Colonel E. E. E. Case).
    1st Battalion The York and Lancaster Regiment (Lieut.-Colonel A. L. Kent-Lemon).
  168th Light Anti-Aircraft Battery, Royal Artillery.
  260th Heavy Anti-Aircraft Battery, Royal Artillery.
  55th Field Company Royal Engineers (less one section).

C. ROYAL AIR FORCE
  No. 263 Squadron, Gladiators (Squadron-Leader J. W. Donaldson).

§ 4. *Operations Based on Mosjöen, Mo, and Bodö*

A. ROYAL NAVY
  Naval escort to Norway: Destroyers.
  Transfers in Norway: Cruiser *Effingham*, Anti-aircraft Cruiser *Cairo*, Repair Ship *Vindictive*, and Destroyers.

B. ARMY (Scissorsforce)[4]
            Brigadier C. McV. Gubbins.[5]
  1. 9th–11th May:
    Nos. 1, 2, 3, 4, 5 Independent Companies.[6]
    One Section 166th Light Anti-Aircraft Battery, Royal Artillery.

---

[1] Sailed from Aandalsnes, etc., on 30th April/1st May under command of Vice-Admiral G. F. B. Edward-Collins.

[2] Sailed from Aandalsnes, etc., on 1st/2nd May under command of Vice-Admiral G. Layton.

[3] Appointed 20th April, before which date the force, consisting of 148th Brigade and 168th Light Anti-Aircraft Battery, was under command of Brigadier H. de R. Morgan.

[4] On 23rd May the name was changed to Bodoforce.

[5] Brigadier The Hon. W. Fraser was in command 12th–17th May.

[6] Recruited from the 52nd, 9th, 54th, 55th and 1st London Divisions respectively. No. 2 Company did not land in Norway until 13th May. One company Scots Guards had been stationed near Bodö since 1st May, but was not under Scissorsforce command.

APPENDIX B   265

2. 12th–22nd May:
   1st Battalion Scots Guards.
   Nos. 1, 2, 3, 4, 5 Independent Companies.
   One Troop, 203rd Field Battery, Royal Artillery.
   One Troop, 55th Light Anti-Aircraft Battery, Royal Artillery.
   Detachment 230th Field Company, Royal Engineers.
3. 23rd–29th May:
   1st Battalion Scots Guards.
   1st Battalion Irish Guards.
   2nd Battalion The South Wales Borderers.[1]
   Nos. 1, 2, 3, 4, 5 Independent Companies.
   One Troop, 203rd Field Battery, Royal Artillery.
   One Troop, 55th Light Anti-Aircraft Battery, Royal Artillery.
   Detachment 230th Field Company, Royal Engineers.

C. ROYAL AIR FORCE
Detachment No. 263 Squadron (three Gladiators).[2]

§ 5. *Operations Based on Harstad (Narvik Area)*

(1) STATE OF FORCES AS AT 17TH APRIL

A. ROYAL NAVY

Flag Officer, Narvik: Admiral of the Fleet the Earl of Cork and Orrery.
Battleship *Warspite*.
Cruisers *Southampton, Effingham, Aurora, Enterprise*.
Repair Ship *Vindictive*.
Destroyers.
Aircraft Carrier *Furious*.

B. ARMY (Avonforce)
            Major-General P. J. Mackesy.
24th (Guards) Brigade (Brigadier the Hon. W. Fraser):
   1st Battalion Scots Guards (Lieut.-Colonel T. B. Trappes-Lomax).
   1st Battalion Irish Guards (Lieut.-Colonel W. B. Faulkner).
   2nd Battalion The South Wales Borderers (Lieut.-Colonel W. Gottwaltz).
3rd Light Anti-Aircraft Battery, Royal Artillery.
229th and 230th Field Companies, Royal Engineers.
Detachment 231st Field Park Company, Royal Engineers.

(2) STATE OF FORCES AS AT 10TH MAY

Flag Officer, Narvik: Admiral of the Fleet the Earl of Cork and Orrery.

A. ROYAL NAVY

Battleship *Resolution*.
Cruisers *Effingham, Aurora, Enterprise*.
Anti-aircraft Cruisers *Cairo, Coventry, Curlew*.

---

[1] Battalion completed its move south on 27th May.
[2] Operated 26th/27th May only.

Repair Ship *Vindictive*.
Aircraft Carrier *Ark Royal*.
Destroyers.

B. ARMY (Rupertforce)
Major-General P. J. Mackesy.

British

24th (Guards) Brigade (Brigadier the Hon. W. Fraser):
    1st Battalion Scots Guards[1]
    1st Battalion Irish Guards.
    2nd Battalion The South Wales Borderers.
One troop 3rd King's Own Hussars (tanks).
203rd Battery, 51st Field Regiment, Royal Artillery.
193rd Heavy Anti-Aircraft Battery, Royal Artillery.
55th Light Anti-Aircraft Regiment, Royal Artillery.
3rd Light Anti-Aircraft Battery, Royal Artillery.
229th and 230th Field Companies, Royal Engineers.
Detachment 231st Field Park Company, Royal Engineers.

French and Polish
Général de Brigade Béthouart.

27th Demi-Brigade Chasseurs Alpins:
    6th Battalion Chasseurs Alpins.
    12th Battalion Chasseurs Alpins.
    14th Battalion Chasseurs Alpins.
13th Demi-Brigade Foreign Legion:
    1st and 2nd Battalions.
Polish Brigade (Chasseurs du Nord), (General Bohucz-szysko):
    1st Demi-Brigade: 1st and 2nd Battalions.
    2nd Demi-Brigade: 3rd and 4th Battalions.
342nd Independent Tank Company.
2nd Independent Group Colonial Artillery.
14th Anti-Tank Company, 13th Chasseurs Alpins.

(3) STATE OF FORCES AS AT 3RD JUNE

Flag Officer, Narvik: Admiral of the Fleet the Earl of Cork and Orrery.

A. ROYAL NAVY

Cruiser *Southampton*.
Anti-aircraft Cruisers *Cairo*, *Coventry*.
Repair Ship *Vindictive*.
Destroyers.
Aircraft Carriers *Ark Royal*, *Glorious*.

B. ARMY (North Western Expeditionary Force)
Lieut.-General C. J. E. Auchinleck.

---

[1] Less one company detached to Bodö.

British

24th (Guards) Brigade.[1]
Nos. 2, 3 and 5 Independent Companies.[1]
One troop 3rd King's Own Hussars.[2]
203rd Battery, 51st Field Regiment, Royal Artillery.
6th Anti-Aircraft Brigade, Royal Artillery (Brigadier F. N. C. Rosseter).
55th Light Anti-Aircraft Regiment (163rd, 164th, 165th Batteries).[3]
56th Light Anti-Aircraft Regiment (3rd, 167th Batteries).
51st Heavy Anti-Aircraft Regiment (151st, 152nd, 153rd Batteries).
82nd Heavy Anti-Aircraft Regiment (156th, 193rd, 256th Batteries).
No. 10 Army Observer Unit, Royal Artillery.
229th and 230th Field Companies, Royal Engineers.
Detachment 231st Field Park Company, Royal Engineers.

French and Polish
As before (§5(2)B. above.)

C. ROYAL AIR FORCE (Air Component)
Group Captain M. Moore.
No. 263 Squadron, Gladiators (Squadron-Leader J. W. Donaldson).
No. 46 Squadron, Hurricanes (Squadron-Leader K. B. B. Cross).
No. 11 Observer Screen.

PART III

Air Operations

§ 1. *Fleet Air Arm Attacks Against Ships in German-held Harbours*

Bergen	.	10th April from Hatston, Orkneys.
Trondheim	.	11th April from H.M.S. *Furious*.
Trondheim	.	25th April from H.M.S. *Glorious*.
Trondheim	.	25th, 28th April, 13th June from H.M.S. *Ark Royal*.

§ 2. *Royal Air Force Attacks Against Ships in German-held Harbours:*

by Squadrons Nos. 220, 224, 233, 269 (Hudsons)	at Bergen	(11th April, 29th May, 13th June)
	Trondheim	(11th June)
	Larvik	(17th April)
	Haugesund	(19th April)
by Bomber Command (Wellingtons and Hampdens)	at Bergen	(9th April)

---

[1] Brought back from Bodö for evacuation on 29th-31st May, Nos. 1 and 4 Independent Companies only being evacuated direct to home ports (see § 4B3 above).

[2] Less tanks.

[3] Less one troop sent to Mo.

§ 3. *Royal Air Force Attacks Against German-held Airfields:*

by Squadrons Nos. 107, 110, 254 (Blenheims)	at Stavanger Trondheim	(18 attacks) (2 attacks)
by Squadrons Nos. 44, 50 (Hampdens)	at Oslo	(30th April)
by Squadrons Nos. 220, 224, 233 (Hudsons)	at Stavanger Trondheim	(2 attacks) (20th May)
by Squadrons Nos. 9, 37, 75, 90, 99, 115, 149 (Wellingtons)	at Kristiansand Stavanger	(20th April) (9 attacks)
by Squadrons Nos. 10, 51, 58, 77, 102 (Whitleys)	at Oslo Stavanger Trondheim	(10 attacks) (6 attacks) (5 attacks)

APPENDIX C
List of Published Sources

(Used to supplement the unpublished official British records of the Campaign)

ASSMANN, KURT: *Deutsche Schicksalsjahre*. Eberhard Brockhaus, Wiesbaden, 1950.

* AUCHINLECK, LIEUT.-GENERAL C. J. E.: Report—*see* Lord Cork's Despatch, Appendix B.

BROCH, THEODOR: *The Mountains Wait*. Joseph, 1943.

* BUCKLEY, CHRISTOPHER: *Norway—The Commandos—Dieppe*. H.M.S.O., 1952.

CHURCHILL, WINSTON S.: *The Second World War*, Volume I. The Gathering Storm. Cassell, 1948.

CLARKE, BRIGADIER DUDLEY: *Seven Assignments*. Cape, 1948.

* CORK AND ORRERY, ADMIRAL OF THE FLEET THE EARL OF: Despatch *London Gazette No. 38011*, 10th July 1947.

DIETL, GERDA-LUISE and HERRMANN, KURT: *General Dietl*. Münchner Buchverlag, Munich, 1951.

FITZGERALD, MAJOR D. J. L.: *History of the Irish Guards in the Second World War*. Gale and Polden, Aldershot, 1949.

GAMELIN, GENERAL: *Servir*. Tome III. La Guerre (*September 1939–19th May 1940*). Plon, Paris, 1947.

GETZ, COLONEL O. B.: *Fra Krigen i Nord-Tröndelag 1940*. Aschehoug, Oslo, 1940.

* HALLIFAX, REAR-ADMIRAL R. H. C.: Despatch *London Gazette No. 38005*, 3rd July 1947.

HINGSTON, LIEUT.-COLONEL WALTER: *Never Give Up* (History of the K.O.Y.L.I., Volume V, 1919–42). Printed by Lund Humphries, 1950.

JENSEN, COLONEL JÖRGEN: *Krigen paa Hedmark*. Tanum, Oslo, 1947.

KOHT, DR HALVDAN: *Fraa Skanse til Skanse*. Tiden Norsk Forlag, Oslo, 1947.

LAPIE, CAPTAIN PIERRE O.: *With the Foreign Legion at Narvik*. Murray, 1941.

MACCLURE, VICTOR A.: *Gladiators in Norway*. Blackwood's Magazine, Volume 249, February and March 1941.

* MACKESY, MAJOR-GENERAL P. J.: Report—*see* Lord Cork's Despatch, Appendix A.

MARTIENSSEN, ANTHONY: *Hitler and His Admirals*. Secker & Warburg, 1948.

* MASSY, LIEUT.-GENERAL H. R. S.: Despatch *London Gazette No. 37584*, 29th May 1946.

MAUND, REAR-ADMIRAL L. E. H.: *Assault from the Sea*. Methuen, 1949.

MOUNTEVANS, ADMIRAL THE LORD: *Adventurous Life*. Hutchinson, 1946.

---

* British official publication.

APPENDIX C

Munthe-Kaas, Colonel O.: *The Campaign in Northern Norway*. Royal Norwegian Information Service, Washington, D.C., 1944.

Nazi Conspiracy and Aggression (*Proceedings of the International Military Tribunal at Nürnberg*) (8 + 2 supplementary volumes). U.S. Government Printing Office, Washington, D.C.

Norges Krig 1940–1945. Sections by H. Smitt Ingebretsen, Professor Arne Ording, and Major-General R. Roscher Nielsen. Gyldendal, Oslo, 1947.

Norwegian Parliamentary Report. *Innstilling fra Undersökelses-kommisjonen av 1945*. (Commission of Enquiry of 1945) 1 + 2 volumes of appendices. Aschehoug, Oslo, 1946, 1947.

Reynaud, Paul: *La France a sauvé l'Europe*. Tome II. Flammarion, Paris, 1947.

Rickman, A. F.: *Swedish Iron Ore*. Faber & Faber, 1939.

Ruge, Major-General Otto: *Krigens Dagbok*, Volume I. Halvorsen & Larsen, Oslo, 1946.

Scheen, Captain Rolf: *Norges Sjökrig 1939–40* (2 volumes). Grieg, Bergen, 1947.

Sereau, Raymond: *L'Expédition de Norvège 1940*. Regie Autonome des Publications Officielles, Baden-Baden, 1949.

Sundell, Colonel Olof: *9 April*. Sohlman, Stockholm, 1948.

Tedder, Marshal of the R.A.F. The Lord: *Air Power in War* (The Lees Knowles Lectures 1947). Hodder & Stoughton, 1948.

* Whitworth, Vice-Admiral W. J.: Despatch *London Gazette No. 38005*, 3rd July 1947.

Zbyszewski, Karol: *The Fight for Narvik*. Lindsay Drummond, 1940.

---

* British official publication.

Index

INDEX

Entries in bold type following place names give the appropriate map number.

Aalborg **7** : Danish airfield, 52; bombed by R.A.F., 53, 133–4

Aalesund **5** : proposed landing at, 69, 97; naval guns landed, 98; telephone centre, 133; evacuation, 139

Aandalsnes **6** : described, 97; its occupation desired by Falkenhorst, 19; possible Allied foothold, 64; operations based on, 97–128; attacked from the air, 114, 130, 136, 138–9; evacuated, 137–9

Aasen **5** : 87–8

Aasmarka **6** : engagement at, 106–8

Acasta, H.M.S. : sunk after torpedoing *Scharnhorst*, 224–5

Admiralty : dispositions made 8th April, 26; information received earlier, 28; orders issued 8th/9th, 31; cancels Bergen attack, 33; sends out *Furious*, 34; new instructions for southern areas, 34; warns Norwegian Legation, 37; instructions to Warburton-Lee, 43–4; instructions for further attack, 46, 48; urges occupation of Narvik, 51; control of Norway operations, 58; and Operation Hammer, 73–4; instructions to Lord Cork, 147; conducts North Norway evacuation, 175, 221; orders *Renown* to return to Home Fleet, 225; interventions in commanders' dispositions appraised, 238–9. *See also* Royal Navy, Churchill

Afridi, H.M.S. : completes Namsos evacuation; sunk by air attack, 142

Agdenes **5** : description, 40, 71–2

Air Ministry : instructions to Bomber Command, 55; direct control of air operations in Norway, 58; choice of Lesjaskog, 115–6; rules against reinforcement, 118; unable to meet General Paget's requests for bombers, 119; Situation Report on Narvik area established, 164; refuses bomber squadron for rearguard, 172; appreciates difficulties prospectively, 234. *See also* Royal Air Force

Allied Military Committee : subordinate functions of, 57, 243; and embarkation of French troops, 78, 165

Altmark : boarding of, 10, 13–14; influence of episode on Hitler, 17–18; influence on Norwegian opinion, 244

Andfiord **10** : 148, 222–3

Anglo-Norwegian relations, history of, 3–5; in winter of 1939–40, 9–14, 21–4; and the mine laying, 25–6, 36; and the German invasion, 37–8, 65–7; affected by evacuation of Central Norway, 143–4, 162, 166, 171; admission of N. to Supreme War Council and Allied Military Committee, 165; and shock of German landing north of Mosjöen, 171; Mowinckel Plan, 173–6; in North Norway generally, 202–3; affected by evacuation of Bodö, 214, 216; and difficulties of North Norway evacuation, 218–9; review of, 243–4; special problem of control of civil population, 244–5. *See also* Norwegian Government

Ankenes **9** : *Cossack* aground off, 49; dominates landing-points in Narvik, 151; General Mackesy plans to capture, 155; objective of advance from Haakvik, 158–9, 200; west end cleared of enemy, 208; final assault on, 210–1

Arab, H.M.T. : sinks German bomber, 140

Ardent, H.M.S. : sunk in escort of *Glorious*, 224

Arendal **4** : 27, 39

Arethusa, H.M.S. : in Aandalsnes expedition, 98, 138,

Ark Royal, H.M.S. : intended employment for 'Hammer', 74; off Trondheim, 114, 134; makes first fighters available in Narvik area, 194, 205–6; covers Bjerkvik attack, 198; in final evacuation, 220, 221, 223, 226–7

Army : *see* Artillery, Brigades, Royal Engineers, Tanks

Artillery, Anti-aircraft : 62; at Namsos, 95; at Aandalsnes, 98, 130; at Otta, 111; at Lesjaskog, 116–7; four batteries lost in Central Norway, 163; at Harstad, 148–50; build-up for Narvik area, 164, 194; additional regiment sent (10th May), 172; at Tromsö, 201; North Norway 'bag', 207; during evacuation, 220; exaggerated hopes regarding, 234; shortage of, 235

Artillery, Field : 62; in action against Ankenes, 159, 207, 210–11; at Stien, 185; at Viskiskoia, 188; at Pothus, 190; details of arrival, 193; in final evacuation, 220

Atcherley, Wing-Cmdr. R. L. R. : 203

Atlantis : hospital ship in company with *Orama*, 224; meets *Valiant* and gives news of attack, 225

Attlee, Rt. Hon. C. R. : on absence of settled plan for Norway, 236

Auchinleck, Lt.-Gen. C. J. E. : appointment to command, 169-70, 200; and retention of Mo, 183, 186; orders to Col. Trappes-Lomax, 188; reports on future needs in North Norway, 201-2, 239; sends all British troops south and gives General Béthouart command in Narvik area; and evacuation, 218, 221; on enemy's provision of fighting requirements, 240; assessment of his troops, 241-2; finds civil situation in North Norway 'Gilbertian', 244-5

Audet, General : arrives at Namsos, 88; prepares counter-attack, 95; letter to Col. Getz, 143; objects to Grong rearguard, 166, 178

Aurora, H.M.S., 25, 26; carries Lord Cork to Harstad, 146-7; reconnoitres Narvik, 153; in bombardment, 154; in patrol of fiords off Narvik, 156; defends Haakvik, 159; in Bjerkvik attack, 198

'Avonmouth' : 145

Balbergkamp **6** : action at, 108-9

Ballangen **10** : German destroyers anchor in fiord, 44; refuge for sailors in village, 46; S.W.B. land at, 158; base for Polish reserve battalion, 208, 210; parachute attack, 220

Banak **End Papers** : proposed as bomber base, 203, 204

Bangsund **5** : as landing-place, 84-6; bridge held by rearguard, 140, 142

Bank of Norway : 138

Bardufoss **10** : Norwegian airfield, 148; British air base established, 192; described, 204; construction work, defences, and use, 204-7; affected by sea fog, 209; planned German *coup* at, 216; evacuation of airfield, 218, 220

Beisfiord **2** : entrance to, 45; advance of Allied forces to, 158-9, 200, 210-11

Beitstadfiord **3** : 86

Bergen **4** : intended Allied base, 13, 15; object for German 'protection', 30; proposed British naval attack on, 33; R.A.F. attacks harbour, 34; captured by Germans, 40; advance along railway from, repelled by Norwegians, 101

Berney-Ficklin, A/Major-General H. P. M. : 72

Béthouart, General : arrives at Namsos, 88; leaves for Narvik area after preparing counter-attack, 95; confers with General Fleischer, 157; proposes immediate landing on Öyjord peninsula, 196; assault on Bjerkvik, 198-9; commands all land forces in Narvik area and prepares assault, 201; assault on Narvik, 209-11; receives news of decision to evacuate, 213; cancels Skjomenfiord attack, 217; relations with Norwegians, 218; sails in *Southampton* from Harstad, 221

Biri **6** : 106, 110

Birmingham, H.M.S., 25

Bison : French destroyer set on fire in evacuation from Namsos, 142

Bittern, H.M.S. : disabled at Namsos and abandoned, 140

Bjerkvik **9** : held by Germans, 154, 156; French objective, 157-8; landing operation, 196-200; capture strengthens demand for assault on Narvik, 172

Björnaa, R. **8a** : action at, 180

Björnfjell **10** : German attack near, 156; site for dropping men and weapons, 195; last German refuge, 216, 217

Blaamannsis **8b** : 213, 214

Black Swan, H.M.S. : damaged in anti-aircraft defence of Aandalsnes, 132

Blücher : heads expedition to Oslo, 27; sunk by Norwegian fortifications, 36

Bodö **8b** : described, 186; minelaying near, 15, 25; one company sent to protect, 159, 167; protection from sea considered, 169; larger garrison for, 170; R.A.F. reconnaissance party bombed at, 179; landing ground, 189, 192, 205; to be held permanently for defence of Narvik, 201; withdrawal to, 213-15; evacuated, 215-6; F.A.A. attack airfield, 220

Bogen **10** : held by Irish Guards, 154, 155, 158; march of Polish battalion from, 199

Bohusz-szyzko, General : 207

Bomber Command : 53, 55. *See* Royal Air Force

Bonte, Commodore : 45

Borkenes **10** : 215

INDEX

Braastad **6** : 106
Braüer, Dr : 37–8
Bremen, S.S., evades blockade, 10; proposed use of, for landing in Lyngenfiord, 216
Brettingen **5** : attempts to engage Germans, 40; fires on British destroyers, 47, 72; armament, 71–2
Brigades, Infantry, 15th : transferred to Norway, 62; assigned to 'Hammer', 72; in Sickleforce, 77; composition, 119; operations, 113, 115, 119–39
    24th (Guards) : situation on 9th April, 60; transfer southwards discussed in London, 69; in 'Avonmouth', 145; composition, 145; operations, 145–9, 154–9
    126th : considered for diversion to Norway, 62
    146th : situation on 9th April, 60; diverted to Namsos, 69, 146; composition, 84; operations, 85–96
    147th : offered for Norway, 62; assigned to 'Hammer', 72; to Mauriceforce, 84
    148th : situation on 9th April, 61; intention of restoring third battalion to, 62; in Mauriceforce, 84; composition, 98; operations, 98–112, 121, 135–6
Broch, Theodor : on German morale, 152; on bombardment of Narvik, 209
Bröttum **6** : 106
Bud **5** : 26
Burgin, Rt. Hon. Leslie : Minister of Supply, 59

Cadart, Rear-Admiral : 142
Cairo, H.M.S. : escorts first Namsos convoy, 85; leads French convoy in and out, 88, 89; as flagship in final bombardment of Narvik, 208, 209
Calcutta, H.M.S. : in pursuit of *Nord-Norge*, 181
Canadian battalions : earmarked for Norway, 62; assigned to 'Hammer', 72; not sent to Norway, 77
Canaris, Admiral, 22
Carlisle, H.M.S. : in expedition to Aandalsnes, 98; in evacuation from Namsos, 141–2
Carton de Wiart, Major-General Sir Adrian, V.C. : in command of Mauriceforce, 77, 78, 83–96; organizes evacuation, 139–43; objects to Grong rearguard, 166, 178; on lack of plan and ignoring of lessons from First World War, 236; and lack of interpreters, 242–3
Casualties, British : at 2nd Battle of Narvik, 51; in Central Norway, 143; in North Norway land operations, 215; in sinking of *Glorious*, 225; total, 230
    Allied : in capture of Bjerkvik, 199; in capture of Narvik, 211; total, 230
    German : total, 230
Cedarbank, M.V. : torpedoed, 111
Chamberlain, Rt. Hon. Neville : *see* Prime Minister
Chasseurs Alpins : raised for intervention in Finland, 61; brigade of, forms light division, 62; recruitment, 63; allocated to Mauriceforce, 77; half transferred to Narvik, 79, 95, 161; in Mauriceforce, 88–90, 93, 95–6; movements for evacuation from Namsos, 140; sufferings in snow referred to by General Mackesy, 151; reported unavailable for Narvik, 153; sail for Narvik, 155; operations north of Narvik, 157–8; in Ankenes area, 159, 200, 207; at Mosjöen, 178; intended employment at Bodö, 189; attempted advance on Bjerkvik, 199; guard Bardufoss, 205; bombed while moving to reserve area, 206; advance along Rombaksfiord, 207; in rearguard at Harstad, 221
Chasseurs de Montagne : 193. *See* Polish Brigade
Chief of Imperial General Staff : *see* Ironside
Chiefs of Staff, consulted before Government declaration on Norway, 9, 10; report on stopping ore-traffic, 11; on intervention in Finland, 13, 14; German move forecast to, 22; arrangements for launching expedition, 23; relations with Military Co-ordination Committee, 58–9; membership, functions, and sub-committees, 59–60; memorandum on available resources (March), 61; meetings of 9th–11th April, 64–5; 13th–14th April, 68–9; paper opposing Operation Hammer, 75–6; consider 'Hammer 2', 80; order plans for evacuation of Central Norway, 129; changes made on 1st May, 165; ruling about naval patrols for Bodö, etc., 169; re-define objects of 'Rupert', 169; and proposed assault on Narvik, 169–70; release anti-aircraft artillery for Norway (10th May), 172; order report on North Norway requirements, 201; General Auchinleck's report to, 201–2; further limitations imposed by, 202; and abandonment of Narvik, 174–5; in direct control of campaign, 237–8. *See also* Ironside, Newall, Pound

Chrobry, M.V. : conveys troops and stores to Namsos, 84–5; returns to Namsos, 96; bombed and sunk near Lofoten Islands, 184

Churchill, Rt. Hon. W. S., First Lord of the Admiralty, proposes to mine the Leads, 11; has in mind measures for Oxelösund and Lulea, 12; christens 'Wilfred', 14; speeches of, 23; chairman of Military Co-ordination Committee, 59; on abandonment of 'Hammer', 75; notes hazardous position of Mauriceforce, 78; urges reinforcement for Narvik, 79; briefs Lord Cork, 147; desires *point d'appui* for mine barrage, 161; presses for transfer of aircraft carrier to Narvik, 164; given powers of control over Co-ordination Committee and Chiefs of Staff, 165; points out danger of Germans moving north by sea, 169; presses Lord Cork for action, 166, 169, 193; minutes on position at Mosjöen, 184; and cancellation of Bergen attack, 239. *See also* Prime Minister

Civil Lord of the Admiralty : 165

Clarke, Lieut.-Colonel D. W. : 133

Climatic conditions : general description, 1–2; influence on timing of operations, 21; Namsos, 85, 91; Gudbrandsdal, 107, 117; Narvik, 151, 193; Grong-Bodö, 178, 183

Clyde, H.M.S. : reports movement of German ships off Trondheim, and later torpedoes *Gneisenau*, 227

Coastal Command : 53, 55, 221. *See* Royal Air Force

Combined Headquarters : set up at Harstad for evacuation, 219; needed for proper conduct of campaign as a whole, 237–8

Combined Operations : Chapters V–XIV *passim*; 234-8; 242

Cork and Orrery, Admiral of the Fleet the Earl of : at meeting of Military Co-ordination Committee, 65, 147; career, 146; relations with General Mackesy, 147, 150–5, 157; in supreme command, 70, 154; bombards military objectives at Narvik, 154–5; is pressed to attack Narvik, 166, 171–2; Narvik assault proposed and postponed, 169–70, 193, 196; to command Independent Companies, 169; reinforcements offered to, 172; sends troops to Bodö and Mo, 170, 182, 187; determination to hold Mo, 183–4; at Bjerkvik attack, 198; meets General Auchinleck, 200–1; transfers headquarters ashore, 201; visits Norwegian King and Government, 202; and evacuation, 176, 213, 218, 221, 223; strikes his flag, 227

Cossack, H.M.S. : boards *Altmark*, 13; hit and aground off Narvik, 49–51

Coventry, H.M.S. : in final bombardment of Narvik, 208, 210; in evacuation of North Norway, 219, 221

Cunningham, Vice-Admiral J. H. D. : sails from Rosyth, 31; examines northern fiords, 51, 156; conducts evacuation from Namsos, 140–2; on special mission, decides not to break wireless silence, 226

Curacoa, H.M.S. : in Aandalsnes expedition, 98

Curlew, H.M.S. : sunk by air attack, 206

Dahl, Colonel T. A. : operates with Group west of Mjösa, 104, 105, 110; expected to re-enter Gudbrandsdal, 111, 123; Group capitulates, 143

Daladier, M. : views on intervention in Finland, 14; receives letter from Darlan, 22; resists use of fluvial mines, 24

Darlan, Admiral : forecasts invasion, 22, 57

Defence Committee : established, 171; decides on evacuation of Narvik, 174–5

Demolitions : material sent and its use urged, 79; protest by Ruge, 103; intended use in Österdal, 124; used in Rosti gorge, 135, 136; other proposed uses, 162, 167

Denmark : non-aggression pact, 6; number of men mobilized, 8th April, 7; Germans consider occupation of, 16; plan of aggression against, 18; Norwegians affected by surrender of, 38; German use of airfield, 52; train ferries destroyed, 54

Denny, Captain M. M. : as naval officer-in-charge, Molde, reports on conditions, 130

Derrien, Admiral : 88

Devonshire, H.M.S. : in Namsos evacuation, 140; carries Norwegian King and Government to Britain, 219, 226

Dietl, General : earlier record, 20, 201; functions in the invasion plan, 27; defence of Narvik, April, 152; clears railway, 156; re-allocates troops 158; contemplates evacuating Narvik, 196; on Björnfjell, 216; re-enters Narvik, 222

Djupvik **2** : 49

Dombaas **5** : objective of 148th Brigade, 99–100, 104; attacked by German paratroops, 99; bombed, 114; British defence, 134–6

INDEX

Dormer, Sir Cecil: 71

Edds, Captain W. F., R.M.: 84
Edward-Collins, Vice-Admiral G. F. B.: movements, 7th-8th April, 29, 31; conducts Aandalsnes evacuation, 30th April, 138
Effingham, H.M.S.: in Narvik bombardment, 154-5; wrecked near Bodö, 185; Bren carriers salvaged from, 188; at Bjerkvik, 198, 200
Egersund **4**: 27, 39
Eidsvold: sunk in defence of Narvik, 41
Elsfiord **8a**: 182, 183
Elvegaard **9**: seizure of military equipment by Germans, 41; stormed by French, 199
Elvenes **10**: 157
Elverum **4**: meeting-place of Norwegian parliament, 38; captured by Germans, 102; proposed objective of French ski patrols, 88
Emile Bertin: damaged on way to Namsos, 88
Empress of Australia, S.S.: conveys troops and stores for Namsos, 84-5
Engelbrecht, General: 27, 36
Enterprise, H.M.S.: in Narvik bombardment, 154-5
Eskimo, H.M.S.: torpedoes *Künne*, 49; severely damaged, 50
Europa, S.S.: proposed use for landing in Lyngenfiord, 216
Evacuations: Central Norway, 80-82, Chapter IX; consequences of Central Norway evacuation, 161-4; Narvik area, 174-5, 192, Chapter XIV
Evans, Admiral Sir Edward: appointed naval commander for Narvik, 25; mission in Sweden and Norway, 66-7

Faaberg **6**: 105, 108
Falkenhorst, General von: appointed to command, 18; debarred from occupying minor ports, 19; transfers troops to Group Pellengahr, 120
Fauske **8b**: terminus of observer posts, 205; defence of isthmus position, 214
Fellingfors **8a**: 180
Fetten **5**: 87
Feurstein, General: 183
Finneid **8b**: position at south-east of Bodö peninsula, 213; abandoned, 214
Finneid **8a**: position on neck of Hemnes peninsula, 182-3, 185
Firedrake, H.M.S.: in final bombardment of Narvik, 208
Fisknes **3**: 92-3
Fleet Air Arm: attacks *Königsberg*, Bergen, 47; attacks supply ships and transports, 52; and Operation Hammer, 73-6; attempt to protect *Suffolk*, 75; attacks Vaernes, 94-5, 114, 134; escorts Gladiators to Lesjaskog, 116; attempt to help Central Norway evacuation, 134; its help sought for Bodö, 189; new role in inshore operations, 235
See also Ark Royal, Furious, Glorious
Fleetwood, H.M.S.: in evacuation from Aandalsnes, 138
Fleischer, General: confers with General Béthouart, 157; opposes withdrawal from Mo, 183-4; freed for operational tasks, 202-3; meeting with General Auchinleck, 203; and use of Bardufoss, 204; at entry into Narvik, 210-11; accompanies Government to Britain, 219; on use of term 'Allies', 243
Follafoss **3**: 86
Forbes, Admiral Sir Charles: revises dispositions, 26; decisions on 7th April, 28-9; on 8th, 30-1; on 9th, 33-4; and Operation Hammer, 73-4, 89; on timing of Namsos evacuation, 141; orders for Lulea operation received by, later cancelled, 176; examines facilities at Mosjöen, 177; and evacuation from Narvik, 221, 223, 225-7
Foreign Legion: two battalions offered for Norway, 62, 63; sent to North Norway, 163, 193; capture Bjerkvik, 197-9; support Norwegian attacks on Kuberg, 207; in assault on Narvik, 208-11; pursue Germans to Straumen, 217
Foreign Office: notes rumour of impending partition of Scandinavia, 22; presses for action in Trondheim area, 68-9; emphasises our intention of capturing Narvik, 162; welcomes Mowinckel Plan, 173, 175

INDEX

Fornebu : *see* Oslo

Fossbakken **10** : held by Norwegian patrols, 148; held by Scots Guards, 156

France, French Government : interest of, in Thyssen's views, 10–11; Petsamo proposal, 12; arrangements for intervention in Finland, 13–14; information prior to German invasion, 22; destroyers in Skagerrak, 52; strong moral position, 9th April, 57; oppose Central Norway evacuation, 81; receive encouraging report from Namsos, 81; favour withdrawal overland from Namsos to safeguard northern area, 166–7; conference with Norwegian Ministers in Paris, 171; and Narvik evacuation, 213; liaison questions, 242–3

Fraser, Brig. the Hon. W. : commands 24th Brigade, 145; wounded on reconnaissance, 158; commands in Mo-Bodö area, 182–3; invalided home, 186; his orders quoted, 187

French War Committee : rejects agreement on fluvial mines, 24; presses for action in Trondheim area, 69

Furious, H.M.S. : intended attack on Bergen, 33; attacks Trondheim, 34, 47; attacks Narvik harbour, 48; and 2nd Battle of Narvik, 48, 49; proposed for 'Hammer', 74; works in fiords as far as Tromsö, 194; flies off Gladiators for Bardufoss, 206

Galatea, H.M.S. : in Aandalsnes expedition, 98, 138

Gällivare **End Papers** : ore deposits at, 10; its control an object of Allied policy, 13, 16, 145, 166

Gamelin, General : generalissimo on Western Front, 57, 62; favours advance inland from Aandalsnes, 69, 78; protests against Central Norway evacuation, 81; urges speed in Narvik operation, 169; orders Grong rearguard, 178

Geiranger **5** : 130

German Air Force : provision for *Weserübung*, 20; attacks on Home Fleet, 9th April, 33; in occupation of Oslo, 36–7; pursuit of King and Ministers, 39; capture of Stavanger and forts at Bergen, 39–40; over Narvik, 13th April, 50; Kristiansand, 52–3; transport activities, 67; attacks *Suffolk*, 74; numbers at Trondheim and Stavanger, 76; attacks on expeditions to Namsos and Aandalsnes, Chapters VI-IX, *passim*; attacks on Narvik expedition, 149–50; scope of action after Central Norway evacuation, 162; dominant in Mo-Bodö area, 182, 184–5, 188, 191, 215; strength and activities in Narvik area in May, 195, 198, 205–7, 209–10; during evacuation period, 220, 226; losses, 231; general achievement, 234–5

German Army : provision for *Weserübung*, 20–1; organization of expedition, 27; reinforcements in Oslo area, 67; operations against Norwegians, 68; numbers in Trondheim area, 76; in attack on Steinkjer, 92, 96; in advance on Lillehammer, 106; in attack on Kvam, 120; in Österdal, 124; situation in Narvik area after naval battles, 151–2, 156; at end of April, 158–9; numbers in advance from Grong to Bodö, 183; size and condition of Narvik force in May, 194–5; numbers defending Narvik and Ankenes in final stages, 207–8, 210; losses, 230; equipment and morale, 240–1

German Naval Staff : judgment of Operation Hammer, 77; and Operation Juno, 223, 225, 227

German Navy : every ship required for *Weserübung*, 19, 27; in invasion of Norway, Chapters III and IV *passim*; achievement appraised, 51–2; Operation Juno, 222–7; losses, 231

German Supreme Command (O.K.W.) : studies Scandinavian operation, 18; temporarily takes direct control of Dietl's force, 195

Getz, Colonel : relations with, 87, 91–2, 95, 143; uses overland route from Grong to Mosjöen, 175; relations affected by lack of interpreters, 243

Gjövik **4** : German approach to, 102, 106

Glasgow, H.M.S. : Operation Henry, 84–5; evacuates King of Norway from Molde, 138

Glomma, R. **4** : 101, 102

Glorious, H.M.S. : to be used in 'Hammer', 74; off Trondheim, 114; Gladiators flown from, 116; returns with new aircraft, 134; flies off Hurricanes for Skaanland, 206; receives Hurricanes and Gladiators for evacuation, 220; attacked and sunk, 224–6

Glowworm, H.M.S. : action v. *Hipper*, 29; enemy report, 30

Gneisenau : escorts Narvik expedition, 27; damaged by *Renown*, 32; returns to Wilhelmshaven, 51–2; in Operation Juno, 222–7

Goltz, General von der : 245

Göring, Marshal : opposes *Weserübung*, 18, 135

Gratangen **10** : location, 148; objective of Norwegian attack, involving heavy losses, 156–7

INDEX

Green Howards, 1st : at Kjörem, 122, 126; at Otta, 126–8; at Dombaas, 136; at Verma, 137
Grom : Polish destroyer sunk off Narvik, 194
Grong **5** : location, 83; detachment sent by railway to, 86; starting-point for intended withdrawal overland, 166, 178
Group Command West : 223–4
Gubbins, Lieut.-Colonel C. McV. : commands Scissorsforce, 168; in defence of Mosjöen, 180–2; commands as brigadier in Bodö-Mo area, 186; instruction to Colonel Trappes-Lomax, 188; orders retirement from Viskiskoia, 189; from Pothus and Rognan, 191–2; informed of evacuation, 192, 213
Gudbrandsdal **6** : King Haakon in, 66; German advance up, 79; Chapters VII-IX *passim*
Günther, Herr : and German iron-ore supplies, 11; discusses Mowinckel Plan, 173, 175–6
Gurkha, H.M.S. : sunk by air attack, 34
Gurkhas : 163
Gustaf V, King of Sweden : confirms neutral status of country, 163

Haakon VII, King of Norway : election to throne, 4; actions of, on 9th-10th April, 38–9; visited by Admiral Evans, 66; departure from Molde, 138; visited by Lord Cork in Maalselvdal, 202; sails for Britain, 219, 226
Haakvik **9** : landing-point of S.W.B., 158–9; held by Irish Guards, 200
Hagelin, Herr : 18
Hallamshire : *see* York and Lancaster Regiment
Hamar **4** : meeting-place of Norwegian Parliament, 38; captured by Germans, 102
Hambaara **5** : fortification unmanned, 40, 71–2; disabled, 76
Hamilton, Captain L. H. K., R.N. : 156
Hammer, Operation : origins, 70–2; forces provided, 72–4; reasons for abandonment, 74–6; assessment, 76–7; revived as 'Hammer 2', 80
Hamnesholm **2** : 48
Hardy, H.M.S. : in Narvik attack, 43–5; sunk, 46; rescue of survivors, 51
Harstad **10** : described, 149; as landing-place, 146–8; base frequently raided, 150, 217; evacuation, 218–21; objective of German naval sortie, 222–3; sinking of *Vandyck* near, 226
Hartvigvatn **9** : wrecking of German aircraft on, 152; angle of German position at, 199
Hattfjelldal **8a** : airfield, 180; not used by Germans, 184
Haugfjell **10** : 217–8
Havelock, H.M.S. : in Bjerkvik attack, 198, 199
Hegra **5** : garrisoned, 67; besieged, 87; surrender (5th May), 144
Heidal **6** : withdrawal of 148th Brigade to, 112, 114
Hemnesberget **8a** : German landing at, 181; attempted recapture, 181–3
Henry, Operation : 84–5
Herjangsfiord **2** : described, 44; scene of Bjerkvik landing, 196; used to embark forces for assault on Narvik, 209
Hinnöy **10** : 147, 220
Hipper : expedition to Trondheim, 27; rammed by *Glowworm*, 29; at Trondheim, 40; returns home, 47, 52; in Operation Juno, 222–7
Hitler, Adolf : peacetime relations with Norway, 6; receives Quisling, 17; supervises plan and selects commander, 18; retains destroyers at Trondheim, 19; seeks excuse for operation, 21; decides date, 23; backs Quisling, 39; fitfully inclined to evacuate Narvik, 152; interchange of letters with King of Sweden, 163; orders air support for Narvik, 195; requires Dietl to hold out in North Norway to the end, 216; orders supply through Leads, 222; and von der Goltz's Finnish operations, 245
Hjelle **3** : 94, 95
Hjerkinn **5** : German threat to, 124; withdrawal of Norwegian defenders from, 135
Hoare, Rt. Hon. Sir Samuel : Secretary of State for Air, 59; on air power, 235
Hogg, Brigadier D. : commands Aandalsnes base, 129–30; proposes evacuation, 129–30; 133, 137–8

Holtermann, Major : 87

Home Fleet : and convoys for Finland, 13; and Operation Wilfred, 15; sails from Scapa, (7th April), 29; searches for enemy, 30–1; suffers air attacks, 34; moves northward, 47; west of Lofoten Is., 48; returns to Scapa, 51; reduced area of control, 52; and Operation Hammer, 73–7, 89; 'Hammer 2', 80; proposed bombardment of Agdenes, 161; June operations, 225–7; Admiralty intervention in command of, 238–9

Hopen **8b** : held by Scots Guards, 179; headquarters of Scissorsforce, 179; withdrawal from, 214–5

Hopwood, Brigadier A. H. : 138

Horten **4** : Norwegian naval base, 25; surrendered, 35

Hostile, H.M.S. : in Narvik attack, 44–5

Hotblack, Major-General F. E. : 72

Hotspur, H.M.S. : in Narvik attack, 44–5; heavily damaged, 46

Hundalen **10** : 155

Hunter, H.M.S. : in Narvik attack, 44; sunk, 46

Hustad **3** : 93

Hvinden Haug, General : commands 2nd Division, 104; orders British relief of forward troops, 106; decides on withdrawal, 107; disappointment of, 109–10; hands over supply system, 123; capitulation of Division, 143

Hysnes **5** : engages German destroyer, 40; fires on British destroyers, 47, 72; armament, 71–2

Icarus, H.M.S. : captures German supply ship, 46

Independent Companies : possible employment as demolition parties in South Norway, 162; sent to Norway, 163, 179; recruitment, organization and functions, 62, 63, 167, 168; transferred to Lord Cork's command, 169; limited usefulness, 170; operations, 180–92; evacuated from Bodö, 214–5; five more companies formed, 163, 172

Inderöy **3** : 91–2

Intelligence (British and French) : before German invasion, 22; 7th-8th April, 28–30; 9th-11th April, 66; collection placed under War Office, which produces daily summary, 66; deficiencies, 233

Intelligence (German) : reports from Norway, 20; concerning Allied intentions, 23; general achievement, 233

Inter-Services Planning Staff : function, 60; to arrange assembly and embarkation of forces, 65; to prepare plans for Central Norway evacuation, 129; report to Chiefs of Staff on capture and evacuation of Narvik, 174

Inter-Service Training Centre : 65, 238

Irish Guards, 1st : embarked, 146; at Harstad, 148–9; in Bogen area, 154; to exploit effects of Narvik bombardment, 155; at Haakvik, 200; attacked in *Chrobry* on way to Bodö, 184; reach Bodö area, 187; action at Pothus, 189–92; withdrawal to Bodö, 214

Iron ore, Swedish : importance, 3, 10–11; stocks at Narvik to be diverted to Britain, 69; German supply through Narvik stopped, 144, 201; plans to destroy mines, 163; flow of ore via Narvik to be restored for our own use, 171; possibility of securing through Mowinckel Plan, 173; hopes abandoned, 176; renewal of export from Narvik estimated to take twelve months, 211; resumption in January, 1941, 229

Ironside, General Sir Edmund : Chief of Imperial General Staff, 59; and arrangements for recapture of Narvik, 64, 65; messages to Brigadier Morgan, 99, 104, 105; receives appeals from Generals Ruge and Paget, 131–2; replies, 132–3; notifies Gamelin of immediacy of Central Norway evacuation, 81; message to General Mackesy, 146; his former command at Archangel, 245

Ismay, Major-General H. L. : head of secretariat for Military Co-ordination Committee, 58, 59; member of Chiefs of Staff Committee, 165

Italy : uncertain state of British relations with, 63, 245–6

Jan Wellem, S.S. : used for refuelling at Narvik, 44; escapes damage, 45; provides supplies, 158–9

Jensen, Colonel : 107, 108

Jernvatnene **10** : 217

Joint Intelligence Sub-Committee : membership, 60

INDEX

Joint Planning Sub-Committee : membership and functions, 59–60; to prepare directive, 65; stress weight of German air attack to be expected at Trondheim, 77, 80; pressure of work due to changes of objective, 237
Jonsvand **5** : 89
Jora, R. **6** : 136
Juniper, H.M.T. : sunk, 223
Juno, German operation : 222–7

Karlsruhe : at Kristiansand, 39; sunk, 34
Keitel, General : and planning of *Weserübung*, 18
Kent-Lemon, Lieut.-Colonel A. L. : takes over command of 15th Brigade, 121; reports on Dombaas action, 136
Keyes, Admiral of the Fleet Sir Roger : presses for naval attack on Trondheim, 80
King's Own Yorkshire Light Infantry, 1/4th : landing at Namsos, 84–5; defence of main road, south of Vist, 92–3; long march round German flank, 94; hold rear area, 95; in evacuation, 140
    1st : at Kvam, 119–22; at Dombaas, 134–6
King-Salter, Lieut.-Colonel E. J. : reports from Norwegian headquarters (14th-18th April), 67–8; and Gudbrandsdal operations, 103, 105; wounded, 112
Kirkenes **End Papers** : 1; metallurgical industries of, 2; visited by 1st Cruiser Squadron, 51, 156; intended garrison for, 170
Kirknesvaag **3** : 92
Kiruna **End Papers** : iron ore deposits at, 10; proposed Allied advance to Finland through, 13; hopes of reaching, 171
Kjörem **6** : location, 122; action at, 124–6
Koht, Dr : actions on 9th and 10th April, 37–8; Paris visit, 171; meeting with Swedish Foreign Minister, 176
Köln : return voyage of, 34
Königsberg : damaged by Bergen forts, 40; destroyed by F.A.A., 47
Kongsberg **4** : 101
Korgen **8a** : 182
Kristiansand **4** : captured by Germans, 39, 101; as German air base, 53
Kristiansund **5** : devastated by German air attack, 132
Krokstrand **8b** : action at, 188
Kuberg **10** : description, 197; key to German position, 200; Norwegian capture of, 207; starting-point for final Norwegian attack, 217
Künne : beached and torpedoed, 49
Kvam **6** : location, 114; Norwegian withdrawal behind, 115; air support at, 117; action at, 119–22
Kyrksaeteröra **5** : 71

Laagen, R. **6** : 111, 114
Labergdal **10** : French advance through, 157–8
Landing craft : six for Operation Hammer, 74; none accompanying Narvik expedition, 151; arrival of 4 ALC and 6 MLC, 193; number insufficient for assault on Narvik, 196; used at Bjerkvik, 198–9; in final assault, 207–9; shortage of, 240
Langset **8b** : 192
Lapphaug **10** : German post attacked by Norwegians, 156–7
Larvik **End Papers** : 66
Laurantzon, General : 87
Layton, Vice-Admiral G. : protecting convoy, 7th April, 29; in proposed attack on Bergen, 33; commands escort to Namsos, 85, 146; completes Aandalsnes evacuation, 139
Leads, The : general description of, 2–3; used by German shipping, 1939-40, 9–10; in Operation Juno, 222; their subsequent protection by German air power, 229
League of Nations : Norwegian support of, 5; in relation to Russo-Finnish War, 12
Leirfiord **8b** : 215

Leksdalsvatn **3** : 92
Lesjaskog **6** : position, 114; used for air operations, 115-8, 122; railway accident at, 136-7
Lessons of Campaign : 232-245
Levanger **3** : 73, 87
Light Divisions, French : 1st, how formed, 62; 2nd, at Brest, 78; waiting in the Clyde, 163, 172; 3rd, at Brest, 78, 163. *See also* Chasseurs Alpins
Lilleberg **9** : 207
Lillehammer **4** : 99; position described, 103; defence, 105-8; bridge destroyed, 110
Lillesand **4** : 30
Lillesjona **8a** : 85
Lofoten Islands **End Papers** : and Vesteraalen, 147; loss of *Chrobry* near, 184; Observer Posts in, 205; evacuation of Norwegian forces from Rösvik to, 214
Lulea **End Papers** : ore exports from, 10; proposed measures at, 12, 15, 171, 173, 176, 201; on route of proposed Finland expedition, 13; date of ice clearance at, 21, 176; danger of German *coup* against, 66, 161; Foreign Ministers meet at, 175
Lundehögda **6** : action at, 106-7
Lütjens, Vice-Admiral : 27
Lutzow : in expedition to Oslo, 27; torpedoed, 35, 48
Lyngenfiord **End Papers** : 216

Mackesy, Major-General P. J. : at Scapa, 11th-12th April, 65; earlier career, 145; instructions, 145-6; sails with advance party, 146-8; relations with Lord Cork, 70, 147, 150-5; conduct of operations, 155-9; sends troops to Bodö and Mo, 170, 182, 200; rejects General Béthouart's initial proposal for landing at Öyjord, 196; plans landing for Narvik, 196; decides on Bjerkvik attack, 197; hands over command to Lieut.- General Auchinleck, 200-1
Maere **3** : 93, 95
Marschall, Admiral : commands in Operation Juno, 222-7
Massy, Lieut.-General H. R. S. : commands Allied forces except for Narvik, 78; memorandum on policy, 94-5; representations of General Paget to, 114; defines bridgehead, 122; notifies German advance in Österdal, 123; evacuation arrangements, 129, 131-2, 138-9; presses for demolition parties in South Norway, 162; policy for Mo-Mosjöen area, 167; its rejection, 168-9; states four essential requirements, 242
Maund, Captain L. E. H., R.N. : accompanies General Mackesy and advance party, 146; agrees with postponement of Narvik attack, 196; reference made to his account of operations, 153 (footnote)
Maurangerfiord **4** : 34
'Mauriceforce' : 68
Military Co-ordination Committee : functions and membership, 58-9; meetings on 9th and 10th April, 64-65; 11th-13th April, 68-70; and Operation Hammer, 72-5; abandons 'Hammer 2', 80; decision to evacuate Central Norway, 80, 129; briefs Lord Cork, 147; re-organized, 165; and possibility of guerrilla warfare, 168; replaced by Defence Committee, 171; concerned with operational details, 237
Military Mission : appointed, 202; reports Norwegian Government's views on Bodö evacuation, 216
Mine-laying : in the Leads proposed, 11, 14-15; timing of, 23-4; carried out, 25-26; first use of magnetic mines, 54-5; results, 234
Ministry of Economic Warfare : views of, on German iron ore supplies, 10-11; paper on retention of Narvik, 175
Mo **8a** : discussion of defence of, 167, 169; to be garrisoned, 170; arrival of Independent Company at, 179; air attacks on, 179; line of approach from Mosjöen cut by Germans, 181-2; attempted defence, 182-6; evacuated, 186
Molde **5** : description, 97; landings at, 99, 113; bombed, 130; use in evacuation, 131, 138-9
Montcalm : in Namsos evacuation, 140
Moore, Group Captain M. M. : 203
Morgan, Brigadier H. de R. : in command of 148th Brigade, 98; operations, 98-112, 114; commands sector of base area, 138

Mosjöen **8a** : first considered, 84, 177; small initial force landed at, 166, 178; discussion of air defence, 167; need for naval protection, 169; rapidity of German advance towards, 168; attempted defence, 180; evacuated, 181–2

Mountain Troops (German) : 3rd Division provided for Narvik, 20, 27; used at Vist, 92; large reinforcements wanted, 96; 2nd Division sent additionally to Norway, 183; mountain infantry dropped in Narvik area, 195; cross-country march to relieve General Dietl, 215–6. *See also* Ski-troops

Mowinckel, Herr : 173

Murmansk : used by *Bremen*, 10; proposal to blockade, 12; rumoured presence of German troops at, 170; Allied convoys to, attacked from Norway, 229

Namdalseid **3** : 91, 94

Namsos **5** : described, 83; intended base for Finland expedition, 13; its occupation desired by Falkenhorst, 19; possible Allied foothold, 64; operations based on, 84–96; attacked from the air, 89–90, 140; evacuated, 142

Narvik Committee : 165

Narvik **9** : location and growth, 3; iron-ore exports, 10–11; Allied landing planned, 13–16; German capture, 40–1; the Allied expedition to, Chapters X, XI, XIII; postponement of assault, 196; assault, 208–11; evacuation, 213, 216–21; heavy German air attack, 217; re-entered by Germans, 222; scene of Hitler's first defeat, 232

Narvik, Mayor of : *see* Broch, Theodor

Naze, The, **End Papers** : 1, 28

Newall, Air Chief Marshal Sir Cyril : Chief of Air Staff, 59; supports Operation Maurice, 68; opposes despatch of bomber squadron to Narvik area, 172

Nicholson, Lieut.-Colonel C. G. C. : 131

Nicholson, Captain R. S. G., R.N. : 85

Nord-Norge, S.S. : transport of German troops, 180–1

Norge : sunk at Narvik, 41

Northern Barrage : efforts to complete, September 1918, 5; decision to reconstruct, November 1939, 11; Bergen to be terminal point, 13; alternative terminal on coast desired, 161

North-Western Expeditionary Force : 201

Norwegian aircraft : numbers, 7; unable to resist at Oslo, 36; withdrawn from Stavanger, 40; support Norwegian attack in mountains, 197; in final evacuation, 219

Norwegian Army : service and training, 6; dispositions prior to invasion, 7; early operations, South Norway, 67–8, 100–3; north of Trondheim, 87, 91–2, 95; south of Lillehammer, 105–7; assistance to British at Tretten, 112; Kvam, 122; and Dombaas, 136; withdrawal from Gudbrandsdal, 123, 135; end of campaign in Central and South Norway, 143–4, 162; contact with British in North Norway, 148; operations, 156–8; in Mosjöen-Bodö area, 179–183, 186–92; advance in mountains, 197, 199, 207; battalion seconded for assault on Narvik, 201, 209–11; in defence and evacuation of Bodö, 214–6; and Allied evacuation, 218–9; relations with, 244

Norwegian Government : complains of *Cossack* action, 14; protests against British minelaying, 24; warned of possible attack on Narvik, 37; actions on 9th and 10th April, 37–9; loses touch with its representatives, 65; its information from Oslo, 67; urges recapture of Trondheim, 71; appoints new Commander-in-Chief, 100; evacuated from Molde, 138; representatives sent to Paris and London, 171; Mowinckel Plan, 173, 175; and Allied evacuation, 175–6, 216, 219; attitude to Polish Brigade sent to Tromsö, 193; visited by Lord Cork, 202; members evacuated in *Devonshire*, 210; requisitioning of mercantile marine, 229; British relations with, 243–5. *See also* Anglo-Norwegian relations

Norwegian mercantile marine : importance of, 2; rise, 4; losses in First World War, 5; agreement for chartering of November 1939, 9; requisitioned by Norwegian Government, 229

Norwegian Navy : strength in 1939, 6; disposition of coast defence ships, 25; patrol of minefield, 26; and German invasion, 35, 39, 41; at Aandalsnes, 130; in final evacuation, 219

Norwegian Royal Family : 38, 138. *See also* Haakon VII

Nubian, H.M.S. : visits Namsos after bombing, 90

Nykirke **6** : 105

Observer Posts : 205
Ofotfiord **2** : 3, 41, 44, 158
Ogndal **3** : 92
Oil Pioneer, S.S. : sunk, 223
Olav Tryggvason : in defence of Horten, 35
Opdal **5** : 123, 124
Operations : *see* Avonmouth, Hammer, Henry, Maurice, Primrose, Rupert, Scissors, Sickle, Wilfred; *also* Juno
Orama, S.S. : empty transport sunk, 223–4
Örnefjell **9** : 199
Orzel : Polish submarine, sinks *Rio de Janeiro*, 30
Oscarsborg **4** : fortress sinks *Blücher* and damages *Lützow*, 36
Oslofiord **4** : penetrated by German warships, 35
Oslo **4** : German capture, 35–7; evacuated by Government, 38; arrival of German reinforcements reported, 67; R.A.F. attacks on Fornebu airfield, 53, 133–4
Österdal **5** : German advance through, reported, 67, 123–4; withdrawal of Norwegian delaying detachment from, 135; resistance in, terminated, 143
Östfold **4** : 101
Otta **6** : guns halted at, 111; position prepared at, 114, 124; described, 126; action at, 127–8
Oxelösund **End Papers** : ore exports from, 10
Öyer **6** : 100, 103, 109
Öyjord **9** : linked with Narvik by ferry, 148; dominates landing-points at Narvik, 151; objective of General Mackesy's plans, 155, 196–7; captured, 199; starting-point for Narvik attack, 208–9; artillery positions, 209

Paget, Major-General B. C. T. : instructed to leave for North, 72; order withdrawn, 75; appointed to Sickleforce, 77; operations, Chapter VIII; evacuation of force, Chapter IX; on mistakes in planning of campaign, 236, 237; on lack of interpreters, 243
Paratroops (German) : in capture of Oslo, 36; in capture of Stavanger, 40; dropped near Dombaas, 99–100; reported in Österdal, 124; expected during retreat from Gudbrandsdal, 135; in Narvik area, 195–6, 217, 220; their use a novelty, 235
Pegram, Captain F. H. : 84
Pellengahr, General : 27, 106, 120
Penelope, H.M.S. : detached with *Repulse*, 30; joins *Renown*, 44; selected for Narvik operation, 46; damaged, 47
Petsamo **End Papers** : proposed attack on, 12–13
Phillips, Brigadier C. G. : commands 146th Brigade, 85; rejoins from Narvik area, 86; confers with Norwegians, 87, 91; report to General, 93; holds base area, 95
Plan R.4 : description, 15–16; timing, 23–4; abandonment, 26; forces made ready for, 60–61; intended transfers from France for, 62
Pol III : 35
Polish Brigade : intended for Finnish expedition, 62; recruitment, 63; sent to North Norway, 163, 193; description, 193; directed first to Tromsö, 193; march from Bogen to Bjerkvik; replace British in Ankenes peninsula, 200; replace French, 207; final attack of, 208, 210–11; pursue Germans beyond head of Beisfiord, 217–8
Pollock, Colonel R. C. G. : 202
Porsangerfiord **End Papers** : 203
Pothus : action at, 189–92
Pound, Admiral Sir Dudley : First Sea Lord, 59; orders disembarkation of troops from cruisers, 26; proposes 'Hammer 2', 80; briefs Lord Cork, 147; and German threat to Mosjöen, etc., 169; and cancellation of Bergen attack, 239
Prime Minister (Rt. Hon. Neville Chamberlain) : surprised by Admiralty decision, 26; presides over Military Co-ordination Committee, 59; statement in House, 9th April, 66; confronted with views adverse to 'Hammer', 75; gives orders for 'Hammer 2', 80; announces evacuation from Aandalsnes, 2nd May, 141, 144; on time factor in capture of Narvik, 161; reorganizes Military Co-ordination Committee, 164–5; agrees to Norway's inclusion in Allied Military Committee, 165; fall of Government, 144, 171; emphasizes German losses, 230; warning against dispersal of forces, 245

INDEX

Prime Minister (Rt. Hon. W. S. Churchill) : formation of Government, 171; presses for action at Narvik, 171–2; desire to bottle up Lulea, 173; and Mowinckel Plan, 173–4; reasons for abandoning Narvik, 174–5; project for self-contained garrison, 175; defers announcement of intended evacuation to Norwegians, 218. *See also* Churchill

Primrose, Operation : 98

Prunella : sights unknown vessels (5th June), 225

'Puffers' : described, 149; bring troops to Bodö area, 187; evacuate from Rognan to Bodö, 189; and assault on Narvik, 209, 210; in withdrawal along Bodö peninsula, 214; in final evacuation, 219; difficulty in maintaining steady supply of, 240

Punjabi, H.M.S. : damaged but returns to Narvik attack, 49

Quisling, Major : visits Hitler, 17; seizes power, 38; his followers, 18, 41; causes lack of confidence, 218, 244

Raeder, Grand-Admiral : on iron-ore traffic, 11; proposes action in Norway, 17; doubts about naval strength, 18; forecasts British intentions, 23; orders ruthless breaking of Norwegian resistance, 35

Rana, R. **8b** : 186–8

Randsfiord **4** : attempt to check German advance at, 102–3, 105

Ranen, S.S. : use as decoyship *Raven*, 216

Ranfiord **8a** : location, 180; entered by *Nord-Norge*, 181; exposed to air attack and lacking naval patrol, 182

Rauenfels, S.S. : 46

Rauma, R. **6** : described, 132; 97, 114, 139

Renown, H.M.S. : covers mine-laying, 25, 26, 29; search for *Glowworm*, 30; engages *Gneisenau* and *Scharnhorst*, 32; diverted from Narvik convoy duty, 225; returns to Scapa and sails with *Renown*, 225–7

Repulse, H.M.S. : leaves Scapa, 29; sent to intercept enemy, 30–31; joins *Renown*, 44; diverted from Narvik convoy duty, 225; sent to join convoys, 226

Resolution, H.M.S. : in Bjerkvik attack, 198; sent home after bombing, 206

Reynaud, M. : becomes prime minister of France, 14; accepts plan of action, including fluvial mines, 24; and evacuation of Central Norway, 81; desires success at Narvik to offset bad news, 173

Rio de Janeiro, S.S. : sinking of, 30; event reported to Norwegian Government, 36; its implications ignored, 233

Roasme **9** : 199

Rodney, H.M.S. : sails from Scapa, 29; deck bombed, 34; returns to Scapa, 51; in June operations, 225–7

Rognan **8b** : position, 187; base for retirement, 189, 191–2

Rombaksfiord **2** : scene of destroyer battle, 13th April, 50; reconnoitred, 150; crossed in final assault, 208–10

Romsdal **6** : described, 132; 97, 114, 135

Roope, Lt-Comdr G. Broadmead : 29

Röra : 86, 91, 93

Röros **5** : 123

Roscher Nielsen, Lieut.-Colonel R. : Norwegian commander in Mo-Bodö area, 183; proposed for command over British troops, 203; quoted, 180, 216

Rosenberg, Herr, 17

Rosti **6** : 135, 136

Rösvik **8b** : terminus of road north, 214–6

Royal Air Force : supplies aircraft to Finland, 12; reports German movements, 28; attacks warships, 28–9; finds German ships, 8th April, 30; reconnaissance work, 9th April, 33; Bergen attack, 34; finds German battle cruisers, 52; attacks ships and airfields, 53–5; sowing of magnetic mines, 54; Operation Hammer, 72–4; attempted raids on Trondheim, 89; Gladiators on Lesjaskog, 114–8; patrols at Aandalsnes, 118, 133; unable to support army as requested, 119; bombs enemy bases to protect evacuation, 133–4; proposals for Narvik area, 164; dispatch of fighters, but no bombers, after 10th May, 172; search for airfield sites, 179; in action at Pothus and near Bodö, 192,

Royal Air Force, *contd.*
215; activities in North Norway, 203–7; in assault on Narvik, 209–10; in evacuation of North Norway, 217–8, 220; help of Coastal Command for Narvik evacuation not requested, 221; attack on German ships in Trondheim and diversionary attack on Vaernes, with main effort at Bergen, 227; losses, 231; general difficulties, 234–5

Royal Engineers : at Verdalsöra bridge, 88, 91; intended demolitions in Österdal, 124; demolitions exploded in Rosti gorge, 135; survey damage in Narvik, 211

Royal Leicestershire Regiment, 1/5th : despatched to Aandalsnes in two flights, 99; at Aasmarka, 106–8; losses on march, 108; at Balbergkamp, 108–9; at Tretten, 112

Royal Lincolnshire Regiment, 1/4th : landing at Namsos, 84–5; War Diary of, 91; in fighting at Vist, 92–4; difficult withdrawal of rear companies, 94; in evacuation, 140

Royal Marines : howitzer battery for 'Hammer', 72; land at Namsos, 84–5; howitzer battery at Namsos, 95; land at Aandalsnes, 98; anti-aircraft battery, 98; in action near Verma, 137; Fortress Unit at Skaanland, 149–50; transfer of base organization, 218

Royal Navy : coast of Norway safeguarded by, 6; action against *Altmark*, 13; Operation Wilfred, 25–6; counter-measures against German expedition, 29–35; Battles of Narvik, 43–51; and Operation Hammer, 73–5; in evacuation of Central Norway, 138–42; force assigned to Lord Cork, 147; and control of coast south of Narvik, 169, 180–1, 182; in evacuation of North Norway, 219–227; losses, 231; effects of German air power on, 234; problems of command, 238–9; shortage of destroyers, 240. *See also* Home Fleet and names of ships

Rudi **6** : 135

Ruge, General : defends barricade, 38; appointed Commander-in-Chief, 10th April, 100; visited by Admiral Evans, 66–7; presses for action at Trondheim, 70–1; operations, 10th–20th April, 101–3; negotiations with King-Salter and Morgan, 103–5; doubts about holding of Lillehammer, 107; requires stand at Tretten, 111–2; pessimistic message, 115; negotiations with Paget, 122–3; receives news of evacuation, 131–3; evacuated from Molde, 138–9; unable to take troops to North Norway, 143; warned of Namsos evacuation, 143; urges importance of stemming advance from south, 182, 183–4; activities as Head of Supreme Defence Command, 202–3; informed of Narvik evacuation, 219; stays in Norway and negotiates armistice, 219, 222; attitude to British, 244

'Rupertforce' : name presumed given by Mr. Churchill, 65

Russia : invasion of Finland by, 7, 12–14; uncertainty regarding intentions of, in North Norway, 63, 170, 193, 201, 245

Rye **7** : 53

Salangen **10** : 148

Saltdal **8b** : 187

Sandnessjöen **8a** : 181, 216

Scharnhorst : escorts Narvik expedition, 27; engaged by *Renown*, 32; returns to Wilhelmshaven, 51–2; in Operation Juno, 222–7; torpedo-hit by *Acasta*, 225

'Scissorsforce' : 168

Scots Guards, 1st : embarked Clyde, 60, 145; advance party, 146–8; operate with Norwegians, 154, 156–7; one company to Bodö, 159; three companies arrive at Mo, 182; action at Stien, 185–6; withdrawal to Bodö, 186–9; welcome fighter aircraft, 194; occupy positions in Bodö peninsula, 214–5

5th : disbanded, 14

Setesdal **4** : 101

Setnesmoen **6** : used as landing-ground, 118

Sheffield, H.M.S. : and Operation Henry, 84–5; in evacuation from Aandalsnes, 138

Sherwood Foresters, 1/8th : embarked without mortar ammunition, 99; at Nykirke and Biri, 105–6; at Lundehögda and Slagbrenna, 106–8; at Balbergkamp, 108–9; at Frydenlund, 110; at Tretten, 112

Shortages of equipment : on disembarkation from cruisers, 61; in Mauriceforce, 86; in Sickleforce, 99; in North Norway, 151; generally, 239–41

'Sickleforce' : 69

Sildvik **10** : on line of German retreat from Narvik, 208, 211

Simpson, Lieut.-Colonel H. W., R.M. : commands naval force at Aandalsnes, 98; commands sector of base area, 138

INDEX

Sjövegan **10** : 148; held by Scots Guards, 154; landing of Chasseurs Alpins near, 157

Skaanland **10** : location of naval base, 149–50; air attacks on, 150; held by S.W.B., 154, 158; project for military base at, 201; attempt to construct airfield at, 204–5; evacuated, 218

Skagerrak **End Papers** : at termination of the Leads, 9; assumed safe area for German reinforcements, 20, 55; control secured by German air action, 52; work of British submarines in, 34, 52; French destroyer sortie into, 52–3

Ski-troops (British) : disbanded, 14, 241
    (French) : land at Namsos without skis, 88; partly equipped, 90; patrols in mountains, 95; in Namsos rearguard, 140; in Narvik area, 157–9; proposed for Grong rearguard, 178; with Poles in Ankenes peninsula, 207; to attack German rear, 208
    (Norwegian) : in Namsos area, 87, 92, 95; at Kvam, 121–2; on British flanks, 134, 137; at Stien, 186
    (German) : in attack on Vist, 92; at Balbergkamp, 109–10; at Narvik, 195

Skjelfiord **End Papers** : naval station and repair depot, 47, 181; intended rendezvous, 147

Skjomenfiord **2** : position, 158; point of departure for proposed attack on German rear, 208, 217

Skjomnes **2** : 45, 158

Slagbrenna **6** : 106–7

Smyth, Brigadier H. E. F. : receives instructions, 113; Morgan's conference with, 114; wounded at Kvam, 121

Snaasavatn **3** : 87, 93, 95

Sognefiord **4** : 115

Sola : *see* Stavanger

Sörreisa **10** : 204

Southampton, H.M.S. : in evacuation from Aandalsnes, 138; carries advance party to Harstad and mainland, 146–8; in final bombardment of Narvik and Ankenes, 208; in Narvik evacuation, 221, 227

South Wales Borderers, 2nd : embarked, 146; at Harstad, 148; at Skaanland, 154; operations towards Ankenes, 158–9, 200; wrecked in *Effingham*, 185; reach Bodö area, 187, 192; occupy position south of Lake Solöi, 215

Sparbu **3** : 93

Spearfish, H.M.S. : torpedoes *Lützow*, 48

Stadland **5** : 15

Stanley, Rt. Hon. Oliver : Secretary of State for War, 59

Stannard, Lieut. R. B. : 140

Stavanger **4** : airfield (Sola) to be demolished, 13, 15; capture by Germans, 39–40; resistance continued in mountains, 101; R.A.F. attacks on airfield, 53–5, 133–4

Steinkjer **3** : held by 146th Brigade, 86; heavily bombed, 93; abandoned, 94; estimate of German garrison at, 96

Steffens, General : 101

Stien **8a** : position, 182; action at, 185–6

Stiklestad **3** : 86, 91, 92

'Stockforce' : 190

Stockwell, Lieut.-Colonel H. C. : 191

Stören **5** : 123, 124

Storfosshei **8b** : 187

Storjord **8b** : 189

Stork, H.M.S. : in escort of *Chrobry*, 184; protects landing craft during assault on Narvik, 208

Storvatn **9** : 158–9, 208

Straight, Squadron-Leader Whitney W. : 115

Straumen **2** : described, 50; approached by French land advance, 207, 217

Straumsnes **9** : 209

Strömmen **3** : 91–3

Stumpff, Col.-General : 195

Submarines : dispositions to protect mine-laying, 25; sinking of *Rio de Janeiro*, 30; reports from Skaw, 31; sinking of *Karlsruhe*, 34; other successes and losses, 35, 48; sow

Submarines, *contd.*
   magnetic mines, 55; proposed use to land demolition parties in South Norway, 162; alarm regarding, delays *Nord-Norge*, 181; success against *Gneisenau*, 227. *See also* U-boats

Suffolk, H.M.S. : bombards Sola and is counter-attacked, 74

Sundlo, Colonel : 41

Sunnan **3** : 94, 95

Sunndal **5** : 118, 122

Supreme War Council : discusses Thyssen memorandum, 11; resolves on intervention in Finland, 13; decisions of, on 28th March, 23–4; delegates command to Britain, 57; accepts British views, 57; meeting on 9th April, 62; meeting on 22nd April, 78; accepts evacuation of Central Norway, 81; plans compensated destruction of Swedish iron mines, 163; admits Norwegian representation, 165; approves evacuation of Narvik, 175

Surna **5** : 71–2

Sweden : relations with Norway (1905–18), 5; iron-ore and Finnish questions, 10–15; source of intelligence for both sides, 22–3; German invasion rumoured, 63; information from Norway, 66; Anglo-French mission sent, 66; facilities allowed to Germans on railway, etc., 152, 194–5; difficult situation after the evacuation of Central Norway, 162–3; and Mowinckel Plan, 173, 175–6; Dietl's force expected at frontier, 218; its isolation from the west as a result of the campaign, 230; operations affected throughout by uncertainties regarding Swedish neutrality, 246

Tanks (British) : requested by Ruge, 103; sunk in *Effingham*, 184
   (French) : in assault at Bjerkvik, 197–9; fail at Narvik and Ankenes, 209, 210
   (German) : in action on 16th April, 102; at Tretten, Kvam, and Otta, 112, 121, 127

Taraldsvikfjell **9** : described, 208; attacked, 209–10

Telemark **4** : 101

Teviot Bank, H.M.S. : 26

Thyssen, Herr Fritz : 10

Tjeldsund **10** : position, 148; location of naval base, 149, 150; mined from the air, 220

Tolstad **6** : 109

Transport problems : of Norway in general, 1; of Mauriceforce, 85–7, 88, 95; of Sickleforce, 99, 103, 132; in Narvik area, 149, 205; of Scissorsforce, 168

Trappes-Lomax, Lieut.-Colonel T. B. : succeeds to command of 24th Brigade, 158; at Stien, 182–3, 186; in withdrawal from Mo, 187–9

Trawlers : three lost at Namsos, 140; six lost at Aandalsnes, 130; fifteen lost at Skaanland, 150; escort for preliminary convoy in Narvik evacuation, 221; particularly vulnerable to air attack, 240

Tretten **6** : action at, 110–12

Tromsö **End Papers** : possibly occupied by Germans, 66; destination of Norwegian Government, 138; use of radio station, 154; additional base and hospital base to be established at, 201, 202, 218; evacuation, 219–221

Trondheim **5** : intended Allied base, 13, 15; captured by Germans with Vaernes airfield, 40; British air attacks, 47, 53, 134, 229; situation at, reported by King-Salter, 67; strategic importance and access, 70–1; direct attack proposed, 72–7; captured by pincer movement attempted, 77–81; Chapters VI–VIII *passim*; German establish relief, 143; German air base, 142, 195; in Operation Juno, 224–7

Truant, H.M.S. : sinks *Karlsruhe*, 34

Trygg : sunk off Aandalsnes, 130

Tynset **5** : 123

Tysfiord **End Papers** : 216

U-boats : protect invasion, 27; in Narvik area, 43, 44; one sunk by aircraft in Herjangsfiord, 48; convey supplies to Trondheim, 76; sinking of *Cedarbank*, 111; three sunk and North Sea dispositions captured in Narvik area, 150; planned use for reinforcing Narvik, 195

Vaagsfiord **10** : 58, 148, 222

Vaernes : *see* Trondheim

Valdres **4** : 103, 115, 143

Valentini, Lieut.-Colonel : 157

INDEX

Valiant, H.M.S. : sails from Scapa, 29; ships special shell for 'Hammer', 74; escorts first transports to Harstad, 148; meets Narvik convoys, 223, 225–6

Vandyck, S.S. : bombed and disabled in Harstad area, 226

Vangsmjösa, L. **4** : 115

Veblungsnes **6** : 139

Vefsenfiord **8a** : 177, 181

Vefsna, R. **8a** : 180

Verdalsöra **3** : Norwegian outpost at, 87; attacked by Germans, 91–2

Verma **6** : 137

Vice-Chiefs of Staff : appointed 23rd April, 59; oppose 'Hammer', 75; estimate for anti-aircraft defence of Narvik, 164

Victoria Cross : awards of, 29, 46, 140

Ville d'Alger, S.S. : difficulties of unloading, at Namsos, 90

Vindictive, H.M.S. : embarks Irish Guards for landing at Narvik, 155; evacuates troops from Bodö, 215; in final evacuation, 221, 223

Vinje **5** : 71

Vinstra **6** : 115

Viskiskoia **8b** : action at, 188–9

Vist **3** : German objective, 91; attacked and captured, 92–3

Vivian, Rear-Admiral J. G. P. : doubts about one-day evacuation of Namsos, 141–2; has charge of ships in Narvik evacuation, 219

Voss **4** : 101

Warburton-Lee, Captain B. A. W., R.N. : attacks German destroyers at Narvik, 43–6

War Cabinet : considers iron-ore problem, 10–12; help to Finland, 12–14; and timing of Norway operation, 22; relaxes rules for attacks on shipping, 35; restricts aircraft raiding Stavanger, 55; relationship with Ministerial Co-ordination Committee and Chiefs of Staff, 58–60; deliberations on 9th–11th April, 64–5; authorizes operations in Trondheim area, 68–9; abandons Trondheim operations, 81; question of instructions to General Mackesy restricting bombardment, 154; and reorganization of 1st May, 165; deals with military objections to attack on Narvik, 169–70; discusses Mowinckel Plan, 173; considers and authorizes withdrawal from Norway, 174–5; concerned with operational details, 237–8

War Office : stands down forces for Finland, 14; on enemy airfield prospects, 53; on inter-Allied command, 58; affected by commitments in France, 60; intelligence arrangements, 66; and subordination of British to Norwegian commander, 103–5; instructions brought to General Mackesy by D.D.M.O., 146; appreciation by D.M.O. of Narvik situation, 70, 152; presses for immediate assault on Narvik, 153; orders one company to Bodö, 159; raises Independent Companies, 167–8; estimates anti-aircraft requirements in North Norway, 202; failures in planning, 236

Warspite, H.M.S. : joins Home Fleet, 34; in 2nd Battle of Narvik, 48–51; and Operation Hammer, 73–5; aircraft from, sinks submarine near Narvik, 150; available for Narvik operation on short-term basis only, 153; in bombardment, 154; replaced by *Resolution*, 194

Wegener, Vice-Admiral, 16–17

Wells, Vice-Admiral L. V. : 134

Weserübung : origins, 16–18; execution, Chapter III; appraised, 51–2

Whitworth, Vice-Admiral W. J. : and the minelaying, 25–30; Narvik orders, 31; engages German battle cruisers, 32; sends destroyers to patrol Vestfiord entrance, 43; considers reinforcement, 44; new Admiralty orders, 46; transfers to *Warspite*, 48; 2nd Battle of Narvik, 48–51; reports situation at Narvik, 51, 147; Narvik reconnoitred by his destroyers, 150

Wilfred, Operation : name and details, 14–5; timing, 23–4; execution, 25–6, 145

Wolverine, H.M.S. : rescues troops from *Chrobry*, 184

York, H.M.S. : in Namsos evacuation, 141–2

York and Lancaster Regiment, 1/4th (Hallamshire) : embarked, 60, 145; landing at Namsos, 84–5; in reserve, 94–5; in evacuation, 140, 142

    1st : at Kvam, 120; at Kjörem, 124–6; return journey to Aandalsnes, 135, 136

Zulu, H.M.S. : in bombardment of Narvik, 154; in pursuit of *Nord-Norge*, 181

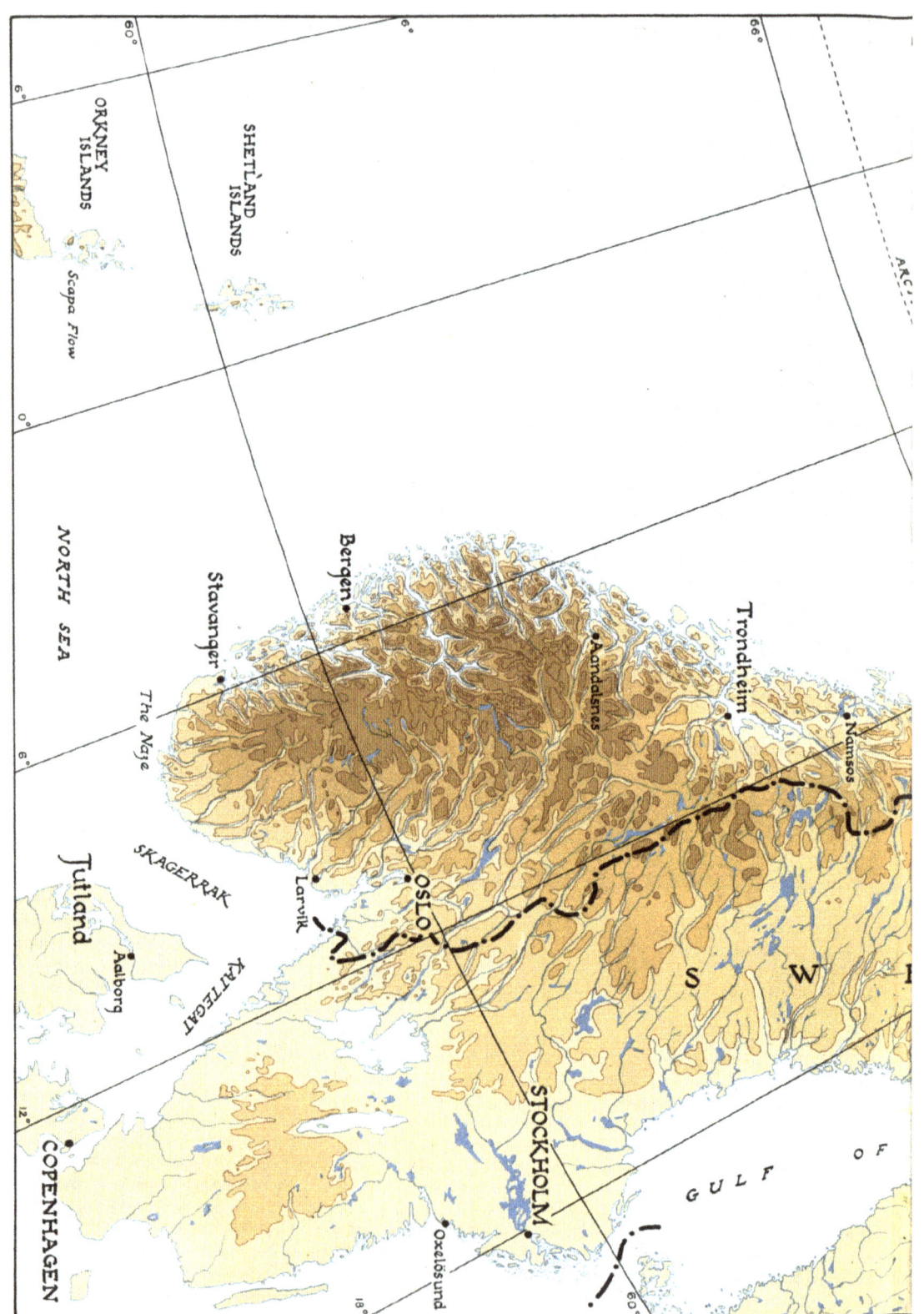

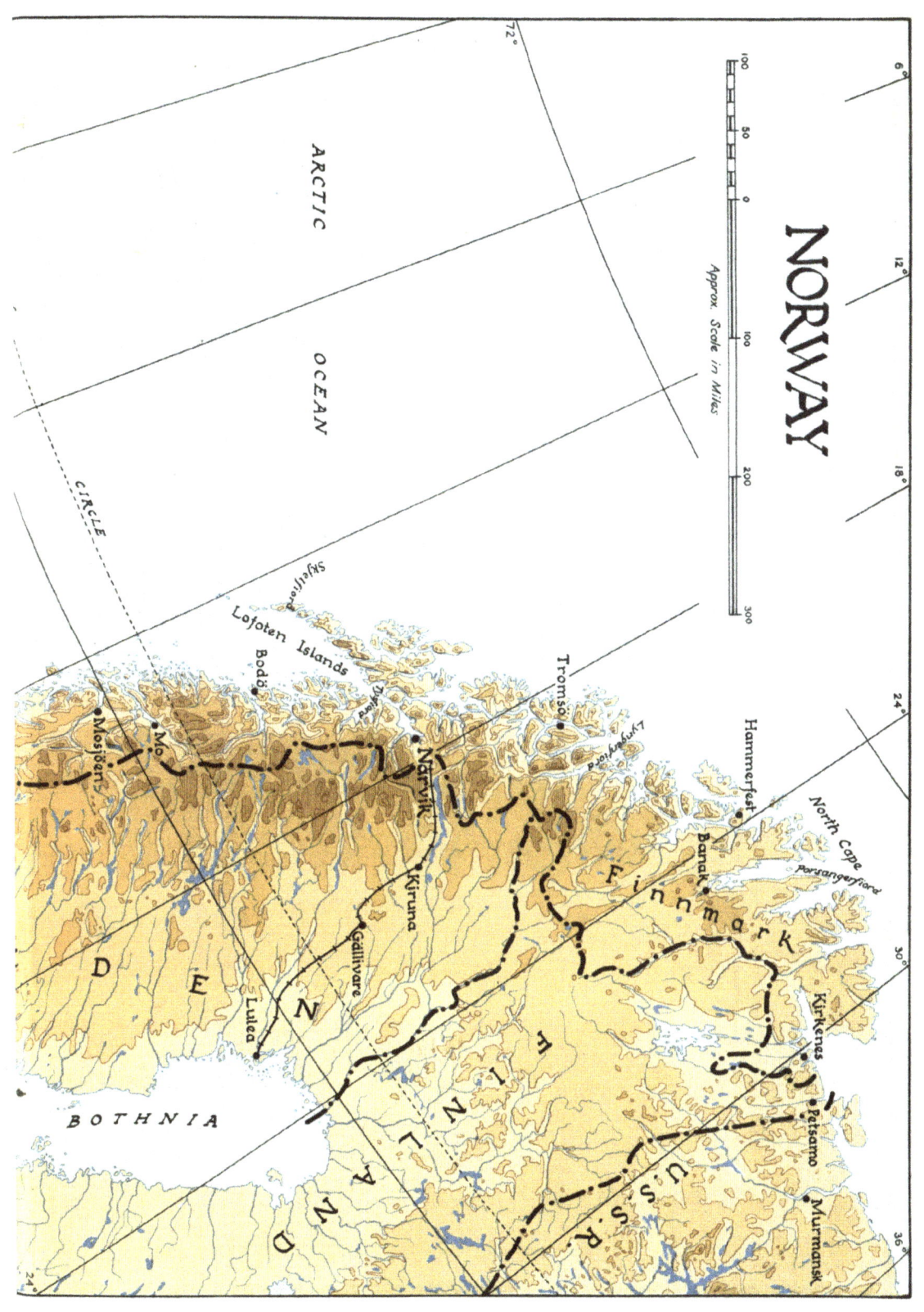

HISTORY OF THE SECOND WORLD WAR

UNITED KINGDOM MILITARY SERIES

Reprinted by the Naval & Military Press in twenty two volumes with the permission of the Controller of HMSO and Queen's Printer for Scotland.

THE DEFENCE OF THE UNITED KINGDOM

Basil Collier

Official history of Britain's home front in the Second World War, from the Phoney War, through the Battle of Britain and the Blitz to victory in Europe.
ISBN SB: 9781474537292
ISBN HB: 9781474537308

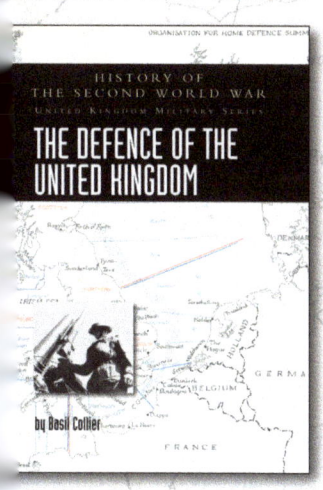

THE CAMPAIGN IN NORWAY

H. Derry

The catastrophic 1940 campaign which caused the downfall of Neville Chamberlain and brought Winston Churchill to power.
ISBN SB: 9781783315369
ISBN HB: 9781783315710

THE WAR IN FRANCE AND FLANDERS 1939-1940

Major L. F. Ellis

The role of the BEF in the fall of France and the retreat to Dunkirk.
ISBN SB: 9781474537063
ISBN HB: 9781474537247

VICTORY IN THE WEST

Volume I: The Battle of Normandy

Major L. F. Ellis

The build-up, execution and consequences of D-Day in 1944.
ISBN SB: 9781783315345
ISBN HB: 9781783315680

Volume II: The Defeat of Germany

Major L. F. Ellis

The final stages of the liberation of western Europe in 1944-45.
ISBN SB: 9781783315338
ISBN HB: 9781474537339

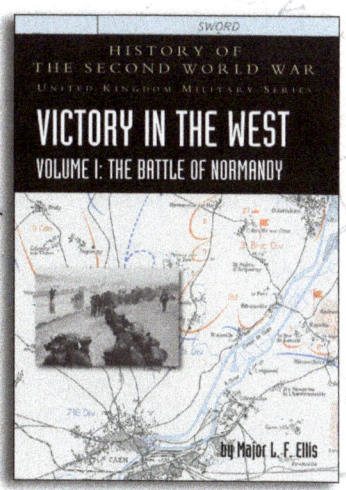

www.naval-military-press.com

THE MEDITERRANEAN AND MIDDLE EAST

Volume I: The Early Successes against Italy (to May 1941)

Major-General I. S. O. Playfair

Britain defeats Italy on land and sea in Africa and the Mediterranean in 1940.
ISBN SB: 9781783317608
ISBN HB: 9781783318148

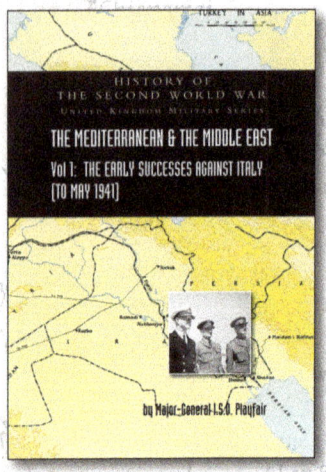

Volume II: The Germans Come to the Help of their Ally (1941)

Major-General I. S. O. Playfair

Rommel rides to Italy's rescue, Malta is bombarded, Yugoslavia, Greece and Crete are lost, and Iraq and Syria are secured for the Allies.
ISBN SB: 9781783317615
ISBN HB: 9781783318155

Volume III: (September 1941 to September 1942) British Fortunes reach their Lowest Ebb

Major-General I. S. O. Playfair

Britain's darkest hour in North Africa and the Mediterranean, 1941-42.
ISBN SB: 9781783317622
ISBN HB: 9781783318162

Volume IV: The Destruction of the Axis Forces in Africa

Major-General I. S. O. Playfair

The battle of El Alamein and 'Operation Torch bring the Allies victory in North Africa, 1942-4
ISBN SB: 9781783317639
ISBN HB: 9781783318179

Volume V: The Campaign in Sicily 1943 and the Campaign in Italy — 3rd Sepember 1943 to 31st March 1944

Major-General I. S. O. Playfair

The Allies invade Sicily and Italy, but encounter determined German defence in 1943-44.
ISBN SB: 9781783317646
ISBN HB: 9781783318186

Volume VI: Victory in the Mediterranean Part I: 1st April to 4th June 1944

Brigadier C. J. C. Molony

The Allies breach the Gustav, Hitler and Caesar Lines and occupy Rome.
ISBN SB: 9781783318032
ISBN HB: 9781783318193

Volume VI: Victory in the Mediterranean Part II: June to October 1944

General Sir William Jackson

The 1944 Italian summer campaign breaches the Gothic Line but then bogs down again.
ISBN SB: 9781783318049
ISBN HB: 9781783318209

Volume VI: Victory in the Mediterranean Part III: November 1944 to May 1945

General Sir William Jackson

The messy end of the war in Italy, Greece and Yugoslavia.
ISBN SB: 9781783317653
ISBN HB: 9781783318216

THE WAR AGAINST JAPAN

Volume I: The Loss of Singapore

Major-General S. Woodburn Kirby

The fall of Hong Kong, Malaya and Singapore in 1941-42.
ISBN SB: 9781783316786
ISBN HB: 9781783316793

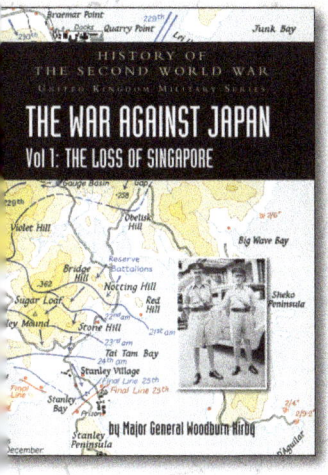

Volume II: India's Most Dangerous Hour

Major-General S. Woodburn Kirby

The loss of Burma and Japan's threat to India in 1941-42.
ISBN SB: 9781783316809
ISBN HB: 9781783316816

Volume III: The Decisive Battles

Major-General S. Woodburn Kirby

Turning the tide in the war against Japan at the battles of Kohima, Imphal and the Chindit campaigns.
ISBN SB: 9781783316823
ISBN HB: 9781783316830

Volume IV: The Reconquest of Burma

Major-General S. Woodburn Kirby

The reconquest of Burma by Bill Slim's 'forgotten' 14th Army.
ISBN SB: 9781783316847
ISBN HB: 9781783316854

Volume V: The Surrender of Japan

Major-General S. Woodburn Kirby

Victory in South-East Asia in 1945 - from Rangoon to Nagasaki.
ISBN SB: 9781783316861
ISBN HB: 9781783316878

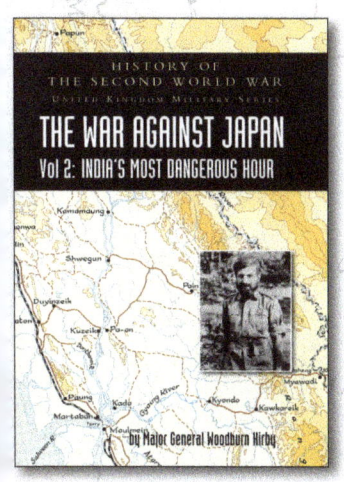
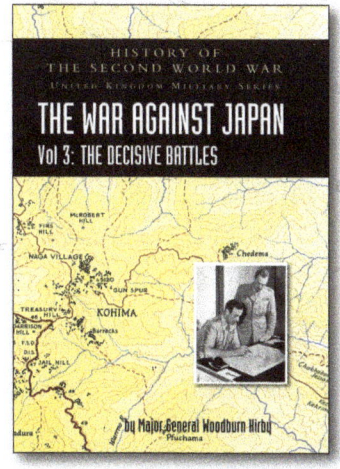

www.naval-military-press.com

THE WAR AT SEA - 1939–1945

Captain Roskill has long been recognised as the leading authority on The Royal Navy's part in the Second World War. His official History is unlikely ever to be superceded. His narrative is highly readable and the analysis is clear. Roskill describes sea battles, convoy actions and the contribution made by technology in the shape of Asdic & Radar.

Volume I: The Defensive

Captain S. W. Roskill, D.S.C., R.N.

2004 N&MP reprint (original pub 1954).
SB. xxii + 664pp with 43 maps and numerous contemporary photos.
ISBN SB: 9781474535694
ISBN HB: 9781474535700

Volume II: The Period of Balance

Captain S. W. Roskill, D.S.C., R.N.

2004 N&MP reprint (original pub 1956).
SB. xvi + 523pp with 42 maps and numerous contemporary photos.
ISBN SB: 9781474535700
ISBN HB: 9781474535724

Volume III: Part 1 The Offensive
1st June 1943-31 May 1944

Captain S. W. Roskill, D.S.C., R.N.

2004 N&MP reprint (original pub 1960).
SB. xv + 413pp with 21 maps and numerous contemporary photos.
ISBN SB: 9781474535731
ISBN HB: 9781474535748

Volume III: Part 2 The Offensive
1st June 1944-14th August 1945

Captain S. W. Roskill, D.S.C., R.N.

2004 N&MP reprint (original pub 1961).
SB. xvi + 502pp with 46 maps and numerous contemporary photos.
ISBN SB: 9781474535755
ISBN HB: 9781474535762

www.naval-military-press.com

www.ingramcontent.com/pod-product-compliance
Lightning Source LLC
Chambersburg PA
CBHW040740300426
44111CB00027B/2994